I0813518

Lydia's Tale

THE MYSTERY of LYDIA DARRAGH, IRISH QUAKER, PATRIOT SPY

ROBERT N. FANELLI

WESTHOLME
Yardley

Westholme Publishing, LLC
904 Edgewood Road
Yardley, Pennsylvania 19067
Visit our Web site at www.westholmepublishing.com

ISBN: 978-1-59416-447-7
Also available as an eBook.

Printed in the United States of America.

CONTENTS

Illustrations

MAPS

A gallery of images follows page 122.

INTRODUCTION

For many years, a story circulated in Philadelphia about a Quaker woman who, in 1777, during the British occupation of the city, crossed the British lines to bring intelligence of an impending surprise attack to George Washington. Some even claimed that her brave action saved the American army from destruction. That woman, Lydia Darragh, the subject of this study, has been written about many times in the last two centuries, though seldom in much depth. Usually, renditions repeat some version of her legend, occasionally augmented by a few stray facts from the historical record. Most celebrate her patriotism without reservation; a few question whether she ever did the things alleged in her story. Despite the various accounts, not much is actually known about her life, and less yet about her mentality—who she was as a person.

Historians are fortunate when they can discern the thoughts and attitudes of women like Elizabeth Drinker, Sally Wister, or Sarah Logan Fisher, three of Lydia Darragh's Philadelphia peers who left behind extensive diaries and other writings. Even a laconic but persistent Maine chronicler, the midwife Martha Ballard, wrote enough that her state of mind could be deduced by a gifted historian. Lydia Darragh left behind no diary, no correspondence. The record of her life is faint, though admittedly there are more traces than for most of her anonymous contemporaries. All we have of Lydia's thinking is the story she related to her acquaintances, fewer than a thousand words in length, and those second-hand.

Though some historians dismiss the Lydia Darragh story, which they perceive to be implausible, even a cursory examination reveals these writers did not examine facts but relied instead on conjecture. Those who simply argue against Lydia Darragh's impact on the outcome of the Revolution walk on surer ground, but their contentions seldom address the reality of her walk to Frankford in an effort to deliver what she saw as vital intelligence.

At this remove in time, we may not be able to determine with absolute certainty whether every particular element of Lydia's Tale is true. But by examining her narrative in its richer historical setting, we may be able to reach an approximate understanding of a person's life, even when much of the evidence is patchy and scattered. Laurel Thatcher Ulrich's magisterial analysis of Martha Ballard's diary demonstrated how fully a spare chronicle might be illuminated by mining the context surrounding her subject's fragmentary writing.[1]

Similarly, in writing about the female Continental soldier Deborah Sampson, Alfred F. Young gave us a practical benchmark for evaluating the likely veracity of story elements. In trying to assess the accuracy of various parts of the lore that grew up around Sampson, Young used a standard that can be applied readily to Lydia's Tale. He suggested that stories "fall into one of three categories of credibility: likely, unlikely and improbable. For the war, the likely events can be confirmed by other evidence and appear credible given the known context; the unlikely events are unsupported by evidence or are supported by only the thinnest proof; the improbable events are negated by contradictory testimony or are improbable because of what we know about the historical context."[2]

In trying to understand how Lydia Darragh thought and felt, her religious culture and beliefs are of more than cursory interest. To that end, I will touch on the Religious Society of Friends—"the people called Quakers," as they identified themselves—as we go on. This investigation leans heavily on Quaker records, which inform us about Lydia's cultural background and which help us understand how she engaged the world and what she thought about what she was doing. This reliance on Friends' records is an artifact of their organizational culture—they were careful recorders of events, more so than many other contemporaneous institutions. Quakers' orderly practices helped ensure the survival of their dissenter religion while other radical sects failed. The Society's explanations of their experiences and their world provide the most numerous records of Lydia's existence, influencing, perhaps disproportionately, what we know of her.

Friends' strict and outspoken adherence to the commandment "Thou shalt not kill" is one of the sect's most notable tenets, a thing that often sets them at odds with the community at large, especially during troubled times. This article of faith is frequently ridiculed by others as an idealistic stance quaintly out of touch with the realities of a cruel world—a practice and belief that threatens to undermine support for society's defensive and militaristic endeavors. Outsiders have often sought to undercut this moral high ground, questioning the common sense, patriotism, and courage of its adherents. For many such, Lydia Darragh's heroism became a morality tale about a woman who was willing to shed an impractical belief in courageous service to her nation. Was that a choice she actually made, and, if so, how did she come to make it?

Lydia Darragh was a unique individual—a determined one at that. She was also a member of a close-knit family. Her changing attitudes during the revolutionary period were not hers alone but were shared with her husband, her children, their extended kin, friends, and neighbors. In this study, I will attempt to shed light on the radicalization of a Quaker family as the conflict grew.

This book actually features two main characters: Lydia Darragh, the woman, who lived from about 1728 till 1789, and Lydia Darragh's Tale, her personal reminiscence and its outgrowth, which took on a life of its own after her death. Though this work deals primarily with Lydia Darragh herself—the person, as best we can reconstruct her life, and her experience during and shortly after the upheavals of the American Revolution—it also focuses on Lydia's Tale, its initial transmission and recording, its growth and gradual transformation from an individual experience story into the celebration of a cultural icon, and her apotheosis as an enduring part of American mythology.

In writing about Lydia's Tale, I contend that it has become a part of American mythology, that amorphous body of stories and ideas that are commonly used to convey the values and ideals of the United States of America. The word *myth* is frequently used today to indicate a misconception, a story or idea that is a falsehood. I do not use the term in that way. Rather, by *myth*, I mean a narrative that points to persistent and underlying truths about American culture.

While exploring Lydia Darragh's world, I tried to examine the veracity of notions that have become commonplaces in writing about the period—things that writers take for granted without actually checking the facts, without bothering to review primary sources to support their statements. For example, some writers blithely assert that William Howe occupied John Cadwalader's house in Philadelphia, while others point to Howe's residence at the Penn house on High Street. Few, if any, tell us how they know these things. Many writers simply make assertions based on long-standing traditions rather than question the underlying facts. I have tried to investigate the accuracy of such commonly held ideas, citing primary sources for them whenever possible.

The first chapter of this book introduces the earliest printed example of Lydia's Tale. For years, Robert Walsh Jr.'s was the best known version of the story, the one that had the greatest influence. Throughout the course of this book, when other versions of the story add information, or contradict Walsh, I cite them as well. Each of the early versions of Lydia's Tale can be found in its entirety in the appendices.

Care has been taken to identify as many records as possible about Lydia Darragh, her family, and associates. Certainly, publication of this book does not shut the door on new information coming to light. There are still many questions and doubtless more to learn. There are also a number of anomalies in the records that might be resolved more clearly in the future; I have tried to point those out for future researchers. In addition to traditional primary sources, this study utilizes many digitized records available online through subscription services, most commonly Ancestry.com for US Quaker records, Findmypast.ie for Irish Quaker records and British newspapers, FamilySearch.org for genealogical information, Fold3.com for US military records, and Genealogybank.com for US newspapers.

A word about quotations used in this work. Rather than paraphrase others' writing, I frequently use direct quotations when available. Though paraphrasing may read more clearly to our eyes today, when we read and "hear" other people's actual words, we learn more directly about how they thought. Hopefully, for the reader, this will result in a kind of immersion in the period, leading to a better understanding of the considerations that shaped the milieu. Generally, I have retained the exact words used but have often normalized spelling and names to something like current usage. For those concerned with the exact appearance of a quoted text, I recommend consulting the primary sources directly. In the records, writers have spelled the Darragh surname in a variety of forms, including Darrah, Darah, Darrach, and Darach. When quoting texts I retain their spelling, but otherwise I follow the spelling Darragh, which Lydia used when signing her name.

It is difficult to compare eighteenth-century prices, wages, and wealth with their values today. It is helpful to understand the monetary system in place throughout Great Britain at the time. Easy appreciation of the period's money is further complicated by the simultaneous use of several different forms of legal tender. In addition to British coins, others were commonly circulated, especially in the North American colonies. Equivalency tables were often printed in the newspapers at the time so that people could understand whether they were receiving fair value.[3]

Chapter 1

Lydia's Tale

IT IS AN ATTRACTIVE STORY: an unlikely heroine, a diminutive Quaker woman, crossing the British lines alone to bring vital information that saves George Washington's army from destruction. Over the years, it became a part of American mythology, a source of pride, a tale told and retold. In particular, it became a focus of traditions celebrating women's roles in creating a new nation. Like many such stories, it has grown in the telling, attracting embellishment and a measure of unquestioning belief. Yet the underlying traces are faint. At such a great remove in time, can we understand what really happened that gave rise to the legend?

Unlike heroic Molly Pitcher, a composite of several women, Lydia Darragh is an easily verifiable historical figure. Her exploit, known to several people in the Philadelphia area, was preserved in their memories for half a century before making the leap to print in 1827. By the time her story reached the public, Lydia had been dead for thirty-seven years, and associated details were difficult to corroborate, resulting in some questionable interpretations of events. This book attempts to resolve those misapprehensions in light of data more readily available in the twenty-first century, as information networks dramatically expand our access to historical records.

To understand the legend's growth, it is important to know the narrative in its earliest published form. Nearly everything that has been written about Lydia Darragh stems from a single published source, journalist Robert Walsh Jr.'s 1827 essay, "American Biography," which appeared in the first issue of his journal *American Quarterly Review*. In it, Walsh presented a tale he had learned from several people who had heard it directly from Lydia Darragh. As we will see in Walsh's next-to-final paragraph, controversy about the story arose even before its first publication.

Here is the basic text, widely distributed throughout America at the time. With minor variations, nearly all later versions followed this form:

> When the British army held possession of Philadelphia, General Howe's head quarters were in Second street, the fourth door below Spruce, in a house which was before occupied by General Cadwalader. Directly opposite, resided William and Lydia Darrah, members of the Society of Friends. A superior officer of the British army, believed to be the Adjutant General, fixed upon one of their chambers, a back room, for private conference; and two of them frequently met there, with fire and candles, in close consultation.
>
> About the 2d of December, the Adjutant General told Lydia that they would be in the room at seven o'clock, and remain late; and that they wished the family to retire early to bed; adding, that when they were going away, they would call her to let them out, and extinguish their fire and candles.
>
> She accordingly sent all the family to bed; but, as the officer had been so particular, her curiosity was excited. She took off her shoes, and put her ear to the key-hole of the conclave. She overheard an order read for all the British troops to march out, late in the evening of the fourth, and attack General Washington's army, then encamped at White Marsh.
>
> On hearing this, she returned to her chamber and laid herself down. Her mind was so much agitated, that, from this moment, she could neither eat or sleep; supposing it to be in her power to save the lives of thousands of her countrymen; but not knowing how she was to convey the necessary information to General Washington, nor daring to confide it even to her husband.

The time left, was, however, short; she quickly determined to make her way, as soon as possible, to the American outposts. She informed her family, that, as they were in want of flour, she would go to Frankford for some; her husband insisted that she should take with her the servant maid; but, to his surprise, she positively refused.

She got access to General Howe, and solicited what he readily granted,—a pass through the British troops on the lines.

Leaving her bag at the mill, she hastened towards the American lines, and encountered on her way an American Lieutenant Colonel (Craig) of the light horse, who, with some of his men, was on the look-out for information. He knew her, and inquired whither she was going. She answered, in quest of her son, an officer in the American army; and prayed the Colonel to alight and walk with her.

He did so, ordering his troops to keep in sight. To him she disclosed her momentous secret, after having obtained from him the most solemn promise never to betray her individually, since her life might be at stake, with the British. He conducted her to a house near at hand, directed a female in it to give her something to eat, and speeded for headquarters, where he brought General Washington acquainted with what he had heard. Washington made, of course, all preparation for baffling the meditated surprise.

Lydia returned home with her flour; sat up alone to watch the movement of the British troops; heard their footsteps; but when they returned, in a few days after, did not dare to ask a question, though solicitous to learn the event.

The next evening, the Adjutant General came in, and requested her to walk up to his room, as he wished to put some questions. She followed him in terror; and when he locked the door, and begged her, with an air of mystery, to be seated, she was sure that she was either suspected, or had been betrayed.

He inquired earnestly whether any of her family were up the last night he and the other officer met:—she told him that they all retired at eight o'clock. He observed —"I know you were asleep, for I knocked at your chamber door three times before you heard me:—I am entirely at a loss to imagine who gave General Washington information of our intended attack, unless the walls of the house could speak. When we arrived near White Marsh,

> we found all their cannon mounted, and the troops prepared to receive us; and we have marched back like a parcel of fools."
>
> Such is the substance of Lydia's narrative, heard from her mouth by several most respectable persons of our acquaintance, and implicitly believed by all of them, who knew her character and situation.
>
> Marshall, in the third volume of the Life of Washington, says, in reference to Howe's scheme—On the fourth of December, Captain M'Lane, having discovered that an attempt to surprise the American camp at White Marsh was about to be made, immediately communicated the information to the Commander-in-chief. In the evening of the same day, Sir William Howe marched out of Philadelphia, with his whole force, &c. Mrs. Darrah's auditors, as we have stated, give Craig, as the name of the officer to whom she communicated the information. Whichsoever may have received it, the public benefit that she conferred, must be pronounced inestimable. The loss of many hundred American lives, and even more disastrous consequences, were, in all likelihood, averted by her courageous stratagem.[1]

The approach of the fiftieth anniversary of the American Revolution in the 1820s generated intense interest in the story of the nation's founding. This was stimulated in part by an awareness that the people who had lived through the period were fast disappearing. Most of those still living who had had significant roles in the tumultuous events were in their seventies or older. Even the young drummer boys were by then in their sixties, already well above the average life expectancy for the time. The Marquis de Lafayette's triumphal return to America in 1824–1825, at the request of President James Monroe and Congress to help celebrate the country's creation, had a strong impact nationwide. The great hero stayed for over a year, touring each of the states, feted in town after town throughout the land, the subject of endless military parades and honorary functions. It was in this atmosphere that people felt a need to record Lydia's Tale before it was lost forever, inspiring three writers to take up their pens between 1827 and 1829.

In sequence, those earliest publications were Robert Walsh Jr.'s essay "American Biography" in *American Quarterly Review* (1827), Alexander Garden's book *Anecdotes of the American Revolution . . .* , 2nd ser. (1828), and John Fanning Watson's manuscript "Annals of Philadelphia" (1829).

The intertwining of these three documents can be confusing. I will attempt to untangle them by explaining their interconnected origins.

Over the years, some myth-busting writers have cast doubt on the story. But both Walsh and Watson believed that what they had heard was essentially true. As we have seen, Walsh accepted it because of the reputations of the people who related it: "Such is the substance of Lydia's narrative, heard from her mouth by several most respectable persons of our acquaintance, and implicitly believed by all of them, who knew her character and situation."[2]

Before the tale's first publication, Walsh shared it with Alexander Garden, and the two engaged in a friendly dispute over the identity of the American officer who was informed by Lydia Darragh of the British plan. Though Garden, himself a veteran of the Revolutionary War, questioned a couple of the details about which he believed he had personal knowledge, his writing is based on his communication with Walsh and follows Walsh's published version closely.

Watson also trusted the account of events he had learned: "I have been well assured of a circumstance in 1777 which saved General Washington and his army, while at Whitemarsh. Mrs. Lydia Darach . . . related it herself afterwards to my particular friend, and may be relied on. . . . Mrs. Hannah Haines, who reads this, tells me she has heard the same from Lydia Darach in substance. She was a woman of excellent repute among Friends, as also her husband too."[3]

As we will see, Hannah Haines, though unnamed by Walsh, turned out to have been his most important source as well. Having recounted Lydia's Tale many times, she finally wrote it down and shared copies of her manuscript with both men.[4]

A second version of Lydia's Tale descended through a separate but verifiable chain of communication. It only came to light much later, in a 1916 pamphlet, *Lydia Darragh One of the Heroines of the Revolution*, by a man named Henry Darrach, which was based on the story as it was told by Ann Darragh, Lydia's daughter. This account was passed down over time inside the Darragh family. It parallels the Walsh and Watson versions but has some striking differences that must be considered when trying to separate fact from fiction to determine exactly what did take place in December 1777. Darrach's version can also be found in the appendices.[5]

While Walsh and Watson were "well assured" that Lydia's Tale was true, others over the years have been skeptical. Was the story an outright fiction? Did those who retold it get the details wrong? Did the story change and morph out of its original shape as it passed through many hands? We will test the various assertions of the tale, bouncing them up against what we can learn of the persons, places, and events of eighteenth-century Philadelphia. Along the way we will see that Lydia Darragh was a real, living person, well known and well regarded in her adopted city. Many details of her experience can be corroborated and ring true. Examining her life reveals a remarkably brave woman who actively engaged her world and left her mark on the people and the times.

Chapter 2

The Barrington and Darragh Families in Ireland

LYDIA DARRAGH's personal story begins not in Philadelphia but in Ireland. She was born in Dublin about 1728. Through her speech, her manner, and her husband's Celtic surname, people in Pennsylvania identified her as an Irishwoman. Though no record of Lydia's birth has been located, her marriage certificate and other documents, found among the minutes of the Society of Friends in Dublin, confirm that she was the daughter of John Barrington, from a Quaker family of English descent, and Mary Aldridge, a woman about whom little can be verified.[1]

As we consider Lydia Darragh's background and experiences, we encounter the Society of Friends, a religious sect who often refer to themselves as "the people called Quakers," in recognition of the term popularly applied to them by outsiders. Lydia's Quaker faith and concomitant Quaker culture were significant constants, permeating many aspects of her life. Members of the religion enforced adherence to their principles collectively through their Meetings for Business, which imposed discipline for deviation. Because Quakers viewed their living as exemplary, moral infractions could never be overlooked. Punishment frequently included disownment—what is sometimes referred to as being "read out of Meeting." The records created as a result of Friends' vigilance and insistence on public corrective measures can make it seem that their members were constantly on the hot seat for violations of moral norms. In examining Lydia's life and times, leading up to her dramatic experience during the American Revolution, it will be helpful to understand how the Friends' faith came into being and how it evolved and functioned during her lifetime. Later, we will take a closer look at her experience as a member of the Society of Friends and how that experience shaped Lydia's Tale. But first we will examine her family background.[2]

While the evidence is fragmentary, we can piece together enough information to get a reasonable picture of Lydia Darragh's antecedents, at least on her father's side. The particular Barrington family from which she seems to have descended was granted land in Queen's County (earlier called Leix, later County Laois), as part of the first English Plantation in Ireland. By 1564, one John Barrington had settled in Laois, in the Barony of Cullenagh, along the slopes of the Cullenagh mountains. There the family maintained a fortified house known as Cullenaghmore. This castle served as a refuge and a local garrison. It was the locus of English military and governmental control in the neighborhood during the frequent troubles that followed, as the supplanted Irish inhabitants waged a guerrilla war against English occupiers.[3]

Starting about 1639, England became engaged in a struggle between King Charles I and Parliament over how to govern the nation. Civil war erupted. Taking advantage of a chaotic situation, Irish Catholics rebelled against English rule and resumed political control of much of their country. The Parliamentary faction gained the upper hand in England by 1649, executing Charles and declaring a commonwealth free from royal rule. Its leaders, however, feared an alliance between remnants of the Royalist faction and the Irish Catholic Confederation. To thwart this, they sent their military commander, Oliver Cromwell, to attack the Irish and reassert Parliamentary control. Many of the soldiers and officers of Cromwell's New Model Army were Puritans or members of other dissenter religions who had broken away from mainstream Anglicanism. Several bore a distinct detestation of Catholicism, and, believing that the Irish had persecuted their Protestant coreligionists, they meant to have revenge.

Having been active in supporting the English cause in Queen's County during the Irish Confederate Wars of the 1640s, the Barrington family of Cullenagh became officers with the Cromwellian force that invaded Ireland in 1649. Three Barrington brothers, Thomas, Nicholas, and Benjamin served as captains in the New Model Army along with their kinsmen and neighbors, including Lieutenant Colonel Walker and Lieutenant Francis Brereton. Thomas was later promoted to major.[4]

In September 1649, a month after landing in Ireland, the Parliamentary army captured the fortified town of Drogheda. Cromwell described the murderous mayhem that followed: "[B]eing in the heat of action, I forbade them to spare any that were in arms in the Town: and, I think, that night they put to the sword about 2,000 men." Many of those who surrendered were butchered, including a group of soldiers in a tower who had initially fought back. Cromwell continued, "When they submitted, their officers were knocked on the head; and every tenth man of the soldiers killed; and the rest shipped for the Barbadoes."[5]

Cromwell intended the slaughter at Drogheda as a lesson in terror for the towns he would assault later. He smugly placed the blame for his soldiers' killings on the victims themselves: "I am persuaded that this is a righteous judgment of God upon these barbarous wretches, who have imbrued their hands in so much innocent blood; and that it will tend to prevent the effusion of blood for the future. Which are the satisfactory grounds to such actions, which otherwise cannot but work remorse and regret."[6]

This massacre at Drogheda set the stage for Cromwell's attack on the port city of Wexford. It is clear that his intent went beyond mere political subjugation and included extirpation of the Catholics in Ireland and their replacement with "an honest people," by which he meant English Protestants. On October 11, upon gaining entry to Wexford, his soldiers killed many Royalists and Anglo-Irish Confederates, visiting their especial hatred upon the Roman Catholics there, particularly the clergy. Writing five days after the event, one of the English officers described the murders of Wexford's priests:

> It was a place settled the most deepe in superstition and darknesse that I have seene or heard of, and a people zealous against anything of better light. God visited both the deceivers and the deceived together. Of their Priests (which deceived and led them) were many slaine. Some (I heard of) came holding forth Crucifixes before them, and conjuring our Souldiers (for his sake that saved us all) to save their lives; yet our souldiers would not owne their dead images for our living Saviour, but struck them dead with their Idols. Many of their Priests being got together in a Church of the Towne, (where, 'tis sayd, many poore Protestants were kept and killed together in the beginning of the Rebellion) were slaine together by our Souldiers about their Altar.[7]

Cromwell used the terror sown by the carnage at Wexford in his threats against the nearby city of Ross six days later, on October 16. Fearing another massacre, Ross's town leaders tried to negotiate terms of surrender. This included requesting "liberty of conscience to such as shall stay" rather than leave the town. Cromwell's response was unequivocal: "[I]f by liberty of conscience you mean a liberty to exercise the Mass, I judge it best to use plain dealing and to let you know, where the Parliament of England have power, that will not be allowed of."[8]

English soldiers spoke virtuously of their motives for depopulating Wexford and the surrounding countryside. The officer who described the slaughter at Wexford explained why the invaders wanted to preserve the city from ruin. They hoped it could "be kept for such honest Families as shall hereafter come out of England to inhabit this Towne, we being desirous by any such encouragements to draw over a Generation and seed of good People (if God see it good) to possesse such places and to plant the Countreyes." Another writer, Hugh Peters, noted the opportunity presented by clearing the area of supposed heathens: "It is a fine spot for some Godly congregation, where house and land wait for Inhabitants and occupiers. I wish they would come."[9]

Oliver Cromwell's offensive set the stage in the mid-seventeenth century for a massive transfer of land from the Celtic Irish to an English and Anglo-Irish aristocracy who prospered at the expense of the original inhabitants. The bloodbath that took place in Wexford was a particularly violent episode in the long history of Ireland's subjugation to English rule. Beneficiaries of this brutal conquest, members of the Barrington family acquired substantial property in Wexford.[10]

In 1668, members of the Queen's County Barrington family entered into an agreement to settle an estate. The original records of this transaction were destroyed, but a surviving extract provides some of the details, though in a somewhat confusing manner. The upshot was a deed of settlement that gave Thomas Barrington use for life of 216 acres of land at Ballymacane, near the south coast of County Wexford, as well as a couple of smaller tracts in the county. This usage extended to Thomas's sons, Thomas II, John, and Mark, and possibly to their heirs as well.[11]

Perhaps it was horror at the inhumane experiences of Cromwellian warfare, or the memory of that conflict, that led some of the Barringtons to join the ranks of the emerging pacifist Quaker religion after the war's end. Many other former soldiers who had fought for the Parliamentary army, such as William Edmundson, William Dewsbury, and Thomas Holme, became convinced by Quaker teachings after the invasion. The first Irish Friends' meeting for worship took place at Mountmellick in 1659. Other Quakers became active near Lambstown, about ten miles from the city of Wexford, where a Meeting developed in the later seventeenth century. The Friends of Lambstown Meeting did not need to look farther than the road through their little village for an example of the violence they abhorred. On October 5, 1650, it had been the site of the sanguinary Battle of Lambstown, which occurred at a place afterward noted on the first Ordnance Survey of Ireland as Bloodygap. In a local tradition that persisted till late in the nineteenth century, the roadside ditches were said to have run red with blood.[12]

Following Cromwell's military activity, the Barrington line in Wexford continued to grow. Thomas Barrington remained in Ballymacane. In 1683, his son Thomas II married Susanna Nunn there. By the time their son John was born on October 25, 1689, they were members of the Friends Meeting at Lambstown.[13]

The Barrington family was active in educating Quaker children. A man named Thomas Barrington, likely either Lydia Darragh's grandfather, Thomas II, or perhaps a cousin, served as the schoolmaster and teacher of Latin for Friends in County Wexford. In 1705, he was one of six Quaker teachers who attended a conference in Dublin "in order to meet with other friends to consider of what good Books they may teach Children, and other good order to be observed in the teaching of Children that they may be as well instructed and kept in the way of Truth as otherwise." The focus of these education efforts was both practical and spiritual. As another record of this conference put it, "They decided what books should be taught by Friends and what laid aside, and what methods used, and among other things it was advised that children should not be corrected in passion, nor for their lessons more than for untruthlike behaviour."[14]

For Friends, "Truth" was more than simply the virtue of honesty; it was a metaphor for "God's Word." Quaker schools conveyed a specific set of values as well as knowledge. When, in 1719, the Leinster Quarterly Meeting was held at Lambstown, highly literate Thomas Barrington was appointed to "Keep the Book." That meeting's first item of business expressed the centrality of Quakers' emphasis on the notion of Truth: "A verbal Account was given by a Friend or Friends from every Monthly Meeting in this Province, that Friends continue their care in the Affairs of Truth for the good of all. . . . It is therefore the Desire of Friends of this Meeting, that they may be zealously concerned for the Honour of the Name of the Lord, and Promotion of Truth, and the Testimony thereof." A generation later, when Lydia Barrington Darragh was being tutored by a convinced Friend, we can be certain that this cultural and familial tenet of Truth held a prominent place in her education. As we will see, Truth was an important subtext lying just beneath the surface of Lydia's Tale.[15]

Sometime in the early 1700s, members of the Barrington family began migrating from County Wexford to the growing city of Dublin. By 1760, the city's population was estimated to be about 141,000, making it the second largest in the United Kingdom, after London, home to around 740,000 people. At mid-century, many of the Barringtons and their extended kin, as well as members of the Darragh family, were involved in Dublin's textile manufacturing industry. Based on addresses for family members between 1751 and 1763, many of these people were living and working in the silk-weaving trade centered on Meath Street, where the principal Quaker Meeting House was also located. Directories for the period show at least forty-two merchants and traders associated with silk weaving whose place of business or abode was within a few blocks of Meath Street. Presumably, those listed were reasonably prosperous people employing the labor of others. Those shown as silk weavers likely owned looms, each of which generally employed about four laborers.[16]

By 1714, John Barrington had moved to Dublin, where, on January 11, 1715, he married Mary Aldridge. A copy of the marriage certificate, which survives in the records of the Dublin Friends Meeting, names John as the "Son of Thomas Barrington of Lambstown in the County of Wexford." Little information survives about Mary's parents, though there is an index listing them as William and Frances Aldridge of Dublin. No identifiable member of Mary's family signed the marriage certificate; her parents seem to have died sometime before the marriage.[17]

Some of John's relatives did witness the marriage and signed their names to the certificate in the column reserved for family members. Prominent among them was John's sister, Frances Barrington Jesop, whose name heads the family section. Her signature is immediately followed by that of her husband, Andrew Jesop. The two had been married just six months earlier. The next two to sign were Nicholas and Mary Barrington, John's brother and sister-in-law, who likely made their way from Lambstown for the occasion. Other witnesses of note included Susanna Jesop and John Nunn, likely a relative of John's mother, Susanna Nunn.[18]

Over the years, John and Mary Aldridge Barrington had at least eight children together: Frances, born in 1715, Susanna, born in 1717, Comfort, born in 1719, Thomas, born in 1720, John, born in 1722, Lydia—the subject of our tale—born about 1728, Anna, birth date unknown, died 1792, Mark, birth date unknown. The naming of these children generally follows a traditional Irish naming pattern.[19]

Though John Barrington's occupation is uncertain, he was prosperous enough to afford a tutor for his children. It is no surprise then that in a time when many ignored schooling for women, Lydia's father should have looked to his daughter's instruction. To this end, he employed a highly literate man named William Darragh. Born about 1719, Darragh was said to be the son of a Presbyterian clergyman who may have been named Charles Darragh. Despite what was probably an upbringing steeped in Presbyterian beliefs, as an adult, William Darragh chose to join the Dublin Friends Meeting, becoming what is known as a "convinced" Quaker, one whose membership was not a birthright but who accepted the doctrine and principles and joined the Religious Society. He had begun attending Friends Meetings for Worship by at least 1748. That year, Dublin Meeting created "A List of Friend[s] Names to be Visited." William Darragh's name appears, crammed in between two others, as though added in afterthought. At this point he was living in Pill Lane (today's Chancery Street), a tony address at the time, suggesting William's origins in a prosperous family.[20]

A later Quaker record from 1763 mentions that William Darragh "came among us several years ago, appearing to be convinced of our Principles, and was sometime after received into Unity and married amongst us." The Friends congregation in Dublin was not large—in 1754, there were only about sixty-five active members of the Men's Meeting for Business. But, adding their families, plus a number of attenders who were not members, there were enough to support at least two meetinghouses and a couple of burying places. The main meetinghouse was on Meath Street, where the Men's Meeting for Business regularly took place, and there was a second meetinghouse in Sycamore Alley. Whether Darragh's conversion was prompted by an earnest conviction or a desire to marry within the endogamous Quaker community, he nonetheless remained a faithful Friend for the rest of his life.[21]

The object of William Darragh's affection was none other than one of his students: John Barrington's daughter Lydia, about nine years his junior. When their courtship may have begun is unknown, but it was not until she was about twenty-five that their relationship moved in the direction of matrimony. Since Lydia seems to be the youngest surviving of the Barrington children, William was probably no longer employed as a tutor by the family at that time, though he may well have been working in that capacity elsewhere in Dublin. It is also possible that he spent some time in London before returning to Dublin to marry. In announcing their intentions to marry, the couple were careful to follow the proper procedures laid out by the rather inflexible Quaker hierarchy. Just the previous year, in 1752, Lydia's first cousin, John Barrington (II) and his spouse, the former Mary Sutton, had been admonished for marrying improperly "out of meeting." John and Mary were required to write a letter acknowledging their error and to read it publicly at Meeting before they could be accepted back into the fold.[22]

No portrait of Lydia Barrington survives; probably none was ever made. But we do have a verbal description of her that came down through her family. She was "of a fair complexion, light hair, blue eyes, very delicate in appearance and extremely neat; conforming in her dress to the rules of the Society of Friends."[23]

This was an unusually stressful period for Lydia. About the time she was making plans to be married, her mother passed away. Worse, as Mary

Barrington was laid to rest on September 18, 1753, the stringent Quaker overseers were watching the mourners for any "Mark of Degeneracy." Since the previous May, the Meeting had been mulling guidance to its members to correct what they considered overly demonstrative grieving, in particular "the Practice of putting on Apparel in token of Mourning," which was "an Occasion for introducing a new Conformity to the World." The unfortunate timing meant that Mary Barrington's funeral, and family members' choice of apparel during the coming wedding, would test their compliance with the Meeting's directives.

Following what was then orthodox procedure, on October 1, 1753, William and Lydia went to the Women's Meeting to say they intended to wed. Alice Gouldby and Isabella Middleton were appointed to escort them the next day to the Men's Meeting. Among its other functions, this Women's Meeting was a so-called "preparatory meeting" that readied business to be discussed at the Men's Meeting for Business, where actual decisions were made. On October 2, the couple reiterated their intent before the men. The potential concern about their mourning behavior must have been very present in the couple's minds; it was a prominent item of business at that very Meeting. Aaron Atkinson and Lydia's kinsman, Thomas Simmons, were appointed "to make needful enquiry into their clearness on account of marriage & whether the young woman's father consents hereto & to make a visit to the young people & advise them to observe the sundries recommended in the paper read to them here." "Clearness" meant their being free of other marriages or engagements as well as their having a clear understanding of the import of marriage itself.

William was directed to publish their intentions in two public Meetings in Dublin, which he did on October 19 and 21. The couple then returned to the Men's Meeting on October 30 to reiterate their intention. John Barrington consenting, and the couple found clear of entanglements, the Meeting approved their marriage: "they are left to their Liberty to accomplish their intentions in any publick meeting in this City at our usual time & place."[24]

Three days later, on November 2, Lydia married William at the Friends Meeting House in Sycamore Alley. They were married in the manner of Friends: No minister or other officiant presided over the rite. Rather, according to the marriage record, during the Meeting for Worship the couple stood up and announced their marriage to those present:

> He the said William Darragh taking the said Lydia Barrington by the hand, did openly Declare as followeth Friends you are witnesses that I take Lydia Barrington to be my wife & I promise through the Assistance of Divine Providence to be unto her a faithful Loving Husband till God by Death Doth us Separate. And then & there in thc Said Assembly, the Said Lydia Barrington did in like manner declare as followeth Friends you are my witnesses that I take William Darragh to be my Husband promising thro Divine Assistance to be unto him a Loving & Faithful wife till it please the Lord by Death to separate us.[25]

The marriage certificate was signed by fifty-two witnesses. A word about the arrangement of the witness list is in order, because it divulges something about Friends' attitudes toward gender equality. The Darragh marriage witness list had four columns. The first two columns contained only male names, while the third column was reserved for females. The fourth column, however, contained a mix of male and female signatures. This special column was reserved for relatives and, perhaps, close friends.

Though Quaker women enjoyed greater freedom of expression than many of their compatriots, there were still restrictions on their degree of personal agency. While Friends' Meetings for Worship were conducted jointly, women could give spiritual testimony if moved to do so. Meetings for Business were segregated by gender. The Women's Meeting could make recommendations to the Men's Meeting, but it was the Men's Meeting for Business that had the final say in most matters. No doubt this division was guided by the legal restrictions of the period. Nonetheless, it exposes a dichotomy regarding the Friends' ideal of equality between the sexes and their perception of practicality.

Most of the witnesses to the Darraghs' wedding were invited guests, rather than random people attending a meeting for worship. Some were clearly relatives. A close examination of the names also reveals some people whose connections to the family are intriguing.

At the head of the special column was the name of Lydia's father, who had signed as "Jno. Barrington." In the next-most-prominent position came Lydia's aunt, Frances Biker, whose romance had caused such a stir in Dublin's Quaker community thirty years earlier.[26] Frances's signature occurred at or near the head of the family columns for several other marriages—including that of nephew Alexander Barrington. Several members of her family also attended these events. These clues about

Frances suggest an active, influential, and forceful personality, very possibly a role model for her niece Lydia.

Other names in this fourth column were also relatives. Susannah Webster and Anna Barrington were Lydia's sisters. Anna continued correspondence with the Darragh family after they removed to Philadelphia. Alear. [Alexander] Barrington is most likely Lydia's first cousin, the son of John Barrington's brother, Nicholas, and Mary Bancroft from Lambstown, County Wexford. Alexander had recently moved to Dublin, where, a couple of years later, he married Elizabeth Jessop.[27]

Two names were missing that we might have expected to see: those of William's sister Mary and brother-in-law James Eddy. They had married in Dublin in 1741. Later, moving to Belfast, they become convinced Quakers. By 1752, they were back in Dublin, where James was involved in the firm Eddy and Darah, Woolen Drapers, on High Street. James was occasionally active in the Dublin Men's Meeting, signing various minutes. He was present early in 1753, when he witnessed the disownment of a man named Joseph Marshall, but in May, Eddy was given a Certificate of Removal from the Meeting. When members moved away from an area, this certificate formally introduced the departing members to the new meeting they were joining. By the time Lydia and William were married that November, James Eddy had sailed with his family for Philadelphia. Ten years later, the Darraghs would follow and reestablish their close family ties.[28]

Lydia and William Darragh had nine children together—six in Ireland and three once they immigrated to Pennsylvania. Records of these births do not seem to have been entered into the Friends records in Dublin or Philadelphia, but late in the nineteenth century, historian Henry Darrach identified Lydia's children from copies of family Bible records that were preserved by her descendants. The six born before leaving Ireland were Mary (1754–1759), Charles (November 18, 1755–June 5, 1801), Ann, "Nancy" (August 12, 1757–August 17, 1840), William (1758, died in infancy), Lydia (died in infancy), and Mary (died in infancy). Those born after arriving in Pennsylvania were John (December 5, 1763–July 24, 1821), William (July 23, 1766–December 11, 1790), and Susannah, "Sukey" (December 19, 1768–September 18, 1792).[29]

It seems probable that Lydia's husband came from a prosperous background. In an autobiographical sketch, William's nephew Thomas Eddy wrote that his mother, Mary Eddy, had inherited £1,000, a substantial sum at the time. That, along with the obvious fact of William's education, suggests that the Darraghs lived comfortably. We don't know exactly how William Darragh was earning a living in the first nine years of his marriage, but by 1762, he had set up shop as a tobacconist in Church Street. The following year, his tobacco shop was listed a few blocks away, on Upper Ormond Quay, between the Ormond and Essex Bridges.

A few months after their wedding, William applied to become a member of the Dublin Men's Meeting. Two trusted members were delegated to run a background check. "William Darragh requesting by a Friend to be admitted a Member of this Meeting Jacob Ford & John Rutty are desired to make enquiry concerning his Conduct & Conversation & return Account to next meeting." Within two weeks, Ford and Rutty had completed their investigation, with happy results: "The Friends appointed to make Enquiry concerning William Darragh return Account that they do not find but that his Conduct & Conversation hath been orderly, they are therefore desired to acquaint him, that he is admitted a Member of this Meeting, & desired diligently to attend the same, & give him such Advice as may appear needful."

From then on, William was able to share the burden of conducting Friends' business and to weigh in on matters of discipline. He was listed as a contributor to the meeting later in 1754, though how much he gave was not recorded. He spent at least one yearly term as a door keeper for the Sycamore Alley meetinghouse, where he had been married. He also spent at least one year on the Committee of the Poor, which oversaw the meeting's charitable works, providing various subsidies, including rent supplements and money for food and heating, as well as schooling poor Friends' children.[30]

Over the years, he remained involved in meeting affairs, signing a number of documents and certificates. He was particularly active in the early 1760s. Dublin Meeting records for 1761 show his signature on a letter to the incoming lord lieutenant of Ireland requesting protection for Quakers from persecution based on their religious persuasion. He signed the disownments of Edward Taylor and Isabella Bewley for marrying out of meeting, and of Hugh McCutchin for "frequenting of Ale houses, & neglecting to take the necessary Care of providing for his Family." The Testimony against Peter Nicholson, which he signed in 1761, noted another kind of improper behavior that merited Friends' discipline: "during his residence here he launched out in precarious en-

The Barrington's and Darragh's Dublin. **1.** Andrew and Frances Barrington Jessop residence, 1718. **2.** Meath Street Quaker Meeting. **3.** Biker & Simmons, Silk Weavers; Alex Barrington, Wool Comber; Susannah Darragh, Dyer. Residences and businesses, 1762. **4.** St. Catherine's, Church of Ireland. **5.** St. Catherine's, Roman Catholic church. **6.** William Darragh residence, 1748. **7.** Eddy & Darragh, Woolen Drapers, 1752. **8.** Sycamore Alley Quaker Meeting. **9.** William Darragh, Tobacconist, business location in 1762. **10.** William Darragh, Tobacconist, business location in 1763. **11.** Lundy Foot, Tobacconist, residence and business, 1760. **12.** John Darragh, Merchant, business 1763. John Roque, *An Exact Survey of the City and Suburbs of Dublin*, 1756, detail. (*Harvard Map Collection, Harvard College Library*)

gagements of trade & having contracted debts to a great amount & some of them in a dishonourable manner he absconded from his Creditors by withdrawing to England." This turned out to be a bit ironic, considering what happened to William just two years later.[31]

One of the duties assigned to William—attending on traveling ministers—seems to have made an impression on him. A word about the concept of a minister in the Quaker religion is in order, since it is quite unlike the common notion of what a religious minister is today. The Society of Friends did not retain a clergy, believing that God spoke directly to individuals and that they needed to seek privately to hear his voice. Meetings were often conducted in silence, as members listened inwardly to God's voice. Occasionally someone might feel a "leading" to speak out if they believed that God had a message for others. Certain inspired persons might speak more frequently, and if their "conversation" seemed good—if the meeting's elders felt they were in "unity" with what was being said—these people could be considered to be "ministers."

Occasionally, some of these inspired ministers requested permission to travel to other meetings, sometimes in other lands, to share their fervor and spiritual insights.[32] Such was the case, for instance, with Elizabeth Ashbridge, noted for writing a spiritual autobiography describing her life and interior struggles, who obtained permission from Goshen Meeting, Chester County, Pennsylvania, to preach abroad: "In the fore part of the year 1753 with the ffree consent of her Husband, and the approbation of ffriends, she embarqued for England, on a religious concern to visit ffriends Meetings." Ashbridge traveled in company with Sarah Worrall, who felt a similar call: "Our Friend Sarah Worrall Requests a Certificate in order to pay a Religious Visit to ffreinds in Wales & some parts of England[.]"

After visiting England, the two headed for Ireland, where they were well received. The perils and strain of travel, however, took their toll. In February 1755, Worrall died at Cork, followed three months later by Ashbridge, who passed away at the home of a Friend in Carlow.[33]

In 1756, two more Friends from the Delaware Valley visited Ireland. The elder of the two, Abraham Farrington, had "acquainted the monthly meeting of Burlington [New Jersey] with a concern that had been at times on his mind for upwards of Ten years past to visit the meetings of Friends in some parts of Great Britain & Ireland." His calling may have been catalyzed by a similar religious visitation to the Philadelphia area by three British Friends, Samuel Fothergill, Mary

Peasley, and Katherine Payton. "Obtaining the proper credentials of the unity of friends at home, he imbarqued at Chester" with those three visiting ministers as fellow passengers, bound for Ireland. Farrington brought along a young man, Samuel Emlen Jr., who also felt a calling but had never acted the role of minister before. Their crossing was an easy one; they had a fair wind all the way, Farrington remarking, "I had but one days illness on the voyage."[34]

Farrington and Emlen traveled about, visiting Friends Meetings in the south of Ireland, then headed for Dublin. Farrington evidently spoke with fervor. In describing his spiritual struggles, he talked of the burning of the Lord's word within him, and his desire for its release: "The word of God is fire."[35] The members of Dublin's Half-Yearly Meeting were entertained and edified by Farrington's visit, forty-nine of them signing a certificate of their approval, sent to the Burlington Monthly Meeting, which described his ministry as "deep, sound and lively." Dublin Friends saw him off to meetings in the north of Ireland, sending William Darragh along to "attend" him and Emlen. Perhaps Darragh was sent because of his familiarity with the area—his sister and brother-in-law Mary and James Eddy had lived near Belfast until just a few years earlier. In this duty, Darragh appears to have covered most of Farrington's immediate travel expenses and acted as a guide. Farrington's horse had cost the meeting £10, plus an additional £1 2s. 9d. for "Horse-hire" when the first mount "failed" during the journey. Darragh's pockets were deep enough for him to bear his own and the others' additional expenses for nearly a year until the meeting agreed to reimburse him for the cost of the trip. During his days with the traveling ministers, William Darragh doubtless learned more about the prosperous Delaware Valley from which they came, supplementing the knowledge he may already have gained from his sister and her husband. Sadly for Farrington, he too, as Elizabeth Ashbridge and Sarah Worrall before him, succumbed to the exposure to hardship that came with extended travel during the period. He passed away in London two years later and was buried there.[36]

With the introduction of Protestantism to Ireland came strain between adherents of the island's various religious sects. Because of Friends' uncompromising insistence on hewing to their own course, both spiritually and socially, relations with their non-Quaker neighbors in Ireland were often difficult. Particularly problematic were those with the Church of Ireland, the officially recognized counterpart of England's Anglican Church. To finance the Church of Ireland's operations, national law sanctioned the practice of involuntary tithing—the collection of money for the financial support of both clergy and church buildings. This meant that adherents of other religions—Catholics, Presbyterians, and Friends alike—were required to pay what amounted to religious taxation, like it or not. If people refused to comply, laymen in the church's employ could distrain goods and money to satisfy the supposed debts. Needless to say, this practice resulted in a great deal of resentment and social unrest.

As part of their rejection of a paid priesthood, Friends had especial doctrinal objections to paying tithes. They refused to pay for "the forced maintenance of ministers," routinely referring to clergymen as "hireling priests." Particularly in the seventeenth century, laws supporting tithes had at times been enforced brutally against Friends who refused to go along with the practice, sometimes resulting in long stretches of imprisonment for those who stood on their principles. But the Friends' organization was adamant about its objection to tithing. Though seldom invoked, payment of tithes could be grounds for disownment. Though imprisonments for failing to pay tithes in the British Isles declined significantly by the first two decades of the eighteenth century, seizure of crops and personal goods remained common.[37]

The Barrington family felt this sting repeatedly over the years. On two occasions in 1712, for instance, one Thomas Barrington "had taken from him for tithes" at a farm near Mountmellick, crops worth £1 9s. 6d., consisting of 106 sheaves of barley, 48 sheaves of rye, 115 sheaves of white oats, and 208 sheaves of wheat. The sight of all this produce being carted off was made the more irritating because the tithe takers had waited to seize the goods till the work of harvesting—the mowing, tying, sheathing, and shocking—had been completed, losing nearly a days' worth of labor in addition to the value of the grain. Such injustice was not ignored by Friends and perhaps never wholly forgiven. Thrifty Quaker record keepers scrupulously calculated their injuries by recording the names of the "tithmongors" (surely not a term applied with love) and the "priests" in whose names their goods were commandeered, noting the value of confiscations to the penny, perhaps in hopes that through remonstrance, the losses might eventually be restored to them.[38]

Tithe collections in cities followed a pattern similar to those in the country, where finished goods were taken instead of crops. In 1742, Lydia Darragh's aunt Frances Biker, by then a widow but still in the business of weaving, was assessed 11s. 6d., a little over half a pound sterling, for tithes. When she refused to pay, "Davis Grew, called Churchwarden, for the use of Henry Echlin, Priest of Katharine's Parish" entered her home and appropriated "Worsted Goods to the value of 0.11.6."[39]

Another difficulty roiled the Quaker community in Dublin about this time. The celebration of military success was antithetical to the Friends' Testimony against War. During the Seven Years' War, their refusal to join in such festivities angered many neighbors who already resented Quaker difference. In 1759, British citizens reveled in an "Annus Mirabilis"—a year of miraculous events—due to a series of triumphs over the French. Several major victories in India, the Caribbean, and Europe made it evident that the tide of this global war was turning in favor of the British. Such military marvels were cause for public festivity, staged by and in support of government, a practice popular throughout Great Britain and, indeed, across Western Europe. Royal anniversaries and martial successes were often feted boisterously in Ireland. The common practice, especially in urban areas, was to rejoice with tolling bells, parades, and the loud firing of military salutes, followed in the evening by bonfires attended by crowds of people in the streets.

A British newspaper described the public joy in Dublin for one such event in 1759:

> Yesterday being the Anniversary of the Birth of his Royal Highness the Prince of Wales, (who then compleated the 21st Year of his Age) the Great Guns were fired in His Majesty's Park the Phœnix, three Rounds, and answered by Vollies from the Regiments in Garrison, (which were drawn out in the Royal Square at the Barracks) and by the Regiments encamped in the Park: At Noon there was a very splendid Appearance of the Nobility, and other Persons of Distinction, at the Castle, to compliment their Excellencies the Lords Justices upon the Occasion: And at Night the Battalion Guns in the Park were fired, and answered by a Feu de sole from the Regiments there, and followed in the same Manner by the Battalion Guns and

the Regiments in the Barracks; and the Night concluded with Bonfires, Illuminations, and all other Demonstrations of Joy.[40]

These evening jubilations were frequently accompanied by "illuminations," when people signaled their joy and allegiance by placing lit candles in their windows, the hundreds of softly glowing panes producing a vision of great beauty. But sometimes the effect was marred by unsightly gaps of darkness—the windows of those who chose not to join in the festive spirit. Quakers, in particular, pointedly abstained from the celebration of military victories, which violated their Testimony against War. Public elation, often marked by drunkenness and exuberant behavior, could easily turn ugly, and the sight of blank windows roused some to fury. During the August celebrations for Prince Ferdinand's victory at Minden (August 1, 1759), when the Quakers of Dublin refused to join in the festivities, some in the crowd became unruly, smashing unlit windows, vandalizing houses, even threatening Friends in the streets. Never acquiescing quietly when they suffered injury at the hands of others, Friends remonstrated with government and the public, carefully recording the cost of damages, and demanding from the lord mayor protection during such events in the future. They published their principled reasons for refusing to join in such "publick rejoicing," supporting their moral position with an array of scriptural quotations, duly noting the expense of paying to print a thousand copies of their complaint for distribution throughout the city. At the same time, the meeting actively disciplined those members who had participated by illuminating their windows, sending teams of weighty Friends to treat with them and guide them toward acknowledgment of their error.[41]

Like other Dublin Friends, Lydia and William Darragh faced a choice about whether to illuminate. If they did not, they could be subjected to vandalism and, perhaps, other forms of reprisal. If they did light their windows, they could expect to share the discipline of those who had "been so weak as to balk their Testimony by complying with the Custom of illuminating Windows." They were active and reliable Friends, close to the business of the meeting. At this time, William was both a doorkeeper and a member of the Committee for the Poor. Would he have jeopardized his position as a trusted member of the Meeting for Business by violating his testimony? The Darraghs would face such a choice again in another land under very different circumstances during the American Revolution.

While Quakers may have turned the other cheek at such insults as vandalism and tithe taking, they did so with a certain amount of unstated resentment. But at least Friends did not need to pay support for their own clergy—they had none. Catholics and Presbyterians were not so acquiescent. For them, tithes were doubly burdensome—they were paying to support two priesthoods, both theirs and the Church of Ireland's. Anger at the unfairness of this periodically erupted into violent resistance. In County Armagh, the sense of grievance boiled over into a protest movement in 1761, which was referred to as the Hearts of Oak because its adherents identified themselves by wearing sprigs of oak in their hats.

Unrest in Armagh and nearby counties was precipitated by the cess, a tax assessment forcing men to work six days a year on county roads, while the local gentry who benefitted most from the roads were exempted from the labor. Men gathered in large numbers to protest. Marching with flags, drums, and music, they descended on the houses of local gentlemen, especially landlords and the magistrates who enforced the laws. Erecting symbolic gallows in some places, they intimidated these men into making pledges to end the practice of cess. Protesters soon included Church of Ireland clergy in their unfriendly visits, demanding that tithes no longer be collected. The alarming movement grew over two years to include resistance in Dublin, most markedly among the weavers. Finally, in July 1763, the government stepped in with military intervention, sending bodies of troops to quell and disperse the marchers.

Though marches and intimidation took place primarily in the north, even in Dublin the sense of unease and concern would have been evident. The Irish newspapers, and indeed papers across the English-speaking domains, regularly reported on the Oakboys with apprehension and dismay. It was just at this time that the Darraghs made a decision to immigrate to America. While they probably embarked from Dublin, it is a distinct possibility that they might have sailed from a northern port, like Londonderry. Had they traveled through the north during late July or early August 1763 to take ship to America, they may well have encountered these protestors or the soldiers along the roads.

The silk-weaving business in Dublin had suffered a serious decline by 1763, which impacted the city's working poor, including Quakers around Meath Street. However, it seems likely that the Darraghs' decision to leave resulted from perceived economic opportunity rather than an escape from financial hardship. Trade between Ireland and Philadelphia burgeoned during the mid-eighteenth century, especially the linen trade with Ulster. The Darraghs knew they would find a welcoming community among the well-established Society of Friends in the city, and especially among their kin who had already made the move to the Delaware Valley. Literate people, they doubtless corresponded directly with their friends and relatives in the New World. Their near relations, the Eddys, were certainly thriving, and there may have been other family members already living there as well. It is likely they had also heard favorable reports from those credible people, especially visiting Friends, who occasionally sojourned in Ireland.[42]

The well-known risks of moving to the New World must also have entered into the family's calculations. War had raged on Britain's North American frontier since 1755, but moving to an affluent and populous city like Philadelphia must have seemed like a safe bet. The restoration of peace, certified by the Treaty of Paris in February 1763, augured well for the region's continued prosperity. With tranquility reestablished, word of ambitious plans for the settlement of a new colony in the Ohio country, to be called New Wales, reached Dublin in June 1763. Four thousand people were expected to march soon from Philadelphia to land grants of three hundred acres apiece in a fertile country where they could expect to raise lucrative crops in their very first year, "particularly tobacco, which in that rich soil is easily cultivated." The prospects for profit must have looked propitious to a man in the tobacco trade.[43]

Uncertain reports of renewed hostilities with Native Americans began showing up in the Dublin press late in July. Later to be known as Pontiac's War, raids, murders, and scalpings were taking place throughout the northern backcountry, from Detroit to Fort Pitt. Three light infantry companies were assembling on Staten Island "in readiness to proceed against the savages, should it appear that there is any thing general intended against the Settlements." While such news may have been somewhat disconcerting, the conflict seemed limited to the frontier, far from the urban centers where they would be settling.[44]

By late June, the Darraghs had committed to leave Ireland for Pennsylvania. The minutes of Dublin Meeting for June 28 show that William requested a Certificate of Removal that his family could take with them to Philadelphia Meeting. That summer, Lydia was expecting another child: her son, John, would be born in America in December. She would travel with two other young ones in tow, Charles, seven, and Ann, six.

Members of Dublin's middle class, William and Lydia were used to living in a household that employed servants, and they may have brought one or two along on the trip.

Despite bright prospects, the decision to move so far away must have been wrenching. Few of those who left Europe for America ever returned to see their families, friends, and the scenes of their childhood again. Leave taking was most always final. The attraction of the New World would have to be compelling for the Darraghs to pull up roots and head off to an unknown future.

Personal monetary considerations were paramount in the family's actual planning. As a practical matter, they needed to liquidate enough of their capital in Ireland to pay their passage and to provide for a new start in their adopted home. At minimum, they required the wherewithal to sustain them financially for several months as they integrated themselves into a new economic network in an unfamiliar city. They also needed to wrap up any business obligations in Ireland, attending especially to debts, before departing. Clearing debt was a particular concern for Friends, whose commitment to truth and honesty demanded that persons leaving the vicinity of a meeting prove themselves free of financial entanglement before they could be granted a Certificate of Removal to a distant meeting.

Rather than apply personally to Dublin Meeting for his certificate, William requested it through a friend. This suggests that he may have been absent from the city at the time. Perhaps he was busy settling his business affairs elsewhere. But this may also have freed him from having to answer direct questions about his arrangements, the answers to which might have been found wanting. The Men's Meeting appointed a well-known Quaker publisher, Isaac Jackson, and silk weaver Robert Unthank "to make the needful Enquiry concerning their Conduct & Conversation & draw a Certificate as they shall find Cause." An imminent departure date hurried the investigation, and a certificate was granted and signed by twenty-one members of the Men's Meeting on July 12, 1763. Still, Jackson and Unthank appeared to have felt their inquiries into William's business affairs were not as thorough as they might have liked. Perhaps they sensed that some stones remained unturned. Their statement was worded less definitely than was common: "we believe he now leaves this City clear of Debt." They believed so because they trusted him, but they were, perhaps, not wholly satisfied.[45]

It was not invariably the practice to make note of the wife's standing when a married couple applied for a certificate. Lydia Darragh, however, was well enough regarded that the meeting made a point of letting Philadelphia Friends know, in their understated way, what kind of woman was joining their community: "with regard to Lydia his Wife; She was educated amongst us, and hath always been as far as we know, of a sober and orderly Conversation, frequently attending our Meetings both for Worship and Discipline: therefore, with Desires for their Welfare and preservation in the Truth, we recommend them to your Christian Care and friendly Notice."

The exact date the Darraghs left Ireland is not known, nor has the ship they sailed on been identified, but we may be able to narrow down the time frame for departure to a period of two weeks. On July 25, the Women's Meeting rushed their normal process for getting the certificate signed because they expected the Darraghs to leave before the next Meeting for Business, scheduled for August 8. Concerned that the certificate might not reach the emigrees in time, they instead asked "that Women Friends stop at the breaking up of first day morning Meeting next [July 31], to read & Sign said Certificate." That Sunday, twenty members of the Women's Meeting endorsed it, including Lydia's sisters, Anna and Susanna Barrington.[46]

The meeting's haste to accommodate the Darraghs quickly came back to bite them. The bad news broke at the Men's Meeting for Business, on August 9: "It appears by the report of the friends appointed that William Darragh hath left this City not clear of Debt as mentioned in his Certificate, Robert Unthank & Isaac Jackson are desired to write to him before he leaves this nation, if possible, and desire him to return the Certificate to this Meeting in order that one more suitable may be drawn and sent after him."[47]

Their embarrassment at having failed to catch Darragh's unresolved financial problems resulted in much review and correspondence with Philadelphia over the next three years, as the meeting tried to correct the situation. They were as much concerned for Dublin Meeting's credulity with Philadelphia Meeting as for the Reputation of Truth. Dublin Meeting determined to issue a new, more accurate document:

> It being understood that William Darragh is gone off to America with the Certificate he received from this Meeting, Isaac Jackson and Samuel Carleton are desired to make further Enquiry con-

> cerning his Conduct draw up a new Certificate agreeable to truth and Justice & bring it to next Meeting to be signed. And it is the Judgement of this Meeting that William Darragh should be immediately written to, by the said Friends not to produce the first Certificate; but return it by the first Opportunity; as the second is to supersede & render it ineffectual.[48]

The substance of the matter (a debt, but how much and to whom) was never revealed in the meeting minutes, though the details were obviously known. The men seem to have felt it a delicate matter, perhaps not entirely to Darragh's discredit. Perhaps there were two sides to the story. It may have been that they did not completely trust the source of the accusation. Being sticklers for accuracy though, their reputation was still on the line. Seven months later, they still could not decide how to word a new document tactfully yet truthfully. Several "weighty Friends" were called in to get the facts straight and the language right, but even they could not agree on how to phrase things. They determined instead to write to Darragh for more clarification.[49]

Another year passed before the matter was taken up again. Though the meeting had received a reply from Darragh in the interim, it was still not wholly satisfactory. Here, the meeting waffled. In July 1765, they agreed to issue another certificate "for William Darragh & Wife," but the next month they once again decided against it. Perhaps at this point their concern was that an injustice was being done to Lydia and her children, who should not be denied acceptance into Philadelphia Meeting merely because of her husband's questionable financial situation.[50]

Eventually, a new Certificate of Removal was created for Lydia and her children. But even that seems to have caused debate and delay. The Men's Meeting signed it on September 9, 1765, yet it took three months before the Women's Meeting members did likewise. In the event, the certificate continued to equivocate William's status, mentioning him, but not by name:

> To the Friends of Philadelphia in America
> Whereas Lydia Darragh hath lately removed from hence along with her husband and Family, in Order to Settle in your Parts; These are to Certify on her Behalf that she was educated and married amongst us in this City, and appeared to be of an Orderly

> Conversation agreeable to our Profession, being a pretty constant attender of our Meetings both for Worship and discipline; We therefore recommend her to your Christian care desiring her Preservation and Prosperity in the Truth, and with dear Love conclude your Loving Friends.[51]

It was not until September 26, 1766, that the Women's Meeting in Philadelphia could finally report that a certificate "from the Monthly Meeting held in Dublin ye 17th 9 Mo. 1765 on Behalf of Lydia Darragh, was Read sent to the Mens Meeting and Accepted." After three years, Lydia had formally become a member of Philadelphia Meeting.[52]

William had not necessarily been fleeing his creditors by moving to America. But he does seem to have dodged at least one debt, at least temporarily. If that debt was large, we might have heard more about it. He may, eventually, have settled that situation, but the blemish persisted, and his status among Friends in Philadelphia remained unclear. While he had been active with the Dublin Men's Meeting, he does not appear ever to have been accepted as a member of Philadelphia's Men's Meeting for Business. This did not mean he could not or did not attend Meetings for Worship, but his involvement in Friends' business affairs seems to have ended.

Chapter 3

The Darraghs Move to Philadelphia

VOYAGES ACROSS THE Atlantic could be perilous, especially because of the risk of disease. That risk was magnified by Lydia Darragh's pregnancy during the crossing. But as relatively prosperous people, William and Lydia are unlikely to have faced the horrific, frequently deadly conditions experienced by poorer emigrants from the British Isles or Germany. The Darraghs most probably paid for passage aboard a ship with reasonable accommodations for a family of four. It is even possible they sailed on a merchant ship belonging to an acquaintance, a ship owner from either Ireland or America. This journey was probably seven-year-old Charles's introduction to the sea, and he seems ever afterward to have been attracted to maritime affairs. Arrived in Philadelphia as people of means, able to demonstrate their financial security, and with established citizens to vouch for them, if necessary, they could debark immediately, while indentured servants might be detained until someone paid for their passage by purchasing their indentures.[1]

At the time, the Atlantic crossing westward might be accomplished in as little as six weeks, though seven or eight might be more normal, and longer voyages of several months' duration were not unheard of. On September 1, the *Pennsylvania Journal* noted, "Last Saturday arrived here the Ship Marquis of Granby, Capt. McIlvaine, in six weeks from Londonderry." It was carrying copies of the *Dublin Gazette* as late as July 7, from which the *Journal* extracted reports. Another ship, which left Dublin on about July 2, took much longer. As the *Pennsylvania Gazette* reported on September 1, "Snow George, Capt. Crannell, from Dublin arrived at Sandy Hook last Saturday after a tedious passage of 13 weeks with 120 passengers."[2]

If, as seems most likely, the Darraghs departed between July 26 and August 8, in the best case they would have been on the ocean until at least September 5. This turned out to be a particularly bad stretch of time to be at sea. Alarming reports reached Philadelphia of a fierce Atlantic hurricane that raged between August 24 and 28. Word of the storm began to filter into the city in early October: "On the 24th ult Captain Rufus Hopkins returned to Newport, Rhode Island, after having been out from thence 62 days, bound to the west Indies. On the 24th of August he met with very hard Gales of Wind, or rather a Hurricane, which lasted 4 Days, in which he lost his Mast, all his Horses on Deck, and received considerable other damage, which obliged him to return. On the First of September he saw a Brigantine, Bermuda built, in Lat. 26. 27. Bottom upwards."[3]

Granted the region where the hurricane was encountered was farther south than the normal sea route between Ireland and Philadelphia, such storms generally track north and east over several days, with strong winds making heavy weather, especially for sailing ships. Those westward bound at the time would likely have been slowed in their passage by contrary winds. By October 27, ships from Ireland were again arriving expeditiously in Philadelphia.

Lists showing ship arrivals and departures were kept by the Philadelphia Custom House and reported in the local papers. Printed records do not show any ships arriving directly from Dublin during the period when we would expect the Darraghs to have landed, roughly between early September and late October. But the published lists show only a ship's most recent port of call. For example, many vessels are shown arriving in Philadelphia from New Castle, Delaware, where ships crossing the Atlantic frequently stopped on their way upriver to the city. It is also possible that the Darraghs departed not from Dublin but from one of the busy northern Irish ports, like Londonderry, which might explain William's absence from Dublin when he requested the Certificate of Removal at the end of June. One possible candidate, for which the timing seems right, was the ship *Culladen*, Captain S. McLane, which was reported on October 6 to have arrived at New Castle from Londonderry and which was noted as an "Inward Entry" from New Castle to Philadelphia on the 16th. In the end, the ship on which the Darraghs sailed and their date of arrival cannot be determined with certainty.[4]

If the news reaching Ireland about frontier troubles had seemed disturbing in early summer, events once the Darraghs arrived in Pennsylvania must have been downright frightening. A major battle took place between British forces and Native Americans at Bushy Run in August, while the Darraghs were at sea. More alarming still, Indigenous warriors stirred up by colonists' ill treatment had gone on brutal killing rampages in nearby Berks and Northampton Counties, only seventy miles from Philadelphia. This was certainly close to home by Irish standards, less than the distance between Dublin and Wexford, or Dublin and Londonderry. The ferocity of these murders as reported by the press must have inspired terror in readers—and fear for safety—especially among bewildered newcomers. Violence between European settlers and Indigenous tribes continued to roil affairs in Pennsylvania that winter, as a group of angry colonists known as the Paxton Boys massacred Conestogas at Lancaster, then marched on Philadelphia intending to slaughter those Indians who had fled to the city for shelter from their sanguinary rage.[5]

Fortunately for the Darraghs, when they did finally set foot on shore, they were immediately able to draw on a local support network. William's sister, Mary, wife of fellow Quaker James Eddy, had immigrated to Pennsylvania with her family in 1753. We know of this relationship through a letter written by Christopher Marshall Jr. to his father in 1778. Christopher Jr. was married to Ann Eddy, the daughter of Mary Darragh and her husband, James Eddy. In the letter, Marshall refers to his wife's aunt as "Aunt Lydia Darragh." The inference is that the relationship is through her husband, William Darragh. As will be seen below, this conclusion is supported by several other close connections between the Darragh and Eddy families.[6]

Mary Darragh was born in Dublin about 1724 "of a respectable and good family" and raised in the Presbyterian faith. In 1741, she married another Presbyterian, James Eddy, a merchant's apprentice, who had been born in Belfast about 1712. After marrying, they left Dublin for Belfast where James established his own import-export business. It seems likely that James's business was well-capitalized from the start: their son, Thomas Eddy, mentioned that Mary brought to the marriage a fortune of about £1,000 sterling.[7]

At some point before his marriage, James became a convinced Friend. Thomas Eddy recalled of his parents:

> They had both been educated Presbyterians, but during their residence in that city, he became acquainted with Robert Bradshaw, a Friend, of considerable estate, who resided at Newtonards, about seven miles from Belfast, and was highly respected and much beloved. He was not a minister, but a meeting was held at his house, which was occasionally attended by some of his tenants. He lent my father some Friend's books, who in this way became acquainted with their principles, and was received as a member in the society.[8]

Mary Eddy, though initially rejecting Quakerism, also became a pious Friend. Thomas remembered: "My mother was warmly attached to the Presbyterians, and much prejudiced against the doctrines and principles of Friends; however, she afterwards became convinced of their rectitude, and was received into membership. She was a pious and valuable woman."

The Eddy family migrated to Pennsylvania in 1753, and James set up an importing business. By the following summer, he was regularly advertising his shop in the *Pennsylvania Gazette*. Located on South Second Street, between Market and Chestnut Streets, Eddy's store was copiously stocked with a wide variety of goods. At first, he was willing to sell items cheaply for cash, probably as much to recoup his initial outlay as to be competitive. The *Gazette* advised customers, "As said Eddy is a new beginner, he is resolved to sell every article at the very lowest price for ready money."[9]

In a short time, James began advertising as a contact who arranged for goods and passengers to be shipped back to Great Britain. This raises the possibility that he may have had a hand in arranging the Darraghs' passage across the Atlantic. He certainly would have been a good person for them to consult. Eddy was also involved in importing and selling servants, arranging their terms of indenture. This, along with his frequent appearance in estate settlements, suggests a considerable familiarity with the law, though he may not have been an attorney himself.[10]

It is useful to explore the distinctions and overlaps between a few classes of business people—merchants, manufacturers, and shopkeepers—especially as those terms were used in colonial America. Generally, a merchant can be described as someone involved in importing or exporting goods or materials, usually on shipboard, but also by land, as might be the case with wood or furs, for instance, or agricultural goods, like tobacco. A manufacturer is someone who takes raw materials and transforms them into a saleable product. A joiner, for example, might fashion finished furniture out of wood. A pharmacist might change herbs into consumable drugs and remedies. A tobacconist might toast and grind snuff out of tobacco leaves. A shopkeeper is in the business of merchandising goods to the public through a fixed venue—a shop. A single person might pursue all three lines of business. For instance, shopkeepers might also be manufacturers, or they might be involved in arranging for goods to be brought to their locations. James Eddy is an example of a person whose primary line of business was shopkeeping, but who also functioned as a merchant who had an interest in the shipping of metalwork to sell in Philadelphia. Though William Darragh was involved in manufacturing snuff, he was generally listed on the tax rolls as a shopkeeper.

Well-established in business by 1759, James Eddy purchased a piece of property that year from the well-known diarist, druggist, and merchant Christopher Marshall, another former Dubliner. This property, on the west side of South Fourth Street, between Locust and Spruce Streets, bordered a more extensive piece of land to the south that would later be divided between Marshall's sons. As two immigrant Irishmen—both convinced Friends—James and Christopher Sr. must have found they had much in common. Two of their children found likewise. The following year, James and Mary Eddy's daughter Ann married Christopher's oldest son and namesake, Christopher Marshall Jr. Following this marriage, James Eddy appears to have conducted some of his business in partnership with Marshall. Through this connection, the Darragh family got to know the Marshalls, with whom they became closely associated.[11]

Other Darraghs were also living in Pennsylvania when William and Lydia arrived, though their exact familial relationships are difficult to uncover. In addition to Mary Darragh Eddy, William seems to have had another sister in Philadelphia, Ann Darragh. Though, as with Mary Darragh, there are no records precisely describing Ann Darragh's relationship to William, there is evidence of close ties between these three people. When Ann Eddy married Christopher Marshall Jr. in 1760, among the witnesses was Ann Darragh. Her signature does not appear in the column reserved for family members, but this may have been because she was not a Quaker. She may have been a Presbyterian at the time, as Mary and William had been.[12]

Two years later, Ann Darragh married another Irish immigrant, Blair McClenachan, at the newly formed St. Paul's Episcopal Church on Third below Walnut Street. The service was performed by a former Presbyterian minister who had converted to Anglicanism, William McClenachan, quite possibly a relative of the groom. The Reverend McClenachan had recently been preaching at well-established Christ Church in Philadelphia. His fervent, extempore style, inspired by George Whitefield, the evangelical architect of the Great Awakening, had attracted many followers. But Christ Church's staid clergy were so disturbed by McClenachan's "wild, incoherent rhapsodies" that they petitioned the bishop of London to keep him from becoming an assistant minister. Days after that decision was publicized in the city, a rebellious group of McClenachan's adherents, said to number as many as three thousand, met at the Pennsylvania State House and voted to found St. Paul's, where they could practice religion in the style they preferred.[13]

The Eddys, Marshalls, and McClenachans remained close. When Ann Eddy Marshall's daughter Ann married former patriot officer Solomon Bush in 1791, the wedding took place at the McClenachans' home, Cliveden, the former house of Benjamin Chew, which had featured so prominently in the Battle of Germantown. We will have more to say later about Ann Darragh and Blair McClenachan and their connections to William and Lydia Darragh.[14]

The Darragh family lodged in several different houses during their years in Philadelphia. They did not purchase property in their adopted city for many years, perhaps because they were undercapitalized. It was not until after William's death in 1783 that the family actually acquired real

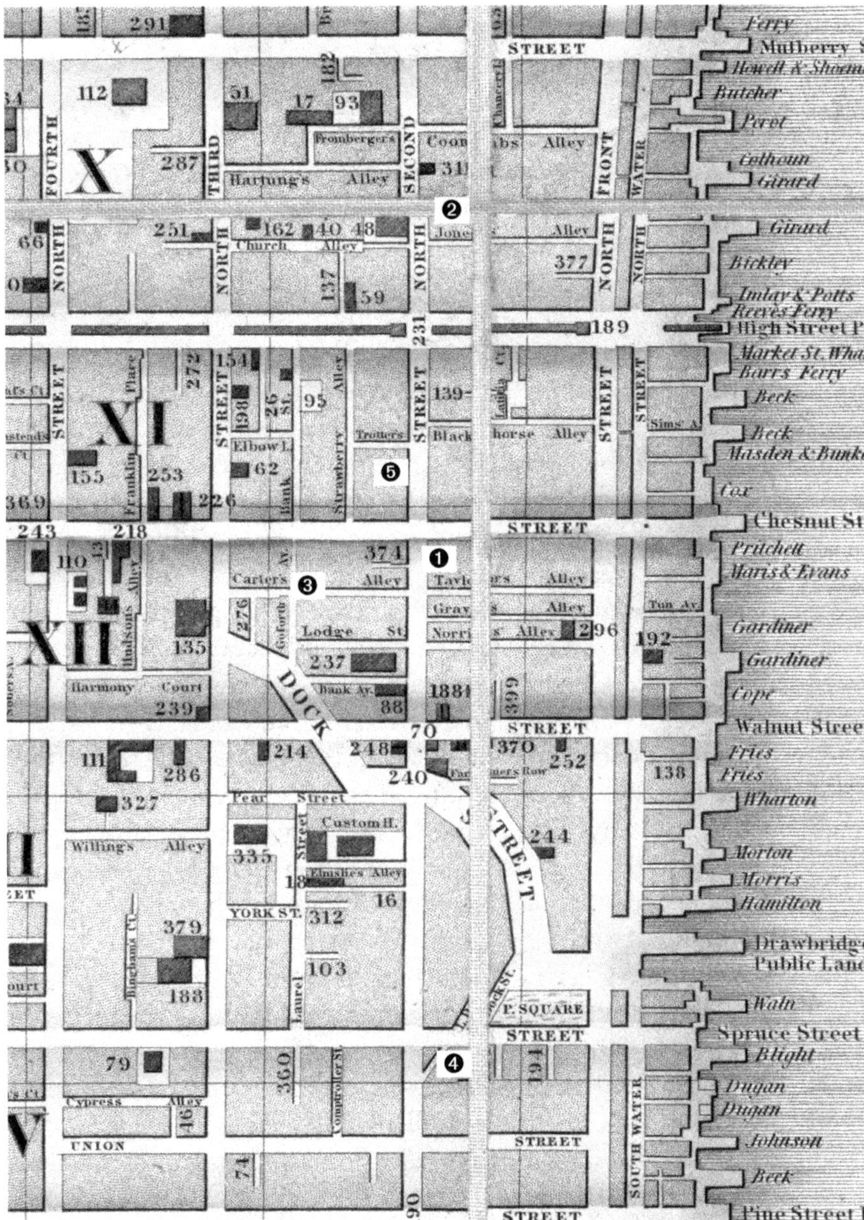

Known Residences of the Darraghs in Philadelphia, 1764–1786. **1.** 1764–1767, corner of Taylor's Alley and Second Street. **2.** 1769, Pewter Platter Alley (also known as Jones' Alley), near Second Street. **3.** 1773–1777, Carter's Alley and Goforth Alley. **4.** 1777-1785, Loxley House on Second Street below Spruce Street. **5.** 1786, west side of Second Street, eleven doors above Chestnut Street. Detail from "Plan of the City of Philadelphia and Adjoining Districts," published in 1830 by H. S. Tanner. (*Library of Congress*)

estate for their own use. Prior to that time, they continued to live and run a shop as renters, though several of the houses they lived in were of good quality and were solid business locations. The fact that they continued to rent for at least twenty years meant they were not tied to a single place in the city. Whether through preference or because they were subject to the whims of landlords who might choose to sell a property they were leasing, as happened to them at least once in the 1770s, they lived a somewhat peripatetic existence within the city confines. Yet by always renting on Second Street, or within a stone's throw of it, they managed to remain visible and easily accessible to their clientele. The properties they are known to have rented were generally attractive, genteelly appointed, and noteworthy in appearance. Three of their four homes up through the Revolution were on corner lots, which usually were more expensive to buy or rent.[15]

While it is possible that they had arranged a place to live before sailing for Pennsylvania, it seems likely that immediately upon arrival in autumn 1763, they stayed with someone already living in the city. They may have moved in for a few days with the Eddy family or another relative until they could secure more-permanent accommodations.

The first place we are certain the Darraghs lived was on the northeast corner of South Second Street and Taylor's Alley, across the street from James Byrne's Golden Fleece tavern. This first residence was a highly visible property where, by summer 1764, they set up a tobacco and dram shop. There they remained for about five years, until 1769, when they moved a few blocks north, to one of Abraham Mitchell's properties along Pewter Platter Alley, a small side street that ran from Second Street, just opposite Christ Church, east to Front Street. They did not remain there long, perhaps finding the site's lower visibility inconvenient for walk-in trade.

By 1773, they were renting more commodious premises that had recently been sold at sheriff sale by William Mitchell to Thomas Barclay, William Mitchell's business partner. That location was only half a block west of their original shop, this time on a corner lot of Carter's Alley, a continuation of Taylor's Alley on the west side of Second Street. In February 1777, they moved again to what was to be their most notable place of residence, the uniquely appointed Loxley House, on the southeast corner of Second and Spruce Streets.

Chapter 4

The Darraghs' Livelihoods

ONCE THEY ARRIVED in Pennsylvania, the Darraghs needed to establish some means of livelihood. William quickly went into business for himself, pursuing the tobacco trade, as he had in Dublin. It took a number of months for him to make arrangements. This turned out to be an inopportune moment to be venturing into a new enterprise; Philadelphia itself was in an economic depression that lasted several years. Nevertheless, in summer 1764, William introduced himself to Philadelphians through a front-page advertisement in the *Pennsylvania Gazette*, from which we learn considerable detail:

> William Darragh, Tobacco and Snuff Manufacturer, takes this method of informing the Publick, that he has opened a Tobacco and Snuff Manufactory, at the Corner of Taylor's Alley, in Second-street, Philadelphia; Where he makes and sells, by Wholesale and Retail, Superfine Scotch Snuff, Strasburgh Violet Rappee, Dublin high Toast Snuff, both coarse and fine; Grass cut, Roll and Pigtail Tobacco. The above named Goods he engages to be

> equal in Goodness to any imported into this Province. Those who please to favor him with their Commands, may be assured they will find an Advantage to deal with him. If any of his Goods should not be liked, he will change, or take them back again. He will give the highest price for the best Tobacco; also Four Shillings a Dozen, for old Snuff Bottles.[1]

Through James Eddy's connection, William Darragh began a business relationship with Christopher Marshall, a fellow Dubliner and convinced Quaker whose son had married William's niece in 1760. In the same issue of the *Gazette* that ran Darragh's first ad, Marshall's chemist's shop, at the "Sign of the Golden Ball in Chesnut Street," began plugging "Darragh's best Scotch snuff, allowed by good judges to be equal in goodness to any imported from abroad."

Often collectively referred to as "SP" or "Spanish snuff," several styles of snorting tobacco were popular at the time, especially three kinds: Scotch snuff; Maccaboy (originally from the island of Martinique); and rappee, sometimes known as Swedish snuff, which was grated. Scotch snuff, described as a dry, strong, unflavored and finely ground powder, generally took about eight weeks to ferment and so was a bit quicker to manufacture than rappee-style snuff. Lundy Foot, one of the best-known producers of this Scotch style, sometimes also referred to as "high toast" or "Irish toast," had begun manufacturing snuff in Dublin in 1753. His shop was just a two-minute walk from the Friends Meeting House in Sycamore Alley. William Darragh was probably familiar with a couple of tales that circulated at the time about how Lundy Foot had hit on this particular style. In a folk etymology, the notion of "Scotch" snuff was said to have derived from the word "scorched" rather than having anything to do with Scotland.[2]

The first story, recounted later by an anonymous author, attributes the discovery of "scorching" to a mistake made by a stereotypical drunken Irishman:

> With respect to the origin of this favourite Snuff, there is a story pretty generally known, about Lundifoot leaving a man up all night to watch an oven or kiln used for drying the scented Snuffs. Poor Paddy amused himself by emptying a whiskey bottle, and forgot his charge. The snuffs were discovered in the morning, burnt into the real high dried; and Lundifoot gave it a name from the Irish Blackguard who caused the fortunate mishap.

The writer, however, did not believe this account of what had happened to be true, and related a second version:

> The real truth is this:—a large Tobacco warehouse had been burnt down in Dublin, and Lundifoot, or rather Lundy Foot, then a poor man—a porter at the same warehouse, purchased, for a mere trifle, a large quantity of scorched and burnt Tobacco from off the ruins. This he ground up into a new sort of Snuff, which he sold excessively cheap among the poorer sort of Irish. It was much admired for its pungency, and soon grew into immense repute. Lundy Foot opened a shop, gave the Snuff his own name, and became a thriving man; but his invention has generally been known as Irish Blackguard, from the persons who first gave publicity to its excellence.[3]

William Darragh found he had plenty of competition. The Philadelphia newspapers for 1763 and 1764 show several shopkeepers selling Scotch snuff, most of it imported. Carrying out his manufacture at a city location rather than at a mill, it is likely that he created relatively small batches. That the scale of his operation was small to start with we can see in his plea for locally sourced tobacco and his need for bottles to package the snuff. But by following a good recipe and using American-grown tobacco, without the added costs of transshipping twice, back and forth across the Atlantic, he stood a good chance of getting a foothold in the local market by offering low prices. The way he advertised his discount pricing reveals his genteel education and refined manner of speaking: "Those who please to favor him with their Commands, may be assured they will find an Advantage to deal with him."

Darragh's tobacco shop, on the northeast corner of Second Street and Taylor's Alley (which today is called Ionic Street) was in a newer section of town, one of a number of buildings that had been erected in the early 1760s by James James. Because James resided in the building prior to the Darraghs, it seems reasonable to suppose that this property was a cut above the others in the new row, as befitted its attractive corner location. The place had been for a few brief years the busy printing shop of James Rivington, before he moved his operation to New York. Rivington, an interesting character in his own right, was notorious for publishing a Tory-slanted newspaper in New York throughout that city's long occupation during the Revolutionary War. Unknown to most people at the time, he used this position as a cover to feed intelligence to the American army.[4]

Situated directly across the street from a popular tavern, James Byrne's Golden Fleece, which opened about 1764, the immediate area around the Darragh shop was new, dynamic, and appealing. The Darragh establishment held allure of its own. To take better advantage of the walk-in trade, William set himself up as a public housekeeper, a person licensed by the governor "to sell spiritous liquors by the small measure." Not only could visitors indulge in tobacco and snuff at the Darraghs' shop, they could also drink and, presumably, engage the voluble proprietor or his wife in friendly conversation. Their host was reputed to be a loquacious person. Samuel Rowland Fisher, who disliked William Darragh, described him in an uncharitable comment as "a talkative, boisterous man." With the infant John, plus seven-year-old Ann and eight-year-old Charles about the premises, the Darragh shop must surely have been a lively place. Rounding out the household, an indentured servant helped Darragh manufacture snuff. They employed a female servant as well.[5]

Philadelphia was a thirsty town. Well over a hundred licensed public houses did business in the city at the time, while many other unlicensed "tippling houses" operated quietly, if not entirely secretly. From the colony's early days, Pennsylvania law spelled out policies that governed the tavern trade, controlling who was permitted to sell alcohol for consumption. Licenses were issued for full-fledged tavern operators, but also for "publick housekeepers," people who dispensed alcoholic drinks in their homes, usually in a front room of the house.

The colony regulated the sale and serving of alcohol carefully, setting the maximum prices that could be charged for a glass of beer or spirits. The city's tavern trade came under close scrutiny from the municipal and provincial governments. Liquor licenses were reviewed and issued annually. Philadelphia's Mayor's Court screened applicants for liquor licenses in the city, accepting some and denying others deemed unfit, recommending people "to his Honor the Governor for his License to sell spirituous Liquors by the small Measure in the Houses where they now dwell in this City." This court also gauged existing license holders' congruence with sound social practice and with the law, being especially mindful of whether they paid their annual licensing fee.

Only a few years of eighteenth-century licensing records survive. Fortunately, among them are records relating to William Darragh. We know that he applied for a license in 1767, paying £2 6s. 0d., the standard fee for a midtier license, as distinct from a less expensive license to sell only beer, or the £3 6s. 0d. tavern license fee that James Byrne was paying for the Golden Fleece across the street. Though public records don't show Darragh applying for a license in prior years, he may well have begun operating his dramshop earlier. Each year in July, many of the "old publick Housekeepers" were recommended to continue. Others were not. For unknown reasons, in 1768, William Darragh's name appeared on the city of Philadelphia's exception list, among thirty-six others whose licenses were recommended for discontinuation. It is unclear whether the governor accepted some or all of those recommendations. While Darragh's license may have lapsed in 1768, he was back in the good graces at least by 1771, authorized once again to operate a dramshop on Second Street.[6]

The presence of the Darraghs' shop on South Second Street appears to have motivated at least one relative to settle close by. In 1766, Blair and Ann McClenachan purchased a property at the southwest corner of Second Street and Carter's Alley, diagonally across from the Darraghs. By that time, the McClenachans had three young daughters who could play with their cousins across the way.[7]

William and Lydia used newspaper advertisements as a means to launch a number of new enterprises. Over twenty-five years, from 1764 to 1789, family members ran at least seven different ads announcing new lines of businesses in Philadelphia. William pursued several distinct occupations, working as a tobacco manufacturer and retailer, dramshop operator, school teacher, and stenographer. Likewise, Lydia promoted several different services, including wet nurse, "layer out of the dead," and shopkeeper. Without appearing to have advertised, she also developed a considerable following as a midwife and nurse. It is not known if she pursued any of these employments while living in Dublin. Additionally, daughter Ann began advertising as a shopkeeper selling imported goods at the family store in 1778, while son John announced his engraving services there in 1783. It was the family's thrifty practice to utilize only one or two initial announcements, afterward trusting to the custom and relationships they were able to cultivate to sustain their various ventures over time.[8]

We can document Lydia Darragh's contributions to the family's income beginning in 1765. In November, William ran a short advertisement offering Lydia's services as a wet or dry nurse, the earliest indication we have of Lydia's involvement in any kind of nursing care. The notice itself was a simple announcement, which didn't mention her by name: "A woman who can be well recommended for either Wet or Dry Nursing wants Employment. Enquire at William Darragh's, Tobacconist, in Second-street, near Chestnut-street."[9] Their son John had been born two years earlier, on December 5, 1763, shortly after they arrived in Philadelphia. Their next surviving child, William, was born in July 1766. Infant mortality at the time was high; Lydia herself had lost three children in infancy between 1758 and 1762.[10] The following year, Lydia paid five shillings to post another ad, this time offering mortuary services. In this one, she identified herself by name.

> The Subscriber, living in Second-street, at the Corner of Taylor's Alley, opposite the Golden Fleece Tavern, takes this Method of informing the Public, that she intends to make Grave-Clothes, and lay out the Dead, in the neatest Manner; and as she is informed a Person in this Business is much wanted in this City, she hopes, by her Care, to give Satisfaction to those who will be pleased to favor her with their Orders.
> Lydia Darragh.[11]

Lydia Darragh was still employed in that business in 1773, when she provided "black Buttons and Buckles" for the funeral clothing of Mary Symonds, a milliner who lived nearby. Lydia may simply have reached into her shop inventory to supply these items. But in the business of making grave clothes, she would have employed the skills of a seamstress to fashion shrouds and other apparel. Today, the term *milliner* denotes a person who makes women's hats, but at the time a milliner was "One who sells ribands and dresses for women." Symonds's millinery shop sold a wide assortment of trimmings for ladies' fashions. Advertisements list her store on the south side of Chestnut Street, six doors east of Second Street, in a property owned by Thomas Doyle, a Lancaster County hatmaker. It may seem odd that the buttons and buckles could not be found within Symonds's own store, but she may not have kept such items in somber black. As a "layer out of the dead," Lydia Darragh may have focused on black grave goods. Such low-key trimmings would have been appropriate if she were selling articles for sober Quaker women's fashions as well. After her passing, the contents of Symonds's shop were sold at discount to large purchasers; it is not hard to imagine Lydia Darragh acquiring some of the inventory to expand her own shop and trade. It is worth noting that later, Lydia Darragh's daughter Ann also pursued the millinery trade while operating out of the family shop, in continuance of one of her mother's lines of business.[12]

We learn from various sources that Lydia Darragh was an active midwife, a role she filled till the end of her life. Because she didn't advertise midwife services, we don't know when she may have begun pursuing that occupation. She certainly had ample personal experience of childbirth before coming to Philadelphia, having already borne at least six children while still in Dublin. She may have begun working at it in Philadelphia shortly after her arrival in 1763, the same year Dr. William Shippen began to offer his services as a "man midwife" to the community. It is clear that her obstetric practice kept her busily engaged. In his discussion of Philadelphia midwives, historian John Fanning Watson praised Lydia Darragh for assisting "in increasing the census of the city more than any other lady of her profession."[13]

Lydia Darragh's obituary bore out Watson's claim, noting that she "applied herself, for the support of her family, to a profession, in which the female part of society experienced her skill, tenderness and assiduity." The article went on to praise her as a model for others to emulate: "Let her example enliven the hope of the industrious, and give strength to the virtuous." An opportunistic midwife, Anne Emes, whom Lydia Darragh may have mentored, lost no time applying this advice. Four days after Lydia's death, Emes ran an ad through which she attempted to pick up Darragh's clientele and assume her mantle as one of the foremost midwives in the burgeoning city.[14] Emes's ad is worth reading, because it sheds light on the practice of midwifery at the time:

> Ann Emes presents her Respects to the Ladies of Philadelphia and informs them, that she has Removed from her late Dwelling in Fourth street to the east side of Third street, three Doors below Church alley, where she is to be found at any Moment, Night or Day. From the long Experience which Ann Emes has had in the Practice of Midwifery, as well as from the good Understanding which ever subsisted between Catharine Patten, Lydia Darrah and herself, she hopes that every future Trial of her Skill and Tender-

ness will justify her Title to the Care of Ladies expecting, and under Confinement.[15]

Midwifery served as an entree to a complex of naturally related professions: midwife, nurse, and "mortician." Midwives were necessarily involved in providing nursing care, often throughout their patient's pregnancy, and especially during confinement. In writing about diarist Martha Ballard, a healer and midwife of the period, who practiced in Maine, historian Laurel Thatcher Ulrich explained how a woman might develop such a skill set:

> As a young matron, she no doubt watched with sick neighbors and assisted at births, until in midlife, with her own child-rearing responsibilities diminished, she became a more frequent helper and eventually a healer and a midwife. Midwives were the best paid of all the female healers, not only because they officiated at births, but because they encompassed more skills, broader experience, longer memory. . . . A midwife was the most visible and experienced person in a community of healers who shared her perspective, her obligations, her training, and her labor.[16]

In the cities, this was a period of increased competition between male doctors, who acted with the authority of a formal education, and female medical practitioners, including midwives, who learned their skills in less formal but still effective ways. To be sure, many women preferred the services of a female midwife to those of a male doctor. A male physician who aided women in childbirth often billed himself as a "man midwife." The distinction was an important one. Many women felt more comfortable with the services of another female in such an intimate situation, despite a doctor's supposedly greater medical expertise. Female midwives came with a considerable amount of proficiency in this particular field, generally having served what amounted to an apprenticeship under more-experienced midwives over a period of years. Many women delivered hundreds of babies in the course of their careers. Most had direct personal experience and could empathize with what a mother was going through, having gone through childbirth themselves, something a "man midwife" could never do. Additionally, women were felt to be more tender and sensitive to their patient's situation and needs, though clearly some midwives could be imperious and impatient, as witnessed in seventeenth century Boston when Alice Tilly was prosecuted because her bedside manner was thought offensive and dangerous. A skilled midwife made use of her credible experience to guide a distressed and fearful woman through the alarming, painful process of childbirth. This intimacy served to create a special relationship of trust between the midwife and patient, and that trust influenced others' opinions of the reliability and veracity of the midwife that oftentimes extended beyond the lying-in room.[17]

Those doctors who were also man midwives had to divide their services among a greater number of patients with a wide variety of problems, many of which required urgent attention. Female midwives generally had more time to spend with an individual patient, being solely focused on her care and comfort during the delivery, even when labor was protracted. Doctors were able to charge a premium for their formal training and so tended to be more expensive. In the later years of the eighteenth century, the decision to call in a midwife instead of a doctor was often an economic one, especially among those with fewer financial resources. Lydia served all women, rich and poor. As her obituary noted, she practiced her skill among the "poor and unfortunate" as well as the wealthy.[18]

The value set on a midwife's services in the eighteenth century varied somewhat by locale and circumstance. In the rural area around Augusta, Maine, late in the eighteenth century, Martha Ballard's usual fee was six to nine shillings, depending on the complexity of the delivery. Her fee was payable in cash, but more often paid in kind and frequently not immediately collectable—a delay in payment of months was more common than not. Even doctors, such as William Shippen, in cosmopolitan Philadelphia, often collected their fees in goods or services rather than in cash, especially from poorer patients. Payment in kind may have been even more likely during the British occupation of 1777–1778, when specie was in short supply. The vital expertise of midwives commanded payment even for those enslaved women who practiced the art. Enslaved midwives of Virginia at this time were collecting fees of between 7s. 6d. and 10 shillings per delivery from plantation owners for increasing their wealth by bringing new slaves into the world.[19]

It is reasonable to think that Lydia Darragh's fees were at least comparable to those being paid in nearby Virginia. By comparison, a fee of 10 shillings would place her economically at least at the level of a successful working man, or possibly even that of one of the lesser gentry. In 1774, a laborer in Philadelphia's shipyards might earn 9 shillings per day, when actually working, while a common laborer might average only 3 shillings daily. A private in a regular unit of foot in the British army earned substantially less—only 8 a pence day, the equivalent of two-thirds of a shilling. Philadelphia politician Joseph Galloway observed that in 1759, for a gentleman to live in Philadelphia "but meanly, and maintain a Horse will cost seven [shillings] at least" per day. Though there is evidence that the Darragh family may have struggled somewhat economically in Philadelphia as late as 1775, as we will see, their financial standing became visibly more comfortable in their later years. Much of this was attributable to Lydia's livelihood.[20]

That livelihood came at considerable personal cost, especially because she was the mother of young children herself. As midwife advertisements noted, she had to be available "day or night at short notice." Midwives were usually called at the onset of labor and remained through delivery and beyond if additional nursing care was required for the mother or child. This urgent and unpredictable calling would have taken Lydia Darragh out of the house, perhaps weekly or more often, sometimes for days at a stretch. Her youngest daughter would not turn ten, an age at which children were often thought old enough to fend for themselves, until late in 1779. In the meantime, with their father occupied at his own professions, responsibility for child care might have been relegated to the older siblings, especially to their oldest daughter, Ann.[21]

Midwives were well known in their communities through the multiple relationships they built while pursuing their practice. It was common for several women to be present at a lying-in. In addition to the mother and the midwife, female relatives or neighbors might attend the birth. Midwives were often joined by assistants, like Ann Emes, who would help with various tasks, while learning the business. These women's gatherings were opportunities for conversation, the sharing of women's knowledge and culture, and the exchange of news. Information passed around in the birthing chamber had acquired the derogatory name among men of "gossip," from a word initially used to describe a child's godparent, that gradually morphed into a term for these gatherings of women. In his famed dictionary, composed in 1755, Lydia Darragh's contemporary Samuel Johnson cited that pejorative sense of the word among men, citing a gossip as, "One who runs about tattling like women at a lying-in." Excluded from this information conduit, men often found themselves surprised, even angered, when they stumbled across things that all the women around them knew and they didn't. But gossip, and trust in its veracity, was tied to the confidence people felt in the person bearing the story; and confidence in midwives, who frequently carry such information from one place to another, was generally strong. Such was the case with Lydia Darragh. In Lydia's Tale, we see her carrying secret information to an American officer, and, knowing her and her reputation, we see him immediately accepting that information as credible.[22]

Lydia's skill as a nurse probably had its genesis in midwifery and was an additional source of income for her. We know that she was reputed to be a capable and compassionate healer, sometimes treating problems that baffled even the most expert physicians in the city. Jacob Hiltzheimer's was a case in point. On October 15, 1776, he was struck with an unidentified but agonizing malady: "About one o'clock Thomas Pryor and I started on horse back to dine over Schuylkill, but we had not gone fifty yards before I was suddenly seized by a great pain in my right hip and forced to return. Doctors Cadwalader, Bond and Kearsley, were immediately summoned to my bedside, but could give me but little relief."

After two days of suffering, he finally called in Lydia Darragh to help. Praising her skill afterward, he wrote: "October 17. My pain still continued excessive, but with the help of a clever little Irish woman named Darrah, I got some relief by a clyster."[23]

It was not uncommon for eighteenth-century women to die in childbirth or shortly afterward. Infant mortality was especially high. The midwife provided nursing care for both mother and child, and she was right by their side if they died. This made her the most immediate and most logical person to compose the deceased for burial. Given her experience in these matters, a midwife might be called on to provide funerary services for others as well. So, while we don't know when Lydia Darragh became a midwife, we can theorize that it was sometime before her 1766 mortuary advertisement, and that these skills stemmed from her obstetric practice. We can confidently say that she earned a decent living, independent of her husband's income, by pursuing several different but related occupations: midwife, mortician, and nurse, in addition to helping keep the family's shop.[24]

We don't know how long William Darragh continued to operate as a tobacconist, but advertisements show he was still at it in 1766, after which notices for his tobacco business ceased. Selling out of a prominent corner location on busy Second Street and augmenting his trade by the sale of spirituous liquors, he may have developed enough regular custom that he didn't feel a need for the expense of further advertising. That the family continued to operate a shop for the walk-in trade beyond the 1760s we know from his application for a liquor license in 1771.

It is clear however that by 1769, Darragh faced significant competition for locally made Scotch snuff. Early that year, as a newspaper ad attests, the partnership of Thomas Gilpin and Joshua Fisher "erected a new snuff-mill, where that article is carefully manufactured. Choice Scotch Snuff of an excellent quality, may be had in any Quantity, of Joshua Fisher and Sons, carefully packed for land carriage or exportation, and considerable allowance made for those who take quantities." Such an enterprise certainly threatened to undercut the Darraghs' own snuff manufactory. As we will see, bad blood eventually developed between William Darragh and the well-heeled Fisher family. This business rivalry may well have been its source.[25]

Also by 1769, the Darraghs' eldest son Charles was thirteen—old enough to be trusted serving customers in the store, which may have allowed William time to pursue other ventures. Whether because of this additional help or the faltering of his tobacco business, Darragh returned to the pursuit of his earlier occupations. In June of that year he began publicizing his services as a teacher as well as a stenographer, a skill he may have learned while still in Dublin.[26]

A dozen different forms of shorthand existed in the English-speaking world by the mid-eighteenth century. Several instructional manuals had been published and were available for Darragh to read, though he may have learned his technique directly from another practitioner. William used both terms, *shorthand* and *stenography*, to describe the method he followed. There were several active shorthand specialists in Dublin, such as John Angell, Sussex Dare, and John Lodge, who gave instruction during the time William Darragh lived there.[27]

Without a sample of Darragh's shorthand writing, it is impossible to say which method he may have followed. We know that Dare taught "the noted Mr. Weston's method" which in turn was based on the shorthand published by Theophilus Metcalf in 1655. Ebenezar Wickes advertised his services as a teacher of "Mr. Weston's Stenography" in

Philadelphia in 1731, but does not seem to have sustained himself long in that business. Judging from the paucity of eighteenth-century American newspaper advertisements for stenography, it would seem that William Darragh did not face a lot of competition in the field.[28]

It is interesting to note, however, that examples of his shorthand still existed in the hands of his descendants many years later. Henry Darrach, who communicated with Darragh's great-granddaughter in the late 1890s, wrote that in his day, some family members had preserved samples of William Darragh's stenography, which they took to be evidence of his direct involvement in espionage. In the absence of any corroboration that William ever acted as a spy, other than a family story, it is more likely that the examples his family saw, but could not decipher, were simple examples of transcription or documents he used in his teaching.[29]

To draw attention to their abilities and to earn additional income, eighteenth-century practitioners of stenography sometimes resorted to transcribing and publishing events of great interest to the public. It was not uncommon for a stenographer to take down the testimony at a sensational trial, as Edward Hodgson did in London when "The Honourable" Cosmo Gordon was tried for murder after killing an opponent in a duel. In peaceable Philadelphia, a good Quaker sermon was as likely to attract favorable attention as a murder trial. To that end, William Darragh took down and published the spontaneous preaching of a visiting Quaker minister, Rachel Wilson, "a female friend from Old England." Though he used the occasion to help stimulate business, his sincere interest was revealed in his literate and earnest introduction to the short twenty-four-page publication.[30]

Presumably hoping to drum up his shorthand business, Darragh advertised his book for sale, as well as promoting his services both as a schoolmaster and teacher of stenography:

> To the Public. This is to give notice there is printed, and now ready to be delivered by the subscriber, at his house in Pewter-Platter-Alley, near Second-Street, the substance of a discourse, taken down in short hand, as was spoken by a female Friend from Old England; also a prayer by another Friend. delivered on the same morning, the third day of last Fifth month, at the friends Meeting-house, in Pine-Street, Philadelphia; being the time a marriage was celebrated; to which is added a short preface by the editor.

> The subscriber still continues keeping school, where youth are carefully taught to read, write, and understand accompts in the most correct manner; also short-hand writing, the same being a most easy and speedy method to write any discourse as delivered; the knowledge of which may be easily attained in a few weeks.
> William Darragh, School-Master, and Teacher of Stenography.

In seeking stenography students, Darragh directly imitated the optimistic promotions of Sussex Dare and other Dublin shorthand instructors, who promised to teach the process quickly "in a few months" and even "in a few weeks." By noting that he "still continues keeping school," the ad reveals that he had already been teaching in the city for a while, possibly since his arrival.[31]

Throughout this period, the Darraghs continued to rent rather than purchase property, which kept the family on the move, though they always remained close to Second Street. The stenography ad indicates that for reasons unknown, but most probably financial, the family had given up their desirable business location at Second and Taylor's Alley and moved to a rather less prominent spot along Pewter Platter Alley, a little north of High Street, the city's main business thoroughfare.[32]

The Darraghs were prosperous enough on arrival in Philadelphia to afford domestic help, a practice that continued throughout Lydia's lifetime. Hannah Haines's rendition of Lydia's Tale mentions that they employed a servant maid in 1777, and Lydia's will shows that she still had a female servant in 1789. William was initially well-enough capitalized to employ an indentured servant in his little snuff manufactory, at least for a brief time. But on September 27, 1764, just as his business was getting started, William ran an ad in the *Pennsylvania Gazette*:

> Forty Shillings reward.
> Run away from the Subscriber, living in Second-street, Philadelphia, on the 21st inst September, an Irish Servant Boy, named Michael Dunn, about 17 Years of Age, 5 Feet 3 Inches high, dark brown Hair, marked somewhat with the Small-Pox, long visaged, and of a pale Complexion; had on, when he went away, a light grey Ratteen Coat, with carved Brass Buttons, a new Check Shirt, and an old Pair of Leather breeches, an old Wool Hat, and Pepper

> and salt coulored Pair of Worsted Stockings. Whoever secures said Servant, so that his Master may have him again, shall have the above reward, and all reasonable Charges, paid by William Darragh.
> N.B. All Masters of Vessels, and others, are forbid to carry him off, or harbour him, at their Peril.[33]

It is possible that the Darraghs purchased Michael Dunn's indenture once they arrived in Philadelphia. But it seems more likely that they had brought him as an apprentice on their voyage to America, paying for his passage. The records for St. Catherine's Roman Catholic Parish in Dublin note on September 23, 1748, the baptism of a boy named Michael Dunn, the son of Matthew and Anne, who is close in age. That this church was four blocks from the Meath Street Quaker Meeting is suggestive. The date he chose to run away was very close to what would have been his sixteenth birthday, an age by which he may have seen himself as an adult capable of deciding his own fate.[34]

The timing was such that Michael may have come to work for Darragh's Church Street tobacco shop about 1762 through one of the charter working schools, which were described in a Dublin almanac.

> The Schools erected proceed hopefully: In most of them, the Children manufacture their own Cloathing, and the Boys cultivate Nurseries of Fruit and Timber Trees. The Children admitted are such only, as are born of Popish Parents, and of sound Health and Limbs. Their Age from 6 to 10 Years old. They are placed in Schools remote from their former Abode, and the Boys at 16, and Girls at 14 Years of Age, are apprenticed in Protestant Families. Since the Opening of these Schools, about 1300 Children have been so apprenticed. The Society give a Portion of Five pounds to every Person educated in the Charter-Schools, upon his or her marrying a Protestant. Gentlemen, Manufacturers, (particularly Linen Weavers) and farmers, may be supplied with Servants and Apprentices, either Boys or Girls, educated in these Schools, by the Secretary, Mr. James Simon in Fleet-street.[35]

Such apprenticeships were qualitatively of a different order from those of highly skilled craftsmen, like goldsmiths, for instance, which ended with the apprentice becoming a journeyman in a lucrative trade.

In the cases of these poor people, the immediate benefit was that poor families were relieved of the burden of a mouth to feed. While the child might learn to be productive at some common labor, it seems unlikely that many of these "apprentices" ended up as master craftsmen, much less merchants and traders. No reliable record of this particular Michael Dunn is to be found after William's runaway announcement. As far as can be told, he made good his escape from the Darraghs and melted into the colonial population along with many another fugitive apprentice.

As we have seen, the Darraghs pursued multiple sources of income simultaneously, and they continued to run a shop out of their home at a number of different addresses between 1764 and 1789. Various records show the family as shopkeepers at several points throughout Lydia's lifetime. Though we don't have direct evidence for the family shop between 1771 and 1778, it seems most probable that they persisted in following this line of business. As noted earlier, William Darragh was licensed as a public housekeeper in 1767 and again in 1771. Though there is no evidence he was authorized in any other year, that does not necessarily mean he stopped selling liquor. Did the Darraghs, like so many others, simply ignore any temporary lack of a license and continue serving alcohol to their customers in their shops at subsequent locations? The question raises an intriguing possibility.

By 1773, the Darraghs were renting a place owned by Thomas Barclay between Second and Third Streets a few doors north of Dock Creek. This property was on the southwest corner of Carter's Alley and a post alley, variously referred to as Smith's or Goforth Alley half a block west of their old Second Street shop. Their family friends, the sons of Christopher Marshall, owned several properties along the alley. Our earliest knowledge of the Darraghs' living there came on April 21, when Barclay ran an ad in the *Pennsylvania Journal and the Weekly Advertiser*: "To be sold by public Vendue at the London Coffee-House, on Saturday the first of May, at six o'clock in the evening, if not disposed of sooner at private sale, A House in Carter's Alley now in the tenure of William Daragh; any person inclining to purchase may know the terms by applying to the subscriber. Thomas Barclay."

In the event, he was unable to sell the property, and the Darraghs remained in residence there another three and a half years.[36]

The corner property they rented from Barclay contained an attractive house, well-appointed with wainscotting, and, in addition to the living quarters, a large room that could be used for commercial purposes. Such a space would have been most convenient as a schoolroom for William to continue his teaching or to house the family store. Fresh water was easily accessed—there was a convenient pump on the alley two doors to the west. Evidence suggests that they may have continued to run their shop, selling tobacco and spirituous liquors, at this location.[37]

Today, the ground where the Darraghs lived on Carter's Alley lies within the boundaries of Independence National Historical Park, beneath the Museum of the American Revolution, on property the museum acquired through a land swap with the National Park Service. Archaeological exploration prior to constructing the museum turned up numerous bottles, glasses, and other discarded remains in a privy pit located on Thomas Barclay's corner property, debris suggesting that a dramshop once operated there. Noted archaeologist Rebecca Yamin, in analyzing the discoveries, attributed this tippling house to Benjamin and Mary Humphreys, who had moved into the house next door to the Darraghs in 1776 and whose property shared the privy pit with them, as was common in the city at that time. While the Humphreys were authorized to sell liquor in 1774 and 1775, their license appears to have lapsed later, just as William Darragh's may have after 1771. The Humphreys may well have run a dramshop on Carter's Alley without a license. While living there in 1783, Mary was charged with keeping a disorderly house, which could have been an unlicensed drinking establishment or a brothel. But it seems possible that at least some of the snuff bottles, punch bowls, tankards, and drinking glasses found in the jointly used privy were residue from the Darraghs' own dramshop. Their four-year tenure was surely long enough for a significant amount of trash to have been dumped down their latrine.[38]

Chapter 5

Lydia Darragh's Quaker Faith

UNDERSTANDING THE Quaker faith can shed light on Lydia Darragh's experience and actions during the Revolution, so it is worth taking time to consider how Quakerism developed and how this religion and its culture shaped her thinking. In the 1530s, taking advantage of the growing Protestant Reformation in Europe, King Henry VIII separated his country's religion from the Roman Catholic Church, establishing the Church of England, with himself as its supreme head. During the following centuries, through disagreements over various matters of faith and practices, a number of nonconformist English Protestants broke away from the state religion, setting up their own separate denominations, much to the aggravation of the Anglican clergy and the government.

Among these dissenters was George Fox, who, in the 1650s, argued that Jesus Christ spoke directly, without an intermediary clergy, to those individuals who would listen for his voice. When hauled before the magistrates for blasphemy, he claimed, "I bade them tremble at the word of the Lord." For this he was dubbed a Quaker, a term intended to be derisive but that he and his followers adopted as their badge of honor, often describing themselves, as did William Penn, as "the people called Quakers."[1]

Rejecting Anglican practices, which channeled authority and knowledge of God through a paid priesthood, Quakers valued direct, personal inner enlightenment from God as preached by Fox. Friends' knowledge of God's will came from listening internally for his voice—seeking the "Inward Light." For Friends, each individual was potentially in contact with the deity personally, if only they could calm their inner turmoil so they could hear God's Word—the Truth.[2]

These early Quaker dissidents were both evangelical—they sought to convert others to their ideas—and demonstrative. They frequently captured attention through outré actions—such as appearing in public naked or scattering money in the streets—that would create an opening for dialogue about their spiritual thinking, a common tactic among evangelists in religions that have not yet become settled and routinized. Quaker activists undermined priestly authority and perhaps worse, their livelihood by visiting churches during services, criticizing ministers, and arguing directly in opposition to them before their own parishioners. Not only did Quakers contest these priests' words in their own sanctuaries, by drawing away worshippers toward their own upstart religion, they threatened the ministers' income. Friends' adherents refused to pay the tithes that supported the Anglican clergy. This infuriated the Anglican priesthood, which clamored for governmental action.[3]

Worse still was the Friends' challenge to established government at all levels. These upstarts actively opposed worldly authority in favor of the divine, symbolized most prominently by their refusal to take oaths. Quakers believed they should speak the Truth at all times, and that swearing to the Truth implied two different kinds of Truth, one with oaths and one without oaths. Many non-Quakers, finding this concept difficult to grasp, resented what they saw as Friends' incomprehensible obstinacy in refusing to conform to common practice. Quakers also rejected outward forms of respect, such as doffing their hats to others or using formal terms of address, instead preferring to address every person, no matter their station, with the familiar "Thee." This was particularly galling to the nobility and other pillars of society who saw themselves as occupying a loftier social stratum than these lowly upstarts. Many saw the Quaker manner of plain dress as a highly visible and insulting repudiation of the vanity of fashion. Quaker rejection of custom extended even to their method of time keeping; rejecting the names of heathen gods for the days of the week and the months of the year, they called these increments simply by number, such as "Fourth Day" for Wednesday and "First Month" for January. Friends' beliefs, religious practices, and mode of living were a critique of norms that set them apart from their neighbors. These differences, and Friends' dogged adherence to them, set the stage for conflict.[4]

Official oppression and persecution followed, beginning about 1650, culminating in England's 1662 Quaker Act, which proscribed their refusal to swear oaths and forbade their assembly "under a pretence of religious Worship." Infractions were punishable by escalating penalties including fines, imprisonment, and hard labor. During this period, as a defensive posture—a matter of survival—Friends gradually withdrew themselves from worldly affairs. They tamed the overtly demonstrative behaviors that caused them to clash with government while still sustaining such basic tenets as plainness and simplicity, rejection of a priesthood, and their testimony against war. At the same time, they gradually refined their initially somewhat inchoate doctrine and practices into a form of consistent orthodoxy.[5]

This "cooling of the spirit" helped pave the way for the 1689 Toleration Act, which finally allowed freedom of worship to religions not conforming to Anglicanism, including Quakerism. In the meantime, many Friends had begun migrating to the newly established British colony of Pennsylvania, William Penn's "Holy Experiment," where religious toleration flourished under the benevolent rule of Quaker leadership. When Pennsylvania's first legislature met at Upland, December 4–7, 1682, it created a series of statutes known as the Great Law. Chapter 1 enshrined religious tolerance as a keystone of Pennsylvania government:

> [N]o Person now or at Any time hereafter Liveing in this Province who Shall Confess and acknowledge one Almighty God to be the Creatour Upholder and Ruler of the World and that professeth him or herselfe Obliged in Conscience to Live Peaceably and Justly under the Civill Government shall in any case be Molested or Prejudiced for his or her Conscientious Perswasion or Practice nor shall he or she at any time be Compelled to frequent or Maintaine any Religious Worshipp place or Ministry whatever Con-

trary to his or her mind but shall freely and fully Enjoy his or her Christian Liberty without any Interuption or reflection.[6]

One consequence of Friends' reliance on the inward and direct voice of God, and their rejection of what they saw as perfunctory priestly conduct, was that they did not codify their doctrine. No explicit credo set forth their religious tenets. Rather, knowledge of key beliefs was shared in oral testimony during Meetings for Worship, in references in the meetings' records and correspondence, and in private conversation. When Friends wrote or spoke of their beliefs, they did not do so following a prescribed formula but rather used the words that occurred to them personally and individually at the moment.[7]

Some of Friends' key beliefs were referred to as testimonies. Many of the testimonies denoted the significant differences that separated the manner of Friends from worldly behavior. Though these testimonies were frequently described using different terminology, among the most important beliefs were the Testimony of Truth, the Testimony against Oaths, the Testimony against War, and the Testimony of Simplicity.

The Testimony of Truth is a central tenet of Quaker belief. "Truth" is a metaphor for Jesus Christ, for the Word of God, and for the Voice of God that can be understood when attending to one's Inward Light. Truth was also the Friend's way of life, which spoke to others by its example. George Fox, one of the most influential early Quakers, urged people to "live in the life of truth and let the truth speak in all things." One aspect of living an exemplary life was that one must always speak the Truth and act honestly. In practice, a Quaker businessman would set a fair price for something and would not bargain in search of greater profit, which would be sinful. Quakers became renowned for honest dealing, which, because they could be trusted, gradually made them prosperous in turn. But when they refused to deviate from their principles to accommodate worldly interests, their insistence on personal integrity proved to be a two-edged sword. This became a serious problem for the leaders of Quaker Philadelphia during the revolutionary period, particularly in regard to swearing allegiance to either side in the conflict.[8]

The testimony against swearing oaths was based on Jesus's Sermon on the Mount, when he said, "But I say unto you, Swear not at all; neither by heaven; for it is God's throne: nor by the earth, for it is his footstool. . . . Neither shalt thou swear by thy head, because thou canst not make one hair white or black. But let your communication be, Yea, yea; Nay, nay: for whatsoever is more than these cometh of evil." If a person said a thing, it should be true, and if it was Truth, it would be wrong to embellish its simplicity.[9]

The peace testimony was particularly obnoxious to government leaders of any stripe. Quakers could not be compelled to perform military service, denying authorities a source of the warm bodies needed to force their political will on others. At first, this was not a problem in Pennsylvania. Under peaceable Quaker leadership, a military establishment was not a necessity. Diplomacy and fair dealing kept relations with the Indigenous peoples amicable. But as non-Quakers' hunger for land grew, so grew the native inhabitants' hostility toward those encroaching on their territory. Ironically, it was William Penn's own sons, by then reverted to Anglicanism, whose greed for land did much to sow the seeds of conflict with the formerly peaceful natives. In 1737, they swindled the trusting Lenape in a land grab known infamously as the Walking Purchase, by which they fraudulently claimed ownership of 1.2 million acres of land. Unscrupulous land speculators and squatters on the colony's fringes intensified the pressure on Native Americans. When they retaliated, the non-Quaker settlers demanded that the government defend them by force of arms. This the Quaker Assemblymen refused to do, leading to their gradual ouster from the legislature and a withdrawal by many Friends from the political arena.[10]

While the other testimonies were generally matters of the inward life, bearing witness to the Testimony of Simplicity was a thing that separated Friends from their neighbors in a way that was highly visible. Though as a result of their honest business practices many Friends became quite prosperous, they shunned flamboyant fashion and displays of material wealth to avoid inciting jealousy in others. Simplicity in dress and speech made Quakers immediately recognizable as different. Such differences in belief and outward appearance gradually became sources of friction as non-Quakers came to dominate the colony of Pennsylvania.

In Philadelphia, as in the British Isles, Quaker adherence to orthodoxy and orderly practice was maintained through a set of queries, which were discussed, reviewed, and certified four times a year, then reported by the Monthly Meetings to the Quarterly Meeting. The queries included questions for the meeting to answer, such as: "What is the state of your meeting? Is there any growth in the truth?" "Do friends, by example and precept, endeavour to train up their children, servants, and those under their care, in all godly conversation, and in frequent reading of the holy scriptures, as also in plainness of speech, behavior and apparel; and are friends faithful in admonishing such as are remiss therein?" "Do you bear a faithful and Christian testimony against the receiving or paying tithes?" "How are the poor among you provided for; and what care is taken for the education of their offspring?" "Do you bear a faithful testimony against bearing arms?"[11]

Friends in Philadelphia generally conducted "unprogrammed 'silent' meetings where the entire meeting for worship is held in expectant waiting on God." They also recognized elders and ministers, those with a special gift who might speak during meetings, but in such cases they valued an impromptu style of sermon preparation and delivery. Rachel Wilson, for instance, was a well-known preacher who paid a religious visit to North America, traveling extensively to various meetings throughout the British colonies. During her second visit to Philadelphia in fall 1769, many anticipated hearing her speak during a marriage ceremony in the city's Southern District meetinghouse.[12]

While Friends generally discouraged recording testimony at Meetings for Worship, they did not forbid it. Prepared to hear something profound that might be instructive for others, William Darragh used his stenographic skill to capture Rachel Wilson's ideas. While publishing her words served as an excellent advertisement of his services, Darragh could have recorded anything—a session of the assembly, a spectacular trial. That he chose a sermon demonstrated business acumen, in analyzing what was likely to sell in Quaker Philadelphia. But Darragh was also moved by his faith. His sincere belief shines through the act, as revealed in his brief preface, where he notes his intent: "The publishing of good books hath oftentimes been of great service, nay, hath often been the means of kindling a holy fire in the hearts of the lukewarm."[13]

Rachel Wilson's talk followed the theme, "Whatsoever he bids you do, that do." The early Friends' imperative, that their actions be exemplary, is echoed here. Quaker religious culture was not passive. Though they had gradually subdued their confrontational evangelism, the validation of faith through personal action remained a key part of their ethos. Wilson expressed the Quaker linkage between apprehending God's voice and taking action: "Since my sitting down here amongst you in this meeting, the thoughts of it came into my mind, without the least study or premeditation. I could not be silent, thinking it to be my duty, in obedience to the divine will; for I desired not the sound of my voice to be heard, but would much rather hear than be heard; but apprehending it to be my duty. . . . Woe be unto me if I preach not the gospel!"[14]

As noted earlier, Pennsylvania was begun intentionally as an exemplary Quaker society—a place people could look to and see Friends' values playing out in a peaceful, prosperous, and beneficial way. Over time, and aided by Quaker toleration, an influx of non-Quakers to this flourishing province gradually transformed it into a pluralistic community.

Many of the inhabitants of Philadelphia and its environs were Friends by culture, even if not especially active practitioners of the religion. While taking part in Quaker civil practices—living in the manner of Friends—not all birthright Quakers in the area adhered closely to the religion or its testimonies. Because they had been born into the Society of Friends, they were listed in their meeting's records as Friends. They may have been raised as Friends and attended meeting when they were younger, but, with time, drifted away from active practice. Yet they retained Quaker modes of dress, speech, and attitude. Others who had become convinced Friends might also drift away from religious practice yet keep Quaker customs.

Once a Quaker community had been established in the Delaware Valley in the late 1600s, and Quakers could govern themselves, those things that had set them apart from the mainstream became societal norms. This did not last. During the course of the eighteenth century, as the region filled with non-Quakers, attracted both by the orderly and prosperous society and the fertility and availability of the land, social friction once again came to dominate relations between Friends and others. A spirit of jealousy over Friends' prosperity and resentment of Quaker political power gradually prevailed in Pennsylvania. Ironically, by the time of the Revolution, the tolerant people, who had permitted others to live side by side with them as equals, became a people barely abided in their own home.

Chapter 6

The Coming of the Revolution

THE DARRAGH FAMILY arrived in Pennsylvania at a time when the relationship between Britain and its North American colonies was increasingly being called into question. The American Revolution did not simply happen overnight. Though the beginning of the trouble is generally associated with the Stamp Act crisis in 1765, its roots went much deeper than that. Over time, Britain and America had become separated by more than just the chasm of the Atlantic Ocean. The widening rift dividing the British and American peoples had several dimensions—economic and political to be sure, but more importantly, cultural.

The physical distance between these two societies was immense: as the crow flies, London and Philadelphia lay 3,500 miles apart—more like 4,000 miles in actual travel distance. Communication between Britain and its colonies was slow, leaving plenty of time for misunderstandings to grow and fester. Simply outfitting and sailing a ship to carry a message across the ocean was a complex, expensive, risky undertaking. Under the best conditions, it might take nearly three months for a single letter to receive a reply, assuming the vessels involved survived both legs of the journey. A notable example drives the point home.

On April 25, 1775, four days after the battles at Lexington and Concord, General Thomas Gage, commander in chief of the British army in North America, wrote to Secretary of War William Barrington and to the Earl of Dartmouth, secretary of state, to explain what had taken place. But the Massachusetts Provincial Congress wanted to get a leg up on its opponents by placing an American version of events in front of the British public before government officials could do so. Despite the need for speed, it took them nine days to collect depositions from the participants and compose an account that presented the revolutionaries' view of how the conflict had started. American ship captain John Darby set sail for England on April 28 in a fast schooner, the *Quero*, empty of cargo, in hopes of overtaking the official British report. Straining all his resources, Darby managed to arrive in London by May 29, where he delivered his packet of information to John Wilkes, who published the news in the *London Evening Post* the next day. Darby's lightning-fast race across the Atlantic had taken thirty-one days.[1]

Over a century and a half, the residents of Britain's North American colonies had gradually become a very different people. Though speaking the same language, their living conditions were quite dissimilar. Most significant, perhaps, was America's lack of a hereditary aristocracy. Certainly, the British nobility owned property and enterprises on the western side of the Atlantic and wielded great influence. But they were not physically present. Americans did not need to pay obeisance on a daily basis. Additionally, in many parts of North America, people from the British Isles lived cheek by jowl with those of other ethnicities: Germans, French, Africans, Dutch, Spanish, and Indigenous peoples, groups who had little familiarity with or reverence for the English gentry.

Another significant difference was the availability and affordability of land in the colonies. Continual migration toward sparsely settled areas by those seeking land pushed American frontiers farther from the more urbanized seacoast. Settlement over the course of generations, in places with scant safety or support networks, engendered a population with strong values of self-reliance and self-sufficiency. These people were well armed for sustenance through hunting and for self-defense against both aggressive neighbors in lawless areas and the aggrieved Indigenous peoples on whose lands they encroached. Habits of local self-government, with little actual influence from centralized British government, developed an expectation of self-determination that went well beyond common notions of English liberty.

Politically, the colonists generally adhered to the factional Whig-Tory dichotomy of the home country. Their thinking was also informed by events of the previous century and a half. Two seventeenth-century precedents auguring in favor of dramatic change lurked not far beneath political consciousness. First was the dramatic upheaval of the English Civil War, in which the reigning king, Charles I, was challenged politically, defeated militarily, and executed. Then there was the relatively bloodless Glorious Revolution of 1688, in which a second monarch, James II, was deposed by his daughter, Mary, and her foreign husband, William of Orange. British citizens, including those in the colonies, knew from these experiences that royal government could not rule absolutely but must be subject to the consent of the people.[2]

As the people in North America drifted away from Britain culturally, developing new dialects and different interests, attitudes, and practices, so too their politics gradually diverged from the mainstream of their parent nation. During the Darraghs' time in Pennsylvania before the Revolutionary War, colonial political affiliation did superficially resemble that of Britain. But American politics were suffused with local concerns, especially economic self-interest.

Because of its peculiar history of settlement, British North America was divided into numerous separate governmental jurisdictions, each with its own legislatures and laws. Granted, colonial legislation and rulings were based in English law, they still tended to diverge over local conditions and local experiences, as do the laws of the various states today. There was, however, a growing recognition that some kind of union of colonial governments might be useful. As early as the outset of the French and Indian War in 1754, when legislators from seven colonies met at the Albany Congress to discuss mutual defense, that persistent innovator Benjamin Franklin proposed a plan for unified colonial government, often referred to as the Albany Plan of Union.[3]

Based on local conditions and interests, politics in each of the colonies took on unique shapes. In Pennsylvania, tensions developed between the dominant European group, the Quakers, who had founded the colony, and a growing body of non-Quakers who did not share the same values. The original plan in the colony, pursued by the Quakers and practiced by the Swedes before them, had been to acquire land from the native inhabitants in a peaceable way, through purchase and treaties. This worked admirably well in the seventeenth and early eighteenth centuries. But as non-Quakers became more numerous, and as greed for land grew stronger, fair dealing was cast by the wayside. By 1737, even William Penn's own sons, now the Proprietors of Pennsylvania, had schemed to defraud the Lenape of an immense tract of land. That year, they perpetrated the infamous Walking Purchase, in which, by mutual agreement, the extent of a land sale in northern Pennsylvania was to be determined by the distance a man might walk in a day. Instead of acting in good faith, the provincial secretary of Pennsylvania, James Logan, sent the colony's three fastest runners to make the "walk," one of whom covered seventy miles. The tally: 1.2 million acres of land for the avaricious Proprietors.[4]

The Friends who dominated the Pennsylvania Assembly found it increasingly difficult to maintain their separatist, moral approach to government, especially when military measures for defense were ordered by Great Britain. In such situations, when the outside world impinged on their value system, they resorted to evasion, attempting to turn a blind eye to the implications of the actions they were required to take. Benjamin Franklin described how, in the 1740s, they could wash their hands clean of responsibility:

> My being many years in the Assembly, the majority of which were constantly Quakers, gave me frequent opportunities of seeing the embarrassment given them by their principle against war, whenever application was made to them, by order of the crown, to grant aids for military purposes. They were unwilling to offend government, on the one hand, by a direct refusal; and their friends, the body of the Quakers, on the other, by compliance contrary to their principles; hence a variety of evasions to avoid complying, and modes of disguising the compliance when it became unavoidable. The common mode at last was, to grant money under the phrase of its being 'for the king's use,' and never to inquire how it was applied.[5]

Franklin cited a humorous example of the hypocritical subterfuges the Quaker assemblymen resorted to:

> But, if the demand was not directly from the crown, that phrase was found not so proper, and some other was to be invented. As, when powder was wanting (I think it was for the garrison at Louisburg), and the government of New England solicited a grant of some from Pennsylvania, which was much urg'd on the House by Governor Thomas, they could not grant money to buy powder, because that was an ingredient of war; but they voted an aid to New England of three thousand pounds, to be put into the hands of the governor, and appropriated it for the purchasing of bread, flour, wheat or other grain. Some of the council, desirous of giving the House still further embarrassment, advis'd the governor not to accept provision, as not being the thing he had demanded; but he repli'd, 'I shall take the money, for I understand very well their meaning; other grain is gunpowder,' which he accordingly bought, and they never objected to it.[6]

Meanwhile, unauthorized squatting on native-owned lands caused increasing trouble in Pennsylvania, especially west of the Susquehanna River. Over time, but increasing with the outbreak of the French and Indian War, depredations against settlers across Pennsylvania made defense a serious bone of contention in the province. In 1755 and 1756 alone, the death toll among Pennsylvania settlers and militiamen exceeded three hundred people killed, men, women and children. Frontier inhabitants petitioned the Quaker government for militant action against the native inhabitants, even going so far as to threaten violence against the Assembly and marching several hundred strong on Philadelphia in fall 1755. Political conflict over militarization and backcountry representation found the community of Friends, which had remained active in provincial government, honoring the peace testimony by withdrawing themselves from the Pennsylvania Assembly and from active governance as war continued to ravage the province over the next several years.[7]

A few weeks before the Darragh family arrived in Philadelphia in 1763, the end of the French and Indian War was blazoned across the front page of the *Pennsylvania Gazette.* In the kind of imperious language that galled many colonists, George III declared:

> By the KING.
> A Proclamation.

George, R.
Whereas a Definitive Treaty of Peace and Friendship between Us, the Most Christian King, and the King of Spain, to which the King of Portugal hath acceded, hath been concluded at Paris on the Tenth Day of this inst. March, in conformity thereunto, we have thought it fit hereby to command, that the same be published throughout all our Dominions. And we do declare to all our loving Subjects our Will and Pleasure, that the said Treaty of Peace and Friendship be observed inviolably, as well by Sea as Land, and in all Places whatsoever, strictly charging and commanding all our loving Subjects to take Notice hereof, and conform themselves unto accordingly.
Given at our Court at St. James, the 21st Day of March, 1763, in the Third Year of Our Reign.[8]

Pennsylvanians had reason to view this announcement as ironic, if not outrageous. In fact, war in America was far from over. In this era of slow-moving information, the king's declaration of peace had already been overtaken by events. Just a few days later, the *Gazette* delivered distressing news:

Extract of a letter from Fort Pitt, May 31.
We have most melancholy Accounts here—The Indians have broke out in several Places, and murdered Colonel Clapham and his Family; also two of our Soldiers at the Saw-mill, near the Fort, and two Scalps are taken from each Man. An Indian has brought a War Belt to Tuscarora, and says Detroit is invested; and that St. Dusky is cut off, and Ensign Pawley made Prisoner. Levy's Goods are stopt at Tuscarora by the Indians. Last Night eleven Men were attacked at Beaver Creek, eight or nine of whom, it is said, were killed. And Twenty-five of Macrae's and Aliton's Horses, loaded with Skins, are all taken.[9]

For months Pontiac's War burned in full flame throughout the province. July saw a major action fought at Bushy Run, when a confederation of Indigenous warriors ambushed a relief column headed for Fort Pitt. After a two-day battle, the British force reported fifty men killed and sixty wounded before finally driving off their opponents. Native American losses were estimated at between twenty and sixty men killed, with an unknown number wounded. While this sanguinary clash brought a measure of peace to western Pennsylvania, hostilities then broke out in the east, not far from Philadelphia. About the time the Darraghs landed that fall, bands of infuriated warriors began murdering farm families as they tried to bring in their harvests. Near Tuscarora and as close as Northampton, a mere fifty miles from the city, dozens of settlers were killed.[10]

Retaliation did not take long. In December, the Paxton Boys took the law into their own hands, slaughtered twenty peaceful Conestogas, even dragging several from the Lancaster jail, where government representatives had tried to protect them. A change was taking place in which irate western settlers showed themselves increasingly willing to challenge government in extralegal fashion. Attempts by authorities to identify and punish those responsible failed when few of their neighbors would cooperate in the effort. Emboldened by their successful defiance, the Paxton Boys turned their attention to Philadelphia, seat of the provincial government, where a group of Indians from Northampton were being sheltered in the city's barracks. In February, hundreds of these men marched on the city, intent on killing the Indians. They got as far as Germantown before negotiations, and a hastily organized militia that outnumbered them considerably, turned them back.[11]

Backcountry discontent and active resistance against government continued to grow. In an effort to quell Indigenous anger, the king issued the Royal Proclamation of 1763, which officially restricted colonial settlement to a line east of the Atlantic watershed along the Appalachians. This did not sit well with frontier people, who frequently expressed their anger against governmental interference, which began to take the shape of armed confrontation in places. As an example, in 1765, a group of Pennsylvania dissidents known as the Black Boys actually laid siege to British soldiers at Fort Loudon in a dispute over supplying arms to Indigenous tribes.[12]

Displeasure with British governance was growing more general throughout the North American colonies. Overextended, with debts reaching £150 million, Parliament enacted the Stamp Act to recover some of the expense of stationing troops in America by levying a tax on the colonies' printed documents. Within weeks, the tenor of relations between the two lands underwent a dramatic shift. Even before organized American resistance began, colonists turned informally to nonimportation and self-reliance as a means of protest. This souring of relations can be seen in a letter that Samuel Morris wrote to a nephew, then in England, who was considering the purchase of furniture for his new house in Philadelphia: "Household goods may be had here as cheap and as well made from English patterns. In the humour people are in here, a man is in danger of becoming Invidiously distinguished, who buys anything in England which our tradesmen can furnish. I have heard the joiners here object this against Dr. Morgan and others who brought their furnishings with them."

Local industry boomed, to the detriment of London merchants, causing Benjamin Marshall to caution one British supplier, "Great Quantitys of home made Cloths, Linnens, Blankits & various other articles are daily brought to this City and Manufactorys erecting."[13]

Protests led to the organization of another American congress. Representatives at the Albany Congress had been focused on mutual defense. Ominously, the Stamp Act Congress saw the colonies join together in a challenge to British rule. Led by Pennsylvanian John Dickinson, they drafted a Declaration of Rights and Grievances, in which they asserted colonists' legal rights as citizens and argued against taxation in which they had no say. In Philadelphia, protesting the unpopular act, importers and retailers formed an association to boycott British goods, a disturbing sign that dissenters were willing to take extralegal action to support their position.[14]

One tenet of the Quaker faith—that Friends should remain aloof from worldly matters—was difficult to maintain in a province where they were, at least initially, the dominant political power. Though by the 1770s Friends no longer led the government of Pennsylvania, yet they retained considerable influence in the colony's governance and finance. As the winds of change blew hotter, it became increasingly difficult for many Friends to preserve a neutral stance. Honoring their Testimony against War became especially problematic because the newly emerging polity required compulsory military service from eligible males. Patriots viewed noncompliance as an indication of Tory affiliation.

From what we can tell, Lydia and William were devout Quakers. The Darraghs must surely have known and associated with many people who supported the Crown, especially early in the conflict, before the broad identification with American separatism that gradually took hold among the majority of Philadelphia's populace, even among Friends.

They remained connected by ties of blood to the Eddys, who seem to have been driven forcibly into the Tory camp when patriots would brook no middle ground. Thomas Eddy noted that even close family relationships, like that with the Darraghs, were being subjected to strain: "Public affairs were in a very unsettled state, and a great deal of bitterness and ill-will subsisted amongst the people, which produced much division and strife between families and near connexions, who had heretofore lived in perfect peace and harmony."[15]

While we have no first-person statements from Lydia or William Darragh attesting their reactions to the political turmoil of the time, we can glimpse the outlines of their gradual radicalization during the period of the American Revolution. Several bits of evidence show where the family's political sympathies lay: The Darraghs' close associations with active patriots, Charles Darragh's enlistment as a Continental officer, Lydia Darragh's walk to Frankford to warn the American army, Lydia's contribution to the Ladies Association when it collected money to support American troops in 1780, a comment by Samuel Rowland Fisher noting that William Darragh Sr. agitated Pennsylvania's courts against supposed Toryism, and the Darraghs' enrollment among the founding members of the breakaway Free Quakers, who, because of their support for the Revolution, separated themselves from the mainstream.

It is clear that the Darraghs had frequent contact with a number of active patriots who may have influenced their thinking. Five in particular stand out: Thomas Barclay, Blair McClenachan, Christopher Marshall, Christopher's son Benjamin Marshall, and Benjamin Loxley. All but Loxley were Irish by birth or, in Benjamin Marshall's case, by immediate descent.

Among those who supported Philadelphia's Nonimportation Agreement in 1765 was Thomas Barclay (1728–1793), who signed on behalf of his firm, Carsan, Barclay and Mitchell. Barclay himself was from Strabane in Ulster, one of the chief linen-producing areas of Ireland, where his father, Robert, was a linen exporter. Samuel Carsan, Thomas Barclay's uncle, had come to Philadelphia in the 1730s to manage the American end of the business, importing finished linen yard goods to be sold in his shop along Water Street by the Delaware riverfront. When Barclay arrived in Philadelphia about 1763, he and Carsan joined with another Irishman, William Mitchell, to import linen and export the high-quality American flaxseed that Irish growers relied on to create the fabric. Mitchell and Barclay maintained a dry goods store, also on Water Street, where their linens were sold. When Mitchell returned to Ireland, his property on Carter's Alley was auctioned off at sheriff's sale. The purchaser was Thomas Barclay, who then rented the house to William Darragh.[16]

As time went on, Barclay's involvement with the dissent leading to revolution grew. He was appointed to Philadelphia's Tea Committee in October 1773, joined the city's Committee of Correspondence beginning in 1774, became a member of the Committee of Inspection and Observation, and, in 1777, was appointed to Pennsylvania's Naval Board. It seems likely that the Darraghs at least knew of, and may well have been influenced by, their compatriot's views on relations with Britain. Barclay's involvement with formal revolutionary institutions paralleled his participation in the informal association of the Friendly Sons of St. Patrick—he was elected its president in 1780. Coming to the New World, many Irish natives brought with them a strong resentment of British authority.[17]

Barclay, who would become the Darraghs' landlord by 1773, was not the only one who found himself increasingly radicalized during the imperial crisis. The controversies that roiled Pennsylvania's political waters were certainly topics of much discussion in Philadelphia's shops and taverns. The Darraghs' shop provided more than just a means of income. It was also a place of conversation where news and ideas could be exchanged. It seems likely that the Darragh family were frequently exposed to such discourse as patrons dropped by their shop for some snuff, a smoke, or, perhaps, a drink and some conversation. Situated as they were across the street from Irishman James Byrne's popular Sign of the Golden Fleece, a venue that promoted politically oriented meetings and festivities, chances are that voluble William Darragh found himself engaged in civic dialogue. He may well have found himself attuned to the tenor of the times.

In 1766, Blair McClenachan purchased the property across Carter's Alley from James Byrne's Golden Fleece. The northeast corner, as we have seen, was occupied by the Darragh family. Now three of the corners at that intersection were occupied by Irishmen who were to become patriots. A few years later, though the Darraghs had left, the fourth corner was occupied by another active patriot, a Danish merchant named Abraham Markoe. When political tensions finally exploded into warfare,

Markoe became honorary captain of Philadelphia's Light Horse and, nominally at least, his neighbor McClenachan's commanding officer.[18]

It was at the Golden Fleece that a group of merchants known as the Irish Club met regularly to play backgammon and whist. When they gathered to celebrate St. Patrick's Day in 1769, thirty-six toasts were offered, many expressing the growing stress in America's relations with Britain, epitomized by the onerous Townshend Duties. Even the first toast hinted at disloyalty. It was made to "The pious and immortal memory of St. Patrick"; "The King, the Queen and Royal Family" only came second. Several other salutes foreshadowed the coming rebellion, including: "May every constitutional effort of the Americans to preserve their liberty be crowned with success. . . . May the liberty of the press remain free from ministerial restraint. . . . May Arbitrary Power and Passive Obedience be always detested by Americans, and the Sons of St. Patrick. . . . May Irish ministers who support illegal taxation be deemed illegitimate, and be excommunicated from Heaven by St. Patrick. . . . May all authors who by their writings support the cause of Liberty be introduced into Heaven by St. Patrick."[19]

The following month, members of the city's Scottish fraternal organization, the St. Andrew's Society, which had been meeting at Byrne's Golden Fleece, organized a highly symbolic birthday party in honor of the Corsican rebel and patriot Pasquale Paoli. Paoli had been elected head of an insurgent government that declared Corsica to be an independent sovereign state, free from control of the Republic of Genoa. When the Genoese ceded their title to Corsica to France in 1768, the French invaded the island, and Paoli led a guerrilla war against them. James Boswell's then-recent book, *An Account of Corsica, The Journal of a Tour to That Island, and Memoirs of Pascal Paoli*, had sold well in Britain and America. Pasquale Paoli was celebrated as a model for the liberty that was every Briton's right, including those living under British dominion in North America. A printed account of the toasts offered for Paoli's birthday party exposes the growing tension between Britain and its colonies. Among those revealing Philadelphians' political temperament: "May Great Britain be always just, and America always free. . . . May every British Minister be convinced, that nothing is lawful but what is just. . . . Liberty to mankind. . . . A speedy export to all the enemies of America, without a drawback. . . . Unanimity to the Colonies."[20]

Philadelphia's social clubs helped cement relationships among those who resisted Britain's increasingly oppressive policies. In March 1771, a number of prosperous men of Irish descent, including many who shortly would oppose British rule, met again at the Golden Fleece to formally found The Society of the Friendly Sons of St. Patrick, an Irish ethnic organization parallel to the Scots' St. Andrew's Society. The fraternal order's first president, Stephen Moylan, went on to become colonel of the 4th Regiment of Continental Dragoons. William Mitchell, the linen importer and business partner of Thomas Barclay, was elected vice president and treasurer. That September, Moylan proposed as an honorary member, though he was not Irish, John Cadwalader, who would soon become colonel of the Philadelphia Associators, a Pennsylvania militia organization that fought at Princeton in 1777. Another honorary member was Robert Morris, frequently referred to as "the financier of the American Revolution."[21]

The mechanisms by which political control in Philadelphia shifted from British-based governance to a system dominated by American insurgents are not well known to the general public today. The extralegal associations that had been formed in the city in response to the Stamp Act paved the way for a host of unofficial citizens' committees. When in 1773 serious opposition to the Tea Act developed, British control of the colonies began to disintegrate. Parliament had hit on a scheme to support the East India Company's lagging trade by undercutting the price of tea smuggled into America. There was one hitch: A small duty had to be paid when the tea arrived. Americans objected strenuously, arguing that since they had no representation in Parliament, that body had no right to tax them.

In Philadelphia, two prominent Friends, merchants Abel James and Henry Drinker, found themselves caught up in the controversy. Both men had been active in supporting the nonimportation agreement in opposition to the Stamp Act eight years before. By 1773, many merchants no longer honored nonimportation; so when James and Drinker were appointed commissioners for the East India Company tea, they felt they were on safe ground. But when *Polly*, the ship carrying their tea consignment sailed up the Delaware in October, Philadelphia erupted. Thousands swarmed the State House, where, on October 18, they passed a series of resolves, declaring it the duty of every American to oppose the Tea Act. Eight resolutions echoed the language of the toasts for St. Patrick and Pasquale Paoli from 1769, including "5. That the Resolution lately entered into by the East-India Company to send out their Tea to America, subject to the Payment of Duties on its being landed here, is an open Attempt to inforce this Ministerial Plan and a violent Attack upon the Liberties of America" and "6. That it is the Duty of every American to oppose this Attempt." Protesters forced the *Polly*'s captain to turn back, his cargo unlanded, causing financial and political embarrassment for the ship's sponsors, who were compelled to abrogate their commitment or face retaliation by the mob.[22]

Meanwhile, the Philadelphia Resolves were sent on to other American ports. At a town meeting on November 5, Boston's citizens adopted Philadelphia's resolutions then took direct action. Shortly afterward, angry protesters dumped Boston's tea into the harbor, in what became known as the Boston Tea Party. Rather than heed the portentous message, the outraged British government dug in its heels. To punish Massachusetts, Parliament passed five drastic measures that Americans called the Intolerable Acts, further fanning the flames of revolution. Referring to governmental retribution, Benjamin Franklin noted, "The Flame of Liberty in North America shall not be extinguished. Cruelty and Oppression and Revenge shall only serve as Oil to increase the Fire."[23]

One of the most significant countermoves was the Continental Congress's adoption of the Association of Nonimportation, Nonexportation and Nonconsumption on October 20, 1774, a trade boycott they hoped would pressure Britain to address colonial grievances and to repeal the Intolerable Acts. The extralegal bodies set up in each of the colonies to enforce this association began an active transfer of power from the governors, assemblies, and colonial institutions into the hands of radical revolutionaries. Philadelphia's Committee of One Hundred saw to it that merchants complied with the association's terms. Those who disagreed vocally with Congress's dictates were publicly and often violently humiliated.

The experience of two men in fall 1775 shows the vehemence with which the extralegal association was enforced, as well as the complete suppression of any further dialogue about continued loyalty to Britain. When attorney John Hunt defended a man accused of not honoring the boycott, Hunt was placed in the back of a cart, vilified, and paraded through the streets. A well-respected doctor, John Kearsley, infuriated by the spectacle, attempted to come to the lawyer's defense, going so far as to fire a pistol into the street toward the mob escorting Hunt. A melee ensued. Kearsley was wounded in the hand by a bayonet and shoved into the cart in Hunt's place, and the parade continued. The tumult was such that Mayor Samuel Rhodes tried to call out the militia because he feared for Kearsley's life. Despite threats of tar and feathering, the doctor was finally released, worse for the wear, but unchastened. Hunt was carted again a few days later and once again led through the streets. He wisely made his apologies at each stop along the way, avoiding more serious punishment. Though on humanitarian principles many witnesses had sympathized with the doctor's physical plight, they nonetheless supported his subsequent arrest and imprisonment on charges of disloyalty to the new American government. Kearsley died in a backcountry Pennsylvania jail two years later, still outspoken and unrepentant.[24]

Another influential acquaintance of the Darraghs was the patriot Blair McClenachan (1734–1812). While no records have been found that spell out precisely the nature of their relationship, it seems likely that McClenachan was a close relative of William Darragh's, most probably his brother-in-law.

Hailing from the north of Ireland, McClenachan became a successful merchant in Philadelphia. He was among the founders in 1751 of the Hibernia Fire Company, one of the city's earliest Irish associations. When the Friendly Sons of St. Patrick organized, McClenachan became a member.[25]

McClenachan managed to avoid involvement in the political committees during the run up to the Revolution, perhaps preferring to concentrate effort on his shipping business. In November 1774, when Philadelphians began to organize militarily to resist British policies by force, McClenachan, said to be of fiery temperament, was among the first men to join the light-horse of the City of Philadelphia. More commonly known as the First City Troop, these cavalrymen saw active service during the coming war. The group was particularly distinguished during the Battles of Trenton and Princeton, where it functioned as a bodyguard for George Washington. Despite his wealth and numerous business pursuits, McClenachan somehow found time to serve as a private and seems to have been present during other engagements throughout the war.[26]

The Revolution proved a boon for McClenachan. Early in the war, he began outfitting privateers to cruise against British shipping. Eventually he owned or was partner in dozens of armed vessels commissioned by Pennsylvania. With a knack for picking the best seamen and investing in the most likely ships, he quickly became one of the richest men in the state, referred to by some as "Midas" and even described by John Adams as "King McClenachan." In 1780, at the urging of his friend Thomas Paine, he pledged £10,000 to support the American army. The only other person matching this level of commitment was Robert Morris, whose wealth had also grown through lucrative privateering. Interestingly, McClenachan took the Darraghs' son Charles into one of his privateering enterprises. The two subscribed the bond for a voyage aboard one of McClenachan's most successful privateer vessels, further evidence of McClenachan's connection with the Darragh family.[27]

Through the Eddy family, as we have seen, the Darraghs were closely connected with the family of Christopher Marshall (1709–1797), with whom James Eddy was tied by the marriage of their children and through various business transactions. Marshall had provided valuable and timely aid by helping William Darragh launch his snuff-manufacturing business just a few months after the latter arrived in Pennsylvania. Though only a part of their extended family, over time, the Marshalls came to treat Lydia Darragh and her sons, Charles and John, as kin.

Christopher Marshall was a successful chemist and apothecary who manufactured and sold drugs and paints in Philadelphia at the Sign of the Golden Ball. It was gold that got him into trouble with Philadelphia's Quaker establishment. In 1729, Marshall came to Pennsylvania, settling in a Bucks County crossroads town called Four Ends Lane, known today as Langhorne. There he became a convinced Friend, and, according to the meeting's minutes, "he hath been carefull in attending Meetings . . . behaved himself in a good degree agreeable to our holy profession." After a few years, he married a Quaker woman, Sarah Thomson, daughter of a Philadelphia merchant, and moved a few miles south to Philadelphia.[28] He began keeping shop as a glazier on Chesnut Street, installing glass, as well as selling glass and lead for glazing houses and ships. He also started dabbling in chemistry, creating and selling lead-based paints. Marshall was a firm believer in advertising, hanging a large golden ball outside his shop and hawking his wares through frequent ads in the newspapers. By 1746, his paint business had eclipsed glazing, and he had launched the pharmaceutical enterprise for which he became principally known, concocting remedies and selling such popular medicines as Bateman's Drops and Daffy's Elixir. Unfortunately, Marshall's enthusiasm for chemistry went a little too far.[29]

Historians often claim, based on supposition, that Marshall was disowned by Philadelphia Meeting because of his support for the Revolution. That was not the case. His standing in Philadelphia's Quaker community came into question in 1750, when a report reached the meeting that he had been involved in scandalous conduct, bringing discredit upon the Society of Friends. The Monthly Meeting Minutes for December 22 reveal that, "Samuel Jackson is charged with being concerned in the Counterfeiting Gold & Silver Coins & that Christopher Marshall is charged with being an Accesary therein & several Friends who have treated with them finding, tho' they deny, their being guilty of the Charge they acknowledge they have been highly imprudent & culpable in their Conduct."

The charge was so concerning that the meeting appointed eight of its weightiest Friends, instead of the usual two, to investigate and "gett aright understanding of the matter and make to report thereon at our next meeting." Jackson, who at this point was incarcerated, admitted his guilt and was disowned, though the meeting looked with pity on his wife and children, who were now "in want of immediate assistance and relief" and took care of them. Marshall submitted a paper in his defense, but it was rejected, and he too was disowned.[30] The Friends' investigation disclosed surprising details about Marshall's part in the counterfeiting scheme. It seems he had been practicing alchemy!

> Whereas Christopher Marshall of this City Glazier hath made profession of the Truth among us, yet for want of a steady adherence to its Dictates hath Espoused & maintained some Erroneous Principles the unhappy effect of which hath lately appeared in his conduct having spent much time & pains in attempting the Transmutation of Metals and thereby been led into an intimacy with dishonest base men pretenders to that Mistery, by some of whom he is now charged with Assisting & encouraging them in making receiving & passing Counterfeit Money—And tho' after a carefull and full Examination he doth not appear to us to be guilty of the groser part of their accusation, yet as by his conduct he hath given much reproach to be cast on our holy profession, We think it necessary to testify that we have not Unity with the said Christopher Marshall & to disown him from being a Member of our Religious Society.[31]

Several men involved in the conspiracy to mint and distribute counterfeit Spanish pieces of eight were tried and convicted. Marshall's role in the ruse is unclear. He seems to have believed, or hoped, that lead could actually be transformed into gold, if he could just find the right formula. At some point, he became aware of the counterfeiters' intent; perhaps they used him to test their false dies' appearance by stamping a batch of metal he created. But through fear of incrimination, once aware of what was taking place, he tried to hide his involvement rather than expose the chicanery. He was tried in the courts on charges of aiding the scheme and found innocent on two counts. However, the jury did rule that "Christopher Marshall is Guilty of a Misdemeanor in knowing of & concealing the Stamps mention'd in the Indictmt. but as to the Residue of the matters charg'd in the Indictment he is not guilty." Though he may have been, at least initially, an unwitting dupe, people thought he should have known better. He was sentenced to two months in the city jail, required to pay a fine of £50, and to post a bond of £100 for a year against his good behavior.[32]

Marshall felt he had been misunderstood and treated poorly. He appealed his disownment first to the Philadelphia Quarterly Meeting, then to the Yearly Meeting, but they confirmed their judgment against him, and he finally gave up. Disownment meant he could no longer participate in the business of the Society of Friends. Though technically he could still attend Meeting for Worship, as a matter of practice this would be very awkward, and Marshall chose not to do so. This did not mean, however, that he would be completely ostracized. Quakers were always solid men of business. Marshall's altered status did not prevent one of the meeting's guiding lights, James Pemberton, from selling him a piece of property within days of the meeting upholding its final judgment against him.[33]

Marshall's wife and sons continued as members of Philadelphia Meeting, though Christopher kept away from all meeting business. Eventually he joined the Free Quakers when that organization began meeting in the 1780s. But he always retained the Sign of the Golden Ball above his shop, perhaps as a way of vindicating himself to the public.[34]

The Marshalls grew to be active patriots in the years leading up to the outbreak of hostilities with Britain. Christopher Sr. signed the nonimportation agreement in 1765, just two years after the Darraghs' arrival. Though limiting imports could have been detrimental for some shopkeepers, because William Darragh's tobacco business relied on an American-grown product, he was not seriously threatened by nonimportation. That might have made it easy for William to remain in sympathy over the issue with the man who had befriended him.

Christopher Marshall retired from business by 1774, leaving his younger sons, Christopher Jr. and Charles, to manage the family enterprise, while his oldest son, Benjamin, operated a separate business as a tin-plate manufacturer and also had interests in shipping—successful enterprises that earned him substantial wealth.[35]

Benjamin Marshall (1737–1778), like many other Quakers, was torn between his political and religious convictions. Amid the furor, he was appointed to Philadelphia's Tea Committee, one of its wealthier members, exceeded only by three others, the richest of whom was the builder Benjamin Loxley. Benjamin Marshall also joined representatives of Philadelphia's major religious denominations gathered at William Bradford's London Coffee House, where much of the city's business was transacted, to discuss their response to the Boston Port Act, which was slated to close that city's harbor on June 1, 1774. They agreed to mark the day with a solemn pause, closing shops, holding special religious services, and ringing muffled church bells throughout the day.[36]

Late in 1774, Benjamin Marshall became a member of Philadelphia's newly formed Committee of Observation and Inspection which was organized to enforce the Continental Congress's Association of Nonimportation, Nonexportation and Nonconsumption. Patriots pledged to "eat drink and wear only what America could produce itself." The city's British imports slowed to a dribble. Some importers, including Quakers James and Drinker, found their imported goods sequestered, the profits from their sale sent for the relief of Boston.[37]

The Friends' Meeting for Sufferings for Pennsylvania and New Jersey drafted an epistle to meetings under their jurisdiction, specifically objecting to the association and seeking to rein in those Quakers involved in implementing it. The meetings were urged to treat with those Friends who served "as Committee Men to carry [the Association] into execution." Of course, this was code for beginning the process of disownment. Benjamin Marshall was accused of "having accepted of a public station where measures contrary to our peaceable principles were carried into execution." Two members from Philadelphia Monthly Meeting began to meet with Marshall to get him to recognize, acknowledge, and abandon his course of deviation.[38]

Though appearing contrite, he vacillated. After several months, the appointed Friends grumbled that though he had given them expectations he would resign his appointment, he had "been reappointed to the same service." Finally, early in 1776, "the Friends who have the case of labouring with Benjamin Marshall informed the Meeting that they have had two conferences with him since last month, which have been more satisfactory than any of the former, and that he has lately withdrawn from the public station in which he has acted for sometime past, which gives some reason to hope he begins to see his conduct has been inconsistent with our Christian testimony and principles."[39]

As late as May 1776, they felt there was some hope of persuading him to abandon his support for the Revolution. In the end, Marshall refused to acknowledge that his actions had been wrong. Worse, at the same time, he manufactured and sold to the American army hundreds of tin cartouche boxes—canisters that were designed to hold thirty-six cartridges of powder and ball. Though good business, this was warlike behavior indeed. Having had enough, the meeting finally disowned him on July 27. Convinced of his personal rectitude, like his father before him, Benjamin Marshall appealed his disownment but was unable to see the appeal through to its conclusion. Early in 1778, his warm support for the revolutionary cause ended up costing him his life.[40]

The meeting had already disowned Benjamin's father, Christopher Marshall, in 1751. When he too became active with the revolutionary committees, there was little the meeting could do to influence him. As part of the nonimportation movement, Christopher Marshall had advocated for homegrown manufacturing to take the place of British goods. Later, as he himself became increasingly radical, he joined the leadership of Pennsylvania's Committee of Observation, along with other hardliners like Thomas McKean and Timothy Matlack. With plenty of free time on his hands after retirement, Christopher Sr. kept a diary, which became an important source document for our understanding of the American Revolution.[41]

Another radical with whom the Darraghs were associated was Benjamin Loxley (1720–1801), who became their landlord in 1777. Born in England, Loxley immigrated to Philadelphia in 1734, and his uncle placed him in apprenticeship to a carpenter whose daughter he later married, gradually becoming a highly successful builder. While still a teen, he joined Pennsylvania's budding militia, quickly becoming an officer. In 1755, he learned "Laboratory work, Gunnery and Bombadoreing" from British military engineers. He then borrowed four ships' cannon and, an able carpenter, mounted them on carriages to aid in the defense of the province, as a result of which he was elected captain lieutenant of the city's artillery company. When the Paxton Boys marched on Philadelphia, it was Loxley who commanded the guns that were brought against them. Alexander Graydon left a humorous description of the man: "Captain Loxley, a very honest, though little, dingy-looking man, with regimentals, considerably war-worn or tarnished; a very salamander or fire drake in the public estimation, whose vital air was deemed the fume of sulphureous explosion, and who, by whatever means he had acquired his science, was always put foremost when great guns were in question."[42]

When in 1775 Loxley was appointed to a local committee of safety, he was initially troubled because he had three times sworn oaths of allegiance to the king. On consideration, he reasoned that "King George had broken his coronation oath with us, wherein he engaged to protect all his subjects in free liberty of conscience and lawful rights, and now he had broken his promise and we were free from ours." He set about preparing the city's ordnance, overseeing the creation of gun carriages, mounting cannon, and readying them for service. In 1776, he joined the Flying Camp in North Jersey with his artillery company to aid in the defense of the New York area. Throughout the rest of the war, he continued to labor on behalf of the army in the manufacture and maintenance of artillery.[43]

These, then, were some of the patriots the Darragh family knew well.

Chapter 7

Lydia Darragh's Neighborhood

THE FIRST SCENE of Lydia's Tale opens upon a definite location—two houses in the neighborhood of Second and Spruce Streets in Philadelphia. The story checks out. Property records show that John Cadwalader did indeed own a home on the west side of Second Street below Spruce. Directly across the street, on the eastern side, was a house rented by William Darragh, one of four properties in that block owned by Benjamin Loxley. A prosperous house carpenter who had come to the city from England in 1734, Loxley held at least eighteen other properties in the city at the time, most of which he rented out.

Second Street was one of Philadelphia's most important arteries. Lined with numerous shops, it connected two of the city's principal markets, the main marketplace on High Street, then considered the center of town, and New Market, which took up the entire widened block of Second Street between Pine and Cedar Streets. Running north from

High Street, Second passed Christ Church, the primary Anglican place of worship, then ran past the British barracks and over the Cohocksink Creek, where it terminated at Germantown Road. South of Cedar Street, it ran deep into a rural farming area called The Neck, today the dense urban neighborhoods known collectively as South Philadelphia.[1]

Second Street was the focus of the Darragh family's livelihood. They lived and maintained a shop on the street for eighteen of their twenty-four years in the city, never perching more than a full city block from it at any other time. By moving to the Loxley House in early 1777, they had selected a prime place to do business, one that stood out clearly from its neighbors.

Their store was located in a distinctive place, by the bridge where Second Street crossed over Little Dock Creek. The long, two-story building, painted blue, sported handsome shop windows across its street side at the ground level. Its façade was surmounted by a generous railed balcony spanning the entire front, protected overhead by a high, jutting roof supported by a large pair of projecting bracket ends that terminated in unique ornamental volutes. Across the way, set back from the street behind an elegant brick wall, stood John Cadwalader's stately home, one of the city's finest, its gardened backyard rising steeply up the flank of Society Hill toward Third Street.[2]

John Cadwalader (1742–1786) and his brother Lambert, sons of the noted Philadelphia physician Thomas Cadwalader, established themselves in the city as successful importers of dry goods. As importers, they opposed Britain's colonial taxation schemes, beginning with the Stamp Act. By signing the Nonimportation Agreement of 1765, they joined the American boycott of British goods. The brothers shared the sentiments of their first cousin, John Dickinson, who, in 1767 and 1768, wrote *Letters from a Farmer in Pennsylvania*, a series of twelve essays published throughout the North American provinces that helped unite the colonists against the Townshend Acts. In 1769, John married Elizabeth Lloyd, daughter of a wealthy planter from Maryland's Eastern Shore. His father-in-law, Colonel Edward Lloyd, took him to visit George Washington at Mount Vernon, and the two struck up a fast friendship. The Cadwaladers soon embarked on an ambitious venture, purchasing several adjacent properties on the west side of Second Street and transforming them into one of the finest homes in North America.[3]

Cadwalader's property was a place once famed for its natural allure—and a certain strangeness. Indeed, Cadwalader's hillside garden must still have been a lovely sight in the 1770s. Before settlers changed the face of the land by filling it with thousands of loads of earth, the ground below the slope, along the creek, was what Benjamin Loxley called a whortleberry swamp. It was particularly soggy by the foot of the hill where Little Dock Creek crossed the line that became Second Street, because a spring ran out of the hill there. The hillside, known by early residents as Bathsheba's Bower, was said to be "a charming hanging garden" with "the choicest fruits and grapes."[4]

The name was an eighteenth century play on words, mixing the spring, or bath, and the hillside bower—a shelter of overhanging vines—with the name Bathsheba Bowers, an actual person who lived at that spot at one time. It is worth considering for a moment who Bathsheba Bowers was, because her intellect, personal power, and sense of agency—and her eccentricity—stood out in her day. By the time the Darraghs moved to the house across the street from Bathsheba's Bower, Lydia's own forceful nature and sense of purpose were well formed and frequently exercised, but the lingering memory of a kindred spirit across the way—a woman who was completely her own person—was probably not lost on her.

Bathsheba Bowers was born in Charlestown, Massachusetts, on June 4, 1671, to a family of considerable notoriety who were embroiled in the religious controversies that raged among the dissenter religions of Old and New England. Bathsheba's father, Benanuel Bowers, declared himself a Quaker, a sect viewed by Puritans in an even worse light than Baptists. He was punished repeatedly—sometimes fined, sometimes jailed, sometimes whipped—for his deviant opinions, for failing to attend Puritan public worship, and for entertaining Quakers in his house.[5]

Bathsheba, Benanuel's youngest daughter, seems to have been deeply impressed with her father's strong-willed spiritual independence and unwavering perseverance in opposition to the community he lived in. About 1689, Benanuel decided to send four of his daughters to the new Quaker colony in Philadelphia, where Friends were the dominant secular and religious power and religious toleration the rule. Reflecting on her own sense of personal agency, Bathsheba noted, "I had heard great talk of great matters in Pennsylvania, and being willing to try that experiment, I prepared myself, and came over." Once there, she turned at least part of her attention to intellectual pursuits and to enhancing what was already a place of natural beauty. "I began to take delight in Gardening, and applied myself, with pleasure, to the Contemplation of Matters Philosophical and Divine."[6]

The four sisters quickly integrated into their new surroundings, three of them marrying into flourishing families. Though remaining single, Bathsheba was particularly industrious and soon became prosperous in her own right. Her niece, Ann Bolton, who went to live with her aunt when she was ten, in about 1701, later explained her financial success: "my Aunt learned to make mantuas [coat-like women's gowns, popular at the time], and became, in a short time, so complete a work woman, that she not only worked for, but pleased the best in the city: by which means she maintained herself genteely." Soon she had made enough money to buy a house and an adjacent property in the growing city. At first, enamored of show and status, she decorated the place extensively, painting both the exterior and interior herself and furnishing the house in an attractive fashion. She turned the adjacent lot into a fine garden, complete with a fence, graveled walkways, and a small summer house. Within three years, her place was said to be as beautiful as anything Eve beheld in the original paradise.[7]

However practical and productive in her business, Bathsheba was a difficult person. As she grew older, she became overbearing, querulous, and argumentative. Though she was intensely spiritual and vocally, even stridently, espoused a high morality, her behavior was utterly contradictory; she treated those around her harshly, sometimes cruelly. Ann observed that she "had never been anything but a torment to herself and everyone about her," most especially her sisters and her poor, innocent niece. As a result, she was likely seen by most as a prickly person, most unpleasant to be around.[8]

Despite personal flaws, Bathsheba was a person of strong principles and held to them strictly, even when, or maybe especially when, those principles lay outside the norm. Ann Bolton tells us, for instance, that as a result of "being crossed in love when about eighteen, she vowed Chastity ever after." Instead of the company of men, she surrounded herself with other women. "She had several young women of the better sort (for she would take no others) to live with her; but they were soon scared away." Though financially well off, once she conquered her phase of outward ostentation, she lived an abstemious existence yet was generous to the poor. "Her station in life and fortune, whilst I remained with her, and many years before, might have been deemed rich.

She was so sparing that she scarcely allowed herself and me, the common supports of life; yet, at the same time, charitable to the poor, even to excess."[9]

Her physical wants satisfied by commercial success, her disposition uneasy, she gradually became something of a recluse. Her detachment from things worldly increasing, Bathsheba left her fancy uptown house and moved to the area of Second and Spruce Streets. Though the street grid had been laid out, this was still a rural place. The land between Spruce and Pine Streets, stretching from the Delaware to the Schuylkill, was owned by the defunct Free Society of Traders, which had ceased active operation a few short years after its inception in 1681. As the city grew, squatters moved onto the Society's unimproved lands. One of them appears to have been Bathsheba Bowers. The area was used by locals as a commons, and as a lovely rural area for picnicking.[10] Ann Bolton wrote, "as nothing ever satisfied her so about one and a half miles distant under Society Hill She built a Small house close by the best Spring of Water perhaps as was in our City. This house she furnished with books a Table a Cup in which she or any that visited her (but they were but few, and seldom) drank of that Spring."[11]

In 1709, Bowers published *An Alarm Sounded to Prepare the Inhabitants of the World to Meet the Lord in the Way of his Judgments.* Though sometimes referred to as an autobiography, this unusual twenty-three-page work dealt primarily with Bathsheba Bowers's spiritual agony and how she gradually attained a semblance of peace. Some interpret her internal conflict as a struggle against cultural expectations of women that limited her own self-understanding and circumscribed her ability both to express herself clearly and, ultimately, to make her way publicly in a male-dominated society. But it might be more productive to respect this powerful woman's well-developed intellect, to take her at her own word, and to assume that she actually believed, as she repeatedly said she did, in the Friends' understanding that God's voice speaks within us and that we can hear it if we will only listen. Bowers's struggles were not so much with worldly expectations of her gendered role. Rather, she waged continual battle between her desire to achieve spiritual perfection, and thereby inner peace, and her self-perceived sinfulness, in the context of a morality derived from her close reading of the words of the Bible. Her spiritual anguish speaks clearly to us across a span of three hundred years.[12]

Bowers's writing shows that she was attracted to and repelled by her desire to preach publicly, a practice for which she was notorious in early

Philadelphia. In the excited and confusing prose style of *An Alarm*, we can catch a glimpse of what her oratory may have sounded like. Her drive to communicate, loudly and combatively, her views on the life of the spirit was unwelcome among Philadelphia's Quakers, whose once fiery and demonstrative religion had been settling, over several generations' remove, into a placid quietism that shunned such vigorous outward display. Eventually frustrated in Philadelphia, she determined to head to the province of South Carolina, where she hoped her preaching would meet with a better reception.

It took courage for a person from a peaceful urban background to brave the wilds of the Carolinas, especially during a period when death and destruction stalked the backcountry. Once there, Bowers was caught up in the Yamassee War, a ferocious conflict between Indigenous tribes and colonists during which hundreds of lives were lost, including those of many civilians. Though at the time her health seems to have deteriorated, her will remained as forceful as ever. She was so completely convinced of her own immortality that she might easily dismiss personal risk from disease or violence. Bolton related an episode that occurred near the end of Bowers's life:

> My Aunt was strong in the belief that she would never die; though this secret she revealed in plain terms, only to my Mother. So fixed was she in the opinion, that fate had decreed that she would never die, that some years after she removed to South Carolina, when the Indians, early one morning, surprized the place, killed and took prisoners several in the house adjoining hers, she moved not out of her bed, but when two men offered their assistance to carry her away, she said Providence would protect her; and indeed so it proved at that time; for those two men, no doubt by the direction of Providence, took her in her bed for she would not rise, conveyed her into their boat, and carried her away in safety, though the Indians pursued and shot after them.[13]

Bathsheba never returned to her bower in Philadelphia. She finally proved mortal after all. In 1718, her unquiet spirit passed from this life. Notorious in her own day, now she is largely forgotten.

When American resistance began to organize militarily, John Cadwalader became captain of a Philadelphia militia company composed of many of the city's elite youth. Cadwalader drilled them on his own extensive property, the gardens of which stretched from Second to Third Streets. Alexander Graydon left a colorful description of the scene in his *Memoirs*:

> [T]hey were sneeringly styled, The silk stocking company, commanded by Mr. John Cadwalader, and which having early associated, had already acquired celebrity. This nickname evinced, that the canker worm, jealousy, already tainted the infantile purity of our patriotism. The command of this company, consisting of the flower of the city, was too fine a feather in the cap of its leader to be passed by unenvied: it was, therefore, branded as an aristocratic assemblage, and Mr. (since general) Mifflin, had the credit of inventing the invidious appellation. To this association I belonged. There were about seventy of us. We met morning and evening, and from the earnest and even enthusiastic devotion of most of us to learn the duty of soldiers, the company, in the course of a summer's training, became a truly respectable militia corps. When it had attained some adroitness in the exercises, we met but once a day. This was in the afternoon, and the place of rendezvous the house of the captain, where capacious demijohns of Madeira, were constantly set out in the yard where we formed, for our refreshment before marching out to exercise. The ample fortune of Mr. Cadwalader had enabled him to fill his cellars with the choicest liquors; and it must be admitted, that he dealt them out with the most gentlemanly liberality. He probably meant it, in part, as an indemnification for our voluntary submission while under arms, to all the essential points, as well as the little etiquette of subordination, required of privates under the most regular discipline.[14]

It may be that Lydia Darragh's son Charles, about twenty at the time and living a few blocks away, was impressed by the militant noise drifting over Cadwalader's iron-spiked brick wall and across the neighborhood. The sound of the drums would have been hard to ignore, as they beat in that natural amphitheater, reverberating through the air, echoing off the brick walls of the neighboring houses. The comings and goings of these patrician men from the city's most prominent families—men whose refinement and prosperity were to be emulated, men who dared to challenge the established order—could not have been lost on young

Charles Darragh, who stood at the brink of manhood. He may also have noticed the comings and goings of influential Whigs, especially during the periods when the Continental Congress met in the city. Among the numerous distinguished callers who could be seen passing down Second Street to be feted at Cadwalader's tony mansion were John Adams, Silas Deane, and, on at least three occasions between 1773 and 1775, the tall, impressive, martial figure of George Washington.

While John Cadwalader pursued his mercantile, political, and military endeavors, he and his wife found time to grow a small family. Between 1771 and 1776, Elizabeth gave birth to three daughters, Anne, Elizabeth, and Maria. The family's early pleasure in one another's company was captured vividly by Charles Willson Peale in a portrait of the happy couple with their infant daughter, Anne. Sadly, on February 15, 1776, eleven days after giving birth to Maria, Elizabeth Lloyd Cadwalader died of complications arising from the childbirth. John was left alone to raise a five-year-old, a two-year-old, and a newborn infant.[15]

We don't know much about the relationship between the Cadwalader family and the Darraghs except that beginning in February 1777, they lived across the street from one another—though it may not have been perceived that way. Their residences were not separated by the street alone, but also by Little Dock Creek. While Robert Walsh wrote that Cadwalader lived "directly opposite" from the Darraghs, Darragh family members stated that the house was "almost opposite" and "nearly opposite." Actually, the differing statements reflect a local reality. The angles of the creek and the bridge that crossed it meant the path between the two houses was anything but direct. Leaving Cadwalader's front gate, one would have to walk north up Second Street to the head of the bridge, then reverse direction, walk south across the bridge, reverse direction again at the foot of the bridge, then walk north once again up the street to reach the Darraghs' front door at Loxley House.[16]

The social gulf between the two families was perhaps less easily bridged. While the Cadwaladers and Darraghs may well have encountered one another face to face, any relationship between them would surely have been tinged by notions of social status.

John Fanning Watson, in the first edition of his *Annals* (1830), said the Loxley House "was memorable in its early day for affording from its gallery a preaching place for the celebrated Whitfield—his audience occupying the street (then out of town) and the opposite hill at the margin of Bathsheba's bath and bower."[17] The preacher mentioned was none other than the famed George Whitefield, leader of the evangelical revival movement known as the First Great Awakening, whose unorthodox views and methods had created quite a stir in English-speaking America as well as at home in Britain. Only twenty-five at the time, he was known for attracting crowds and often preached out of doors to reach a larger audience. His journals confirm that he visited Philadelphia in 1739 and gave his farewell sermon from a balcony at Society Hill, a venue he revisited the following year.[18]

Whitefield was no stranger to controversy, and when he returned to Philadelphia in 1740, he found himself *persona non grata* among many of the town's clergy. Someone had paved the way. Knowing that Whitefield was headed for the city, an anonymous contributor sent one of the preacher's letters to the city's chief newspaper. The headline on the *Pennsylvania Gazette*'s lead article on Sunday, April 10, 1740, was intended to stoke controversy: "A Letter from the Rev. Mr. Whitefield, at Georgia, to a friend in London, wherein he vindicates his Asserting, that Archbishop Tillotson knew no more of Christianity than Mahomet." Though Tillotson, the late archbishop of Canterbury, had been dead for forty-five years, his memory was still revered by Anglican churchmen. The letter also criticized the Anglican hierarchy as fatuous, hypocritical, and insincere, disparaging the current bishop of London.[19]

On arriving in Philadelphia five days later, Whitefield asked Archibald Cummings, rector of Christ Church and commissary for the bishop of London, if he might be allowed to preach from his pulpit. The rector refused. He regretted having let the fiery young minister use his church the previous year.

> When Mr. Whitefield arrived here last Year, I gave him at first the use of our Church; and looked upon him at first as a well-meaning tho' rash Young Man, who had imbibed some mistaken Notions of Religion; for which reason I advised him, in the most serious and tender Manner I could, to examine the Principles he went upon with greater Deliberation; adding; that I was sorry he had lost the esteem of the Clergy in England, whom even their Enemies allowed to be generally eminent for Learning and Lenity.[20]

Undeterred, Whitfield returned to the Loxley House. Feeling "that Divine Fire," he spoke once again from the balcony. Inspired by the story of the blind beggar who called out to Jesus despite the crowd telling him to be silent, and who testified before the disbelieving Pharisees that Jesus had made him see, Whitefield railed against Tillotson's writings and against those churchmen "who had the Form of Religion, but never felt the effectual Power of it in their Hearts!"[21]

The next day, he preached from the balcony there twice, in the morning to six thousand people and in the evening to eight thousand. If the numbers seem extraordinary, it must be noted that the house faced west, across Little Dock Creek, toward the rising ground of Society Hill, which formed a natural amphitheater and could easily accommodate the hordes of listeners Whitefield described.[22]

About the quality of Whitefield's voice, Benjamin Franklin observed, in his typically scientific manner:

> He had a loud and clear voice, and articulated his words and sentences so perfectly, that he might be heard and understood at a great distance, especially as his auditories, however numerous, observ'd the most exact silence. He preach'd one evening from the top of the Courthouse steps, which are in the middle of Market-street, and on the west side of Second-street, which crosses it at right angles. Both streets were fill'd with his hearers to a considerable distance. Being among the hindmost in Market-street, I had the curiosity to learn how far he could be heard, by retiring backwards down the street towards the river; and I found his voice distinct till I came near Front-street, when some noise in that street obscur'd it. Imagining then a semicircle, of which my distance should be the radius, and that it were fill'd with auditors, to each of whom I allow'd two square feet, I computed that he might well be heard by more than thirty thousand. This reconcil'd me to the newspaper accounts of his having preach'd to twenty-five thousand people in the fields, and to the ancient histories of generals haranguing whole armies, of which I had sometimes doubted.[23]

Years later, another story about the sermons from the Loxley House was attributed to Franklin:

George preached instead in the open, on Society Hill, to thousands upon thousands. He was not unopposed at first. Some wags bribed a drummer boy to stand right beside the 'pulpit' and drown the preacher with noise. Whitefield spoke louder; the boy drummed harder, and no one could hear a word.

Whitefield stopped. The boy stopped, glad of a rest. Whitefield looked at the boy and laughed and said, for all to hear, 'Friend, you and I serve the two greatest masters existing, though in different callings. You beat up for volunteers for King George, I for the Lord Jesus. In God's name let's not interrupt one another. The world is wide enough for us both and we'll get recruits in abundance.'

The boy grinned and never touched his drum for the rest of the evening.[24]

From this house once graced by one of the great religious personalities of the age, Lydia Darragh would find her faith tested by events unfolding around her.

Chapter 8

The Seat of War

Reacting to the Boston Tea Party, in 1774 Parliament imposed drastic strictures on Massachusetts. Especially galling, and portentous of worse things to come for the colonies, were the closing of the port of Boston and revocation of the Massachusetts charter, severely limiting local self-governance. General Thomas Gage, the commander in chief of British forces in North America, was appointed military governor of the province. Rather than cowing the colonies, as Benjamin Franklin predicted, "Cruelty and Oppression and Revenge" only served "as Oil to increase the Fire." Instead of capitulating and seeking reconciliation, Americans began to take extralegal political measures and prepared themselves for armed conflict with the home country.

Seeking to force their will on obstreperous colonists, the British increased their military presence in Boston. But in what would become a regular pattern, limited by a hostile countryside and a debilitating reliance on their navy for protection, the British military could not project its authority much beyond the ground its soldiers occupied at any given moment. The situation quickly deteriorated. Hoping to increase its control, Britain sent three generals, William Howe, Henry Clinton, and John Burgoyne, to Boston in spring 1775. They arrived to find chaos; fighting had broken out at Lexington and Concord, and their army, humiliated, lay bottled up in the port city. Faced with forces from three colonies now, Connecticut and New Hampshire militiamen having come to the support of Massachusetts, General Howe determined to break the siege by attacking American positions at the Battle of Bunker Hill on June 17. The result was a pyrrhic victory and a second rude awakening for the British: Casualty figures demonstrated clearly that their superior army, small in numbers as it was and with a vulnerable supply line stretching three thousand miles across the ocean, was too meager to force its will upon New England, much less the entire continent. This revelation was borne out repeatedly in the coming months.

On June 15, the Second Continental Congress, meeting in Philadelphia, appointed a Virginia delegate, George Washington—who had signaled his eagerness to fight by arriving decked out in a military uniform—commander in chief of a new American army. The day before, it had voted to have three additional colonies raise elite companies of riflemen to come to the aid of Boston, thus establishing a Continental Army. Pennsylvania was directed to recruit six companies of these soldiers, with another two companies each to come from Maryland and Virginia. Recruitment was so successful that Congress quickly authorized Pennsylvania to add another three companies, and the whole were placed under command of Colonel William Thompson. Pennsylvania had gone from the least militaristic of the thirteen colonies to one of its most militant.

Britain pursued several strategies to bring the rebellious colonies to heel: economic strangulation by blockade to punish them into submission; winning the hearts and minds of inhabitants through attempts at compromise, always however, offering too little too late, and that generally with a tone-deaf, supercilious attitude that grated on colonists' nerves; and destruction of the American army in the field, thereby breaking their will and means of resistance.

British efforts met with mixed results. Local setbacks throughout the colonies included the loss of a key post at Ticonderoga in New York with its store of artillery, and the banishment of Royal forces in the Chesapeake Bay to a few barely habitable islands. There was also a string of embarrassing failures. In March 1776, the American besiegers mounted the Ticonderoga guns on Dorchester Heights, within range to devastate the British fleet, forcing General Howe, who had replaced Gage, to evacuate Boston entirely. The number two commander, Henry Clinton, led an expedition to South Carolina that ended in frustration that June. To the north, in what should have been an ominous warning to Britain, another major operation turned out badly. John Burgoyne, who had been relegated to a minor role, accompanied General Guy Carleton's Canadian force, which was initially successful at pushing the Americans out of what they had hoped would become the fourteenth colony. But this army was stalled in its thrust down the Champlain-Hudson corridor, thwarted by American delaying tactics.

The primary military campaign of 1776, however, unrolled brilliantly. Britain had wisely appointed William Howe's accomplished older brother, Admiral Richard Howe, naval commander in chief of the North American Station, setting the stage for unusually harmonious coordination between their land and naval forces. The brothers, who were somewhat receptive to American complaints of injustice, were also assigned the role of peace commissioners in hopes they could negotiate an honorable settlement with the colonies' less radical elements. From August through the end of the year, the Howes' joint operations in New York handed the Americans defeat after defeat. British troops drove Washington's army clear across the Jersies to the Delaware River. There, near Trenton, the Americans had stemmed the British tide by crossing over to Pennsylvania, taking all the boats along the river with them. Nearby Philadelphia went into a panic. Fearing that the British would soon be in the city, many people, especially politicians, fled in the first of three mass evacuations that took place over eighteen months.

Despite success, William Howe's 1776 campaign failed to achieve its chief strategic goal: ending the rebellion. The main American army remained in the field under the capable leadership of George Washington. Faced with the army's imminent dissolution due to soldiers' enlistments expiring at the end of the year, he launched a startling counteroffensive. Over the course of ten days, between December 25 and January 3, Washington mounted a brilliant campaign of his own in which he outmaneuvered the British, bringing his strength to bear against isolated detachments while avoiding pitched battle with General Charles Cornwallis's main army. Their spirit reinvigorated, the Americans wintered at Morristown, a mere twenty miles from their enemy's main force at Manhattan.[1]

To reward the success of his campaign around New York, King George had knighted William Howe, conferring upon him, in absentia, the Order of the Bath. That was before word arrived of Washington's resurgence, giving the new-minted knight something of a black eye. During the winter, Howe proposed a plan for 1777—sieze the rebel capital at Philadelphia—that was approved by the government, though his request for a substantial troop increase to cover all bases was turned down. Not only was the city the seat of Congress, but it was the center of the nascent American military-industrial complex, where much of the young nation's military supplies were either manufactured or stored. Howe was reasonably certain that Washington would attempt to interpose himself between the British army and its objective, forcing a decisive showdown on the battlefield that he reckoned he could win easily.

Meanwhile, as Henry Clinton sulked in Howe's shadow, John Burgoyne sailed back to England to tout a move he hoped would cover him in glory. Since the days of the French and Indian War, the British government had been obsessed with the strategic importance of the Lake Champlain-Hudson River corridor, which it believed could be used to somehow isolate New England from the rest of the colonies. Having learned little about logistics from his participation in the failed attempt to invade New York from the north, Burgoyne bent the king's ear about leading a second invasion from Canada that would link up with the army already in Manhattan. He argued that control of the Hudson River could split boisterous New England from the rest of the colonies, somehow throttling the rebellious region into submission. The plan was absurd, requiring the British army to garrison a cordon hundreds of miles in length, but it was nonetheless accepted as an augmentation to Howe's main effort. In the event, this sideshow would prove disastrous for British arms.[2]

Winter 1777 was spent in wary watchfulness. Occupying the low country of North Jersey, General Howe's army faced off against the Americans who had passed the winter in strong defensive positions behind the steep hills of the Watchung Mountains, which rose precipitately from the coastal plain. Seeking decisive battle, Howe tried to draw Washington's army out of its mountainous stronghold at Morristown, but to no avail. The spring passed in a series of cat-and-mouse maneuvers where neither side was able to gain advantage. Without the reinforcements he had requested, Howe was chary of marching toward Philadelphia while leaving Washington in his rear, threatening to cut his supply line to New York. Instead, in his typical deliberate, even dilatory fashion, Howe gradually embarked an invasion force aboard his brother's fleet and, finally in July, sailed for Pennsylvania.

For the people of Philadelphia, the third year of the Revolution was shaping up to be a momentous one. In late June, word began to filter into the city about the change in General Howe's plans. On the 23rd, Tory sympathizer Sarah Logan Fisher wrote:

> An express came in today bringing an account that General Howe with all his army have actually left Brunswick & gone to Amboy, which conduct appears to be a great mystery to us, or what intentions they can possibly have in thus leaving the Jersies & their friends in it wholly exposed to the ravages & insults of an incensed army, who will greatly exult & rejoice in this retreat of the English. How much to be pitied are those men who had fled to the English for protection, in hopes of soon returning under the shelter of their wing to their families, & who now are obliged to follow them, let them go where they will.[3]

From the time the British army departed New York harbor, suspicions grew that Philadelphia was to be its target. Tory and Whig alike did their best to track Howe's progress, either with hopeful anticipation or foreboding dread. Sightings along the Jersey coast increased tension in the city. On July 30, when the fleet rendezvoused with Captain Andrew Snape Hamond's squadron at the Delaware Capes, the destination seemed clear. Then, puzzlement again as the fleet mysteriously sailed away. The British continued sailing south, but this fact was unknown to observers on land. The next day, Sarah Logan Fisher noted in her diary:

> All day at home. Spent the evening at Sammy Pleasants'. No further account of the fleet today till evening, when an express came in which says the fleet yesterday morning stood N.E. & have entirely disappeared, which gives great joy to the Whigs & causes them greatly to exult, as they say now that Howe is afraid to come here, & dare not encounter with our troops, & they suppose when he heard that Washington & his army were come down here to oppose him, they were struck with great trepidation & have sailed to some other place where they will not have so powerful an army to encounter with.[4]

On August 1, patriot Christopher Marshall reported, in a somewhat different vein, "No news of any moment by the post last night, except that the enemy was seen off the Capes, that Philadelphia was pretty quiet, and the Militia all ready to turn out." The rumor mill continued to grind. Later in the day, Marshall added, "News that some of the enemy's ships were got to Reedy Island [about forty-five miles downriver from the city]; whether true or not remains doubtful." It turned out to be untrue, but the apprehension that Howe's fleet spelled menace for Philadelphia was well founded.[5]

South Carolina Congressman Henry Laurens, soon to become president of the Congress, wrote on August 5, "the late Motions of Lord and Gen' Howe have puzzled every body on our Side of the Question." He noted that the fleet "finally disappear'd about four days ago and whither they are now wandering we know not." Reflecting the general perplexity, he even speculated that "probably they may have reenter'd North River, possibly landed at Rhode Island and part of the Fleet may be gone to bombard Boston."[6]

Instead of taking the most direct route and attempting to force American riverine defenses on the hazardous and shoaly Delaware, the Howes determined on a circuitous course up Chesapeake Bay. They landed at the Head of Elk, fifty miles southwest of Philadelphia and only seventeen miles west of the initially proposed Delaware landing place near Reedy Island. This indirect route had several benefits: misleading Washington about British intentions, threatening American supply bases at York and Carlisle, and avoiding potentially catastrophic losses on the well-defended Delaware. But adding over three hundred miles to the voyage left the soldiers sweltering in the August heat aboard the transports an additional three weeks, depleting troop strength and supplies and causing the loss of many of the army's horses, which were needed not just for the cavalry but to carry all of the expedition's equipment and baggage wagons. This delay ultimately had an adverse impact on the campaign. Once in control of Philadelphia, the army would need to be supplied up the Delaware River before it froze over in December. The roundabout route consumed valuable time that would be needed to free the river of American defenses: fortifications, obstructions, and the pesky Pennsylvania navy, a collection of small but dangerous vessels capable of much destruction.[7]

On August 21, word reached Philadelphia that the British fleet had been seen high up in Chesapeake Bay. By the 24th, they began debarking near the mouth of the Elk River in Maryland, about forty-five miles southwest of the city. The British then spent several days reorganizing and recovering from the long sea voyage before heading north toward their main objective. Washington moved his men south to interpose them between Howe and the capital city.[8]

At this time, General John Sullivan sent to Congress a set of bogus documents, known as the Spanktown Papers, that suggested there was a continent-wide Quaker espionage network feeding military intelligence to the British. Already disposed to distrust these disaffected people and fearing the oncoming British invasion, on August 28, Congress ordered Pennsylvania's Supreme Executive Council to detain those of Philadelphia's Quaker leaders who might compromise patriots' plans. On September 2, Pennsylvania militiamen arrested several influential Friends, jailing them initially in the Free Mason's Lodge, on Lodge Alley, just around the corner from Lydia Darragh's Carter's Alley home. Among those rounded up and marched to the lodge was Lydia's nephew, Charles Eddy, the youngest of the exiles, then twenty-three years old. Though Eddy's brother Thomas was later accused of treason, he was not arrested at this time. Born September 5, 1758, he was not quite nineteen and may have been deemed too young. Arrested and held without charges or trial, twenty men were summarily exiled from the city and transported to Winchester, Virginia, where they were imprisoned for several months.[9]

The earliest concrete indicator we have of Lydia Darragh's family favoring the American cause over the British is when her son Charles began working for the American military in 1776. His involvement may have begun to drive a wedge between Lydia and her more-staid Quaker neighbors and kin. Though Mary Darragh Eddy had initially resisted changing from Presbyterian beliefs to Quakerism, once she became a convinced Friend, she had become a faithful adherent. She minded the meeting's guidance that Friends should remain aloof from the troubles and supported their *sotto voce* support for the Crown. Charles's military service probably caused tension between the once-close Darragh and Eddy families. Thomas Eddy provided a glimpse of this strain in his memoir: "a great deal of bitterness and ill-will subsisted amongst the people, which produced much division and strife between families and near connexions, who had heretofore lived in perfect peace and harmony."[10]

As a youth, Charles Darragh was surely aware of the growing anti-British sentiment in the city, dating from the Stamp Act Crisis in 1765. If he were present in the main room of the family's shop, possibly even serving drinks to visitors, he may well have caught the tenor of conversation as increasing numbers of residents expressed dissatisfaction with the actions of Parliament. As various committees of resistance were being created in the city, and public meetings taking place in 1773 and 1774, the conversation became more strident and increasingly militant. Judging from his later actions, Charles's father may well have taken an active role in this defiant discourse. By the time the First Continental Congress met in Philadelphia to plan a unified response to Britain's heavy-handed and threatening actions aimed at reining in the colonies, armed resistance seemed to be just over the horizon, and militia units began organizing.

In September 1776, Pennsylvania's Committee of Safety resolved, "That Thomas Seymour, Esq., be appointed Commodore and Commander-in-Chief of all the Naval Armaments in the service of this State." Christopher Marshall Sr. was a member of that committee, and it may be through his connection that Charles Darragh was appointed as Seymour's clerk. As he had for his paying students, William Darragh evidently had taught his son "to read, write, and understand accompts in the most correct manner." The position as clerk would have required Darragh to "give receipts for all the provisions he receives, . . . superintend the delivery of them and keep lists of the men employed," accounting skills Charles employed later in his career as well. In March 1777, after Charles left the post to join the army, the Pennsylvania Navy Board authorized the next incumbent of the clerk job to be paid at a rate of \$14 per month; Charles's clerk pay may have been about the same.[11]

On February 5, 1777, Charles Darragh obtained an ensign's commission in the 2nd Pennsylvania Regiment, despite his Quaker background. Charles's military service can be understood in outline, but because records are spotty, personal details are hard to come by. While it is certainly possible he had joined a Pennsylvania militia unit earlier, no evidence of such service has been found. His service in the Pennsylvania Line quickly found favor; by April, the young ensign was promoted to lieutenant.[12]

Though newly formed, Darragh's regiment had a substantial nucleus of veteran soldiers: 339 enlisted men, largely from Philadelphia and the surrounding area, who had served with the former 1st Pennsylvania Battalion, which had participated in the Canadian Campaign the previous year. Darragh likely joined the unit at the American army's winter encampment at Morristown, New Jersey, where it formed part of General Anthony Wayne's brigade. The regiment saw hard service throughout 1777. That spring it was involved in skirmishing near Bound Brook and Amboy. While not major battles, such actions could be quite hazardous for the participants, and the 2nd Pennsylvania suffered casualties during this time. Fighting at Bound Brook in June, one of the men from Darragh's company was captured. When the British landed in Maryland in August, Darragh's unit marched down to meet them. Elements of his regiment encountered a British advance party at Iron Hill in Delaware on September 3. Eight days later, they engaged again while guarding Chadd's Ford, at the Battle of Brandywine.[13]

The 2nd Pennsylvania Regiment was severely mauled at the Battle of Paoli on September 20, suffering twenty-two casualties, including at least four men from Captain Roger Stayner's 5th Company, to which Darragh was assigned. Their lieutenant and a private were killed, a sergeant wounded, and another private listed as missing in action. In addition, according to Elizabeth Jacobs, her husband, Peter, a private who served in Stayner's company, was hurt at Paoli: "Peter was wounded by a bayonet, in the left side, which he often exhibited to her after her intermarriage with him."[14]

On September 26, when the British finally marched into Philadelphia, they captured Captain Stayner at his home in the city. Reports from the front surely caused Lydia concern, especially the news that filtered through about Paoli. While Lydia may have heard about it from her son by letter, it is unlikely he was able to visit her before the British occupied the town.[15]

The 2nd Pennsylvania saw action again on October 4 at Germantown, where it lost many men, including the regiment's acting commander, Major William Williams, who was wounded and captured. Over the course of several months, Darragh's regiment was drastically reduced by combat, sickness, and detaching men to other units. According to John B. B. Trussell, a careful historian of the Pennsylvania Line, by the end of the month, the regiment had dwindled to two captains, nine junior officers, including Darragh, three staff officers, and seventy-four enlisted men.[16]

Darragh's whereabouts in December, when his mother made her walk to the American lines to warn him, are unclear. His company's payroll for that month shows him simply as "on command," a phrase meaning he had been detailed away from his usual assignment to some other duty. What might that duty have been? Did it last the entire month or for some shorter period? Some writers suggest, without adducing any evidence, that he was employed in espionage. By Lydia's own account, she did not actually encounter Charles when she walked out of the city; instead, she gave her information to Captain Charles Craig.[17]

As the British approached Philadelphia in earnest, fear of catastrophe seized much of the population. Panicked, the government, politicians, and committed patriots fled the city. Once American military forces withdrew, concern about actual fighting in the city lessened. But fear spread that Philadelphia might catch fire and burn, whether intentionally or by accident. Though over the years residents had taken many civic measures to reduce the possibility of a general conflagration, this ever-present threat was always on people's minds, even more so during this period of civil unrest, with its increased level of public distrust.

Normally when an urban fire did break out, it drew swift public action, such as the fire that occurred in Philadelphia on October 13, 1776. Christopher Marshall noted the event in his diary: "About eleven o'clock last night alarmed by cry of fire, which proved to be just above Pool's Bridge, near the Magazine, in a baker's shop, but it was soon extinguished."[18]

City residents, many of whose families had come from London, certainly would have heard stories about a catastrophe their great grandparents had lived through: the Great Fire of 1666, which destroyed thousands of houses in that city. The fire had likely begun by accident in Thomas Farriner's bakery, though many believed it was intentionally set. In the hysterical aftermath, several men, mostly foreigners, were tried, convicted, and executed for arson. Many in Philadelphia were concerned that unscrupulous partisans—Whig or Tory—would stop at nothing in their quest for political dominance. They also feared that miscreant evildoers might take advantage of a chaotic situation to wreak havoc on innocent people.[19]

Once an urban fire began to spread, a chief means of controlling it was to create fire breaks by pulling down the buildings in the blaze's path. Firefighters had leveled whole blocks of buildings in their attempt to stem the Great Fire of London, which raged for four days. On January

15, 1778, when fire broke out in Charleston, South Carolina, once again in a bakehouse, firefighters again began pulling down buildings to stop the flames from spreading. Over 250 houses were destroyed by fire and the effort to stop it from spreading.[20]

Fear that the British might burn Philadelphia had run high toward the end of 1776, as they pursued Washington's army across the Jersies. That concern was not without reason—five American towns and cities had already suffered catastrophic fires since the outbreak of war.

First to burn was Charlestown, Massachusetts, situated on a peninsula across the harbor from Boston. On the night of June 16, 1775, the American force investing Boston had erected a redoubt on Breed's Hill, a threatening position, just a quarter mile from Charlestown, which overlooked Boston's North End. The next day, the British sent a strong force to dislodge them, precipitating the Battle of Bunker Hill. Part of the American force—about three hundred men—was posted in Charlestown itself, from which they could enfilade any advance against the hilltop. As Brigadier General Robert Pigot led his men past the town, they suffered a galling fire in their left flank from the town. Unable to dislodge them in house-to-house fighting, Pigot withdrew so that Admiral Samuel Graves could set the town afire with incendiary bombs from the support ships.

Four months later, on October 18, two British ships repeated this performance, firing on the town of Falmouth, a haven for American privateers in what is now Maine. Men were sent ashore to set buildings afire, eventually razing the city to the ground. Then, on December 10, British troops again set fires that ruined Jamestown on Conanicut Island, Rhode Island.

Next to burn was Norfolk, Virginia's largest city. Virginia's colonial governor, John Murray, Lord Dunmore, had taken refuge from American forces by boarding ships in Norfolk harbor. From there, he demanded the city supply his men with food and forage. Instead of sending aid, American riflemen sniped at the ships from long range. On January 1, 1776, Murray retaliated by bombarding the city and sending landing parties to torch the warehouses by the waterfront. American forces reacted by setting fire to Tories' houses. It being a windy day, Norfolk was soon engulfed in flames that raged for two days, destroying much of the city.

Closer to home, the city of Newcastle, Delaware, came under threat. On May 8, 1776, two Royal Navy warships, the *Roebuck* and the *Liv-*

erpool, sailed up the Delaware to reconnoiter and refresh their provisions from onshore. As many Newcastle residents closed up their houses and fled, the Pennsylvania navy dropped down the river to engage the British ships. The battle was a standoff, but the *Roebuck* suffered considerable damage. Seeking vengeance, its captain, Andrew Snape Hamond, decided to burn the town. According to William Barry, being held a prisoner aboard the *Roebuck* at the time, Hamond detailed a group of crewmen "to be ready to go ashore at Newcastle, under cover of the cannon, to plunder the town, and afterwards to burn and destroy it that night, but they were prevented by the [American] row-gallies following to close." That plan thwarted, "After the vessels had passed Newcastle they came to, in the bite below the town, that night to repair the rigging, &c. and next day the vessels went down to Reedy-Island, where Captain Hammond hailed the Liverpool, and ordered her to go in betwixt the island and the main, and destroy the town of Port-Penn (we heard drums beating ashore) accordingly he went, and soon after returned, and informed there was not depth of water to get nigh enough, and was afraid his vessel would get aground." Fortune spared the Delaware towns, but the British intent to destroy them was made known to Philadelphians through an article published in the *Pennsylvania Evening Post* the next month.[21]

Finally, the city of New York, just eighty miles from Philadelphia, suffered a calamitous fire on September 20, 1776, five days after British forces occupied it. Though no one knew exactly how it began, most believed that incendiaries set the fire on purpose, each side pointing an accusing finger at the other. Several people, supposed incendiaries, were apprehended and summarily executed by British soldiers and sailors, including a woman, caught "with Matches and Combustibles" who "was tossed into the flames by the soldiers."[22]

On September 11, 1777, the two armies clashed at Brandywine Creek in the war's largest battle. Howe once again displayed tactical brilliance in using German General Wilhelm von Knyphausen to fix Washington in position along the creek while he led his main force around the American right flank, striking it hard before his surprised enemy could organize an effective defense, driving it from the field. While Howe was victorious, both armies suffered severe casualties, with hundreds of men killed and over a thousand wounded. After several days' maneuvering toward the city, Howe was able to cross the Schuylkill River on the 22nd and 23rd, halting his troops around Germantown.[23]

As the British approached Philadelphia in earnest, fear of catastrophe seized much of the population. Since American military forces had largely withdrawn from the city, concern about actual fighting in the city lessened. But worry that a devastating fire might break out grew rampant. On September 23, three days before Cornwallis's entry to the city, sixteen-year-old Robert Morton confided that unease in his diary: "In the evening the inhabitants were exceedingly alarmed by an apprehension of the City being set on fire. The British troops being within 11 miles of the City, caused the disturbance, and gave rise to those womanish fears which seize upon weak kinds at those occasions. Set up till 1 o'clock [on fire watch], not to please myself, but other people."[24]

Not only was there concern that miscreants might set the city ablaze, but people were worried that even the organizational will to fight fire may have lapsed. The normal means of controlling conflagration seemed to be missing. Elizabeth Drinker observed, "it is likely from the present prospect of things, that we shall have a Noisy Night." She went on to express the reasons for concern: "all the Bells in the City are certainly took away, and there is talk of Pump handles and Fire-Buckets being taken also."[25]

The next day, she noted curtly, "the report continues of the English approaching us . . . talk of the City being set on fire." Such talk spread far. From Lancaster, sixty-five miles away, Christopher Marshall heard that "the City was all in flames," though he discredited the report, noting the populace's eagerness to hear the worst: "Thus are many of the people in this place imposed upon."[26]

On the 25th, the British army, camped at Germantown five miles north of town, was also apprehensive. British leaders sought to calm the inhabitants. When one resident, G. Napper, went out to consult with them, Joseph Galloway, whom Howe had designated to govern the civilian populace of Philadelphia, "told him that the inhabitants must take care of the Town this night." A letter was sent into the city, presumably by Galloway, to Thomas Willing, a former mayor, "desiring him to inform the inhabitants to remain quietly and peaceably in their own dwellings and they should not be molested in their persons or property."[27]

In this atmosphere of uncertainty, Elizabeth Drinker worried, "tis said that tar'd faggots &c [sticks coated with flammable tar to set fires] are laid in several out Houses in different parts," but expressed her faith that "should any be so wicked as to attempt fireing the Town, Rain which seems to be coming on, may Providentially prevent it." Citizens assembled to foil arson. According to Drinker, "Numbers mett at the State-House since nine o'clock to form themselves into different Companyes to watch the city . . . the Watch-Men crying the hour." Sarah Logan Fisher confirmed the panic, noting that "many people were apprehensive of the city's being set on fire, & near half the inhabitants, I was told, sat up to watch." Among them was Robert Morton: "Set up till 1 o'clock patrolling the streets for fear of fire. 2 men were taken up who acknowledged their intentions of doing it."[28]

Despite the rumors, it is not clear that anyone actually planned to commit arson. As had happened a century earlier in London, and in New York a year earlier, such fear could lead to fatal accusations against suspicious-looking people. Philadelphians believed that their vigilance and a providential storm had averted catastrophe. Late that evening, Elizabeth Drinker was able to voice relief: "it is now near 11 o'clock, and has been raining for several hours, which I look upon as a remarkable favor."[29]

The next day, the 26th, a contingent of the British army finally marched into the city proper from Germantown. General Cornwallis was given the honor of leading the troops in a parade down the length of Second Street, past the Darraghs' house, to a camping spot below the city. The noble Cornwallis, however, did not choose to stay with his troops. Instead, while the others bivouacked out of doors, he moved into Richard Penn's large house on the south side of High Street, between Fifth and Sixth Streets.[30]

In the meantime, William Howe kept his headquarters at Stenton, a large country house near the bulk of the army at Germantown. Once the defensive works north of the city were completed, Howe and his entourage chose John Cadwalader's house to be the general's residence and headquarters, moving there on October 19. Cadwalader's house was selected for several reasons. Though the Richard Penn House might be a more desirable location because of its size, it was already occupied by Earl Cornwallis, a man Howe was not about to preempt. Cadwalader's recently completed home was reputed to be among the finest and most elegantly appointed in the city, a setting fit for a commander in chief. The Cadwalader place was also near the southern margin of the city, more than a mile below the line of redoubts. The site was closer to Howe's next objective: Fort Mifflin, which perched on Mud Island, just below the confluence of the Delaware and Schuylkill Rivers. With the city's landward defenses secured, Howe turned his attention to reducing the fort and opening the Delaware navigation before the river froze over, so that the army could be supplied for the winter.[31]

When the two armies descended on the Delaware Valley, they brought with them war and famine, with terrible impact on the civilian population of this formerly prosperous and peaceable region. With their arrival, the area's population ballooned. Food became scarce. Local farming had already been disrupted when numerous men left farms for military service. Restricting access to food became a weapon of war, as the Americans attempted to cordon off supplies from reaching the occupied city.

When revolution had broken out in America, the rebels quickly seized civil control of nearly all the land the British army did not occupy physically. Throughout the countryside, Americans exerted almost total control of local government, including the courts, which administered the law, the militia, which enforced the law, and taxation, which supported the revolutionary government at each level. British forces lost access to most of the continent's food production. As a great naval power, Britain was able to project its military might virtually any place within a day or two's march of the sea. Its military strategy relied on the ability to supply its troops from their ships, but this was at best a short-term solution.

While urging a takeover of Philadelphia, Tories like Joseph Galloway and Andrew Allen had assured William Howe that the people of Pennsylvania would welcome a return to British rule. But they were wrong. Patriot domination of local governance, enforced by the militia, was strong. The size of the British force sent to Pennsylvania was small compared to the number of rebels. British patrolling, and thus the army's immediate sphere of influence, was limited to about seven or eight miles, about as far out from camp and back as a soldier could reasonably walk in a day. Cavalry could extend that range and cover longer distances quickly in an emergency. They did occasionally launch raids up to twenty miles away, in places such as Gwynedd, Newtown, and Crooked Billet, but knowing they could not hold the ground long lest they be surrounded and overwhelmed, they found it expedient to return within their lines quickly.

To those Philadelphians who applauded the reappearance of British authority, it quickly became clear that military occupation was nothing like the old status quo. Those who wished to remain neutral, and even Tory friends of government, were confronted with a harsh reality—the army must eat, and the army would eat them out of house and home. With cold calculation, the military would see first to its own needs, feeding its soldiers before the populace. With food in short supply, even British camp followers and Hessian auxiliaries would feel the pinch before the regulars.

Inside the city's perimeter, British and German soldiers found it necessary to supplement their rations by simply requisitioning food from people's gardens and farms, and by stealing their farm animals. Soldiers who plundered the inhabitants, stealing money, personal goods, and furnishings from private residences, were liable to harsh punishment if caught. But hungry people will resort to desperate measures when needing to feed themselves and their families. On September 28, Robert Morton went down into The Neck to check on the plantation of his exiled stepfather, James Pemberton.

> About 10 o'clock this morning some of the Light Dragoons stationed near Plantation broke open the house, 2 desks, 1 Book Case and 1 closet besides several drawers and other things, and ransacked them all. I apply'd to their officer, who informed me that if the men were found out they should be severely punished. I have been informed that a soldier this day rec'd 400 lashes for some crime, which I do not know.[32]

The next day, Morton inspected his uncle Israel Pemberton's plantation across the road, "where we found a destruction similar to that at our Plantation, 3 closets being broke open, 6 doz. wine taken, some silver spoons, the Bedcloaths taken off 4 Beds, 1 rip'd open, the Tick being taken off, and other Destruction about the Plantation. The officers were so obliging as to plant a centry there without application." Then he noted with horror, "Upon our return home we pass'd thro' part of the camp and saw a man hanging." Feeling guilt at having exposed some soldier to a similar fate, the following day, September 30, he and his mother tried to stave off another execution:

> This morning my mother and I went to Col. Harcourt, Com. of the Light Dragoons, near our plantation, to make intercession for

> the men who are apprehended for breaking and ransacking our plantation and house. The Col. upon my application, behaved very unlike a Gent'n by asking me 'what I wanted' in an ungenteel manner, and told me he could not attend to what I had to say, and said that the trial was coming on and I must attend to prosecute them. I informed him there was a lady who would be glad to speak with him. He then came to my mother and behaved in a very polite genteel manner, and assured her that he could not admit her application as the orders of the General must be obeyed, and that the soldiers were not suffered to commit such depredations upon the King's subjects with impunity.[33]

While a private soldier might be flogged or hung for stealing, when it came to supplying the army itself with forage, Morton noticed a dual standard. With ironic chagrin, he continued, "Some of the British troops came to my mother's pasture on 6th and 1st days last and took away 2 loads of hay without giving a Rec't or offering Payment."

On October 1, he was somewhat relieved on finding that "the man who was found guilty of robbing our Plantation rec'd punishment this day, which was—lashes." At least he hadn't been hung. But then Morton learned, "The man found coming out of Mary Pemberton's plantation House is sentenced to be executed. M. P. has petitioned the Gen'l for a mitigation of the punishment." Mary Pemberton might have hoped she had a little extra moral leverage with the general, because "during the time he stayed in Philadelphia," Howe had "seized and kept for his own use Pemberton's coach and horses."[34]

The British, like the Americans before them, seized what they needed. While the king's men may have been clear on the distinction between requisitioning and theft, residents of the city could not always tell whether their actions were military policy or plundering. Elizabeth Drinker was disturbed on November 5 when a British soldier came to her house demanding blankets. When she refused, "he went upstairs and took one, and with seeming good nature begged I would excuse his borrowing it, as it was by G. Howe's orders." Penalties for looting were so harsh that many Quakers were unwilling to lodge complaints.[35]

Looting of property was one thing, but officers would often turn a blind eye toward those taking food, especially when harvesting someone else's garden. Troubles in The Neck continued for Robert Morton and his neighbors. After noting that "Provisions are very scarce" and worrying about "a prospect of starvation," Morton returned to his family's plantation on October 19 to harvest cabbages:

> When I had got as far as I. Pemberton's Place, I see about 100 Hessians coming down the road on a foraging, or rather plundering, party. As soon as they came to the corner of the road, their com. gave them permission to take all the cabbage and Potatoes they could find. Being afraid that they would take our cabbage, I applied for a guard to the House and Garden, which was immediately granted, and by that means prevented our cabbage from being plundered. After they had taken all Jno. King's Cabbage and Potatoes they marched off. Brought our cabbage home. It was surprising to see with what rapidity they run to, and with what voraciousness they seized upon Jno. King's Cabbage and Potatoes, who remained a silent spectator to their infamous depredations.

Anxious to protect the family food supply, Morton returned the next day. There he found the relentless German soldiers mounting a full-scale operation:

> Went to the plantation to see about the potatoes, &c, and when I got to the corner of ye road I see another party of Hessians coming down with Horses, Carts, bags, &c, to carry off Hay, potatoes, &c. The commander rode up to Jno. King's House, and I followed him. He said he was come by orders of the General to take the Hay and Potatoes. I told him who it belonged to, but to no purpose. By this time a guard which Col. Harcourt had sent came up and declared they should not take it. From thence they went to J. Bringhurst's Place where they took all the Hay and most of ye Potatoes which belonged to the Tenant, to the distress of the family.[36]

As time passed and supply ships were prevented from getting up the Delaware, only a trickle of food could be brought overland from the victualers at anchor lower down on the river. If provisions were short for the soldiers, things were worse for the populace, most especially the poor, who faced a real prospect of starvation.

Space in the crowded city was at a premium. Officers jockeyed for the best accommodations, sometimes nudging out those of lower status. General Howe occupied John Cadwalader's fine town home, across the way from the Darragh family in the Benjamin Loxley House. Though it was a large house, elegantly appointed, the general and his staff found the space where they lived and worked rather cramped.[37] To get an idea of how much space was available, and how best to apportion it to the army, the British commissioned a census of houses and people, which was supervised by Joseph Galloway and carried out by a number of trustworthy assistants. A summary report exists. It includes separate totals for the city proper, broken out by ward, and the two adjacent suburbs, the Northern Liberties and Southwark. While many find fault with the numbers, there is no reason to suppose the compliers strove for anything but accuracy. Its intended use was as a management tool rather than a piece of propaganda. Such accounts are never completely accurate, but this report seems reasonably reliable, if not near perfect. Galloway estimated that about ten thousand people had fled Philadelphia, leaving at least 21,757 inhabitants, not including men older than sixty, who were left out of the count.[38]

Out of 5,460 dwelling houses, 597, or 11 percent, were unoccupied. Merchants and shopkeepers—who were generally people of some prosperity, with something to lose—seem to have fled from the British in greater proportion than the regular population. Of 287 stores documented, 224 were listed as empty—a staggering 78 percent.

The Darraghs were among the small number of shopkeepers who chose to remain. Never wealthy, perhaps they could not afford to leave. They kept their store open during the occupation, though they probably had difficulties keeping up their inventory, as the volume of supplies of all kinds coming into the city was seriously curtailed by the American cordon. They would also have faced the cash-flow problems that affected so many others in the city. Those merchants who were able to bring goods into town insisted on being paid in specie—hard, cold cash made of precious gold and silver. Bills of credit and the old paper money issued by Pennsylvania were not accepted, while passing Continental scrip in the occupied city was deemed treasonous and could lead to arrest.

As William Howe's staff scrambled to find accommodations, a top priority would be to lodge as close to headquarters as possible. The proximity and attractive appearance of the Darraghs' house across the street, with its appealing glass store front and airy balcony, made it an ideal location. But when officers came to requisition her home, Lydia Darragh balked.

Family stories, collected by Henry Darrach at the end of the nineteenth century, shed light on her resistance. Because the accounts were collected many years after the event, they may not be wholly reliable, but they may contain some kernels of truth. Darrach elaborated:

> William Darragh was ordered to open his house for the accommodation of some of the troops and find other quarters for his family. It was a cold winter, the city was crowded and he knew not what to do, but finally Lydia determined to go herself to General Howe and ask for relief. While she was waiting for an audience one of the staff officers entered into conversation with her and finding she was as well as himself, a native of Ireland, became rather interested in her statement of her difficulties and asked General Howe to relieve her from the order. This he declined to do, saying they also were very much pressed for room, but at length decided to take only one room for a council chamber. This was large and at the back of the house.[39]

Given the press of managing the army, as well as Howe's well-documented impatience when being forced to deal with those of lower status who attempted to set his agenda, it seems unlikely that the general would have granted audience to a middle-class woman about a simple domestic matter, even though she was a neighbor. Instead, he would have assigned staff to run interference. The staff officer who took her case under advisement may have spoken with Howe, but, more likely, only pretended to do so and resolved the matter himself under a simple delegation of authority.

Writing in an earlier article, which was based on communication with Darragh descendants and his own genealogical research, Henry Darrach related the following: "Family tradition states that 'the house in which she resided, Second Street, below Spruce Street, was selected as a place of meeting for the British officers by her cousin, Lieutenant Barrington, who was an officer in General Howe's Army.'" He included a footnote to support this assertion: "History of the Seventh Regiment of Foot, known as the Royal Regiment of Fusiliers. Said regiment formed a part of the army under Sir William Howe at Philadelphia. Lieutenant William Barrington (captain, June 1777) transferred to Seventieth Foot; retired September 2, 1779."[40]

In his recounting of Lydia's Tale in 1916, Darrach mentioned William Barrington again: "In Howe's army was a Captain William Barrington, said to be a relation of Lydia Darragh." Interestingly, he placed this reference in the prefatory remarks. He did not include the assertion in his recitation of Lydia's Tale itself, which was based on a written version he received from Margaret Porter Darragh Newton. Evidently someone, either a relative or Henry Darrach himself, did some cursory investigation in an attempt to put a name to the "staff officer" who was "a native of Ireland." The researcher, on finding an officer with Lydia's maiden name, transformed this person into a cousin. But they identified the wrong man.

The young officer in question, William Wildman Barrington II (1758–1801), was a gentleman of ample fortune and some bad luck. He was born into a prominent English family, one of the sons of Major General John Barrington, who was famed for forcing the surrender of the French island of Guadeloupe in 1759. William was about six when his father died, supposedly due to illness contracted during his West Indies campaign. His uncle and namesake, William Wildman Barrington (1717–1793), second Viscount Barrington of Ardglass, was the British secretary of war during both the Seven Years' War and the American War of Independence. On his brother's passing, the viscount took responsibility for the general's orphaned boys, supervising William's education at Louis Lochée's military academy at Chelsea and using personal influence to secure him a post in the army.[41]

Commissioned a lieutenant in the 7th Regiment of Foot, the Royal Fusiliers, William Barrington was sent to Canada, where he was part of the garrison of Fort Chambly on the Richelieu River, which guarded the upper end of the Lake Champlain corridor and the approach to Montreal. During the American invasion of Canada in 1775, the fort withstood two days of bombardment before capitulating. Seventeen-year-old Lieutenant Barrington was captured, along with eighty-two other officers and men from the 7th and 26th Regiments of Foot. Learning of this and sensing advantage, John Adams crowed in his diary, "We had two valuable Prizes among the Prisoners, taken at Chambly and St. Johns—a Mr. Barrington Nephew of Lord Barrington, and a Captain Williams."[42]

A prisoner of war, William Barrington was sent to Lebanon, Pennsylvania, along with four other officers—evidently all Irishmen—and their servants. They were put on parole and lodged in Matthew McHugh's tavern, the Sign of the Bear, where they were expected to pay their own expenses. On June 15, 1776, Barrington's fellow officers took off and headed to Canada to rejoin their units. Young William remained behind. Having given his word, he may have viewed flight as beneath his honor, or, perhaps, the others preferred not to be burdened with a companion so young. In either event, the angry Americans revoked Barrington's parole and sent him to a jail in Lancaster, where he remained for several weeks in the company of common criminals.[43]

William Barrington was further discommoded by being deprived of his personal possessions. The goods he had brought with him from Fort Chambly were considerable. Among the contents were "a small trunk full of books and a case of liquors." When the other officers absconded from Lebanon, they had left behind "upwards of twenty trunks and boxes, besides some bales and portmanteaus." By contrast, the captured enlisted men, who were accompanied by numerous women and children, arrived in Pennsylvania without their baggage and were in danger of freezing during their first winter in captivity.[44]

The escape resulted in outrage and, perhaps even worse, paperwork. In addition to their substantial baggage, the fugitive officers left behind them a bill from the tavern owner for £100. Such exorbitant charges may have been one reason the officers decided to decamp. This resulted in a flurry of correspondence as Pennsylvania authorities consulted with each other, and even with the Continental Congress, to see if they could auction off the baggage to pay the debt. In the process, Pennsylvania officials tacked on their own expenses for advertising and pursuing the runaways, adding another £30 2s. 2d. to the amount they hoped to recover.[45]

As the nephew of Britain's secretary of war, William Barrington was no ordinary prisoner. Powerful people were solicitous of his welfare. Admiral Lord Richard Howe contacted George Washington and Benjamin Franklin to inquire after the youth's well-being, doubtless prompted by his subordinate, William's uncle, Admiral Samuel Barrington. Shortly after this inquiry, William Barrington was released from the Lancaster jail, granted parole again, and allowed to join other captive officers at York. He was eventually exchanged, probably in December 1776 or January 1777. Following his internment, he was assigned as an aide-de-camp to Major General Richard Prescott, who took over command of the British force occupying Rhode Island in May 1777. While this may have seemed a proper measure for keeping the young man out of harm's way, things did not work out as planned.[46]

On the night of July 10-11, American soldiers under Captain William Barton launched a daring raid on Prescott's headquarters at the Overing house near Newport. They broke into the house and seized the general in his nightclothes. William Barrington, sleeping in a nearby bedroom, heard what was happening, took time to don his britches, and jumped out of a window. The alert raiders snatched him up as well. Prescott and Barrington were hustled off to Providence. They were then taken to the town serving as the capital of Connecticut. Somewhat ironically for the unlucky Barrington, this town too was called Lebanon. Here they were granted parole under the supervision of Governor Jonathan Trumbull, in more-comfortable circumstances than those of Barrington's first captivity. The Americans hoped to exchange Prescott for Major General Charles Lee, who had been captured by the British the previous December. Fearing an attempt to recapture Prescott, they soon moved the general, along with his personal servant, deeper into the country to New Windsor, Connecticut, where, according to Governor Trumbull, "he is genteely accommodated; but strongly guarded." Trumbull appeased his aggravated captive further: "At his request I sufferd his Aid Du Camp Lieut: Barrington to attend him."[47]

Arrangements to exchange them took some time, because, for leverage in negotiating, the British claimed not to recognize Lee, a former British officer, as a prisoner of war, but as a traitor, thereby threatening his execution. As talks ground on, Washington grudgingly allowed Prescott and Barrington to be sent to New York, where they could await their eventual exchange within the British lines. They did not arrive in the city until sometime in mid to late January 1778, which meant Barrington could not have been present in Philadelphia when Lydia Darragh supposedly sought relief from an Irish staff officer. While still on parole, William Barrington took the time to be married to Teresa Clarke in Greenwich, Connecticut, in early April. He may have met her in the weeks after he arrived in New York, but it is also possible they met during his imprisonment in Lebanon or New Windsor. Once exchanged, he returned to Newport with General Prescott and resumed his duties. His trials, however, were not yet at an end. On December 20, 1778, while aboard a British transport headed from Newport to New York, his ship ran aground on Point Judith, near Narragansett, Rhode Island. Here the hapless Barrington was captured yet a third time. His captors, probably shaking their heads at the man's incredibly bad luck, seem to have released him quickly.[48]

William Barrington retired from the army in fall 1779 or early 1780. Back in England, he married again, on July 8, 1781, this time to Anne Murrell. What became of his marriage to Teresa Clarke is unknown. Eventually he succeeded to his namesake's title, becoming, on February 1, 1793, the third Viscount Barrington of Ardglass. His wealthy uncle, however, seemed to have doubts about Barrington's ability to manage business affairs. Instead of bequeathing his full estate to him, he put the assets into a trust managed by Barrington's surviving uncles, granting his heir an annuity of £600 per year, with the proviso that the trustees could manage the spending if they felt him incapable of managing his finances. William Barrington died July 31, 1801, leaving no children.[49]

It is possible that an Irish officer was somehow involved in requisitioning the Darragh home in 1777, whether identifying it as a desirable place for quartering officers or, sympathizing with Lydia's plight, interceding on her behalf to reduce the requirement to an occasional meeting place. It is even possible that the officer was a cousin of Lydia Darragh's, though who it could have been is unknown. But that man was not William Wildman Barrington II. He was not present in Philadelphia in October 1777 when the British asked to use the house, nor was he in the city during Lydia's trek to Frankford that December. Further, as a member of the Shute-Barrington family, he was not related to Lydia by blood. Nor was he even Irish—the very suggestion of which he might have found insulting. While the remote possibility exists that Lydia Darragh and William Barrington actually met at some point, in reality all they had in common was a surname. The identity of the Irish staff officer who intervened in the occupation of the Darragh home remains a mystery. If it even happened at all.[50]

A discrepancy between the Robert Walsh and Henry Darrach versions must be reconciled at this point. Darrach never mentioned the rank of the officer who requisitioned or met in the Darragh house. In Walsh's account, that person was "A superior officer of the British army, believed to be the Adjutant General, [who] fixed upon one of their chambers, a back room, for private conference." Walsh tentatively identified the officer as adjutant general because he faithfully recorded the hesitancy of his informant, Hannah Haines. She had written, "Two officers had frequently met there, one I think the Adjutant General." Alexander Garden, in his version of the story, stated confidently that "the Adjutant General of the army desired Lydia to have an apartment prepared for the reception of himself and friends." Though Garden's account appeared in print after Walsh's account, the two men had nonetheless discussed the differences in their approaches to the story as early as 1822. But neither man ever identified the adjutant general by name. Later writers felt a need to fill this attractive gap in the story. They believed they knew who this adjutant general must have been: no less glorious a figure than the British spymaster Major John André.[51]

But who actually was the British adjutant general during the occupation of Philadelphia? An adjutant general was an officer charged with managing the business affairs of an army. As no formal appointment seems to have been made at the time, it is difficult to determine who had the job in December 1777. Lieutenant Colonel James Paterson, who held the position in 1776, had returned to England that spring. Paterson's successor, Major Cornelius Cuyler, referred to as Howe's first aide-de-camp, personally carried Howe's dispatches about the Battles of Brandywine and Germantown to George Germaine, leaving Philadelphia in mid-October 1777, and delivering them by December 1. After Cuyler's departure, the adjutant general duties devolved onto another of Howe's aides-de-camp, the general's trusted confidant, Major Nisbet Balfour. Balfour's appointment to the position, lasting less than four months, may never have been formalized, since the general intended to promote him to lieutenant colonel of the 23rd Regiment of Foot, which he did the following February 5. Upon that promotion, Howe's German aide, Friedrich von Muenchhausen, noted that Balfour had been Howe's "second adjutant." John Graves Simcoe, commanding the Queen's Rangers, described Balfour as the man who had successfully managed intelligence for the army during the occupation of Philadelphia.[52]

Seeking, as legend tellers often do, to make heroic exploits ever grander through association with famous people, later accounts of Lydia's Tale conjecture that the adjutant general had to have been the tragic André. Once introduced to the legend in 1884, John André became a regular part of the story. Cutting a dashing figure, André was an intelligent, artistic, energetic, and ambitious young officer. He was celebrated in Philadelphia history as one of the men who staged the elaborate and colorful Mischianza celebration, an extravagant farewell party for William Howe when the general gave up his command in Philadelphia. André did eventually become the British adjutant general, but only in 1779, and, as such, supervised the army's collection of intelligence. In 1780, he worked with Benedict Arnold in a plan to betray the fortress at West Point, which could have given the British control of the vital Hudson River corridor. He was arrested by American soldiers in New York after a clandestine meeting with Arnold. Dressed in civilian garb, he was carrying incriminating evidence of the conspiracy. His capture unmasked Arnold as a traitor and led to his own trial for espionage. Found guilty, John André was executed as a spy—ignominiously hung, despite numerous pleas for clemency by sympathetic American officers. And so he passed into the mythology of the American Revolution as a romantic and tragic symbol.[53]

Over time, John André's story became bound up with Lydia's Tale, but the association was a false one. Major André was indeed a member of the British officer corps in 1777, but he was not part of the general staff during the occupation of Philadelphia. Instead, Captain André, as he was at the time, was an aide-de-camp to Major General Charles Grey. He did not reside with Howe at the Cadwalader House but was comfortably lodged in Benjamin Franklin's home, near Fourth and High Streets. Lodged a little too comfortably perhaps. When the British evacuated the city the following June, a reliable witness caught André packing up Franklin's books for shipment as though, after months of familiarity, they had become his own.[54]

In anticipation of the possible British occupation of Philadelphia, Washington had subordinates establish contact with well-affected persons inside the city who would be willing to supply useful information to the Americans. Though some of the British troops marched into the city on September 26, the main force remained at Germantown until fortifications could be built across the neck of land between the Delaware and Schuylkill Rivers. Once the British withdrew inside that defensive perimeter, Washington assigned reliable, enterprising officers to patrol near the enemy lines for several purposes: to serve as a tripwire preventing surprise movements by the enemy, to restrict the flow of supplies into the city, and to gather intelligence. A controversy concerning two of the officers commanding these advanced troops figures prominently in Lydia's Tale. Those men were Captains Charles Craig and Allen McLane.[55]

Throughout the occupation, patrolling forces of both sides waged a deadly cat-and-mouse game of skirmishes and ambuscades. McLane's detachment was assigned to guard the road leading to Germantown, one of three main land routes out of the occupied capital. He also had a broad responsibility to keep a watch on the area between the two rivers. Three miles to the east, watching the King's Road near the village of Frankford, was Charles Craig's troop of light dragoons. Though both were valiant officers, well regarded by their peers, through the accidents of history, Allen McLane became a figure of legend while the name of Charles Craig sank into obscurity. The identities and supposed roles of these two soldiers in Lydia's Tale have generated much confusion and controversy over the years. Both men merit a closer look. We will talk more about them later.[56]

Despite a string of British victories during the Philadelphia Campaign—Brandywine, Germantown, the destruction of the Delaware River fortifications—the American army was still in the field, posted strongly along the hills above Whitemarsh, near enough to threaten the city. After securing the city's defenses and opening the Delaware for navigation, Howe turned his eyes toward another of his key objectives: breaking the enemy's ability to resist. Under pressure to take decisive action, Howe planned a final attempt to bring the American force to a decisive battle before winter set in. Once General Cornwallis's force returned from foraging in New Jersey in late November, preparations began.[57]

Though his primary goal at this point was to destroy Washington's army in the field, Howe's intent in moving against Whitemarsh was at least partly preemptive. British intelligence noted the arrival of American reinforcements from the northern armies at Saratoga and the Hudson Highlands. As an observant British sergeant, Thomas Sullivan, put it:

> The Enemy being joined by upwards of 4000 men, with Cannon, from the northern Army, assembled their whole force in a strong camp at Whitemarsh, covered in part by Sandy Run, 14 miles distant from Philadelphia, with their right to Wissahichon creek. Upon a Presumption that a forward move might tempt the Enemy, after receiving such reinforcement, to give battle for the

British outposts north of Philadelphia, 1777. **1.** Gates by the Cohocksink Creek. **2.** The Norris House, Fair Hill, burnt November, 1777. **3.** The Rising Sun Tavern. **4.** Swedish Mill, north of the bridge at Frankford. **5.** Chalkley Hall, estate of Abel James. **6.** Bush Hill, occupied by General Wilhelm von Knyphausen until after the Battle of Whitemarsh. 7. Lukens' Mill near Germantown. Detail from *A Plan of the City and Environs of Philadelphia, Surveyed by N. Scull and G. Heap, Engraved by William Faden*, 1777. (*Library of Congress*)

> recovery of the City, or that a vulnerable part might be found to admit of an attack upon their camp.[58]

That the nearby rebel army was capable of launching a bold stroke against its opponents was hardly lost on William Howe. Washington's December surprise at Trenton the previous year had shocked the British. Just when the Americans had seemed on the verge of dissolution and defeat, the daring campaign at year's end reinvigorated their flagging military efforts. The American attack at Germantown, coming just three weeks after a major loss at Brandywine, had been both audacious and potentially successful. Rather than allowing the newly reinforced enemy the opportunity of another potentially unbalancing winter surprise, it seemed best to Howe to set Washington's agenda by taking the initiative and launching a surprise attack of his own. It was this plan that Lydia Darragh got hold of while eavesdropping on a meeting in her back room.

Christopher Marshall (1709-1797). Born in Dublin, Marshall was a highly successful druggist in Philadelphia. The famed Revolutionary diarist became a patron of the Darragh family. (*Illustrated Christopher Marshall Papers, Historical Society of Pennsylvania*)

Hannah Marshall Haines (1765-1828), artist unknown. A granddaughter of Christopher Marshall, she knew Lydia Darragh since childhood and preserved Lydia's Tale for future generations. (*Courtesy of The Wyck Association*)

Robert Walsh, Jr. (1784-1859), by John Neagle, 1822. Walsh, a leading American journalist, learned Lydia's Tale from Hannah Haines and was the first to publish it in 1827. (*Booth Family Center for Special Collections, Georgetown University*)

John Fanning Watson (1779-1860), by Abraham B. Rockey, 1849. The preeminent historian of Philadelphia, Watson also learned of Lydia Darragh from Hannah Haines and added several important details to Lydia's Tale. (*Drexel University, Atwater Kent Collection*)

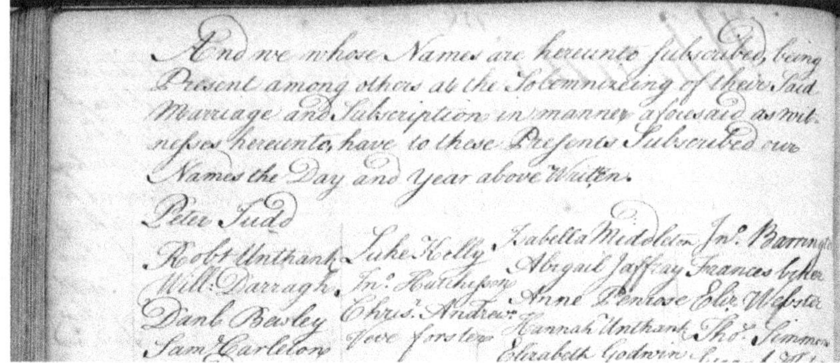

And we whose Names are hereunto subscribed, being Present among others at the Solemnizing of their Said Marriage and Subscription in manner aforesaid as witnesses hereunto, have to these Presents Subscribed our Names the Day and Year above Written.

Peter Judd
Robt Unthank
Will: Darragh
Danl. Bewley
Sam Carleton
Luke Kelly
Jno. Hutcheson
Chris: Andrews
Izabella Middleton
Abigail Jaffray
Anne Penrose
Hannah Unthank
Elizabeth Godwin
Jno. Barrington
Frances Biker
Eliz. Webster
Thos. Simmons

Witnesses to William and Lydia Darragh's marriage, November 2, 1753. Note the family column at the right, beginning with Lydia's father, John Barrington and her aunt, Frances Biker. (*Society of Friends, Dublin Meeting*)

A WOMAN who can be well recommended for either Wet or Dry Nurſing, wants Employment. Enquire at William Darragh's, Tobacconiſt, in Second-ſtreet, near Cheſtnut-ſtreet. †

An ad for Lydia Darragh's services as a nurse. This is the first advertisement for Lydia's nursing services, through which she played an important role in the Philadelphia community. (*Pennsylvania Gazette, November 28, 1765*)

Timothy Matlack (1736-1829) by Charles Willson Peale, 1826. Best known as the man who inscribed the Declaration of Independence, he was the stepbrother of Hannah Marshall Haines's father-in-law. The irascible Matlack is shown here with his famous walking stick. (*Independence National Historical Park*)

Blair McClenachan (1734-1812). A wealthy merchant, the Irish-born McClenachan was a family friend of the Darraghs. Though a major financier of the Revolution, he served humbly as a private in the Philadelphia Light Horse, which accompanied Washington during the Trenton Campaign. (*Trenton Battle Monument, New Jersey State Park Service*)

Top: Benjamin Loxley's House on Second Street rented by William and Lydia Darragh, watercolor by William Breton, 1828. From the second floor porch Reverend George Whitfield preached in 1739-1740. It was in this spacious, uniquely designed house that Lydia Darragh eavesdropped on a meeting of the British Army's senior staff in 1777. (*Athenaeum of Philadelphia*) Bottom: "Lydia Darragh House, Little Dock Creek and 2nd Street," photographed by Frederick De Bourg Richards, c. 1854. By the time this photograph was taken, the southern half of the house had been demolished and the pent roof over the balcony reconfigured. Note the distinctive scroll brackets and porch railing finials in both images. (*Library of Congress*)

"John and Elizabeth Lloyd Cadwalader and Their Daughter Anne," 1772, by Charles Willson Peale. While Cadwalader was serving with George Washington as a general of Pennsylvania militia in December 1777, his elegant home across the street from Lydia Darragh was British general William Howe's headquarters. (*Philadelphia Museum of Art*)

HEAD-QUARTERS, 21st Nov 1777

THE Bearer John Fore

has the Commander in Chief's Permiſſion to paſs the out Poſts, without Moleſtation.

To all Concerned.

N Balfour

Aid de Camp

Nisbet Balfour Pass, November 21, 1777. Major Balfour, an aide to General Howe, was the acting adjutant general of the British army during the occupation of Philadelphia. So many people requested to leave the city daily that forms were printed for the passes. (*Library of Congress*)

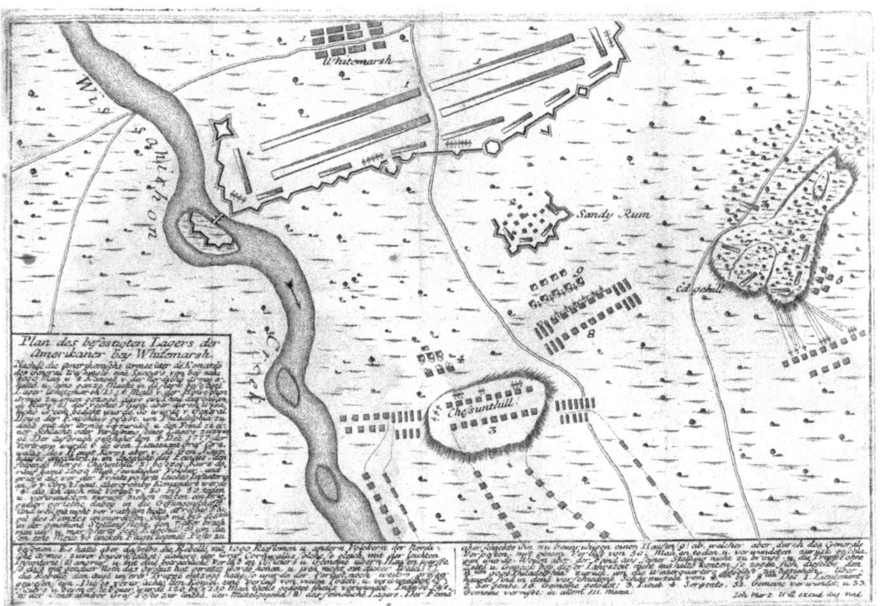

Top: *Plan des befestigten Lagers der Amerikaner bey Whitemarsh* [Plan of the American Fortified Camp near Whitemarsh], Johann Martin Will, 1778. European audiences wanted to "see" the conflict in America, as well as to read about it. A German engraver based this somewhat conjectural map on testimony from an actual participant in the actions around Whitemarsh. Note Edgehill at right. Bottom: *Vorstellung nach dem Plan so d. 4. bis zum 8ten Dec. 1777* [View of the Battlefield from the 4th to the 8th of December, 1777], Johann Martin Will, 1778. This fanciful panorama shows the American positions on the hills above Sandy Run at the upper left and the engagement on Edge Hill at the upper right, with a heroic German General Knyphausen in the foreground. (*Library of Congress*)

Free Quaker Meeting House, Fifth and Arch Streets, Philadelphia. A number of Quakers who had been disowned for involvement with the American Revolution formed a splinter sect, the Society of Free Quakers. They built their own meeting house in 1783. (*Independence National Historical Park*)

Cradle used by Lydia Darragh for her children. Historian Henry Darrach worked with a descendant of Lydia Darragh to place this cradle in the Independence Hall Collection. (*Photograph by Karie Diethorn, Independence National Historical Park*)

Lydia Darragh Chair. This chair, one of a set mentioned in Lydia Darragh's estate, was owned by Margaret Darragh Newton (1823-1894), who told a variant of Lydia's Tale to Henry Darrach. Her daughter, Sallie Newton Page, placed a plaque on the chair when she lent it for an exhibition, possibly during the Sesquicentennial. (*Courtesy Kelly Kinzle*)

Sallie Newton Page (1857-1930). She based her application to the Daughters of the American Revolution on the exploits of her great-great grandmother, Lydia Darragh, and later founded the Great Bridge, Virginia, Chapter of the DAR. (*Great Bridge Chapter, National Society Daughters of the American Revolution*)

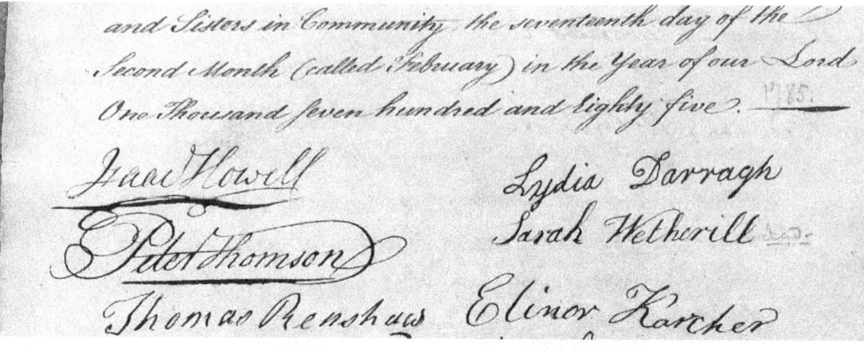

and Sisters in Community the seventeenth day of the
Second Month (called February) in the Year of our Lord
One Thousand seven hundred and eighty five. 1785.

Isaac Howell Lydia Darragh
Peter Thomson Sarah Wetherill
Thomas Renshaw Elinor Karcher

Lydia Darragh's signature, Free Quaker Records, February 2, 1785. One of only two known signatures by Lydia Darragh, this appeared on an epistle to a group of Free Quakers in Massachusetts. The only other surviving sample of Lydia Darragh's writing is the signature on her will. (*American Philosophical Society*)

"Quaker Heroism" (Lydia Darragh Meets Charles Craig), *Godey's Lady's Book*, Volume XXX, January to June 1845. Elizabeth Ellet authored a number of articles about women patriots from the American Revolution, leading off the series with a piece about Lydia Darragh. This engraving eventually became the best known image of the heroine. There are no known portraits of Lydia Darragh. (*Library Company of Philadelphia*)

Chapter 9

Lydia Darragh Eavesdrops on the British

According to the Haines and Walsh versions of Lydia's Tale, on about December 2, an adjutant general told Lydia that he and other officers,

> would be in the room at seven o'clock, and remain late; and that they wished the family to retire early to bed; adding, that when they were going away, they would call her to let them out, and extinguish their fire and candles. She accordingly sent all the family to bed; but, as the officer had been so particular, her curiosity was excited. She took off her shoes, and put her ear to the keyhole of the conclave. She overheard an order read for all the British troops to march out, late in the evening of the fourth, and attack General Washington's army, then encamped at White Marsh."[1]

The British officer in question was thought to have been the adjutant general, though it may have been another staff officer. If the adjutant, then that person is most likely to have been Nisbet Balfour. In any event, the officer's special precautions about the planned meeting aroused Lydia Darragh's curiosity. By early December, she would have been used to meetings taking place in her back room, though not, perhaps, at night. This time, she believed she had gotten wind that something bigger than usual was in the air, and she felt she had to know what.

Walsh's source, Hannah Haines, hadn't been exact in specifying the night Darragh's eavesdropping occurred. Using the sequence of events in the story he had learned, and working backward from the actual date of the march to Whitemarsh, Walsh estimated the date as the evening of December 2, 1777. A careful comparison of contemporary sources with the other early versions of Lydia's Tale confirms this timing but raises a question. Which of the evolving British plans did Lydia Darragh overhear?

William Howe's preparation for the move to Whitemarsh did not unfold in a simple manner. Surviving British accounts of the actual march are somewhat contradictory. As best as can be determined, Howe initially planned the march to begin on the morning of December 4. Yet his order book for November 30 gives no hint about an expected movement. As happened regularly, on that day rations were issued for the coming four days: "The troops to receive four Days provisions to Morrow to the 4th December Inclusive." Preparing for the colder weather ahead, new blankets and mitts were to be distributed to the men as well.[2]

Though doubtless ruminating on his plans by early December, as late as December 2, Howe's official orders make no mention of moving against the Americans. Though observers agreed that a move had been in contemplation for several days, the exact date may have remained undetermined. Did Howe covertly release a plan to his top staff on the 2nd, so they could be ready to move? An army of the period—even a highly agile one—required a certain amount of notice to put into operation a plan demanding coordination as complex as this one, which would require so many units to assemble at an exact time and to move in a precise order.

Perhaps the official orders were silent on the subject in an effort to maintain secrecy. Certainly, there was reason to attempt concealment. Referring to the planned march, Major Carl Baurmeister, adjutant general of the German force, complained, "unfortunately, the enemy is informed of everything as soon as our generals get their orders."[3]

Keeping a secret involving thousands of troops was no simple feat. As the British juggernaut gradually roused itself, soldiers could tell an operation was in the offing—the signs were everywhere. On November 27, Scottish military engineer Archibald Robertson observed, "From this day by the Preparations that were made it was easily seen that a move was intended accordingly." Indeed, civilians in the city, living cheek by jowl with the military, were well aware that something was stirring. On November 30, Robert Morton noted that "reports are prevalent that the main part of the army will soon move off." Elizabeth Drinker confirmed this the next day: "There is talk to day, as if a great part of ye English army were making ready to depart on some secret expedition." Such civilian rumors were doubtless heard by Lydia Darragh, raising her level of suspicion about what might be brewing well in advance of the meeting in her house.[4]

In the days leading up to Howe's move, word leaked through British lines to the American listening posts from a number of sources. Washington's extensive correspondence, generally unavailable to historians in the 1820s, when Lydia's Tale was first written down, demonstrates clearly that while the British hoped to surprise the Americans, Washington was well aware of Howe's intentions.

On November 28, Captain Allen McLane wrote to Washington, "Evry Intelligence from the City agree that the enemy is in motion and intend a Grand stroke." Major John Clark wrote on December 1, "Orders were given to the Troops to hold themselves in readiness to march . . . they either meant to attempt to surprize your Army, or to prevent you making an attack on them." Writing from Frankford, Captain Charles Craig warned Washington on the 2nd that "the enemy intend to make a push out—and endeavour to drive Your Excellency from the present encampment." From Germantown that evening, Robert Smith, a captain in Baylor's 3rd Continental Light Dragoons, reported the enemy's readiness to march: "the Accots from the british Officers are to be attended to a Movement will take Place early tomorrow Morning."

Clark wrote again, on the 3rd, "this morning a Serjeant a Countryman of my Spies, assured him the Troops had received Orders to hold themselves in readiness when call'd for, and to draw two Days provision . . . 'twas the current language in the City among the Troops, & Citizens that they were going to make a move."[5]

As late as December 4, just hours before the British marched out of the city, William Dewees, writing from Frankford, alerted headquarters of the imminent action: "I Have Just Recd Information which I Beleive to be the Best Can be Obtaind that the British Army had Last Night Packd up all their Baggage & each Man four Days Provision Coock'd; their Horses hitchd to their Artillery & every Appearance of marching out Immediately . . . it is Expected they are Determind to Attack you where you Now Are."[6]

Despite the obvious preparations, it was not until December 3 that the official order book hinted that a movement was about to occur. Though that morning's orders still did not mention a plan to march, by late afternoon Howe had decided how and when he would move. Orders issued the evening of December 3 spelled out his expectations:

> After Orders—Evening Gun Firing
> The following Corps to be in readiness to march by 6 o'clock to-morrow morning in two Columns. The Left Column under the Command of Lt. Genl. Knyphausen to march by the left. . . . The Column on the Right under the Command Lt. Genl. Earl Cornwallis to march by the left.

In his diary entry for the 3rd, Archibald Robertson observed: "Orders were given out for the Army to march next morning in Two Columns. This Order was again Countermanded that night." At 11:00 P.M., these orders were changed. A new marching order was issued the next day. The force, now augmented by the addition of several units, would march that night.[7]

Lieutenant John Peebles thought he knew why the march had been postponed: "An order came out late last night countermanding the former, & that the Troops were not to march till further orders, owing it is said to a Sergeant of Artillery having deserted with the orders. The troops desired to be in readiness to march at the shortest notice without baggage."[8]

Johan Evald, whose Hessian jaegers were immediately behind Howe's vanguard during the march, also thought the plans had been discovered: "The 4th. Yesterday evening the army received orders to draw six days' rations and to be ready to march at any time, which the enemy must have discovered at once. For toward midnight our patrols instantly ran into theirs, and at daybreak we found the enemy outposts pushed up in front of ours."[9]

In the event, Howe's troops did not march out as planned beginning at 6:00 A.M. on Wednesday the 4th because sometime during the night, the general had second thoughts about his arrangements and the number of men needed to accomplish them. He issued new orders on Thursday morning that completely overturned the planned order of march. Instead of Knyphausen leading the way, Cornwallis was given a stronger force and placed in command of the army's leading elements, the vanguard. No fewer than eight units were shuffled between commanders during the night, and another seven units were added to the plan of attack. Evidently, Howe's misgivings caused him to strengthen the expedition. All of this took a good deal of sorting out at the ground level, where officers leading the troops needed to know who was following whom.

Though we can be fairly sure that Lydia Darragh's eavesdropping took place on December 2, accounts of the meeting's timing disagree. Hannah Haines, informant for both Walsh and Watson, wrote somewhat confusedly that the officers "would be there, at seven o'clock, should stay late, & wished the family all to retire early to their chambers" but then reported that Lydia "sent her family to bed, at 8 a clock also her husband." When Watson related what Haines had told him, he wrote that the family was "to go to bed by 9 O'Clock." Darrach simply said it was "at an early hour."

Describing Lydia Darragh's eavesdropping, Hannah Haines noted that "she applied her Ear near the chamber door." In this instance, Watson used the identical phrase, "she applied her Ear near the chamber door," indicating he worked from Haines's manuscript as well as his memories of her conversation. Walsh, however, added two additional features, about shoes and a keyhole, which he may have learned from the group discussion he participated in: "She took off her shoes, and put her ear to the key-hole of the conclave." Garden, tracking Walsh closely, had Lydia "Approaching without shoes, the room in which the conference was held, and placing her ear to the key-hole." Henry Darrach, writing much later, brought in a surprising variation: "hearing loud talking, [she] went into a closet, separated from the council room by a thin board partition covered with paper, just in time to hear the reading of the minutes of the council." The Darrach version suggests that at some point, an alteration had been made to the original form of the house, possibly even in order to accommodate use of the back room as a meeting place. In the eighteenth century, the closet mentioned would have been a small room, not necessarily the kind of closet we think of today.[10]

What plans Lydia Darragh actually overheard would depend on who was present for this night meeting. Haines, and Walsh following her lead, mentioned two people frequently meeting in the room, but both were indefinite about the exact number present at the night meeting. Watson referred to "several persons" being present, while Darrach described the meeting as a "council." The nature of the conference seems to indicate more than two people attending. All the early sources agree on one thing: Lydia Darragh overheard not merely a conversation but a reading of something that had been written. For Haines and Walsh, it was "an order read"; for Watson, they were, "reading the whole plan of attack"; while for Darrach, Lydia was "just in time to hear the reading of the minutes of the council, then concluding." In a meeting of only two people, there would be no need to read aloud; one person could simply look over the document presented by the other. But if several people were together, reading an order aloud would save time and inject an air of seemly formality: "This is an order; you will follow it."

The clandestine nature of the meeting's arrangement, and the fact that it occurred before the official version of Howe's orders were written and recorded, suggest that the meeting's details were intended to remain secret. In that case, those present were likely to have been either generals themselves, their trusted aides-de-camp, or their adjutants charged with the logistical aspects of arranging the actual march. The secretiveness surrounding the meeting implies that the British intended to surprise their enemies. The planned march as described in the different versions emphasized this idea of surprise. The movement was to occur under cover of darkness "at 12 o'clock at night" and to be a "silent march." While the word "surprise" may have been used at the meeting, given the military situation and Washington's alertness, actual surprise would have been more an aspiration than an expectation.

While all early versions of Lydia's Tale agree that the secret British march was to take place at night, there is still a problem with the story: the British actually planned to march out on the morning of December 4. As noted above, the plan was altered late on December 3. That means that what Lydia Darragh overheard at the secretive meeting on the night of the 2nd would have been orders for the troops "to be in readiness to march by 6 o'clock" the morning of the 4th, not the evening.

What was it that could have caused the story to stray from reality here? The alterations stemmed from narrative necessities felt by those relating Lydia's Tale. The first was a need to simplify the story to make it believable by conforming to actual events: the march actually took place at night, as many listeners, especially early on, would have known. Second, storytellers do not want untidy facts to get in the way of their story. There should not be questions about the accuracy, and therefore the utility, of the information the heroine carried to the American army. Third was a desire for dramatic effect: Surprises originate in secrecy. A march taking place in broad daylight can be seen by everyone; a night march better serves the narrative need for mysterious concealment, heightening the potential peril.

Who created these narrative accommodations? Because threads of the story came through two distinct chains of transmission, any alterations most likely occurred early in the narrative's development. The story was structured to have dramatic impact. Though it is possible that second-generation or later auditor/transmitters reached similar conclusions about what would make a better story, these artful changes were most likely incorporated into the story by its original narrator, Lydia Darragh herself.

Lydia's discovery was alarming. Not only would there be another battle, but this one might catch the American army unawares. Her son Charles could be in immediate danger. His regiment, the 2nd Pennsylvania, in Anthony Wayne's brigade, was posted in the first line atop the hill above Whitemarsh, a part of the right wing under command of General John Sullivan.[11]

A military outsider, and presumably a pacifist like most of her fellow Quakers, Lydia Darragh seems to have had only a rudimentary idea of Washington's preparations to prevent surprise. But the concept of surprise had taken hold of the public imagination. Some of the most notorious actions to date had been actual surprises. Ticonderoga? Taken by surprise. Trenton? Taken in a bloody surprise. Closer to home, just eleven weeks before, the surprise at Paoli and its devastating impact on the Pennsylvania Line was well known and much discussed inside the city. Many of those killed and wounded were, after all, neighbors—even relatives—of the city's residents.

If Darragh had been able to hold any communication with Charles, she would have learned of the dreadful Paoli attack. Had she not heard from him directly, the rumors and news reports must still have inspired great fear for his safety. Significantly, one dire account of the action appeared in the press on December 3, just about the time Darragh was contemplating her course of action:

On the 21st [of September] at one in the morning, two brigades of rebels, who had been ordered to harrass our rear, were attacked at the Great Flats by a detachment of our troops under Major General Grey. They formed at different avenues outside the rebels, the General having ordered his men to take their flints out of their firelocks, entered their encampment, charged the enemy with bayonet only, killed above 400, took some prisoners, and entirely routed the rest.[12]

That eight weeks earlier Washington had launched his own surprise at nearby Germantown, just ten miles away, was more than just a rumor. City dwellers heard the roar of battle, and it had put them in a tizzy. Elizabeth Drinker recorded her unease:

While I was writing I heard cannon fire, and indeed I heard them before I was up; understood, upon inquiry, that a party of Washington's army had attacked ye English piquet guard at Chesnut Hill. I went before dinner to C. Greenleaf's to look for Rachel Hollingsworth; she was gone out; called upon my return at J. Drinker's. I have not been from home before, except to meeting, since my dear left me.

Rattled by the war's sudden proximity, Drinker and many others continued to scurry about, seeking news and comfort from their neighbors. Though she had not gone out for several days, she went visiting half a dozen times on October 4. Her diary reveals the town's fright:

I stepped down to neighbor James'; Josey is very ill; Nanny Eve, and Gibbon's wife at ye mill, were there. They came to town through fear—ye Battle appeared to be very near them, and some of ye Provincials were about Frankford. They have taken away Joseph Paul and some others.

After dinner C. Greenleaf sent me word that Rachel was at home—I took Billy with me and went again. Tho' Afflick's wife and several others were there. I left my note, bid the Friends farewell, (Rachel and Betty Jollif), and then went round to Chesnut street—called at A. Benezet's and went over to S. Pleasants', where we drank tea. We met several Friends there. . . . This had been a sorrowful day at Philada, and much more so at Germantown and thereabouts.

> It was reported in ye forenoon that 1000 of ye English were slain, but Chalkley James who lodges here tonight, as Henry is out on guard, tells us—that he has been to day as far as B. Chew's place, and could not learn of more than 30 of ye English being killed, tho' a great number were wounded, and brought into the City. He counted 18 of ye Americans lying dead in ye lane from ye Road to Chew's House. Ye House is very much damaged, as a few of ye English troops had taken shelter there, and were fired upon from ye road by great numbers of ye others.[13]

The horror inspired by first-person reports of carnage made a deep impression on people's minds. Lydia Darragh was no exception. Overhearing Howe's orders must have caused great concern. It was horrible enough to learn that another battle loomed—one that would almost certainly involve her son. But hearing mention of a planned surprise would have been positively frightening to such a caring soul.

Lydia Darragh's eavesdropping was a spontaneous act, not part of an elaborate espionage scheme. Characterized in later years as a kind of secret agent, she was, rather, an impromptu spy, acting on her own on the spur of the moment. Intrigued by the officer's special precautions and arrangements, spurred by curiosity, and troubled by fears for her son, she decided to find out what was afoot. A practical woman—worldly enough, despite Quaker exhortations against worldliness—she certainly understood the potential consequences of being caught in the act.

The first dangerous encounter of the story shows off Lydia Darragh's cleverness. Having gained the forbidden knowledge, she put over a ruse to cover her tracks, diverting suspicion by feigning sleep. The primary versions of Lydia's Tale set the stage for this subterfuge with slightly different words, but all required Darragh to lock the door after the British departed.

Walsh, following Haines's manuscript fairly carefully, set up the encounter with an expectation that the British would need to be let out of the house. The "Adjutant General told Lydia that they would be in the room at seven o'clock, and remain late; and that they wished the family to retire early to bed; adding, that when they were going away, they would call her to let them out, and extinguish their fire and candles. . . . [S]he returned to her chamber and laid herself down. Soon after, the officers knocked at her door, but she rose only at the third summons, having feigned to be asleep."[14]

In his first draft in 1829, Watson contradicted himself while handling this scene. First, he noted, parenthetically, that the adjutant general could come and go as he pleased: "(The General kept his own Key to go in & out when he chose.)" Then, ignoring the detail about fire and candles, Watson explained that the officer would have to waken Lydia to let him out: "When she returned to her bed some time, the General rapped at the door to say he was withdrawing, & the front door might be locked."

Possibly from a desire to economize space for the printed word, Watson's later published versions abbreviated the story even more, ignoring entirely the business of the officer trying to awaken Lydia. All he included in those versions was a single brief reference: "She overheard them when she was expected to have been asleep in bed."[15]

The family's version of this story, as related by Henry Darrach, also omitted mention of extinguishing fire and candles. But it did include the setup for the story's dramatic conclusion: "She returned to bed, and when an officer knocked to waken her to fasten up the house after their departure she did not answer until the third summons."[16]

Robert Walsh continues the story: "[S]he returned to her chamber and laid herself down. Her mind was so much agitated, that, from this moment, she could neither eat or sleep; supposing it to be in her power to save the lives of thousands of her countrymen."[17] After letting the officers out of her home, it was a very anxious woman who took to her bed again. Ever the careful journalist, Walsh had simplified Hannah Haines's prose. A Friend herself, Haines had been more explicit in showcasing the Quaker dimensions of her kinswoman's reaction to what she had surreptitiously overheard, a nuance that might have gone over Walsh's head:

> Her mind was so agitated that she could neither eat, drink or sleep, believing it was in her power to save the lives, perhaps thousands, but knew not in what way to give the information to General Washington, not daring to confide, even to her husband, the important secret she possessed. She was sensible that if discovered, her own life & perhaps that of her family would be taken. It was

> an awful situation & she fervently prayed to the Almighty to direct her what to do. The time was short & after much reflection concluded to go herself.[18]

Paraphrasing Haines, Watson also described Lydia Darragh's unease in Quakerly terms: "After this she lay meditating how she might prevent the effusion of blood."[19]

Darragh spent that night in troubled contemplation. Listening for the voice of God inside her, she sought clarity about what to do. It was not simply the danger she might face; that, she had the heart for. She struggled with a dilemma, torn not between right and wrong but between two "right" actions: adhering to Friends' duty to stay aloof from the worldly fray or acting on her conviction that by revealing her ill-gotten secret, she might be able to avert bloodshed.

Lydia Darragh was by nature an active person. Every day, her occupation as a nurse required her to intervene in human affairs. She inherited from her grandmother a family predilection that favored action, even at the cost of violating societal norms. And Darragh was not contemplating the well-being of American soldiers alone. The family version offered an editorial observation. By its speculative, third-person nature this observation probably was not part of Lydia's original narrative, but it gave insight into her final decision: "A sharp pang shot through her heart. Patriotic she was, but perhaps motherly love had a large share in forming a resolution to do something to save the army of which her son was a member."[20]

By morning, the divine guidance she had sought within herself had manifested clearly. Lydia Darragh resolved to act on that clarity. The form that action would take, and its timing, varies in the two major accounts—the Philadelphia version, as propounded by Haines, Walsh, and Watson, and the family version, given by Darrach. We will take a closer look at those differing plans of action in the next chapter. For now, we will consider the timing.

Most probably Lydia Darragh walked out of the city to divulge General Howe's plan to the Americans on the very next morning, December 3, after she listened in on the meeting in her back room. But because there are no records attributing information directly to her, and because the early accounts were vague on the issue, it is hard to be certain. Hannah Haines noting that "the time was short" was indefinite and unsatisfactory, implying, but not stating, that Darragh took immediate action the next morning. Walsh, who generally tended to write with more precision, skirted the issue in this case, merely saying that as the time was short, "she quickly determined to make her way, as soon as possible, to the American outposts." Watson, writing later, after Walsh's publication was widespread, but also in direct consultation with his source, Hannah Haines, was more definite, stating, "She executed her plan early next morning."

Darrach, however, recounting the family version that came through Ann Darragh, stated that Lydia took an additional day in preparation before acting: "The next day (Wednesday, December 3d) was spent in planning some mode of action." While possible, there is no external evidence to either support or disprove the idea that Darragh took her walk on December 4, the day the British army marched.

Darrach was motivated to resolve conflicts between the version he received and those of Walsh, Watson, and, indeed, a later version yet—that of Elias Boudinot's great niece. His 1916 article devoted several pages to answering doubts about the story's authenticity by arguing how the various versions could possibly be made congruent. He personally attempted to clarify the sequence of events by adding dates to the original narrative, elaborating on Walsh's start. Fortunately, we can sort out Darrach's emendations. He was scrupulous about editorial intrusion, being careful to present his comments, including his conjectural dates, within parentheses.

In the absence of solid corroboration of the timing presented in the original versions of Lydia's Tale (Haines, Walsh, Watson, and Darrach), we are left with unsatisfying ambiguity. But while there are some inconsistencies between the four, all agree in their narrative structures, presenting the identical elements. All four share a certain sequence: eavesdropping; feigning sleep; planning (though the timing is implicit in Walsh and Watson, Watson does mention it as "early next morning"); the "walk"; the return; and the night march. This unity indicates, once again, ultimate derivation from a single source, Lydia Darragh's verbal tale. As we examine the "walk" in the following section, we will see how Lydia's Tale bumps up against the reality of the period. While some elements of the story remain ambiguous, many others come into sharper focus.

Chapter 10

Lydia Darragh's Walk to the American Lines

When considering Lydia Darragh's trip to the American lines, we are faced with competing narratives. The first, as described by Robert Walsh Jr. and John Fanning Watson, derived from the same source between about 1822 and 1828: Hannah Marshall Haines. The second came down through Lydia Darragh's direct descendants. It was published by Henry Darrach nearly ninety years after Walsh's version of Lydia's Tale began to circulate, almost 140 years after the actual event. Though they match closely in detail and structure, there are three substantial differences between these two versions: Lydia's excuse to her husband, how Lydia got a pass, and Lydia's destination and route.

Both versions agree that Lydia Darragh felt a need to deceive her husband about her intentions in undertaking a potentially hazardous journey into no-man's-land. Both affirm Lydia's belief that William should not be trusted with her secret, either because the knowledge might endanger him or perhaps because he might inadvertently reveal the truth and so endanger them both. The accounts differ, however, on the excuse she presented to allay his suspicions. In Walsh's telling, Lydia concealed her intention from William by telling him she needed to go to the mill for flour. Walsh's version was backed up by Watson. They both agreed, too, that she needed to obtain a pass to get through the city gates and cross the British lines.

The story as captured by Henry Darrach described the execution of Lydia's plan in somewhat different terms: "[S]he told her husband she was going to use a pass she had obtained some time before to go to the country to see her children, and, starting early the next morning, and going in the direction named in her pass, but soon changing her course, after a long and weary walk, came near the American camp."[1]

The first version has Lydia walking out to Frankford by the most direct route, then changing her destination once she got to the mill. In the second, she attempts to deceive the watchers at the gates by heading toward a place named in her pass then shifting direction toward the American lines. Though it may not be possible to resolve these contradictions, we can explore the likelihood of each version. We will begin by looking first at Walsh's account of the trip to Frankford and then consider Darrach's version. There are two reasons for this: Walsh's account was written closer to the time of the event, and it came through fewer intermediaries—only one for Walsh, as opposed to at least two in Darrach's case. Before examining Walsh's story in detail, we must first address some questions that have been raised about its plausibility.

As we consider the realities of Lydia's Tale and attempt to separate fact from fiction, we encounter a bit of erroneous scholarship that to this day continues to influence a debate about the story's legitimacy. In 1910, Henry Leffmann challenged the story as "fake."[2] Leffmann (1847–1930) was a physician and chemist by training. A busy man, he served his fellow citizens of Philadelphia in several important capacities, including as a professor of chemistry, toxicology and hygiene at the Women's Medical College of Pennsylvania. He taught at several other Philadelphia medical institutions as well. A prolific writer, he published over 250 articles in his areas of expertise between 1866 and 1905, including a book about his experiences as the port physician of Philadelphia. Taking a personal interest in history, he even gave papers on subjects tangentially related to his discipline, such as "Ancient Metallurgy" and "The Water Supply of Rome." Leffmann sometimes delved into more speculative topics, such as his article "George Washington as an Engineer" and his intriguing hypothesis "The Mental Condition and Career of Jesus of Nazareth." Given his wide-ranging intellect, it should not be surprising that he found himself up to the task of writing about any historical subject, including espionage during the Revolution.[3] In a paper read to the City History Society of Philadelphia, Leffmann challenged Lydia Darragh's story:

> To accept the story we must believe that a woman was allowed to go alone on a journey in early December over a territory between the lines of the armies, such intermediate "no man's land" being well known during this period to be extremely dangerous. The excuse for the errand was that she needed flour. There is no reason to think that so serious a scarcity of flour then existed in the city. These features are alone sufficient to show that the story is a lie made out of whole cloth.[4]

A twenty-first-century writer working for the Central Intelligence Agency felt compelled to lend his organization's credibility to Leffmann's doubts. As a federal agency, the CIA is required to provide general information about its work to the American public, including information about its history and its antecedent organizations. To answer that need, the agency's Office of Public Affairs, assisted by its own history staff of the Center for the Study of Intelligence, prepared a publication, *Intelligence During the War of Independence*, intended to provide a popular overview of spying during that period. The publication discusses how the nascent American government, including Congress and the military, organized itself to manage an intelligence-gathering network; enumerates techniques used by spies; describes various instances of espionage during the war; and covers many of the better-known exemplars, such as the Culper Spy Ring, Benedict Arnold, and Nathan Hale. The document wraps up with the take on Lydia's Tale as a "colorful but uncorroborated story," casting suspicion on its believability:

> Some espionage historians have questioned the credibility of the best-known story of Darragh's espionage—that she supposedly

> overheard British commanders planning a surprise night attack against Washington's army at Whitemarsh, Pennsylvania, on the 4th and 5th of December 1777. The cover story she purportedly used to leave Philadelphia—she was filling a flour sack at a nearby mill outside the British lines because there was a flour shortage in the city—is implausible because there was no shortage, and a lone woman would not have been allowed to roam around at night, least of all in the area between the armies.[5]

The CIA version paraphrases Leffmann's erroneous concerns closely without citing the source, stating them as though they had been raised through research done independently within the agency.

Leffmann, it turns out, was not the first to challenge the veracity of Lydia's Tale. He took his lead from an earlier history of Philadelphia produced by J. Thomas Scharf and Thompson Westcott in 1884. Those authors rejected the story entirely based on documentary evidence that the Americans were already aware of Howe's planned march against Whitemarsh prior to Lydia Darragh's famous walk. They followed this dismissal with a piece of unwarranted speculation that Leffmann adopted and that eventually crept, third-hand, into the CIA assessment: "if Howe had contemplated a surprise his pickets and sentinels would scarcely have let a woman pass the lines, and enter the enemy's lines and return, unquestioned." But neither Scharf and Westcott, nor Leffmann had performed extensive research, something perhaps unknown to the Central Intelligence writer.[6]

We know that in pursuit of her employment as a nurse, Lydia Darragh did travel beyond the city limits during the British occupation of Philadelphia. Existing accounts indicate that besides the trip in December 1777, she made at least two other excursions between the lines during the city's occupation. On January 28, 1778, she went out to Providence, where the Marshall sons were living in exile, to nurse Benjamin Marshall. She paid a return visit to Providence on May 6, bringing word to the Marshalls about British plans to evacuate the city.[7]

Despite Leffmann's assurance that "There is no reason to think that so serious a scarcity of flour then existed in the city," Philadelphians were, in fact, starving in fall 1777. The region's expanded population, the blocking of the Delaware River port, the cordon around the city that interfered with food distribution, and the war's incidental destruction of local crops and livestock all conspired to limit the amount of available food. Sustenance became a serious concern. Disrupted farming and commerce, and the increase of local population with two armies perched in the vicinity, impacted available supplies of foodstuffs.

Washington wrote of his efforts at the time to feed his army and stop the British from getting access to food: "Congress may be assured, that no exertions of mine, as far as circumstances will admit, shall be wanting to provide our own Troops with Supplies on the one hand, and to prevent the Enemy from them on the Other." He explained how the countryside between the two armies had been stripped of food, making special reference to flour:

> All the Forage for the Army has been constantly drawn from Bucks & Philadelphia Counties & those parts most contiguous to the City, insomuch that it was nearly exhausted, and entirely so in the Country below our Camp. From these too, were obtained All the Supplies of Flour that circumstances would admit of. The Millers in most instances were unwilling to grind either from their dissaffection or from motives of fear. This made the Supplies less than they Otherwise might have been, and the quantity which are drawn from thence was little besides what the Guards, placed at the Mills compelled them to manufacture.[8]

Flour became a most-sought-after commodity—so much so that some people were willing to go to considerable lengths, even illegal lengths, to profit from it. As people fled the city in expectation of a British advance, civil order began to break down. One target for opportunistic predation was flour. Elizabeth Drinker reported on September 16, "Our stable cellar was last night broken open, and several of Jos. Scott's Barrels of Flour stolen."[9]

This theft was not a simple snatch, like pocketing a handful of coins or paper currency. Rather, it required considerable planning and effort on the part of the burglars: after all, a single barrel of flour weighed 196 pounds. Did the thieves roll those barrels, at least three in number, possibly more, through the streets to wherever they planned to hide or sell them? Did they load them into a wagon in the night and haul them off? They might not have had far to go. The Drinker home was only about two hundred feet from the waterfront for which Front Street was named. At night, once into the maze of warehouses, docks, and wharfs, there would be few prying eyes. Of course, the thieves needed to be on the lookout for the town watch, but at least the man who walked about the streets crying the hour would have been easy to avoid.

The weight of those stolen barrels might seem an unusual number today, but it was a customary measure for flour at the time. The base unit of weight was the fourteen-pound *stone*, or stone weight, literally a standard-sized stone to be placed on a scale—an ancient unit of measure still used occasionally in the United Kingdom, particularly for body weight. A standard barrel was the equivalent of 14 stone units weighing 14 pounds each, hence 196 pounds. In quantity, flour might be sold by the barrel, but for a family's immediate needs, it was commonly sold in lesser units that were easier for one person to carry.

When reckoning the cost of flour, merchants generally talked about a value per hundredweight. By today's reckoning in the United States, a hundredweight would be 100 pounds of flour. But at the time, in English measurement, a hundredweight was 8 stone, or 112 pounds. Flour was sold at the mills where it was ground, or through shopkeepers, by the stone—14 pounds. Typically, if someone was planning to carry a bag of flour on foot, they might fill a two-stone bag, 28 pounds—commonly referred to as a quarter, meaning a quarter of a hundredweight. As we will see, ten-year-old Jacob Coats was used to purchasing and carrying a 28-pound bag of flour when visiting the mill at Frankford.

During the occupation of Philadelphia, the law of supply and demand meant prices for the little food that was available were enormously inflated. Flour, when it could be gotten at all, sold at many times its prewar cost, putting it out of the reach of inhabitants of middling means, much less the poor. In May 1776, a hundredweight of flour in Philadelphia was quoted at 12 shillings, 6 pence (12/6). War drove up the cost significantly in 1777. Even in Virginia, 150 miles from the military confrontation, the cost of a hundredweight rose 50 percent, to 18 shillings—nearly a full pound sterling.[10]

Once the British army arrived, the price of flour in the city soared. Diarists recorded the impact on food prices and the people's distress. On November 12, six weeks after the British marched in, Elizabeth Drinker cited the cost of flour, "what little there is," at £3 per hundredweight, nearly five times what it had been the previous year. This was no exaggeration; others in the area confirmed the inflated price. In Reading, Jacob Hiltzheimer learned from George Mifflin, father of General Thomas Mifflin, who had come out from the city on December

10, that a hundredweight was selling for £3/10 /-. When a group of Philadelphia Friends sought assistance in feeding the city's inhabitants by pleading for help from their counterparts in London, they noted that "flour is sold for near three guineas per hundred [£3/3/-]." Sarah Logan Fisher noted even higher prices: "Flour £5 a hundred, & what is to be bought of that very ordinary. Such is the distressed situation we are in."[11]

William Howe's decision to move the seat of war to Philadelphia flooded the area with thousands more mouths to feed. The number of people living in the city is generally thought to have been about thirty-five thousand in 1777. Granted that many people fled the city itself during the occupation, most of them remained nearby. Historians Gary Ecelbarger and Michael C. Harris estimate the Continental force surrounding Philadelphia at over twenty-four thousand by December. Add to that the size of the British army, which has been put at about sixteen thousand soldiers, plus naval personnel, and we see that the number of people in Philadelphia and its immediate hinterland had swelled considerably. Inflated by as many as forty thousand additional souls, the population of the region had doubled, straining local food allocation. With supplies disrupted and twice the number of people, bread—the "staff of life"—was unobtainable for many.[12]

Making matters worse, especially for the poor, those few purveyors who did have food to sell, especially British factors who had followed the army to the city, would accept only specie—hard currency in silver or gold—for their provisions. Pennsylvania's paper currency, despite organized efforts by the citizenry to support its value, was simply not accepted by British merchants. Those holding Continental currency found it less than useless under the occupation—attempting to pass it could be viewed as a sign of disloyalty to the Crown.[13]

Though the British had finally seized Fort Mifflin on Mud Island on November 16, it took considerable time and labor to remove enough of the river obstructions still blocking the Delaware channel to allow supply ships to move up to Philadelphia. Among other riverine defenses, the Americans had placed dozens of long, iron-tipped poles, known as *chevaux de frise*, anchored in the riverbed by massive rock-filled boxes, weighing fifteen to twenty tons. Even once a narrow passage had been opened, wind, current, tides, and other vagaries of river navigation continued to drive ships onto the treacherous *chevaux*, ripping gaping holes in their bottoms. On December 1, just a couple of days before Lydia

Darragh's walk to Frankford, the British victualler *Juliana* was holed by one, its cargo of food all spoiled. Meanwhile, the city's populace grew hungrier.[14]

Because Philadelphia lay on a neck of land between two tidal rivers, military acccss to the city was relatively easy to control. The British quickly threw up a series of ten redoubts in a line north of the city and connected them with entrenchments, abatis, and other works. The regiments of foot were strung out behind this defensive line, ready to man the fortifications on short notice if attacked. Four advanced posts of light infantry were posted beyond the lines as a trip wire to prevent surprise and to skirmish with approaching enemy forces, delaying them before they could reach the main line. A few gates through the works were set up on the main roads out of town. These were manned by small details of soldiers, usually a sergeant and a few privates, and one or two functionaries from the civil government.

The military on both sides recognized that civilians would need to pass out of and into the city for a variety of reasons: visiting family, conducting business, and, most commonly, carrying food for personal sustenance or to sell. From a practical perspective, each side wished to control access for its own purposes. For security, they needed to control access carefully to avoid ambushes and surprises, and to control the flow of intelligence. The British had a strong interest in obtaining food for the army, as well as ensuring the populace did not starve. They permitted civilians to pass through the lines daily, subject to searches and interrogation.

Americans wanted to restrict the flow of food to the enemy's soldiers, but they did not want the people to starve. Though Washington ordered Allen McLane's party of observation "to suffer no body to carry provisions into the city," as a practical matter this was difficult to enforce. "Multitudes of women" left the city daily, seeking food. The soldiers were too few to police them all. American officers drew a distinction between women trying to sustain their families and farmers bringing quantities of food to sell in town. Sympathetic to the women's plight, soldiers routinely made exceptions. This behavior became increasingly common as the weeks went on, and eventually Washington relented, allowing people to come out to the mills to obtain flour. Colonel Elias Boudinot, who was gathering information near the Rising Sun tavern on December 4, encountered an old woman there who requested permission to pass his outpost "to go into the country to buy some flour."[15]

Travel in the area between the armies could certainly be dangerous. However, those most at risk between the lines were not women, or even children, but males of military age. If taken up by patrolling soldiers of either side, noncombatant men—those unaffiliated with either army—were apt to be detained and investigated as deserters, shirkers from military service, bad actors, marauders, even spies, with potentially dire consequences. Women and children, by contrast, had a reasonable degree of assurance that soldiers would behave toward them in a more gentlemanly fashion, though this was not invariably the case.

Suspicions of betrayal swirled throughout the area. Men apprehended by patrols proved to be an excellent source of intelligence about the enemy. After all, many deserters had left in the first place because of their dissatisfaction with the army that had employed them, so they were often willing to share what they knew. Deserters presented such a danger that officers serving outpost duty would change their location immediately on finding that a soldier was missing. Take for example an incident reported by Sally Wister at Gwynedd on June 3, 1778. A unit of Sheldon's 2nd Regiment of Light Dragoons was staying in the vicinity of the farm where she lived. "Imagine my consternation," she wrote, "when our girl came running in, and said the lane was filled with light horse. I flew to the side door. It was true." Recognizing them for the Americans who were camped nearby, she invited the officers into the house:

> They sat a few minutes; told us that two of their men had deserted, and when that was the case, they generally mov'd their quarters . . . then rose, and after the politest adieus, departed. All the horse followed about one hundred and fifty. I never saw more regularity observed, or so undisturb'd a silence kept up when so large a number of people were together. Not a voice was heard, except that of the officer who gave the word of command. The moon at intervals broke thro' the heavy black clouds. No noise was perceiv'd, save that which the horses made as they trotted o'er the wooden bridge across the race. Echo a while gave us back the sound. At last nothing was left but the remembrance of them.[16]

An instance of humanity serves to illustrate the potentially lethal danger in store for those operating between the lines. Beyond the northeastern gates that led up the Frankford Road, the countryside was patrolled by a regiment of Loyalists known as the Queen's Rangers. They occupied the easternmost redoubt, number one, which lay between the flooded arm of the Cohocksink Creek and the Delaware River. The rangers' commander, John Graves Simcoe, related the following incident:

> Parties of the Rangers every day went to Frankfort, where the enemy no longer kept a fixed post, though they frequently sent a patrole to stop the market people. A patrolling party of the Rangers approached undiscovered so close to a rebel sentinel, posted upon the bridge, that it would have been easy to have killed him. A boy, whom he had just examined, was sent back to inform him of this, and to direct him immediately to quit his post or that he should be shot; he ran off, and the whole party, on his arrival at the guard, fled with equal precipitation; nor were there any more sentinels placed there: a matter of some consequence to the poor people of Philadelphia, as they were not prevented from getting their flour ground at Frankfort mills.[17]

The rangers' decision to warn off the enemy sentinel rather than open fire was a prudent move that gave them at least temporary control of the area by the bridge without having to resort to fighting and, potentially, the loss of their own men. Simcoe was correct that the Americans permitted civilians to come out to Frankford for flour but incorrect in saying that Washington's force abandoned its post there. Rather, they were kept on the move by British patrolling, being forced to change the locations of their outposts in the area frequently to avoid surprise. Throughout the occupation, patrolling forces of both sides waged a deadly game of skirmishes and ambuscades outside the city.[18]

Civilians seeking to cross the lines were not permitted through the gates without passes, though those were relatively easy to acquire. In fact, hundreds were issued every day. The demand was so high that the British resorted to printing a form to reduce the amount of time the harried gatekeepers had to spend controlling passage. To be sure, travelers might be subjected to a certain level of controlled harassment. Persons headed out through the gates were searched to prevent contraband from inside the city reaching the enemy. Coming back at night could be a risky proposition because, by General Howe's orders, the gates were

The "Gates of Philadelphia." The British set up a series of gates along roads in and out of Philadelphia along with crémaillère, defensive entrenchments, roughly following the course of Cohocksink Creek which they dammed to flood the surrounding meadows. This detail from John Montresor's map shows Redoubts 2 and 3, manned by British regulars, protecting Second Street, to the left of number 2, and Front Street and the road to Frankford to the right. The Queen's Rangers loyalist unit manned Redoubt 1. John Montresor, *A Survey of the City of Philadelphia and its Environs Shewing the Several Works*, 1777. (*Library of Congress*)

to be closed at dusk and none permitted to pass. As of November 2, the plan was, "No person in future to be permitted to pass the out Posts from Evening Gun firing till Nine in the Morning, without a written passport from Head Quarters, and all passports are to be returned every morning." At sunset, the end of the official military day, a bugle sounded the retreat. The evening gun was fired after the last note of the bugle call as a signal to lower the flag.[19]

The procedure was revised and clarified on November 20: "No Person from town is to be Permitted to pass the out Posts except between the Hours of Eight in the Morning & Five in the Evening, every Person Coming in between those Hours in the Night & not requiring to be Immediately Forwarded to Head Quarters, are to be detain'd by the Post that Shall Receive them & Reported to the Field Officer of the Piquets in the Morning."[20]

Despite General Howe's admonitions, some managed to pass in through the gates at night without being detained, as long as they did not appear to be threatening. An unpublished story from John Fanning Watson's manuscript "Annals" elucidates the experiences of those wandering between the lines. In 1826, Jacob Coats wrote a letter in which he responded to a list of Watson's queries "respecting the conduct of the British Army on entering and while in possession of the City of Phila., together of the feelings—fears, and conduct of the inhabitants." Coats, ten years old at the time these events took place, describes a night encounter with an American light dragoon. Here is a transcription from Watson's notes, somewhat cleaned up for readability:

> The Market [was] ill and scantily supplied generally, from the scarcity of animal food. Several persons were detected selling horse meat, particularly before the evacuation of Fort Mifflin. In truth before that period, provisions of all kinds were so scarce with many, that the chaps like myself—and young females of delicate breeding (arrived to womanhood)—were obliged to go sometimes twenty miles from the City on foot for provisions to Keep alive our all but starving Parents and helpless infancy of our respective families.
>
> On my return to Philadelphia from one of these exertions with 28 lbs. of flour (my customary load), I got to the houses (not then tenanted but lately occupied and owned by John Dober) near Frankford bridge about ten o'clock at night where [there] were twelve or fourteen others [who] had collected on their return to the city with an intent to stop and rest themselves till morning. [They were] weighed down with their burdens. There were no doors to the house, weather cold, had made a fire. As respected myself, I felt comfortable and contented.
>
> Two young females, addressing me said, "Little boy, we apprehend insult from the light horsemen (American Piquet) stationed here. Will you protect us?"
>
> "With all my heart. You must be my sisters—I will call you so. Leave the rest to me," said I.
>
> About eleven o'clock, a trooper absolutely rode his horse in among us. The screaming, etc., I will leave you to imagine. He did it, I fancy, for a scarecrow or frolic. One of my adopted sisters caught his eye. He rode out and immediately after returned on

foot, made up to her, addressing her familiarly and rudely.

"Let my sister alone, you!" said I, and accompanied my request with [as] violent a push as my strength would admit, and acted the part of a cry baby, as he called me, that I affected my purpose and he retired.

I now proposed to my adopted sisters to start for the city. They hesitated, thinking it unsafe to trust themselves with so weak an escort; but the majority agreeing to accompany us, we started from our untenable quarters somewhat apast midnight and got in the English piquets about two o'clock in the morning.

There I left my company and at my request the Captain of the Guard suffered me to proceed, on my telling him that I resided at the quarters of Colonel Abercromby at my father's house in Vine [Street], between Front and Second Streets. The guard house (English) for Frankford Road was about two hundred yards below the sign of the Black Horse, and I had to pass many sentinels and avoid many, particularly the Hessians, by going a Zig-Zag kind of way to my home.

The sentinels guarded the officers' quarters of their respective corps. Every field officer entitled to a sergeant's guard, made them within speaking distance throughout the city. I arrived safe at home about three o'clock in the morning. I have entered the British lines often on these excursions in the night, for the purpose of avoiding the American scouting parties, fearful [they] would from me take my provisions, particularly if they were animals.[21]

Even during periods of intense military activity, civilians were granted passes that allowed them into the area of operations. Sarah Logan Fisher wrote about her cousin Polly, who was so desperate to obtain flour to feed her family that on December 6, while the British perched on Chestnut Hill skirmishing with Washington's army, she risked heading out near where the fighting was taking place: "Coz. P. Pleasants sent to borrow our chaise to go out to John Shoemaker's to endeavor to get some flour &c for her large family of little children. A very great scarcity of that & everything else in town, & no money likely at present to pass but hard money, & few, very few, families even of the first rank have much of that & the poorer kind of people are likely to be in a most distressed situation."[22]

Shoemaker's mill, where York Road crossed Tookany Creek in Cheltenham, was just two miles behind the British area of operations when they marched out to confront Washington at Whitemarsh. Skirmishing swirled around the fringes of the two armies; small-scale combat was liable to break out anywhere in the vicinity with little notice. The firing could be heard in the city. Polly Pleasants must have felt desperate, indeed, to risk venturing so close to battle in her quest for flour. She was fortunate in not encountering marauders or demanding soldiers from either side.

Others besides Polly Pleasants took advantage of the British march toward Whitemarsh to go out beyond the British lines on December 6. Perhaps thinking that having the British army between her and the Americans would protect her, Mary Stiles decided it would be a good time to try to fetch in some of her possessions from Port Royal, her husband's elegant house near Frankford. American or British troops, or perhaps local bandits, had already ransacked the place. That day, as Elizabeth Drinker noted, she was not so lucky as Polly Pleasants:

> Our neighbor Stiles sent over this morning to borrow our good Horse, Tomson, but as he was not shod we denied him; she sent again and we lent him to her to go to Frankford—her boy Sam with her. She returned in ye evening on foot, having lost her Chaise and our Horse; they were taken from her by ye English Light-horse just as she was getting in ye Chaise at their place. They have been plundered at their country House lately of all ye valuable Furniture, Provisions, Coach, Chariot, Horses, 8 or 10 negroes, etc. to a great amount.[23]

While passes were being issued by the British routinely, it is worth noting that on some days there may have been restrictions. That was the opinion of Robert Smith, an American captain of dragoons who was patrolling near Germantown on December 2. In a letter conveying intelligence to General Washington, he noted: "Hardly any thing has come out to Day. No Passes have been granted from Town. Some Ladies who got out by special Favor say as far as the Accots from the british Officers are to be attended to a Movement will take Place early tomorrow Morning." Perhaps fewer passes were issued that day, or perhaps fewer women made it as far as Germantown, but it is clear that the rules could be bent and favors granted to women in need.[24]

Despite Leffmann's, and consequently the CIA's, doubts that a woman would not be allowed into the area between the lines, Lydia

Darragh's account is, as we have seen from other examples, quite plausible. She would have had no substantial difficulty obtaining a pass and could have gone out through the gates despite planned military action in the area. The detail, that she received her pass from General William Howe, however, should probably not be taken literally. A British pass granted to someone could be said figuratively to have been given by Howe, but in practice, his subordinates were the ones actually writing the passes. Howe's myriad duties as commander in chief kept him far too busy to speak directly with the hundreds of people daily requesting passes. While it is possible Lydia applied directly to William Howe, it seems unlikely she needed to reach so high for a routine pass to buy flour, nor would she have wanted to draw attention to herself. Those applying for passes at headquarters, across the street from the Darraghs, would have dealt with one of Howe's aides-de-camp, or even someone of lesser rank designated to handle mundane matters.

A preprinted pass signed on November 20 by Nisbet Balfour, Howe's aide at headquarters, survives. Briefly worded, it indicates that "The Bearer John Fox has the Commander in Chief's Permission to pass the out Posts, without Molestation." It would be easy to construe the wording to mean that the pass was granted by General Howe. The fact that the pass was a printed form, with only a few details to be filled in—date, name, and signature—indicates how common such passes were.

But if the outspoken, rebel-hating Balfour was, as we surmised earlier, the acting adjutant general, Lydia Darragh would hardly have wanted to raise his suspicions the morning after he had met clandestinely in her house. Instead, she could readily have gotten a pass from the official charged with administering business at the main gates to the city, at the northern end of Front Street. Hundreds of passes were issued there daily by a man named Abraham Carlile. Elizabeth Drinker noted in her diary for November 24 that "the poor people have been allow'd for some time past to go to Frankford Mill, and other Mills that way, for Flour, Abraham Carlile who gives them passes, has his Door very much crowded every morning." Drinker knew Carlile well. He lived just two doors south of her on North Front Street. Those crowds she witnessed before his door, however, were not in front of Carlile's home but rather outside the door to a small frame building he had erected as an office, near the gates themselves, a few blocks away.[25]

To oversee the civil administration in occupied Philadelphia, Howe appointed Joseph Galloway as superintendent general of the city. Galloway enlisted a corps of assistants to serve in various capacities: the police, the night watch, supervising the ports and markets. To oversee civilian passage through the city gates, he solicited the aid of Abraham Carlile. Though some passes would continue to be issued through British headquarters, Carlile handled the main press of business, issuing most passports for people leaving town along the roads to Germantown and Frankford. Galloway also prevailed on a miller, Peter Deshong, to grant passes through the less-traveled gate out the Wissahickon Road, northwest of the city. Both men agreed to do this work reluctantly, finding it troubling in many ways. Not only was it a great imposition on their time, but it involved them in conflict daily as they made decisions about which persons and goods should be allowed to pass. Neither man felt free to refuse the work. The duty also placed them firmly in the pro-British camp, branding them as Tory collaborators in the eyes of the revolutionary government—a fact of which they were well aware but which may have seemed of little importance if they believed that British arms would prevail. As it turned out, Carlile's cooperation with Howe's military, and his religious affiliation as a Friend, placed him in extreme jeopardy once the British evacuated Philadelphia.[26]

Born about 1720, Carlile belonged to a prosperous Quaker family from Burlington, New Jersey, eighteen miles upriver from the city. Moving to Philadelphia, Carlile became a house carpenter and lumber supplier, acquiring a fine property along Front Street, the main thoroughfare paralleling the Delaware waterfront. A master builder and active member of the Carpenters Company, in the 1770s he was one of the largest contributors toward the construction of Carpenters' Hall, which later became the meeting place of the First Continental Congress. When the Revolution arrived, many from the Carpenters Company—men like Benjamin Loxley, Thomas Proctor, and Robert Smith—became committed patriots. Carlile took a different path.

Though Carlile was a birthright Quaker, his name does not stand out in Friends' records. His chief involvement with the Philadelphia Monthly Meeting was in a practical, secular capacity as a carpenter and master builder. In 1753, he was reimbursed for repairs to the aging Bank Street Meeting House. He constructed the large and commodious Friends Meeting House at Second and High Streets in 1755, quietly leaving his initials by hammering rose head nails into a basement joist. Six years later, he was included on a committee to decide whether to expand the existing meetinghouse or build an additional one, presumably because of his technical expertise, since cost estimates were to be part of the recommendations. In a statement near the end of his life, he noted that "he had always had a Regard for the Society [of Friends]," but in general, he seemed to distance himself from active membership.

How Galloway settled on Carlile as the man for the job is unclear. Public records show little about his activities beyond his business as a builder. Before accepting the proffered job, he sought advice from the Quaker establishment. He believed it might put him in a position to do good for people, especially those less well off, by easing their passage between the lines as they sought to buy food at affordable prices or to visit relatives. His neighbor Henry Drinker, one of the inner circle of the Meeting for Sufferings, which had been guiding the Friends' reactions to the growing revolution, was not available to him to consult, having been exiled to Virginia in September with many other Quaker leaders. The lesser luminaries he conferred with hinted that such a post might not be a good idea but failed to express themselves clearly or forcefully. Carlile came away from the conversation having heard nothing to dissuade him.[27]

He may have had other motives as well. Pejorative comments later attributed to him by pro-patriot witnesses make it sound as though he strongly disapproved of the rebellion and its adherents. Money may also have been a motivator. The building trade, and the lumber business dependent on it, had come to a virtual standstill with the city's occupation.

The primary land access through the line of redoubts to Philadelphia's hinterland was along two roads springing from the north end of Front Street, the north-south throughfare that paralleled the Delaware waterfront. One road led northwest to the village of Germantown. The other headed northeast toward Frankford village. To protect the redoubts near the Delaware, the British dammed the Cohocksink Creek, turning its meadows into a moat. A pair of gates were set up just south of the creek, and a defensive line was erected between them along the top of the bluff. The post was guarded by a detail of soldiers under command of a sergeant and covered by redoubts numbers 1 and 2, which could enfilade any approach by the enemy. A 1777 map, drawn by the British chief engineer, John Montresor, shows the location of these two gates clearly.

The British officers' scramble for winter housing was resolved more or less according to rank, with higher ranking officers claiming the best residences, sometimes preempting lower ranks who had gotten to a desirable house first. Such was the case with the house where Jacob Weaver lived, near the top of Front Street, which had been claimed initially by a Hessian officer. Because it was just by the gates, Carlile began using part of it as an office to manage the business of granting passes and examining outgoing people for contraband. When the British attempted to evict Weaver, Carlile intervened on his behalf, allowing him to continue living in the house, an arrangement common in many homes appropriated by officers. After about three weeks, Carlile was preempted by another officer, Captain Frederick Thomas of the Foot Guards, whose unit was stationed at redoubt number 2. This was probably when Carlile, experienced house carpenter and lumber-yard owner that he was, erected a two story "office" on Weaver's property, allowing him to continue doing business at the gates.[28]

A person wishing to pass through the lines would first visit Carlile's office, referred to by some as "the search house," where a printed pass would be filled out and signed. Then the person would show the pass to the British piquet posted at the gate. These soldiers would inquire if the traveler had any contraband items and would search the person to ensure they were telling the truth. If they found what seemed to be forbidden items, they would escort the person back to the office to have Carlile decide whether to let those items pass out through the gates. Salt, in particular, was one contraband item they focused on. Weapons were another.[29]

Once he assumed management of the gates, Carlile took his official position seriously, lending his full support to the British cause. Throughout, he displayed commendable consideration for the poor, who were especially negatively affected by the occupation. But the volume of activity was more than Carlile had bargained for. Each day, numerous people clamored for and received passes. Called on to identify Carlile at a treason trial the following year, Margaret Sweeble testified to just how busy Carlile was at the gates and provided insight into how that business was conducted:

> She knows Mr. A Carlile and saw him in Front Street, where he searched her [pockets and bag she carried under her arm] when she went out for flour. He asked her if she had any salt carrying

out for the rebels. Upon being told no, he said he had given 800 papers that day and had no more, but went to the soldiers and passed her along. Two other times he granted papers when hundreds were with her. He stopped nobody, but let everybody go out. They paid nothing for their paper. She never saw him search anybody else.[30]

While the number eight hundred sounds like an exaggeration, witnesses confirm that those seeking passes could number in the hundreds. Jacob Weaver, who owned the property where the "search house" was located, testified about the large crowds at the gates. "He hath seen him [Carlile] give paper to hundreds of a day, to go into the country for meal, flour and other provisions, 200 or 300 of a day sometimes. The house was quite surrounded with people for papers. He continually granted papers."[31]

Carlile behaved so leniently toward those in need that he was castigated by Howe's aide, Nisbet Balfour, who threatened to fire him. According to a witness: "I saw Carlile pass many people of doubtful character at different times. He showed so much lenity as to be greatly blamed on this account, and threatened to be turned from his place. This I heard Colonel Balfour tell him."[32]

Though Carlile was kind to the poor, there was another side to his personality—one that ultimately spelled his doom. An irascible man, when harried by the press of business he showed little tolerance for people, man or woman, he thought might be patriots. Those he suspected of rebel sympathies were subjected to verbal abuse and harassment. He called one a "terrible Rebel," another a "Rebel son of a bitch," even bragging to others that Washington had "offered 500 dollars to take him up" and that he personally "could kill an hundred rebels and pity not." He was to pay a heavy price for these indiscretions.[33]

As Jacob Hiltzheimer pointed out, Lydia Darragh was a clever woman. Knowing she needed a believable cover story to pass the lines without suspicion, she concocted a perfectly reasonable excuse about why she had to leave the city—one that should both convince her husband and allay distrust when she sought permission to pass the guards at the gates. While in wartime any person might be suspect, women, who were not likely to become combatants, tended to seem less dubious than men, and a woman in need even less so. Given that there was an acute shortage of food, and flour in particular, it is hard to imagine a more plausible reason for leaving town than the need to feed her family.

Two gates left the city at the head of Front Street, just south of the Cohocksink Creek and its flooded meadows. The roads leading out of those gates diverged. The eastern gate led to a long causeway across the Cohocksink, then out King's Highway northeast toward Frankford, a village that stretched for half a mile along the road beyond Frankford Creek. The westerly gate crossed the Cohocksink via a small bridge, then headed northwest out Germantown Road, branching into Old York Road at the Rising Sun Tavern, three miles north of the gates.

In choosing a flour mill to visit, Lydia Darragh selected one that had been providing flour for residents of Philadelphia since the city's earliest days. In fact, the mill was originally erected by Swedish settlers in the 1660s, predating the city's founding by several years. By 1687, the two-hundred-acre mill tract had been purchased by the Free Society of Traders, the same entrepreneurs who had acquired the twenty-thousand-acre tract south of the city, which included Lydia Darragh's neighborhood, and whose memory was enshrined in the name of Society Hill. The old Swedish Mill, as it was frequently called, was four miles out from the city where King's Highway, also known as Frankford Road, crossed Frankford Creek. Darragh used her need to buy flour as a cover for her real goal: reaching the American lines. The Frankford mill area was well known to be frequented by American dragoons, the cavalrymen who were the eyes and ears of Washington's army.[34]

The mill itself was a locus of contention. In 1776, two Quaker millers, Joshua Gibson and Moses Grubb, had begun renting the mill from its recently widowed owner, Elizabeth Fletcher Ashbridge. The rent was considerable—over £280 in 1777—so it was in their best interest to continue operations despite the warfare that had engulfed them. Business at the mill became perilous for its owners almost as soon as the British occupied Philadelphia. On September 30, Elizabeth Drinker mentioned, "Abel James and family are come to Town, thinking it more safe to be here, as a number of ye Americans are skulking near and about Frankford. Old Joshua Gibson whose son lives at Ashbridge's mill, was last week taken from thence by one horseman, but was quickly rescued by one or 2 of ye English Light-Horse."[35]

A few days later, on October 4, when a major battle erupted at Germantown, Gibson's wife fled into the city for protection from marauding Americans. Drinker encountered her at Abel James's town house: "I stepped down to neighbor James'; Josey is very ill; Nanny Eve, and Gibbon's [*sic*] wife at ye mill, were there. They came to town through fear—ye Battle appeared to be very near them, and some of ye Provincials were about Frankford. They have taken away Joseph Paul and some others."[36]

Had Lydia Darragh chosen to do so, she could have reached an American military outpost closer to the city's gates, only three miles away at the Rising Sun. But going that way may have presented problems. While two other mills could be reached by going out the Germantown Road, both were farther away and would make for a longer trip on foot. The Roberts Mill in Germantown, where Church Lane crossed the Wingohocking Creek, was about six miles from the lines. When, on December 6, Sally Pleasants headed out toward Germantown for flour, she chose to go up to Shoemaker Mill, two miles farther yet than Roberts Mill. It may be that Roberts Mill was not thought a good bet for flour at that moment. In any event, Pleasants was riding in Sarah Logan Fisher's borrowed chaise, so she would not have to carry the flour herself. A woman traveling on foot, especially one wishing to keep her real intentions secret, would reasonably choose the Frankford mill, which was closest and was known to have a supply of flour.

But Lydia Darragh also had another good reason to traipse out to Frankford. According to her story, she was personally acquainted with Captain Charles Craig, the officer whose men guarded Frankford. According to the earliest version of Lydia's Tale, "he knew her."

After leaving the east gate at the head of Front Street, Lydia Darragh had to cross the Causeway, an elevated east-west roadway set on pilings that spanned the flooded swale of the Cohocksink Creek toward the foot of King's Highway. Depending on the traveler's destination, the road was also referred to variously as Frankford Road, Bristol Road, or New York Road.[37]

Darragh's walk out to the mill would hardly have been a solitary passage through a barren wasteland. The road to Frankford had been busy in peaceful times. Coaches from several stage lines regularly plied the route between Philadelphia and New York. Numerous wagons full of farm produce and other goods passed along it, especially on market days. Even in this time of war, scores, if not hundreds, of civilians, along with at least a handful of carriages and other conveyances, made their way to Frankford and beyond daily. Despite difficulties, taverns and inns—such as the Sign of the Lamb in Kensington and the Jolly Post in Frankford—maintained their operations along the busy highway. Many local residents continued to live on and operate their farms and other businesses, hoping to avoid the troubles.

John Graves Simcoe, who commanded the British advanced guard patrolling the area, described the disputed countryside that Darragh passed through on her trip to the mill:

> The country in front of Philadelphia, where the Queen's Rangers were employed, was in general cleared ground, but intersected with many woods; the fields were fenced out with very high railing: the main road led straight from Philadelphia to Bristol Ferry on the Delaware; about five miles from Philadelphia, on this road, was Frankfort Creek which fell into the Delaware nearly at that distance, and the angle that it formed was called Point-no-Point, within which were many good houses and plantations. Beyond the bridge over the creek, on a height, was the village of Frankfort; below the bridge it was not fordable, but it was easily passed in many places above it. The rebels frequently patrolled as far as Frankfort, and to a place called the Rocks, about a mile beyond it.[38]

A popular woman with a wide social network in the city through her storekeeping, midwifery, and nursing, Lydia Darragh likely encountered acquaintances along the road that morning, people she knew by sight or by name, perhaps even friends. Garrulous and genial, she may well have made the walk out in the company of other folks, especially women and children. Walking with a group would have provided a measure of protection and comfort, and also served to make her less conspicuous, though she may have had to field uncomfortable questions from her fellow travelers about her motives.

Walking through the countryside north of the city had been a regular source of enjoyment for Philadelphians, the landscape filled with prosperous farms and stately country houses. That pleasant scene changed dramatically when the two armies descended on the region. Now, roving patrols of horsemen daily threatened mayhem. The area had been stripped of anything that could feed men and horses. To warm the soldiers in the city, woodcutters systematically denuded the region of what-

A map published during the British occupation of Philadelphia. Lydia Darragh lived toward the southern end of the city. The British controlled the roads going in and out of Philadelphia; the closest American outposts were at Frankford, shown at the upper right on the map, and along the road to Germantown, north of the Cohocksink Creek. The Battle of Edge Hill occurred just north of Chestnut Hill, labeled at the very top. "A map of that part of Pennsylvania now the principle seat of war in America, wherein may be seen the situation of Philadelphia, Red Bank, Mud Island, & Germantown," by Nicholas Scull, 1777, detail. (*Library of Congress*)

ever would burn. When Lydia Darragh passed through the area that December, many places, their windows shattered, had been looted, while others loomed empty, their fires cold, their people fled. Still other buildings, among them several of the largest and finest estates, were nothing but burned-out hulks. On November 22, city residents had been filled with horror when the British set fire to them so they could not be used as outposts for rebels. Deborah Norris watched the destruction from the roof of her mother's Chestnut Street home as the conflagration consumed her family's summer place, Fairhill, out along Germantown Road, along with sixteen other houses. The ways to Germantown and Frankford were rife with the portents of apocalypse.[39]

Here we must pause to entertain the alternate version of Lydia's Tale, Ann Darragh's account, mentioned earlier. In that telling, Lydia Darragh explained her plan to leave the city by saying she intended to visit her children ("she told her husband she was going to use a pass she had obtained some time before to go to the country to see her children."[40]) Though it was not recorded until much later, this version of the story is also plausible. Her two younger children, William and Susannah, were eleven and eight at the time, and the Darraghs may well have sent them out of town to stay with a relative. It is also possible she sent their son, John, who was just approaching his fourteenth birthday.

Where could she have sent them? William Darragh seems to have had several relatives living in Pennsylvania, siblings or at least cousins, though records of the ties to them are slim. There was a man named Charles Darragh for whom he had witnessed a land warrant in 1766. Another possibility was Ann Darragh McClenachan, who had moved across the street from him in 1766. She and her husband, Blair, a known patriot, most likely left the city prior to its occupation. It is not known for certain where they sheltered, but Blair had kin living in Easttown Township, twenty-five miles west of the city, a ways out in Chester County.[41]

William did have one confirmed relative living in Philadelphia in 1777: his sister Mary Darragh Eddy. The Eddys had several children, including one whose family is a likely candidate to have sheltered the Darragh children during the occupation: their daughter Ann. Ann Eddy was born in Ireland in 1743 and came to Philadelphia with her parents in 1753. In 1760, she married Christopher Marshall Jr., son of James Eddy's sometime business partner, druggist Christopher Marshall. The couple had three daughters, Isabella, Sarah, and Ann, first cousins to the younger Darragh children, with whom they were close in age. Though Ann died at the end of 1775, her husband continued to refer to Lydia Darragh as an "Aunt." When the British occupied Philadelphia, the Marshall sons, ardent patriots, decamped and moved to Providence Township, about twenty-five miles northwest of the city. Lydia Darragh is known to have made the trek out to Providence to see them in January 1778 and again that May. The Darraghs' son, John, stayed with Christopher Marshall Jr. for an extended period in September 1778. If the Darragh children were staying at "the country home of a relative of her husband," there is a strong possibility they were staying with the Marshall families in Providence. Arguing against this possibility, however, it should be noted that Hannah Marshall Haines never mentioned anything in her writing about the Darragh children, who were close to her in age, staying in the vicinity in winter 1777–1778.[42]

If her children were staying outside the city, there is also a strong likelihood that Lydia Darragh had been given a blanket pass, like the one issued by Nisbet Balfour discussed above, that would allow her to pass the lines at any time. Such a pass would not have named the exact location to which she was headed, but she would certainly have been questioned about her destination, a routine practice when passing through the city's gates. Having given that information to the gate guards, it would have been most prudent to then head in the direction of that destination in order to allay suspicion. Avoiding discovery was certainly on her mind. If her named destination were Providence, there were two sets of gates through which she might reasonably walk. The western gate was on Ridge Road that headed northwest paralleling the Schuylkill River and passing through Providence.

For Lydia Darragh, who lived on Second Street, the twin gates at the head of Second Street were more conveniently located. While the easternmost of these gates led to King's Highway and Frankford, the western gate led to Germantown Road, which paralleled Ridge Road closely and also headed to Providence, before the two roads merged near the crossing of the Perkiomen Creek. This would seem to be a better choice for her point of departure from the city because it was the more direct route from her home and it would bring her closer to the known outposts of American soldiers.

There is a detail in Hannah Marshall Haines's unpublished account, reiterated by Watson in his manuscript, likewise unpublished, that may bear on this version of the story. It says that Darragh encountered an American officer prior to meeting the one with whom she shared her information: "While between the two armies, an American officer stopped her, to inquire where she came from. She looked at him, but did not like his countenance, and was fearful he might betray her. . . . She soon met Colonel Craig of the Light Horse."[43]

Watson identified this first officer as Captain Allen McLane, who maintained the American outpost at the Rising Sun, while Craig was posted a few miles to the east, near Frankford. Lydia could have walked all the way out Germantown Road to the Rising Sun before heading east toward Frankford via Nicetown Lane. Or she could have switched direction earlier, after crossing the Cohocksink Creek and out of view of the guards, by using one of the farm lanes headed east from Germantown Road. In either case, she might have encountered McLane or his troopers first, since they patrolled all the way down toward the British lines. But in the end, we cannot say with certainty whether Lydia Darragh's pretext for her trip was a visit to her children or a quest for flour, or even some combination of the two.

Returning to the earliest version of the narrative, Robert Walsh described the moment when Lydia Darragh finally divulged her secret to an American officer:

> Leaving her bag at the mill, she hastened towards the American lines, and encountered on her way an American Lieutenant Colonel (Craig) of the light horse, who, with some of his men, was on the look-out for information. He knew her, and inquired whither she was going. She answered, in quest of her son, an officer in the American army; and prayed the Colonel to alight and walk with her.
>
> He did so, ordering his troops to keep in sight. To him she disclosed her momentous secret, after having obtained from him the most solemn promise never to betray her individually, since her life might be at stake, with the British. He conducted her to a house near at hand, directed a female in it to give her something to eat, and speeded for headquarters, where he brought General Washington acquainted with what he had heard. Washington made, of course, all preparation for baffling the meditated surprise.[44]

Watson confirmed this version of Lydia's Tale, adding some details not found in Walsh:

> Arrived at Frankford, she ordered 25 lbs Flour, & pushed on, hoping to meet some American officer to whom she might communicate. At some distance she met Colonel Craig (who shot himself) with about a dozen horse going to the lines for information. She knew him & begged him to send on his men, & speak with her alone. To him she revealed the whole, & he set off immediately to communicate to Washington.[45]

The story that came down through Lydia Darragh's descendants put the event somewhat differently:

> She saw an officer approaching on horseback. It proved to be Colonel Craig, of the Light Infantry, whom she knew. He was greatly surprised to see her, and asked, "Why, Mrs. Darragh, what are you doing so far from home?" She asked him to walk beside her, which he did, leading his horse. In low tones she told him the important intelligence she had risked so much to bring, and he at once rode with it to headquarters.[46]

Hannah Marshall Haines's version, the earliest we know of, added a detail Walsh left out, revealing Lydia Darragh's ease with Craig, as well as something of her affectionate and persuasive nature: "She took his arm & then told him she was going to put her life into his hands. She then related to him the important information."[47]

The original versions of the story agree well on certain points: The officer was named Craig, she met him on her way toward the American lines, the officer was mounted, he recognized her and asked where she was going, she disclosed her secret to him privately, he rode off to headquarters with the intelligence. These accounts all stressed the hazardous nature of her undertaking: She risked so much that her life was at stake.

But questions arise about the man she met. Was he a lieutenant colonel or a colonel? Was he an officer of the light horse or the light infantry? Later versions of the story introduced more conflicting evidence, particularly about the identity of the officer. A careful analysis and concordance with other primary sources can decide most of these questions, though some unknowns remain. Different writers tried to resolve the incongruities in different ways. Henry Darrach, writing in 1916, tried to bring many divergences into alignment, but the accuracy of his attempt to merge the conflicting narratives into a harmonious whole is suspect. Such conflation of contradictory details continues, however, to this day.

Because of a tragedy, the echoes of which were barely remembered by the time Lydia's Tale first went public, the original versions of the story misidentify Craig, the American officer whom Lydia Darragh met. Hannah Haines identified the officer as "Colonel Craig of the Light Horse." John Watson, following Haines, called him "Colonel Craig (who shot himself)." Robert Walsh, after checking his information with "some military gentlemen whom he deemed the best judges," men who probably had knowledge of the career of General Thomas Craig, who was still living at the time, denoted the man as "Lieutenant Colonel (Craig) of the light horse," accurately citing Thomas's rank as it had been in 1777.[48]

There were multiple American officers from Pennsylvania named Craig, several of them related. The identities of two brothers from Northampton County, Thomas and Charles Craig, were mixed together by those writing half a century later. When Robert Walsh first published Lydia's Tale, the elder brother, Thomas Craig, was well known as a general of Pennsylvania militia. The reputation of Charles, who committed suicide in 1782, a valiant but sad casualty of the horrors of war, had faded from living memory. Let us disentangle these two men.

On June 14, 1775, the Continental Congress authorized the creation of the first American army: six rifle companies from Pennsylvania, as well as two each from Maryland and Virginia. When the new military establishment was created, Northampton's Committee of Correspondence directed its newly formed rifle company to vote for officers; they selected Abraham Miller as captain, Charles Craig first lieutenant, and Thomas Craig second lieutenant. This caused Charles some embarrassment since it put him in line to succeed to the captaincy over his more experienced older brother. Soon afterward, political pressure was brought to bear on Abraham Miller to resign in favor of Charles.[49]

In January 1776, Thomas Craig was appointed captain of a Northampton infantry company in the newly raised 2nd Pennsylvania Battalion. Under command of Colonel Arthur St. Clair and Lieutenant Colonel William Allen Jr., Thomas Craig's unit marched to Canada where it fought in the Battle of Trois-Rivieres on June 8. His performance was such that he was soon promoted to colonel in his battalion's successor organization, the 3rd Pennsylvania Regiment.

At the start of 1777, the American army underwent a reorganization. With the establishment of Colonel Stephen Moylan's Regiment of Light Dragoons, Charles Craig was appointed captain of the new regiment's 1st Troop. Moylan was so impressed with Craig's conduct that by July, he recommended him to General Washington for promotion to lieutenant colonel. Moylan thought Craig "the Oldest Captain in the Service," noting that he was "brave, modest, the latter part of his character is, I verily believe, the reason he is still a Captain." The promotion, however, did not materialize.[50]

After the British occupation of Philadelphia, the American army perched on a series of ridges at Whitemarsh, fifteen miles from the city, maintaining a stranglehold on the British, denying them easy access to the surrounding countryside, rich in food, forage, and military supplies, while remaining a military threat. Washington relied on cavalry units as his eyes and ears in the no-man's-land between the two armies. Cavalry on the lines performed several functions: serving as a warning system about enemy movement; controlling access and the flow of information, goods, and supplies between the occupied city and the hinterland; and gathering intelligence. Any of these activities was likely to provoke skirmishes with enemy horsemen engaged in the same business; fighting between small units occurred frequently.

Major John Clark and Colonel Elias Boudinot took over espionage responsibilities. To aid them, Washington designated two trusted officers to gather intelligence between the Delaware and Schuylkill Rivers: Allen McLane, who was assigned command of one hundred infantrymen and light horsemen with rotating personnel, and Charles Craig of Moylan's Light Dragoons. These men guarded the major roads out of Philadelphia: McLane the Germantown and York Roads, Craig, the King's Highway through Frankford.[51]

Espionage was viewed as a sordid but necessary business. Requiring dishonesty and subterfuge through intermediaries in contact with the enemy, such involvement could jeopardize an officer's integrity. Many of those contacts might be former friends, neighbors, or relatives of ambivalent allegiance, even active Tories. Information gathering naturally involved some quid pro quo, including exchange of nonmilitary reports about the condition of family, friends, and businesses. Because information flowed in both directions, intelligence officers were vulnerable to accusations of double dealing.

Such may have been the case as Charles Craig sought news about British preparations for their final attempt at dislodging, defeating, and dispersing the Americans before winter brought an end to the campaign season. The light horse had been supplying headquarters with a steady stream of intelligence about Howe's plans. On the evening of December 3, the night before the British were to march on Whitemarsh, Charles Craig crossed the bridge over Frankford Creek and rode into the British lines for a talk with two acquaintances: a defector, William Allen Jr., known to Craig from Northampton, who was once his brother's commander but now a Tory colonel, and Abel James, a prominent Quaker merchant and business partner of Henry Drinker's. In the eyes of Pennsylvania's radical faction, Charles Craig's connections to these two men compromised him. Some thought he acted as a double agent.

The meeting was obviously prearranged. Messengers had to have passed the lines in one direction with a proposed time and place, then back again with an acceptance. The rendezvous location was convenient; James' elegant country estate, Chalkley Hall, lay a few hundred yards from the Frankford crossing, about five miles northeast of Philadelphia. Pickets from both sides watched the bridge over Frankford Creek. Others were also watching. An informant later sent an accusation to the American headquarters charging that Craig had met with the enemy and that "Captain Craig had been their spy ever since they [the British] came to town." The letter also claimed that Craig periodically stole into the woods "exchanging clothes," presumably to disguise his appearance when slipping into Philadelphia.[52]

Craig's letters to Washington on December 2nd and 3rd contained misleading information about how the British would approach the hills above Whitemarsh. Howe's military intelligence apparatus—possibly assisted by William Allen, Jr.—seems to have planted disinformation with Craig in hopes of unbalancing and weakening Washington's strong defensive position. We will have more to say about Craig's information shortly.[53]

Involvement with the questionable but necessary business of espionage rendered Charles Craig vulnerable to passing misinformation and to questions about his loyalty—questions that continued to rankle him throughout his few remaining years. As will be seen below, the sting of these aspersions festered, ultimately leading to Craig's final effort to defend his honor. By the time Lydia's Tale was published in the 1820s, knowledge of only the celebrated Colonel—by-then General—Thomas Craig survived in the popular consciousness. The younger of the brothers, Charles Craig, had long passed from public memory.[54]

Recognizing Lydia Darragh's fatigue after her long walk to find him, Charles Craig "conducted her to a house near at hand, directed a female in it to give her something to eat." While she refreshed herself, he "speeded for headquarters, where he brought General Washington acquainted with what he had heard."[55]

Meanwhile, the physical trial for Lydia Darragh was about to begin: the return walk to Second and Spruce Streets, carrying "a quarter of a hundred" weight of flour. Though Walsh simply noted that "Lydia returned home with her flour," consideration of the toil involved caused Watson to elaborate on what he had heard: "To make good her story on her return, she (although a woman of 40 & of weakly habit) actually carried her 25 lbs flour into Philadelphia."[56]

The distance from Lydia Darragh's house to the Frankford mill was at least five-and-a-half miles by the most direct route. Sunrise on December 3 was at about 7:10 A.M. While she may have left home even earlier, she could not have attempted to pass through the gates before 8:00 A.M. without drawing attention. The guards were under orders not to allow anyone to pass the gates at night. In the event, they did not always follow this order strictly, which led Howe to admonish them to perform better. But city dwellers were aware that the gates were to be used only during the day. Given the requirement to check in with Carlile or his staff at the gates, and the press of people trying to go out each morning, Lydia Darragh may well have encountered delay. The walk out to Frankford would have taken her at least a couple of hours, followed by additional time as she transacted her business at the mill. If she then set out for the American lines, it must have been late morning or early afternoon before she finally met the officer she sought.[57]

To make the round trip, she needed to walk at least eleven miles. But she also went an indeterminate distance beyond the mill until she encountered Charles Craig, perhaps as much as another mile or even two, which would have lengthened the total distance she covered to as much as fifteen miles. If she had gone from the mill all the way to the Rising Sun, by way of Nicetown Lane, that would have added three miles to the trip each way, for a total of about seventeen miles, a long weary way to walk for a person in her late forties. Watson continued to think this through, perhaps in continued conversation with Hannah Haines, remarking a few years after his initial rendition, "Mrs. Darrach, although a small and weakly woman, walked the whole distance out and in, bringing with her, to save appearances, twenty-five pounds of flour, borne upon her arms all the way from Frankford."[58]

Surely the return trip must have been an onerous undertaking for Lydia Darragh, an ordeal of several hours of labor and discomfort. Anyone who has tried carrying a heavy weight for five or six miles knows how wearying such a walk can be. To lug an unstable load of twenty-eight pounds of grain or flour in a constantly shifting and sagging bag is a trial indeed. No position is tolerable for long, as gravity gradually tugs the unwieldy mass toward the ground. Lydia would have needed to pause often to redistribute its weight. At times, she would need to lower her burden to ease the burning pain in her muscles, especially her forearms. That she did all this with a troubled heart, fearing discovery, must have made her travail all the sorer.

General Howe's orders specified that any person coming in after 5:00 P.M. would either be detained or forwarded to headquarters. Lydia Darragh's knowledge that the gates would be closed to her by then, and her fear of seeming conspicuous, must have spurred her to make the best speed she could as she hurried back to town. Watching this struggling woman passing back into the city may have aroused the sympathy of the guards, who might have spared her from harassment as she came back through their gate. Even when she finally reached home, across from the busy British headquarters, her fear did not abate, and she found it difficult to rest.[59]

Robert Walsh practiced concision in retelling Lydia's Tale for publication, dropping several revealing details his source had included. The fuller stories, imparted by people who knew her, inform us about Lydia Darragh's state of mind in a way that Walsh's dry recitation of the facts does not. Both the Haines and Darrach versions emphasize Lydia's continued deception of her husband and her reason for doing so. Hannah Haines had originally given Walsh more to work with: "[T]he next night, she told her husband she had something that would occupy her till late & wished him to go to bed. She went into a front chamber, lowered the Shutters & set down to watch their movements. At 12, they marched from Headquarters without a word being spoken; she could only hear their footsteps."[60]

Evidence of Lydia Darragh's very real fear resounds in the words that came down through her daughter Ann:

> Lydia then returned home, but did not tell her husband the real object of her errand to the country until she thought all danger over. He little knew the part his wife had played in the drama of that eventful night. She feared the least suspicion of his having taken information out of the city might endanger his life and kept her secret. That night she sat at a front window, wrapped in a cloak, and watched the soldiery march by on their way to attack Washington.[61]

These threads also say something about another aspect of Lydia Darragh's personality: her curiosity. She was a person who actively sought out information about what was going on around her. This was especially true concerning the activities of the British army. It was curiosity that had led her to listen in on the British officers' conversation and curiosity that kept her up late the night the army marched out of the city. Certainly, the officers' contingent from the headquarters across the street would have passed by her house on the night of December 4. But who were the "soldiery" she heard trudging past on their way to Whitemarsh?

The British army was posted along the line of redoubts north of the city, on the south side of the Cohocksink Creek, in the vicinity of present-day Spring Garden Street. Yet Lydia's Tale claims she listened as troops marched past her house at Second and Spruce Streets, a mile south of the army's encampment. Is this evidence that her story was a fantasy, or that it was unreliable—that people got the particulars wrong after so many years? This seemingly mistaken detail actually corroborates her account because it points to a fact not likely to have been well known by the 1820s. If there was such a group of soldiers, what outfit could it have been?

It turns out there were some British soldiers posted south of the city whose unit did march out with the rest of the army that night. To reach the main force, they would have had to march right past Lydia Darragh's house. Two maps give a clue to the unit's identity. One, published by

William Faden in 1779, shows the 43rd Regiment of Foot posted south of Christian Street, between Second and Third Streets, near Wharton's place, and behind a set of three British batteries that front the Delaware River. This map indicates that there were soldiers who could have marched by Darragh's house and explains why: They were present to support the British guns in case of attack.[62]

But there is a problem: At this time, the 43rd Regiment was not actually in Philadelphia. It was posted at Rhode Island in 1777, under nominal command of William Prescott, the general officer who had been captured in a raid by American forces along with his aide, the hapless Lieutenant William Barrington.

An unpublished manuscript map, which seems to have been the original source for Faden's map, shows the same thing but with slight differences. This map locates the 49th Regiment of Foot at the same spot, though the streets are labeled Front and Second Streets, instead of Second and Third. Evidently the information on the published map was incorrectly transcribed. In the style that the regiment's designation is written on the manuscript map, the "9" in "49 Regt." can easily be mistaken for a "3" at a quick glance. Whoever copied the information onto the published Faden map seems to have made a simple transcription error.[63]

The 49th Regiment was at Philadelphia. It was part of the 1st Brigade, along with the 4th, 23rd, and 28th Regiments. According to General Howe's orders, the 49th Regiment did indeed march to Whitemarsh. On December 4, when Howe added reinforcements to his expedition against Whitemarsh, he revised the planned order of march, shifting the position of the 1st Brigade from the vanguard, under General Cornwallis, to the middle of the column, under General Knyphausen. Thomas Sullivan, a sergeant in the 49th Regiment, also listed his unit as part of the 1st Brigade present at Whitemarsh. Reporting on casualties, he noted that while the 49th suffered no men killed or wounded, there were five rank and file missing in action, probably deserters, but some possibly captives.[64]

Men of the 49th Regiment, then, would have been the soldiers marching past Lydia Darragh's house, their heavy tread causing the bridge to rumble as they passed over Little Dock Creek, which lay between her house and British headquarters. En route to Whitemarsh, they would find themselves marching two miles farther than their comrades in arms who were posted by the redoubts north of the city.

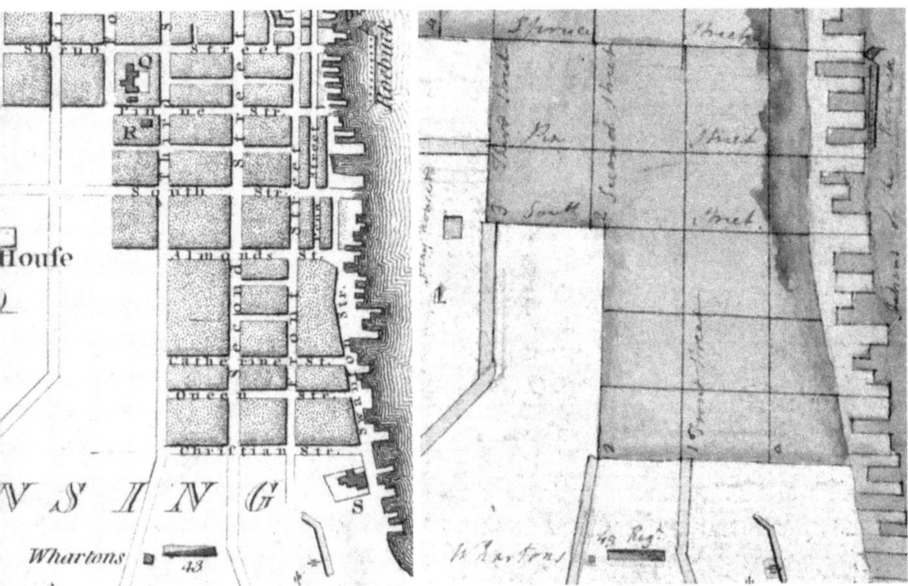

William Faden's 1779 map of Philadelphia, left, was based on an unpublished manuscript map, right, from 1778. Faden introduced a number of errors, including labeling Spruce Street as "Shrub" and Water Street as Front Street, with the result that all of the north-south streets are one block to the east from their actual locations. The 43rd Regiment is shown at the bottom of Faden's map; they were not there. The 49th was instead, as correctly labeled in the unpublished map. *A Plan of the City and Environs of Philadelphia*, William Faden, 1779, detail; "Philadelphia and Neighborhood," manuscript map, 1778, detail. (*Library of Congress*)

Watson added a visual detail about this march that seems a fanciful elaboration on his part: "Next night, she arose, and at the appointed hour saw the silent march, through her window, and the arms beaming by moon light." If their arms beamed by moonlight, it must have been a very faint beaming, because the waxing crescent moon was only four days past the new moon, assuming the sky that night was even clear.[65]

Chapter 11

Whitemarsh and the Battle of Edge Hill

All four early accounts of Lydia's Tale say that after receiving Lydia Darragh's intelligence, Captain Charles Craig immediately rode off to headquarters, eleven or twelve miles away, to inform Washington of what he had learned. Perhaps he did. In the Haines-generated strain, Lydia was led to a house where she got something to eat while Craig immediately rode off. Whether she witnessed him riding off alone, or in company with his men, was not specified.

The speed with which Craig was supposed to have departed underscores the importance, in the mind of the narrators, of the information Darragh had imparted. That perceived importance was also emphasized by the idea that only Craig himself, and no one else, could be trusted to deliver the vital secret.

On December 3, most probably the day Darragh met with Craig, the captain sent a message to George Washington, carried by one of his dragoons, which contained information about the British plans:

Frankford 3rd Decemr 1777
Sir
The enemy have not made any movement since I had the Honour of Adressing Your Excellency.
I have been inform'd since my last, that, the Number that Crossed Schoolkill Consisted of Three Thousand Men, with six field pieces, The[y] Took a Number of flat Bottom'd Boats, with which the[y] intend to Cross on your Excellencys rear, the enemy are very Diserous to Know where our Stores and Baggage are at present, the[y] are making great preparations, But I believe dread the Consequences of Makeing an Attackt. I am With great Truth & respect Your Excellencys Most Obt Servt
C. Craig[1]

The letter itself is an objective fact. But who gave this bit of intelligence to Craig? Might it have been Lydia Darragh? Did its content originate from William Allen Jr., with whom Craig met the evening of December 3? Or could it have come from another, unknown person? Whichever the source, the information was incorrect. While it could simply have been mixed up or mistaken, it might have been a trick intended to confuse General Washington.

At 1:00 P.M. on the 3rd, Major John Clark, based on "a Letter just from the city," also told the commander in chief that the British were bringing boats with them: "The Enemy are in motion have a number of flat bottom'd Boats on Carriages & Scantling—& are busy pressing Horses & Waggons—no persons permitted to come out except those on whom they can depend." But if, as he noted, the British were only letting people whom they trusted cross the lines, what does that say about the reliability of the letter Clark received?[2]

It is intriguing that the following day, Elias Boudinot, the American commissary of prisoners, personally brought a message to Washington that contained several similarities. Because Boudinot's intelligence eventually became entangled with Lydia's Tale, it is worth investigating it further.

Elias Boudinot (1740–1821) was well known during his lifetime and afterward was regarded as one of the American nation's founders. He was a congressman from 1779 through 1795, was president of Congress in 1782–1783, and was director of the US Mint, located in Philadelphia, from 1795 to 1805. A vigorous and devout Presbyterian, he is revered today as an early abolitionist, an advocate for women's rights, and a founder of the American Bible Society. Born in Philadelphia, he was baptized by that luminary of the Great Awakening, George Whitefield, not long after that divine preached from the balcony of the Loxley House. When Elias was about twelve, his family moved to Princeton, where he eventually studied law with Richard Stockton, who would later become a signer of the Declaration of Independence. In 1757, Stockton married Elias's sister, the celebrated poet Annis Boudinot. Further strengthening their familial bonds, Boudinot married Stockton's sister Hannah in 1762. As the troubles between Britain and America grew, the brothers-in-law became firm Whigs and active supporters of revolution. In 1777, George Washington appointed Boudinot to be commissary of prisoners, adding another role as well: "I intend to annex another duty to this Office; and that is, the procuring of Intelligence. The Gentleman ingaged in the department of Commissary of Prisoners will have as much leizure, and better oppertunities, than most other Officers in the Army, to obtain knowledge of the Enemys Situation—Motions—and (as far as may be) designs."[3]

On December 4, 1777, while Boudinot was gathering intelligence near the lines at Philadelphia, he met a mysterious woman. His account of the event follows:

> I dined at a small Post at the Rising Sun abt three Miles from the City. After Dinner, a little poor looking, insignificant old Woman, came in & solicited leave to go into the Country to buy some flour. While we were asking some Questions She walked up to me, and put into my hands a dirty old needle book, with various small pockets in it. Surprised at this, I told her to retire, she should have an Answer. On opening the needlebook, I could not find any thing, till I got to the last Pockett, where I found a piece of Paper rolled up into the form of a Pipe Shank. On unrolling it, I found information that General Howe was coming out the next morning with 5000 Men—13 pieces of Cannon—Baggage Waggons, and 11 Boats on Waggon Wheels. On chequing this, with other Information, I found it true, and immediately rode Post to Headquarters. According to my usual Custom, and agreeable to orders recd from Gen. W., I first related to him the naked Facts without comment or opinion. He recd it with much Thoughtfulness. I then gave him my Opinions, that Gen'l Howe's design

> was to cross the Delaware under pretense of going for New York. Then in the Night to recross the Delaware above Bristol & come suddenly on our Rear, when we were totally unguarded, and cut off all our Baggage, if not the whole Army. He heard me without a single observation, being deep in Thought. I repeated my observations. He still was silent. Supposing myself unattended to— I earnestly repeated my Opinion, with urging him to order a few Redoubts thrown up in our Rear, as it was growing late. The Genl answered me, Mr. Boudinot the Enemy have no business in our Rear, the Boats are designed to deceive us. To morrow Morning by daylight you will find them coming down such a by Road to our left. Then calling an Aide du Camp ordered a line thrown up along our whole front at the foot of the Hill. As I was quartered on that very Bye Road with 6 or 8 other Officers, a Mile in front of our Army, and no Pickett advanced of us, this opinion made a deep Impression upon me, tho I thot the General under a manifest mistake. I returned to my Quarters first obtaining a Pickett to be put on that Road in Advance. When I got home, the Officers were in formed of the News, and my opinion that we should loose our Baggage at least, the next Morning. That our General was at last out in his Judgment, but repeated his last words. Proposed it as a Matter of prudence to have our Horses saddled and the Servt. ordered to have them at the door on the first alarm Gun being fired. About three o'Clock in the Morning we were roused by the Alarm Guns. We immediately mounted and by Sunrise, the British was in possession of our Quarters down the bye Road, mentioned by Genl Washington. I then said that I never would again set up my Judgment agt. his.[4]

When we compare Boudinot's information with Charles Craig's message, we see that there are several similar elements, especially the mention of boats, the army's baggage, and a supposed British attempt to get into the American rear. Another dragoon captain, reporting on December 2 about British readiness, also noted "they have a very considerable number of flat bottom'd Boats on Carriages."[5]

When Boudinot brought his intelligence to Washington's attention, he probably didn't realize that the general had heard these things previously. That this suspect information came on three separate days, from seemingly separate sources, raises the possibility that what we are witnessing was a deliberate ruse—a bit of counterintelligence—on the part of the British. If so, Washington's reaction, "Mr. Boudinot the Enemy have no business in our Rear, the Boats are designed to deceive us," shows us that he was not taken in.

It is possible that people actually witnessed flat-bottomed boats mounted on wheels as part of the British preparations. However, in the several British accounts of the order of march, there is no mention of boats being brought along. Howe and his staff were aware that they could not conceal their extensive preparations. Could disinformation about boats landing in Washington's rear have been part of an intentional effort to cause the Americans to disarrange their defensive positions by shifting their attention in the wrong direction?

Other, related questions arise. Could the "little poor looking, insignificant old Woman" who gave Boudinot the needlebook actually have been Lydia Darragh? Or was it possible that a second woman was also roaming the area, seeking to give information to the Americans about the very visible signs of a British move?

Boudinot's description could match Lydia Darragh in some respects, but not in others. Her daughter Ann, in speaking with a niece, portrayed her mother somewhat differently. According to that account, Lydia was "of a fair complexion, light hair, blue eyes, very delicate in appearance and extremely neat; conforming in her dress to the rules of the Society of Friends."

She may have been small in stature. Just the year before, Jacob Hiltzheimer had described her as a "clever little Irish woman." Hannah Haines, who knew Lydia personally, described her to Watson as "of weakly habit" and "a small weakly woman."[6]

Whoever Boudinot's woman was, if she were tired after trudging out to the Rising Sun, she might not have been looking her best by the time Elias Boudinot met her. Lydia Darragh was not elderly at this time; she was about forty-nine. It is possible she might appear aged to Boudinot's eyes, though he himself was only twelve years younger.[7]

It is true that Quaker dress could appear "poor looking" to those unfamiliar with it, but Boudinot was raised in Philadelphia. He was surely familiar with the range of quality in sober-looking Quaker habiliment and could distinguish between clothing worn by impoverished Friends and that of their more prosperous neighbors. The Darraghs' relative wealth and the care Lydia took of her personal appearance suggest a more refined presence than that described by Boudinot.

Boudinot's detail, that the woman "solicited leave to go into the Country to buy some flour" does accord with Lydia Darragh's quest for flour. But as we have seen, that was an especially common reason for women to leave the city, which was why Darragh used it as an excuse in the first place. There were likely several women moving about in a similar search at that time.

There are some aspects of Elias Boudinot's account that might support the possibility that Lydia Darragh was his informant. For instance, Boudinot was a colonel, which accords with the rank mentioned in the accounts of Haines, Watson, and Darrach, though those accounts specify the name of the colonel as Craig. From Boudinot's evidence alone, we cannot rule out that Lydia Darragh was the woman he met at the Rising Sun. But the idea raises more questions than it answers.

Were Lydia Darragh's auditors mistaken in identifying Craig as the man to whom she delivered her information? If so, how was it that they recalled the name of a soldier who was so obscure as to be virtually unknown by the time the stories were taken down instead of the name of a man like Elias Boudinot, who was justly famous and well remembered?

Might Lydia Darragh, who supposedly told Charles Craig that she was entrusting him with her life and the safety of her family, have disclosed her secret to multiple people, including someone she didn't know personally? If she was so concerned about discovery, and the risk to her family, would this intelligent woman have committed damning information to paper, readily discoverable even though hidden and "rolled up into the form of a pipe shank"?

Elias Boudinot did not accept the old woman's information at face value but checked it against other sources before deciding to share it with Washington. If Boudinot's informant was Lydia Darragh, could apparent reticence on his part have left her so unsatisfied that she continued her walk to seek out a second officer, trying to be certain her message got through? The fact that Boudinot's information tracks with Charles Craig's could argue that Lydia Darragh was in contact with both men. Of course, we don't know for certain that the information contained in Craig's December 3 letter was received from Darragh; he might have learned that from a different source, sent his letter, heard from Lydia afterward, then, as Lydia's Tale suggests, delivered her intelligence to Washington verbally.

We know that numerous people were bringing information to the Americans at that moment. The surviving instances might not represent the totality of that information but only a sampling. The simplest solution would be that two women tried to warn the Americans on the same day, but we cannot say that with certainty.

Boudinot's memoir, written years after the events described, lay buried among his papers for many years, not seeing the light of day until the latter part of the nineteenth century. It first reached print in 1894, through the efforts of an anonymous editor. Seeing a similarity between Boudinot's account and the Lydia Darragh story, the editor decided to highlight it by adding a spurious chapter header to the section detailing the events of December 4 (which was quoted above): "Lydia Darrah Conveys the News of General Howe's Movements to Elias Boudinot, when the British were in Possession of Philadelphia." The actual chapter header in Boudinot's manuscript simply reads, "*British Army at Chesnut Hill.*" There is no mention of Lydia Darragh's name anywhere in Boudinot's manuscript.[8]

Despite his spurious chapter title, the editor prefaced the book with a blanket statement, proclaiming the work's historical accuracy: "This Journal or Diary of Events which occurred during our Revolutionary War, is published, verbatim, literatim et punctuatim, from a faithful copy, made in 1874, of the original Journal written by Elias Boudinot."[9]

Since that time, this identification of Lydia Darragh with the person Boudinot met at the Rising Sun has been accepted as an unquestioned matter of fact by many writers. But the identity of the "little poor looking, insignificant old Woman" who handed the colonel a needlebook remains far from certain.

By the final month of 1777, both George Washington and William Howe were under considerable pressure, from politicians and their own officers, to fight a decisive battle. Neither Charles Craig nor Elias Boudinot was able to provide Washington with exact information about the forces that soon challenged the American army. But the general was well aware that the British were coming. In fact, he welcomed the confrontation since he had the advantage of fighting from prepared positions on his own chosen ground.

Evidence that Washington was planning for the encounter can be seen in his order of battle at Whitemarsh for November 28. On December 3, knowing that the British were about to march, he made minor alterations to his dispositions, ordering the infantry operating on his flanks "to skirmish with & harass the enemy as much as possible." Cavalry units were instructed "to watch the movements of the Enemy, give intelligence thereof & see that the Enemy do not gain our flanks without their knowledge." After hearing from Allen McLane on December 4, Washington increased the captain's hundred-man command by an additional eighty soldiers to guard the enemy's most likely route out of the city.[10]

After von Donop's failed attempt to capture Fort Mercer at Red Bank, New Jersey, Howe sent Major General Cornwallis with a large expeditionary force to accomplish the task. Once the British forces were consolidated again in Philadelphia following Cornwallis's return, Howe turned his attention to organizing his force for battle against Washington. He had to decide which units would march out to Whitemarsh and which left behind to guard the city against attack. In moving against the enemy, he also needed to determine the order in which they would march. Though moving a large mass of men was a complex undertaking, Howe and his officer corps were highly experienced and could pull off the logistical aspects competently. It was important to dispose the units so they were ready for engagement at any point along the road should the enemy choose to make a move of its own. Howe's initial orders, issued on December 3, had the army marching in two columns the next morning. The column on the right was to be led by Cornwallis, with Knyphausen commanding that on the left. But after consideration, Howe countermanded the orders late on the evening of the 3rd. He moved the march time forward to the evening of the 4th, beefed up the entire force with additional troops, and placed Cornwallis in charge of the vanguard, the troops who would spearhead the push out to Whitemarsh. Expecting trouble, he put his most elite units up front: the two battalions of British light infantry and the Jager Corps, followed by the battalions of British and Hessian grenadiers.[11]

To support the army in combat, adequate supplies of ammunition, along with rum wagons and hospital wagons, had to be brought along, as well as enough animals to pull them and men to protect them, a duty assigned to the Queen's Rangers. Beyond that, as Baurmeister and others reported, about one hundred empty wagons were brought, some to carry the wounded back into Philadelphia, others in anticipation of forage, provender, and plunder.[12]

The expedition set out late on the night of December 4, marching in the dark along the axis of the Germantown Road. About 11:00 P.M., as they approached the Three Mile Run, a small creek half a mile south of the Rising Sun, the head of the column was ambushed by McLane's men. Lieutenant Jonathan Cass of New Hampshire attacked the British left flank, while Lieutenant John Dover, operating on his home ground, attacked the right. Commanding the center, McLane "amused [them] in front by a well directed fire of Musketry from 50 men within 20 paces of his Collum." The light infantry in the lead halted and deployed, driving McLane back. Skirmishing continued through the night as the British vanguard forged forward six miles to the top of Chestnut Hill. About 3:00 A.M., the American alarm guns sounded, rousing the troops. As the British assembled along the ridge, they could see the fires of Washington's positions, stretching along the Whitemarsh hills, four miles across the valley.[13]

If Howe had actually expected to catch Washington flatfooted, it had been but a faint hope. Despite Lydia Darragh's unsophisticated but very genuine fears of a devastating surprise, the Americans were prepared for the British sortie. Given their strong position, they genuinely hoped Howe would attack. As a Connecticut private, Joseph Plumb Martin, recalled it years later in a memoir, "We were kept constantly on the alert, and wished nothing more than to have them engage us, for we were sure of giving them a drubbing, being in excellent fighting trim, as we were starved and as cross and ill natured as curs."[14]

The soldiers in this British force had marched at least nine miles through the night to reach Chestnut Hill. Howe made no attempt to surprise the enemy; that had not really been his intent. Instead, the army spent the morning of December 5 resting. Their repose was disturbed, however, by an assault made by the Pennsylvania Militia near the foot of Chestnut Hill. Once again, the light infantry, placed as usual in the foremost exposed position, absorbed the brunt of the attack. A green-coated light company, formerly belonging to Patrick Ferguson and still toting his unique breech-loading rifles, found itself nearly surrounded before the two light battalions came to its rescue, driving the Americans back after a few volleys, killing and wounding several men and capturing several prisoners. Patrolling and skirmishing continued throughout the day, but Washington's army was not to be drawn into the valley for a set-piece battle. While British patrols clashed with American outposts and militiamen between the lines, Charles Craig's dragoons filtered behind the British main body, rounding up enemy soldiers: "[T]hose taken the first day by small parties of horse in Germantown, in the rear of the enemy, were for the most part drunk. These parties of ours had been posted at Frankford, and as the enemy did not extend themselves to the right of Germantown, they fell in upon the enemy's rear, and collected stragglers with impunity."[15]

The 6th passed in much the same way, neither side venturing an all-out attack. In the relative quiet, at least as could be heard in Philadelphia, women like Polly Pleasants and Mrs. Stiles, desperate to feed their families, again filled the roads behind the British army, headed for the mills. His soldiers having recovered from the night march, Howe decided on one final attempt to slip around Washington's flank. Leaving their fires burning on Chestnut Hill, the British marched back to Germantown, passing once again the Chew House, scene of great carnage during the Battle of Germantown on October 4, then turned north again into Abington Lane. While this was supposed to be a secret movement, frustrated troops took the occasion to burn a number of houses in Beggarstown along the way. The light from these fires was surely visible from the Whitemarsh hills. By morning, the army had covered another six miles as they approached Jenkintown on Old York Road. Here Howe split his forces, sending General Charles Grey to demonstrate against the American center, hoping to draw Washington's attention, while the main force worked its way around the American left.[16]

Realizing they had lost track of the British, the Americans sent another detachment of the Pennsylvania Militia, stiffened by addition of the 2nd Connecticut, a veteran Continental regiment, forward from their right to reestablish contact with the enemy. This group spotted Grey's column as it neared the village of Edge Hill and raced it to take up a dominating position on the hill where Grey would have to pass through Edge Hill Gap. Serious fighting broke out when Grey sent his lead elements, highly experienced light troops, to drive the Americans from the ridge above the gap. A combination of elite troops—provincial, German, and British—executed a double envelopment, catching the Connecticut men in a withering crossfire that quickly reduced their ranks. Seeing this, the militia fled back toward their lines, while the regulars were forced to make their way out of the trap as best they could.[17]

Meanwhile, Howe's main force had continued up Old York Road another two miles beyond Jenkintown, the advance reconnoitered by light dragoons. Washington had cautiously pulled his own dragoons back closer to the main army. Guarding the American left were Charles Craig's horsemen, stationed on a spur of the Edge Hill ridge at Abington, near the intersection of York and Susquehanna Street Roads. Early on the 7th, British cavalrymen fell on Craig's detachment, driving them from their post. Washington received a warning that morning from Dr. Enoch Edwards, who was at Abington Presbyterian Meeting, within sight of the cavalry outpost: "The Enemy are moving across the Old York road about a mile below this Place . . . & continuing on to our Left. It appears to be a large Body. Their Horse was up here about two hours ago & I believe Capt. Craig is taken. His Men is gone off & there is no reconnoitering Party here at present."[18]

Though he may have had a close call, when the dust settled, Craig had not been captured. A local story about how he escaped pursuit continued to circulate in the area into the late nineteenth century:

> Captain Craig, an American officer was pursued by a British officer. Both were mounted, and the American captain, knowing of a cellar which had been dug on John Newbold's place in Jenkintown, and was covered with bushes, got ahead of his pursuer, and concealed himself and horse in this opening safely. The British officer rode round for a time, and gave up the chase.[19]

But Craig's separation from his men—once again—and his miraculous escape, while believable, may well have heightened suspicions among his detractors, especially in the following week, when the mysterious letter questioning his loyalty was received at headquarters.[20]

When Cornwallis's force reached the Susquehanna Street Road it turned left, headed toward the left flank of the American position on Camp Hill. But first it needed to pass over the crest of Edge Hill. To buy time while he shifted his troops northeast to counter the British move, Washington sent forward Daniel Morgan's riflemen and the Maryland Militia under Colonel Mordecai Gist. They crossed the Sandy Run valley, taking post along the Edge Hill ridge ahead of the advancing enemy. As the light infantry, once again the vanguard, crested the ridge, Morgan's men ambushed them with a deadly accurate volley of rifle fire, killing and wounding many. The lights responded with a bayonet charge, initially pushing the Americans back. But Washington had ordered the riflemen to execute a fighting withdrawal, keeping the enemy engaged and drawing them up against the formidable American defenses lining Camp Hill.

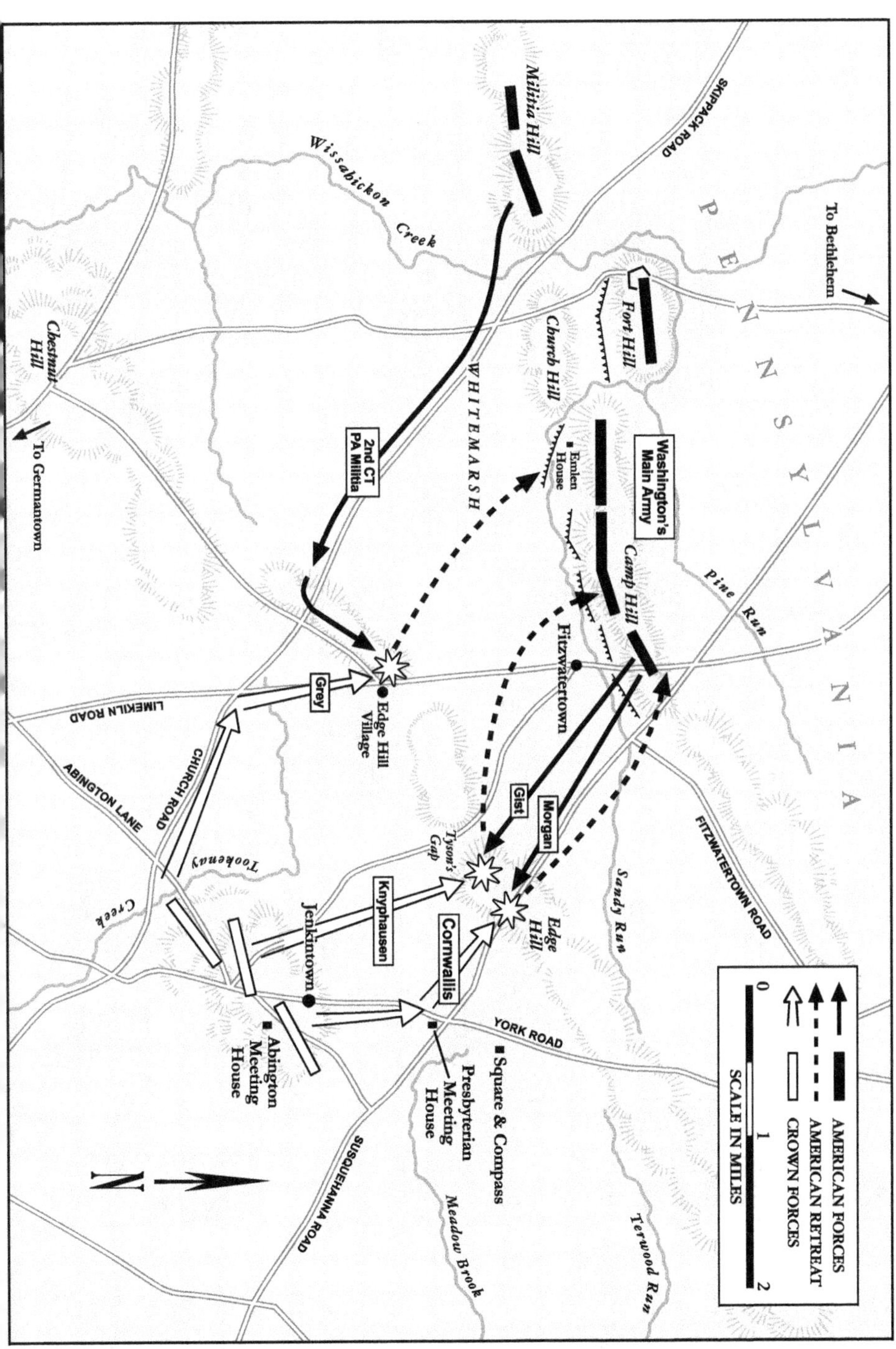

The Battle of Edge Hill, December 7, 1777.

Late on the afternoon of the 7th, Howe led his army across the Sandy Run. As they approached the Americans, they could see cannon mounted all along the line. The Continental infantry lay in wait, entrenched across the steeply rising hill, their front covered by felled trees with sharpened branches, obstacles meant to slow down the British advance while keeping them under a deadly fire. The flank march had taken too long; the Americans were too well prepared. An assault would be costly, risking a decisive defeat that could end the war right there and then. As darkness descended, Howe's men glumly retraced their steps, marching back to camp for the night on Edge Hill. The next day, as Joseph Plumb Martin wryly observed, "The British . . . thought better of the matter, and . . . very civilly walked off into Philadelphia again."[21]

Casualty figures for the four-day venture vary, but from available records it appears the British suffered at least 125 killed, wounded, and missing. American losses were similar, about 126 killed, wounded, and missing. While a full-scale battle had been avoided, the consequences for those units engaged in combat were serious. Years afterward, Lewis Hurd, of the 2nd Connecticut, remembered the battle somberly and simply as the day "where so many were killed." The British were frustrated, once again spending men who were hard to replace, losing comrades for no tangible gain, marching off with nothing to show for their effort. They took out their anger on the local populace, burning and looting all the way back to their lines at Philadelphia. Colonel Israel Angell, no stranger to the devastation of war, observed, "[The] Ravages and Destruction the British troops had made, . . . was Shocking to behold. . . . They had destroyed everything in their power Except the Buildings, and Some of them they had Burnt."

The experience of the Tyson family, who lived on the Edge Hill ridge at Tyson's Gap, was a common one. They reported that the enemy seized all their grain and fed it to their horses, wasting what was not used, a calamitous event for farmers at the start of winter.[22]

Meanwhile, at her house on Second Street, Lydia Darragh awaited the army's return with trepidation.

The returning British officers were in a foul mood. Lydia Darragh had reason to be wary. As Watson put it, "She afterwards saw them return, wearied & chagrined." To avoid the least suspicion of her role in transmitting their secrets to the enemy, Darragh remained silent upon the army's reappearance. She was careful to display no interest in where they had been or what they had been doing, especially because she was living cheek by jowl with the top military brass. With headquarters just across the way, British officers were all around her, many of them probably frequenting her store, possibly buying tobacco or stopping by the shop for a glass of spirits. Who knows what her voluble husband might have said to them had he an inkling of what she had done?[23]

The family version of the story provided more insight into this hazardous situation:

> Lydia . . . did not tell her husband the real object of her errand to the country until she thought all danger over. He little knew the part his wife had played in the drama of that eventful night. She feared the least suspicion of his having taken information out of the city might endanger his life and kept her secret. . . . There were many rumors, but she did not dare to ask a question.[24]

This is the point in Lydia's Tale where the narrative builds toward its dramatic climax. The final scene accentuates Lydia Darragh's naiveté about military matters, the idea that her secret information was of momentous import. She knew only what she had experienced; she was not privy to the wider view of events known to generals or, today, to historians. To her understanding, her daring actions seemed to have borne fruit and had a real impact on the military contest's outcome.

For Lydia Darragh and her auditors, events could only have unfolded in one manner. The British failure to surprise Washington could have but one source: Lydia's disclosure of their secret plan. How else could the word have leaked out? More ominously, whom might the British suspect? They reasoned that the plan could only have been unveiled one time—that night in the Darraghs' back room. There the solution must lay. And so, the adjutant general of the British army, the man who had pronounced the plan, must seek the answer. How had they been discovered? According to Lydia's Tale, it did not take long for the adjutant to confront Darragh with the question:

> The next evening, the Adjutant General came in, and requested her to walk up to his room, as he wished to put some questions. She followed him in terror; and when he locked the

> door, and begged her, with an air of mystery, to be seated, she was sure that she was either suspected, or had been betrayed.
>
> He inquired earnestly whether any of her family were up the last night he and the other officer met:—she told him that they all retired at eight o'clock. He observed —"I know you were asleep, for I knocked at your chamber door three times before you heard me:—I am entirely at a loss to imagine who gave General Washington information of our intended attack, unless the walls of the house could speak. When we arrived near White Marsh, we found all their cannon mounted, and the troops prepared to receive us; and we have marched back like a parcel of fools."[25]

Other versions of the tale provide details that Walsh left out, especially about Lydia's fear and her concern that the expression on her face might give her away: "That evening the adjutant came in, & asked Lydia Daragh to walk up to his room, as he had some questions to ask her. She followed him. He locked the door, placed a chair and requested her to be seated. Providently, the candle was behind her or, she said, he need not have said one word; her countenance would have betrayed her. Her hair felt, as though it arose under her cap when he asked her if any of her family was up, the night they last met."[26]

"The General came straightway & asked her into his Room, by candle light, & began solemnly to question her about there being a possibility of any person in her house to listen to & betray secrets. Happily her face was not to the light or it might have betrayed her."[27]

"When nearly dusk an officer came to the house, called her to the council room, and then locked the door. She was so faint she would have fallen if he had not handed her a chair and asked her to be seated. The room was nearly dark, and he could not see the pallor of her face. Then he inquired if any of her family were awake on the night of their last council."[28]

This part of the story can be understood in several ways. There is the appealing resolution, accessible to any listener, wherein the adjutant reaches his own erroneous conclusion about Lydia's innocence. Despite his power and brilliance, the hero escapes and he is confounded.

But this story had a deeper resonance among the Quaker community in which it originally circulated. Friends had a deep-seated belief in Providence, the concept of benevolent divine intervention in human affairs. "Providently," as Hannah Haines put it, the situation was such that Darragh, though in terror, did not give herself away: "the candle was behind her or . . . her countenance would have betrayed her"; "her face was not to the light or it might have betrayed her"; "The room was nearly dark and he could not see the pallor of her face."[29]

The Friends' value of silence also played a role here, but in an ironic sense. By refraining from speech, by carrying out Quaker silence, she allowed her enemy to deceive himself without saying a word or telling a lie. This was certainly deception but accorded well with the common Friends' practice of worldly accommodation, a central tension around which revolved much of Quaker humor.

The adjutant knew something was amiss, a thing that must have happened in the very room where he conducted his interview with her, but he could not put his finger on it. In the absence of rational evidence, he turned to traditional expression in his fatalistic summation, explaining the outcome by use of a variant of the old proverb about unproved suspicions—"the walls have ears."

Another phrase put into the adjutant's mouth, "parcel of fools," was doubly humiliating. It was bad enough to be fooled, but the term *parcel* here is a collective noun normally reserved for a group of inanimate objects gathered together, "a small bundle," in Samuel Johnson's definition. When applied to a group of people it acquired a different meaning, "A number of persons: in contempt," and that is the meaning intended. If spoken by the adjutant, those words were certainly self-deprecating.[30]

But perhaps such contempt was actually on the other side. Could the adjutant general, Nisbet Balfour, have been toying with Lydia Darragh? One of an adjutant's roles was to conduct espionage and counterespionage, a role Balfour is known to have carried out for the British army during the occupation of Philadelphia. As such, he was the person most likely to have been behind the British attempt to spread disinformation about their plans, as seen in the false intelligence about boats being used to help capture the American baggage train in the army's rear. This may well have been the information Darragh conveyed to Charles Craig. In spreading disinformation, it is best to use unwitting people who are convinced of the truth of what they have learned. It is also important to distribute a false message through multiple conduits so the ultimate target of disinformation can corroborate several accounts, making the information seem more genuine.[31]

Could Balfour have deliberately used Lydia Darragh to spread misinformation? He was scornful and distrustful of American "rebels." That

Darragh's son served as an American officer was probably no great secret to him. Telling her to send her family to bed so no one could overhear the secret conference in her back room obviously roused her suspicions. Hannah Haines observed that, "As he had been so particular, her curiosity was excited." Might she have been duped? If so, when the adjutant conducted his menacing interview with her, was he actually laughing up his sleeve? At this remove in time, and without additional information, the possibility cannot be dismissed out of hand.

Chapter 12

The Aftermath of Lydia Darragh's Adventure

A FEW WEEKS AFTER her expedition to Frankford, Lydia Darragh was back on the road, this time on a different kind of errand—a mission of mercy. Despite American efforts to restrict the flow of people into and out of the city, the lines remained porous, and information continually passed in both directions. In late January, word reached Darragh that Benjamin Marshall lay seriously ill at Providence, twenty-five miles up the Schuylkill, just across the river from the American encampment at Valley Forge. Like hundreds of other patriot families, the Marshall brothers had fled to the hinterlands as the British advanced on Philadelphia. The brothers planned to ride out the occupation close to one another, near the Ridge Road, a bit northwest of Matson's Ford, an area where several other revolutionaries waited for the British to depart (if they ever would), including the Darraghs' landlord, Benjamin Loxley and their neighbor, Samuel Wetherill. The location was a full day's march from the British lines, far enough away from the city that residents would have time to flee toward Reading in the event of a sortie in their direction.

Providence must have seemed a safe place to hide. Initially, when Washington's army marched into nearby Valley Forge on December 19, the refugees may have been comforted by their presence, but soon disease began burning through the army, sickening thousands, felling hundreds. Though the danger was grave, Benjamin Marshall opened his home to tend to some of the sick officers. Soon, he too was ill.

Benjamin's brother, Christopher Marshall Jr., wrote their father in Lancaster:

> I am now at Brother Benny's & have been up with him these two last nights past to attend him in his Illness, which I have been anxious to communicate to thee from time to time . . . thou wast before appriz'd by Letters from Charles & Self as well as personally by Dr. Phyle who saw him, of the Situation he was in. . . . Dr. Morgan & Hutchinson who attended him declare it to be the Putrid Fever.[1]

Benjamin's wife, Sarah, seven months pregnant at the time, was exhausted through caring for him when Lydia Darragh got wind of the situation. A compassionate person, Lydia did not always wait to be called, nor, as a nurse, was she deterred by fear of falling ill herself. On learning of Benjamin's condition, she undertook to trudge out to Providence despite the bitter winter weather to lend what aid she could. Given the two armies' rapacious acquisition of horses throughout the area, it is unlikely she could have procured a conveyance to carry her. Instead, she faced a two-day trek along difficult roads alternately muddy or uneven with hard-frozen wheel ruts. She may have been able to shelter for the night at an inn on Ridge Road or to stay with one of the Quaker families around Plymouth Meeting, the halfway point on her journey.

Christopher Jr. briefed his father about Benjamin's condition: "Sister Sally . . . almost constantly with him . . . her Bodily fatigue is much lessened by having Aunt Lydia Darragh here who heard dismal accounts of Sickness amongst us [which] induced her to come out of Town, so that its great Ease to all our minds to have her here, as thou knows she's so tender hearted, skillfull & willing to do any thing about a Sick person."[2]

While under her care, Benjamin experienced a brief rally, a not-uncommon experience in the final stages of death. Shortly after, however, Charles Marshall reported an ominous turn: "Betwixt 10 & 11 o'clock at night . . . instead of his appearing better . . . we were surprized to find that he was considerably worse . . . so that we called up Sister Sally (whom we had a little before perswaded to go to Bed) & sent for Bro Chris & Sister Betsy who had gone over to David Rittenhouse's to lodge . . . we think he cannot survive over this night."[3]

Sadly, he did not; he passed away during the night of January 29, at age thirty-six. Lydia Darragh's kindheartedness strengthened her ties to the Marshall family, and especially those with Benjamin's twelve-year-old daughter, Hannah, who went on to memorialize her in a way that led to lasting fame. How long Darragh stayed with the Marshalls is not clear. Since she was present when Benjamin died and was experienced, she may well have been the person who laid him out for a wake and burial. It being unsafe for the family to venture into the city for a funeral, Benjamin Marshall was initially interred somewhere close to Providence, perhaps at nearby Plymouth Friends Meeting. Records show that the family paid a grave digger twelve shillings on February 12. Once the British departed Philadelphia, Marshall's body was exhumed, brought into town, and reburied in the Friends burial ground at Fourth and Arch Streets.[4]

It may be that while Darragh was visiting Providence, she was able to spend some time with her son, Charles. His regiment was stationed nearby at Valley Forge, and he was on active duty at the time. While she might have remained several days with the Marshall family, she equally well may have hurried back to town. Someone, perhaps Lydia Darragh, brought the news of Benjamin Marshall's death to the Philadelphia Quarterly Meeting within four days of his passing, just as they were taking up the question of his appeal for disownment. The point by then being moot, they desisted.[5]

Midwives were often characterized uncharitably as gossips. But people looked to them for news, an expectation Lydia Darragh readily obliged. During the British occupation, she was frequently abroad, sharing not just tales from the birthing chamber but also carrying news of goings on in the city. When she traipsed back out to Providence in May, the Marshalls were excited to hear rumors of British plans to evacuate the city. "Lydia Darrah came out on the Sixth from Philadelphia. Little news, but that Howe was there then; that the English troops were cutting down very fast the wood in the Jersies opposite Philadelphia for the transports, as also for fear that the Americans might come there and have the advantage of the woods to cover them." Sharing such information might seem innocent, but Darragh was well aware that her information would be sent to Christopher Marshall Sr. and through him would likely reach deeply into patriot councils.[6]

In the meantime, the Darraghs continued to do business out of their shop at the Loxley House. Daughter Ann, only twenty at the time, ventured into commerce with an ad she took out in the *Pennsylvania Ledger* on May 20: "To be Sold by Wholesale, European Goods. Enquire at Ann Darragh's, opposite General Knyphausen, in Second-street." Perhaps Ann Darragh was taking advantage of the departing British merchants who, getting wind of the city's pending evacuation, had begun dumping their goods in large lots. There was not likely to be room aboard the transports to carry their wares back to New York; the military could scarcely accommodate all of the Loyalist civilians clamoring for passage.[7]

Once the British finally abandoned Philadelphia in June, tensions in the region eased somewhat. People once again traveled freely throughout the area. On September 11, while young John Darragh was visiting with the Marshalls at Providence, Benjamin Loxley, who owned property nearby, came out from the city with news that Christopher Sr.'s wife was very ill at Lancaster. "This," Marshall wrote, "gave me great concern and I immediately concluded for home." Arising at four next morning, and despite the rain, he set out in his phaeton, a fast, four-wheeled light carriage. "Kitty [his son Christopher Jr.] went with me and took John Darragh to be as company on his return." Quarters must have been cramped aboard the phaeton, which was likely of the kind with a pull-out side seat that could hold three people. In their hurry, they took the northernly way, via today's Route 23, a fifty-mile journey that led them over French Creek. They had hoped it would be quicker than heading down to the main route between Philadelphia and Lancaster Road. But this turned out to be a rough road: "both we and horses were tired as the roads were so exceedingly hilly and stony, I think longer and worse than the great road is over the Valley Hills." Nevertheless, they completed the trip in thirty hours, even after spending an uncomfortable night at Captain Thomas Reese's tavern at Blue Ball, where the weary but wary travelers "slept in our great coats, stockings, &c., for fear of fleas and bugs." Much to his relief, Christopher found his wife already recovering. Her troublesome young charge, Polly, a vivacious, amorous girl John's age, whipped them up a welcome "breakfast of good coffee, gammon, &c., of which we partook cheerfully, as we had by that time got a good appetite." Then, though they must have been sore from their long and difficult trip, undaunted, Kitty and John set off for Providence again.[8]

Two months after the Battle of Edge Hill, in February 1778, we find Charles Darragh serving in the army but still "on command." By this time, the Pennsylvania Line had been depleted by battle causalities, desertion, and disease. Perhaps Charles's company was by then so small that he was at loose ends, considered to be supernumerary, with no definite assignment. The threat of battle during the winter encampment at Valley Forge was relatively remote, and many officers were allowed to be away from their regiments for extended periods. For some reason, Darragh made a trip to Lancaster in April, possibly on some government business. He turned up at Christopher Marshall's door there on April 26, delivering "one pound fine Green Tea," a gift from Marshall's friend, the storekeeper Grace Hastings, which had been spirited out of the occupied city.[9]

Shortly afterward, Charles Darragh's military career ended. In July 1778, Colonel Walter Stewart's short-lived 13th Pennsylvania Regiment was folded in with the shrunken 2nd Pennsylvania, and Stewart got the command. As with business mergers and consolidations today, this downsizing forced decisions about which people in overlapping positions would stay and which would go. Henry Bicker, colonel of the 2nd, explained that "a new arrangement took place in the army: which displac'd him from his command, and he was constrained for the general good to retire from service with many deserving Officers." Details are sparse. We only know that Charles Darragh was one of those listed as supernumerary—officers whose service was no longer needed. It is possible that an outburst of bad behavior at an inopportune moment, just a month before, influenced the choice that cut Darragh from the rolls.[10]

A passage in Washington's General Orders for June 18, 1778, as the army prepared to leave Valley Forge, touches on the incident:

> At a General Court-Martial June 15th 1778—Coll Livingston President—Captain Bowen of 9th Pennsylvania Regt Lieutenants

> Darrah and Pursill of the 2nd Pennsylvania Regiment, tried 1st—for entering the Encampment of the 3rd Pennsylvania Regiment in a riotous and mutinous manner.
> 2ndly—for attempting to enter Coll Craige's house between the hours of twelve and one in the morning of the 4th of June instant with drawn swords.
> The Court are unanimously of Opinion that they are not guilty of the Charges exhibited against them and do acquit them with honor.
> The Commander in Chief confirms the opinion of the Court.[11]

We may never know exactly what took place, or why three experienced and evidently honorable officers were incensed enough to draw their swords. Were they pursuing someone who took refuge in Colonel Thomas Craig's residence? Possibly. Were they angry with Craig or members of his organization, the 3rd Pennsylvania Regiment, for some reason? The men were lucky to have gotten off without serious consequences. In a squabble the previous November, for instance, an enraged John Eager Howard, then a major, bared his blade and cut a fellow officer. He was convicted of aiding and abetting a riot in camp. In any event, the other two officers charged along with Darragh remained in the army; Charles did not.[12]

The Colonel Craig in question was the same man whom legend has confused as the officer to whom Lydia Darragh divulged her secret in Lydia's Tale. As we have seen, Lydia actually communicated with Charles Craig, Thomas's, younger brother. It is fortunate that the three interlopers did not actually end up in a brawl with Thomas Craig when they invaded his quarters in the night. Courageous in a fight, he had personally led the storming of Fort Durkee in the Wyoming Valley during the First Pennamite War in 1770. He was also hot-tempered and violent, especially when in his cups. A few years after this confrontation with Charles Darragh, he very publicly murdered a servant in a drunken rage at City Tavern by running the man through with his sword, a crime hushed up and ignored. Such was the clout wielded by prominent officers in Pennsylvania at this time that the powers that be never charged him.[13]

Perhaps Charles Darragh could have found a berth with another unit. That he did not do so suggests he did not mind cutting his service short. After leaving the army, Darragh remained in the Philadelphia area for a number of years. His military service was not yet at an end. Indeed, he remained active with the fledgling nation's military affairs in a variety of ways. Even though he had already served in the army, because he remained an eligible male, he was enrolled in the Pennsylvania Militia. Given his experience as clerk to Commodore Seymour, it is not surprising to learn that he served as quartermaster for one of the Philadelphia militia battalions, commanded by Major David Reese in 1781.[14]

Charles Darragh evidently had access to enough capital to make an investment in the brig *Holker*, a ship owned by Blair McClenachan, whom Darragh had known since a boy when living across the street from him. McClenachan was married to Ann Darragh, who may have been Charles's aunt, or possibly a cousin. This deal was no ordinary maritime venture, risky enough as such things were, but a military project—a dangerous, but potentially lucrative proposition. Charles helped put up a bond of $10,000 for the ship, which had been granted a letter of marque. This was a government license that authorized a private vessel, known as a privateer, to attack and capture British shipping. The bond was meant to ensure legal behavior by the ship's officers and crew. When initially fitted out, *Holker* carried ten guns and a small crew of thirty-five men. On its maiden voyage, in April 1779, the *Holker* sailed to St. Eustatius with a light cargo. Returning, it captured a prize off the Delaware Capes, the snow *Friendship*, bound from Georgia for British-occupied New York, and brought it into Egg Harbor, where the cargo was condemned and sold.[15]

McClenachan's and Darragh's profits from this voyage were endangered, however, when the *Holker's* captain, George Geddes, freed the *Friendship's* crew and signed them aboard his own ship in a seeming violation of Congress's orders concerning prizes. Pennsylvania's Supreme Executive Council ordered the $10,000 bond prosecuted, threatening McClenaghan and Darragh with a serious loss. In the event, Geddes argued successfully that since the crew were Americans, not British seamen, he was entitled to sign them to crew the *Holker*. The council agreed but ordered him to turn over the ship's mate and master, presumably Britons, to the deputy commissary of prisoners. Though we don't know what percentage of the bond Charles had advanced, presumably he made a tidy sum on his investment. He did not underwrite the *Holker*'s next recorded bond, in November 1779. Having nearly lost his stake, he may have recognized the precarity of such a gamble, preferring to quit while he was ahead.[16]

Charles Darragh was a promising young man of good standing in his community. On August 24, 1779, he was accepted as a member of Masonic Lodge No. 4 in Philadelphia. Well educated by his father, he was not only highly literate but was a skilled accountant. At some point, he went to work for the Marshall brothers, ten to fifteen years his senior, functioning much as he had for Commodore Seymour.[17]

His was not the station of a regular employee but rather that of a trusted confidante. Christopher Marshall Sr. frequently mentioned breakfasting or dining with Charles Darragh at his son's house. When Christopher Marshall Jr.'s young daughter, Betsey, grew ill, she was visited by Lydia Darragh, then sent to stay with another woman referred to as Nurse Warner, who could care for her. Charles Darragh was periodically sent to check on Betsey's condition. He was also entrusted with taking the Marshalls' cash payments to the tax collector.[18]

Perhaps trading on his familiarity with the druggist trade, Charles Darragh had entered into some kind of business relationship with two men from New Jersey, Joseph and Samuel Shober, who opened stores in Philadelphia in 1783. That year, Joseph Shober began selling imported goods from East and West India, while Samuel Shober went into the apothecary business, also selling paint and glass, in direct competition with Christopher Marshall's sons. How the Marshall family may have taken Charles Darragh's involvement with another druggist was not revealed in Christopher Marshall's diary. Samuel Shober ran frequent ads in the Philadelphia newspapers through March 1785, but by that May he had become insolvent. Both he and Joseph were jailed as debtors, their goods and properties gradually sold off over the next six years to satisfy their liabilities. Charles Darragh was somehow caught up in the Shobers' financial crisis. He himself became insolvent at that time. He was one of seventy-two Philadelphians who applied to the Court of Common Pleas for relief under the Insolvent Act and who, in June 1785, had their debts discharged. With this discharge, Charles's business problems might seem to have been resolved, but, as his mother's will and his subsequent transactions were to reveal, threats from these financial difficulties continued to hang over his head.[19]

After the British evacuated Philadelphia, the revolutionaries returned to the devastated city to begin the process of healing. But life did not return to its former placid channels. The political rift between Whigs and Tories was exacerbated by the damage that had been done to person and property during the occupation. Someone had to pay. Pennsylvania's government, centered in the city, sought vengeance against those Loyalists who had not cleared out with the departing army. Many who had supported the British administration were accused of treason and were subject to arrest, imprisonment, prosecution, and confiscation of property and even execution.

The Religious Society of Friends had dominated public life in Pennsylvania during its early years, but their policy of religious tolerance, and the colony's rapid prosperity, attracted many non-Quakers, gradually shifting the balance of population by the mid-1750s. Throughout the eighteenth century, animosity had grown against the Quakers, who held the reins of political and economic power. With the onset of the French and Indian War, frontier inhabitants, predominantly Presbyterian, resented Friends' pacifist stand in the Pennsylvania Assembly, which they felt left them to defend their settlements against Indian attacks without military aid. The ensuing struggle for power weakened the Quakers' grip, as many of them chose to withdraw from active involvement in governance. That hostility was magnified with the coming of the Revolution, when radical patriots seized control of the government. The British occupation had interrupted the ascendant faction's *sotto voce* program of settling old political scores with the city's once-powerful Quakers. In the minds of those back in power again, the actions of Friends who had collaborated with the British confirmed that disaffected Quakers were not merely neutral, but disloyal.

The most notable Friends to be tried for treason were a miller, John Roberts, who had served as a guide for a British foraging expedition, and Abraham Carlile, who had supervised passage through the gates at the head of Front Street during the occupation. Along with several others accused of treason against the state, these two men, who had remained in Philadelphia after the evacuation, were arrested and tried before Pennsylvania's Supreme Court in September 1778. They were convicted, and Pennsylvania Chief Justice Thomas McKean decreed a harsh punishment for each man: "Judgement—that he be hanged by the neck till he be dead."

Few believed the extreme sentence would actually be carried out. Hundreds of people signed petitions to spare the men's lives. Indeed, two of the three judges and twenty-two of the twenty-four jurors in the cases petitioned Pennsylvania's Supreme Executive Council for mercy, but they didn't reckon with the vengeful attitude of the revolutionary leaders. Working behind the scenes, George Bryan, acting president of the council, and Joseph Reed, who had prosecuted the cases, managed to avoid a stay of execution. The government unrelenting, however, late on the morning of November 4, Carlile and Roberts were led from jail to the gallows erected on the commons. Overseers of justice at this time often contrived to issue a dramatic last-minute pardon to inspire the guilty person to change his ways, but no such reprieve arrived. Instead, at noon, before a large crowd, the sentence was carried out.[20]

Shocking though it had been, even to its perpetrators, the execution of Abraham Carlile and John Roberts by no means cooled Pennsylvania patriots' ardor for the political persecution of Friends. Samuel Rowland Fisher's was a particularly egregious case of harassment, and it seems that William Darragh, though a Quaker himself, may have colluded in it. Darragh was among those Friends known to have sided with the revolutionaries. If the details in Fisher's account are true, and though uncorroborated there is no reason to doubt them, Darragh was one of those "warm people" who supported the American cause vociferously.[21]

Early in 1779, just months after the executions, Fisher ran afoul of some powerful men running the state's justice system. It seems he sent a letter across the lines to a brother, Jabez Maud Fisher in New York. The letter was intercepted. Though innocent of political intent, Pennsylvania authorities viewed it as treasonous, because it mentioned the precarious economic situation in the state, particularly the high prices and depreciated Continental money. This information was hardly a secret, but Fisher's disdain for the current rulers rankled. Fisher had already suffered injustice at the hands of radical Pennsylvanians—he was one of the Quakers who had been exiled to Virginia in 1777, along with two of his brothers, Thomas and Miers, for refusing to take an oath of allegiance to the new government. Incidentally, the letter also mentioned that in another instance of perceived injustice, Thomas Eddy had been "taken up in Jersey." The authorities did not immediately arrest Fisher—the grounds were not that serious. Rather, an incident of personal pique prompted them to go after him, much to their regret, as it turned out, for Samuel Rowland Fisher proved to be a very difficult person.

Throughout the conflict, the Friends Meeting had routinely investigated and disciplined any of its members known to have supported the war in any way, whether they had borne arms or even simply acknowledged the revolutionaries' legitimacy by such tokens as paying militia fines in lieu of serving. One day, Friends Thomas Fisher and John James came to treat with Timothy Matlack's nineteen-year-old son, William, for "having taken Arms." Timothy Matlack had been disowned by the meeting in 1765 for bankruptcy. The father, by now exasperated by the frequent visits to his son, lost his temper. Fisher's brother Samuel described what happened next. "He gave them some little very abusive language & immediately taking up a Hickory Walking Stick, way lay'd them in the passage, gave them many hard blows over the head & shoulders, following them some distance in the street till he had broken his stick."[22]

Incensed, Matlack demanded that authorities take action against the troublesome and supposedly disloyal Fishers. The same day, Chief Justice McKean swore out a warrant, and the sheriff was sent to arrest Thomas Fisher's brother, Samuel, on a charge of treason connected to the suspicious letter. Thus began a long test of wills between the Pennsylvania government and Samuel Rowland Fisher. Convinced of his own rectitude, Fisher proved to be so thoroughly intransigent that he remained in jail, despite all friends, family and, indeed, the Pennsylvania courts could do to convince him to make the smallest concession to be released. He insisted that since he had done nothing wrong, he would accept nothing but his unconditional release. But he would not ask to be freed, because he refused to recognize the authority of those who had imprisoned him, referring to the revolutionary government and its institutions frequently as "so called," using a long-standing Quaker term that questioned the legitimacy of worldly conventions. "I am suffering for the Testimony of Truth," he argued, though he also mentioned another, political motivation: "I wish to keep my Fidelity to the King and Government inviolate."[23]

One of those who came to visit him in jail was Mary Eddy, who had been contacted by the British commissary general of naval prisoners asking if he might seek Fisher's exchange for an American prisoner. Fisher refused, as she had predicted he would. He believed that Mary Eddy's brother, William Darragh, had been among those who had threatened "those called Magistrates . . . because they appear'd to hesitate to pass sentence on me & send me to Gaol." Fisher's health deteriorated as the months wore on, and he made certain that people were aware of his declining condition. Without the least sign of yielding on the martyr's part, even those who had been involved in his incarceration began to lobby for his freedom. In July 1781, he reported with a sense of vindication that the Free Quakers—a group of Friends who sided actively with the rebellion—were planning to send a petition to Joseph Reed and his associates asking for his release. He took occasion to voice his low opinion of his former rival, William Darragh, whose fledgling snuff business his family had stifled: "And my Brother Thomas informed me that Wm. Darragh stopt him in the Street & said 'Thy Brother Sammy will be out of Goal soon, for we are sending a petition to the Council on his account.' I should not have thought it worth mentioning any thing about such a talkative boisterous man, formerly very low in the opinion of his fellow citizens."[24]

Fisher's extreme inflexibility proved an embarrassment to Philadelphia's Friends, who felt their reputation was being held up to public ridicule. To their relief, the Pennsylvania government finally threw up its hands and released Fisher after two years of incarceration. When the jailer, John Reynolds, finally came to inform him of his release, the hardheaded victor reported their exchange: "'You may get ready to go home as soon as you please, for I have seen the Vice-President & he informed me there is a Pardon ordered to be drawn out for you.' I only said Pardon, Pardon, upon which Reynolds said, 'Oh, I suppose it is a discharge for you & I am very glad of it.'"[25]

Pennsylvania's radicals were glad to get stubborn Samuel Fisher off their minds and consciences. Nonetheless, they continued their efforts to bring all into line with their new government, the wealthy as well as those of the lower sort. In 1782, the Pennsylvania Assembly passed an act to punish any who abetted escaping prisoners of war. As we saw earlier in the case of William Barrington, loss of their captives was a serious problem for the revolutionaries, who forfeited a bargaining chip with each escape. Perhaps ill advisedly, the act provided that half the fines assessed to offenders would go to those who prosecuted them. It was not long before a group of enterprising officers hatched a scheme to punish those aiding escapees while at the same time lining their own pockets, and not necessarily in that order of concern. Using three imprisoned British officers as bait, General Moses Hazen, responsible for the prison camp at Lancaster, ran a sting operation in which he had men pretend to be escapees needing help. Those who gave them food, shelter, or directions were arrested and fined £50 for each escapee. If the accused could not raise £150, as was often the case, they were to be whipped with thirty-nine lashes for each offense.[26]

One kind-hearted lady who fell victim to the ruse was Rachel Hammer of Philadelphia County. The mother of four small children, with a sick husband at home, she was approached by the three soldiers, who probably offered payment for her assistance. The trap sprung, she was tried and convicted. Unable to pay £150, she was sentenced to be flogged—139 lashes in all. When her plight came to the attention of Christopher Marshall, however, he intervened. A patriot in high standing with the men of the court and the state government, he submitted a petition for clemency on her behalf. Marshall went to see the judges and was able to sway Chief Justice McKean, but not fiery George Bryan. Undaunted, he went instead to the Pennsylvania State House to plead before the president and council for mercy, where he was more successful. He noted the happy outcome: "Council debated but forgave her. She greatly rejoiced."[27]

Soon enough, the problem of escaping prisoners abated. As part of the pending settlement with Great Britain, those British prisoners of war held in Pennsylvania were marched under guard to New York. Christopher Marshall watched 1,100 of them pass through the city one day in May 1783, accompanied by an American band derisively playing "Yankee Doodle." The following day, wagons carrying as many as five hundred of the prisoners' wives and children arrived in town, their journey north interrupted by a brief hailstorm so intense it shattered windows and even killed a cow. Then, off to the north and a better situation—or, at least, freedom.[28]

By 1780, the British war effort had moved south. In May, the city of Charleston and its five thousand defenders surrendered to Henry Clinton's army after a six-week siege, a serious blow to the Americans' capability and morale. A few weeks later, with the city of Philadelphia firmly within the patriots' grip, the *Pennsylvania Packet* reported an unusual development:

> Philadelphia, June 16.
> Thirty-six Ladies of this city have undertaken to solicit contributions from their sex, as an extraordinary bounty for our soldiery, and dividing the city into ten wards, have made their applications from house to house with great success, almost everyone offering with the greatest cheerfulness, their proportion, according to their circumstances and their ability.[29]

These activities marked just how extraordinary and socially volatile this revolutionary period had become. Such actions would previously have been thought a violation of the expectation of women's roles. The idea that women, especially those of high social standing, would undertake to personally solicit contributions door to door was a remarkable demonstration of both patriotism and freedom. They were inspired and led by Esther DeBerdt Reed, wife of Joseph Reed, by this time president of Pennsylvania's Supreme Executive Council, effectively the state's governor. She initiated the project to provide funds directly to soldiers serving in the American army.[30]

Four ladies, including the wives of Chief Justice Thomas McKean and financier Robert Morris, took on the task of visiting the houses between Spruce and Pine Streets. It is difficult to discern the order of their visits. Indeed, several of those persons they collected from do not seem to have actually lived within the bounds of their assigned area. The contributions came in a bewildering variety of currencies: Portuguese half joes and moidores, French louisdores (louis d'or), Spanish pistoles and pistreens, Dutch silver dollars, English guineas, shillings, and coppers. Not surprisingly, however, the bulk of the money came in the form of Continental dollars, viewed realistically even by patriots as unstable and liable to devaluation. Ironically, in terms of real value, a contribution in foreign gold or silver coins was actually a greater patriotic gesture than giving American money.[31]

The ladies assigned to the Spruce to Pine neighborhood collected funds amounting to between $12,800 and $14,300. They tried to visit every house, and if men answered the door, they did not hesitate to collect from them in their wives' names. They even visited taverns and, perhaps more surprising yet, the homes of Quakers. Though some felt the Quakers would be likely to support a charitable project, their effort did not meet with large success among Friends. However, among the contributors was one Friend, "Mrs. Darrah," who gave them 100 Continental dollars, about the median contribution for her area. This was yet another indication that Lydia Darragh was willing to buck the Meeting in support of the Revolution.

The Philadelphia project's success led to similar collections in other parts of Pennsylvania, New Jersey, Maryland, and Virginia. The total amount collected was thought to be enough for a two-dollar bounty to be put straight into soldiers' pockets. But though the original intent had been to give the money directly to soldiers, to spend as they would,

George Washington, to whom the money was actually sent, thought that would produce more harm than good. In particular, he felt the men would likely spend it on drink. Instead, he proposed that the funds be spent to buy shirts. After some wrangling, the ladies agreed and took up the task of buying linen and making the shirts themselves. To demonstrate their personal support for the soldiers, each shirt bore the name of the woman who had made it. In addition to the much-needed article of clothing, that personal touch likely provided a boost for at least some of the men's morale.[32]

The Pennsylvania government was not the only entity to settle scores in the wake of the British evacuation. While Friends claimed the moral high ground in their dispute with the revolutionaries, they retaliated in their own way. As the threat to Philadelphia receded, the Quaker establishment disowned many members who had been active partisans during the war. In 1781, the Philadelphia Quarterly Meeting, the central Friends establishment, sometimes referred to as the Arch Street Meeting, dealt with at least forty-four cases requiring inquiry, "loving treatment," and, potentially, disownment. Twenty-two of those cases were initiated that year, the others being continued from prior years.[33]

In 1772, to ease crowding at meetings for worship, Friends had established two subordinate local Monthly Meetings in the city, known as the Northern and Southern Districts, with Walnut Street as the dividing line. These district meetings, though populous, often deferred to superior knowledge and guidance of their parent meeting, especially in matters of discipline. Further, many of the members whose cases arose during this time had migrated back and forth across the district boundaries, sometimes without having secured a Certificate of Removal recommending their membership to the meeting within whose jurisdiction they resided. The upshot was that the Quarterly Meeting, because of its centrality and de facto authority, generally took on cases that originated in, or should have been within the purview of, the district meetings.

The process of forcible separation from the Society of Friends was anything but anonymous or impersonal. Disciplinary proceedings began with some observation of wrongdoing on the part of a member. This information generally arose in a Preparative Meeting that essentially created the agenda for the Meeting for Business. Often, the Preparative Meeting would discuss allegations of impropriety before sending a team of overseers to inquire about their accuracy. If warranted, those appointed to inquire might also begin treating with accused persons to get them to acknowledge their errors and change their behavior.

If the infractions were serious, or the person was reluctant to admit their faults, the case would then be brought before the Business Meeting, where the task of further investigation and persuasion would be assigned to an ad hoc committee of two trusted members. They were responsible for personally visiting the accused, with whom they would "treat lovingly" to help them recognize their deviation from good order. If those assigned were unable to reach the person, the case would be continued until contact could be made. Depending on the team's sense of progress in bringing the person to an understanding of wrongdoing, a case might also be continued from month to month.

Cases could be resolved in two ways. A person could submit a written acknowledgment of error with a promise to reform, to be read personally before the meeting. If the person was judged to be sincere, and the prospect of reform seemed likely, the meeting would accept the acknowledgment. If they were skeptical of the person's sincerity or ability to reform, they might take the case under advisement for further treatment with the individual. Team members who perceived a possibility of change on the part of the subject were given free latitude to continue meeting with the person. Such advising could go on for months, or even years, before the meeting was satisfied.

If the subject of discipline rejected valid charges outright, or justified their behavior for too long a time, the team would be directed to draft a disownment essay, testifying to the person's disunity with the meeting. That testimony would be delivered to the person, noting their right to appeal the decision to the Quarterly Meeting. The team would then report back to the meeting that the testimony had been delivered and how the person reacted.

Sometimes, disownment could follow a more streamlined process, especially in cases of "breach of discipline in marriage." Friends practiced endogamy—marriage with non-Quakers was forbidden—and followed a strict marriage process. Couples would appear twice before the Women's Meeting for Business to announce their intentions to marry and their parents' consent. The couple was assigned two capable Friends to ascertain their clearness about what it meant to marry as a Quaker and to ensure they were clear of other entanglements or obstacles, such as previous engagements, unchaste behavior, or children born out of wedlock.

Problems frequently arose when young people developed romantic relationships with non-Quakers. If the prospective partner worked to become a "convinced" Friend, a process that might take several months, all would be well. But when someone seemed headed toward deviation by marrying outside of the meeting, Friends would counsel the individual. If that person persisted, the case was brought to the Meeting for Business, which could authorize a testimony disowning the person immediately, because they had already been treated with. While such testimonies of disownment followed a general format, the writers used their own words rather than following a precise prescription. Because Friends did not have a codified doctrine but experienced the word of God individually, each might express things somewhat differently.

Records for the Philadelphia Monthly Meeting do not shed light on the conversations that took place when an accusation was made. Nor do they go into much detail, beyond a simple charge or charges, about the nature of an individual's deviation. Friends were concerned to maintain decorum and to avoid descending into "gossip and backbiting" in such matters. Indeed, one of the queries that Monthly Meetings responded to several times a year addressed the need to "discourage Tale-bearing and the spreading of evil Reports." When deviant behavior was discussed, it is clear that despite good intentions, the conversations could verge on gossip. This apparently happened sometimes when multiple members of the same family might come under scrutiny at the same time but for different transgressions. The multiple disownments of the Biddle and Darragh families are cases in point.[34]

In March 1775, the Friends began disciplinary action against Owen Biddle for "joining with & promoting measures pursued by the People for asserting their civil privileges in such manner as are inconsistent with our peaceable profession & principles." His brother Clement was disowned the next year for serving in the patriot military establishment. When their sister, Ann Biddle, married high-ranking rebel officer James Wilkinson at Episcopalian Christ Church on November 12, 1778, the meeting lost no time taking action against her. On November 27, it began disciplining Ann and her sister Lydia, proceeding quickly to disownment by January 29. While the Friends tried to abstain from gossip, such serial accusations might still appear in that light. Allegations against one family member seem to have led directly to claims about another. Testimonies against the Biddle sisters accused them of frequenting "places of dancing and diversion" as well as "dress, address and deportment . . . inconsistent with our religious profession." The charge that Ann Biddle "accomplished her marriage with a man who is not in membership with us before an hireling priest" appears only after citing "those vain and irreligious practices." Ann, referred to by her husband as a "sprightly Quakeress," was notorious for her fashionable appearance. While her beauty may not have aroused jealousy in the bosom of the Women's Meeting, her scandalous behavior and appearance certainly required repudiation. That her sister was dragged into the pious conversation is suggestive.[35]

In March 1781, the Philadelphia Monthly Meeting began pushing Lydia Darragh and her family out of the Society of Friends. It started by examining Charles Darragh's behavior, well after the fact. He had been commissioned an officer on February 5, 1777, and had worked for Pennsylvania's naval establishment the previous fall. The meeting had been zealous in pursuing cases of military service that contradicted the Testimony against War, addressing deviations quickly. But it was not until four years later that the meeting expressed concern about Charles Darragh. Why the long delay? More importantly, what finally turned the meeting's attention to him so long after his transgression?

Once proceedings were initiated, Friends were sent to talk with Charles Darragh and seek acknowledgement of his error, but to no avail. In conversation with them, Darragh disavowed his traditional Quaker faith. Disownment followed quickly, the whole process taking less than a month:

> Charles Darragh of this City, having been reputed a Member, has been treated with for engaging in matters of a Warlike Nature, but disclaiming a Right amongst us, the Meeting judges it expedient to testify that we do not esteem him as a Member of our Religious Society. And Thomas Rogers & James Whiteall are appointed to deliver him a Copy of this Minute.

On June 29, the meeting reported "that a Copy of the minute, respecting the right of Membership of Charles Darragh, has been delivered to him, & that he acquiesced therewith."[36]

The meeting next took action against Ann Darragh for marrying out of meeting. In her case, the Monthly Meeting also appeared to expedite its actions. She had wed James Darrah, who does not appear to have been a Quaker, on January 27, 1781. The couple were married outside the meeting by a minister, "an hireling Priest" in the language of Friends. Three months later, on April 27, the same day it disowned her brother, Charles, the Women's Meeting took exception to Ann's marriage:

> This meeting being informed that Ann Darrow hath contrary to a known Rule of our Discipline accomplished her Marriage before a Priest, without the Consent of her parents, notwithstanding she was cautioned against such a procedure. Her Case is therefore sent to the Men's meeting for further proceeding agreeable to the direction of our Discipline.[37]

The Men's Meeting wasted no time in disowning Ann. The very same afternoon, it decreed: "Ann Darragh, who has been reputed a Member, has accomplished her Marriage before an hireling Priest for which breach of our Discipline we are lead to testify that we do not esteem her as a Member of our Religious Society."[38]

Two members of the Women's Meeting were appointed to deliver the letter disowning Ann, but they hesitated initially, feeling the timing indelicate, tenderly noting "that they were prevented delivering it by the Death of her Husband." Tactfully, they waited a month before completing their task, reporting that Ann "informed them it was what she expected & appeared satisfied."[39]

Marriages such as Ann Darragh's were commonly grounds for disownment, but usually the meeting sent two members to treat with the person, requesting an acknowledgment of the fault and a promise to reform. Depending on the likelihood of contrition, this process could require several visits over a period of months. In Ann's case, the Women's Meeting appears to have gotten wind of her planned marriage beforehand and advised her against it, though there is no record that she had formally announced her intention. But other cases were handled differently.

For example, Mary Goshart was first cited in February 1780 for "breach of discipline in the accomplishment of her marriage," the same offense committed by Ann Darragh. But in this case, they were willing to consider the possibility of reform. Friends appointed to treat with

Goshart reported that "she took kindly the Care of frds., appeared in a tender disposition on the occasion, and gave expectation of offering an acknowledgement to the meeting in some future time." Perhaps the fact that Ann Darragh had been "cautioned against such a procedure" beforehand precipitated the rush to judgment on April 27. But given her brother's disownment the same day, the coincidence of timing is suspect, especially because shortly afterward, the meeting began proceedings against their mother.[40]

Next in line for dismissal was Lydia Darragh, and perhaps she was the real target in the first place. The case against her began with a seemingly innocent pretext. It seemed she had been missed at Meetings for Worship in the Southern District. Perhaps, they argued disingenuously, she did not realize that since her move to South Second Street in 1777, she was actually a member of the Southern District Meeting? Perhaps she required a Minute of Recommendation that formally reassigned her from the Northern District? Perhaps.

The meetinghouse was just around the corner from the Darragh residence, on the south side of Pine Street, between Front and Second, a fairly obvious landmark in the immediate vicinity. Neighboring Friends must have filtered past Lydia Darragh's house each First Day morning on their way to worship there. In case Lydia had somehow missed this, two women were appointed "to make inquiry respecting Lydia Daragh wife of William Daragh, who hath for sometime past resided within the limits of the Mo: Meeting of the Southern District, in order that she may be recommended" for an official notification of her reassignment.[41]

Since the flap about his own Certificate of Removal in 1763, William Darragh had never become an actual member of Philadelphia Meeting. Though he had probably attended Meetings for Worship, he was not part of the meeting's business establishment, so his behavior did not come under their purview. Yet the Women's Meeting still felt it necessary to identify Lydia through her wayward husband. Their inquiry resulted in further action.

On July 27, the meeting took a somewhat unusual, unilateral step. Immediately following announcement of the delivery of Ann Darragh's testimony of disownment, the women addressed the next piece of business on their agenda: "Minutes of removal were produced, read & signed. Viz. One to the monthly meeting for the southern District for Joseph Baker his Wife Esther & their Children Rachel, Esther, Samuel & Elizabeth, likewise one to the same meeting on behalf of Lydia Darragh."

While the Bakers had formally requested removal to the Southern District, the women kindly issued a minute of recommendation "on *behalf* of Lydia Darragh." She had not requested one. Nor did that minute include the names of her three minor children, who had yet to be disowned.[42]

What was going on here? Were these three supposedly separate but sequential actions by Philadelphia Meeting actually the product of some animus, of "tale bearing and evil reports," "gossip and backbiting," in Meetings for Business? What could Lydia Darragh and her family have done to attract such attention?

Throughout the troubled Revolutionary period, the number of people disowned by Philadelphia Friends continued to grow, in particular those who had been disowned for military service or for taking sides in the worldly conflict by serving the patriot government. They had been disowned specifically because they were "friends to the present revolution." Many felt that their "disunity" with mainstream Friends was a matter of conscience rather than religious doctrine. Though technically they were still permitted to attend Meeting for Worship, such attendance would certainly have been awkward and emotionally painful. Yet most of those disowned had never renounced their faith; they still yearned for spiritual nourishment and felt sorrow that this important aspect of their lives had been denied them.

Distressed at being unable to join in weekly religious services, several disowned Quakers began to meet for worship among themselves. The clerk of this ad hoc assembly was a merchant named Samuel Wetherill, who had been disowned in 1779 for his activities supporting the Revolution. He lived directly across Pine Street from the Southern District meetinghouse. It was in his house that this group of outcasts began their meetings. Each First Day, several of these pariahs could be seen gathering for worship, no longer lone exiles but organized and defiant. It was a move directly out of the Quaker playbook of quiet activism intended to show the meeting that these people refused to be shorn of their birthright over matters of conscience.

On February 20, 1781, they conducted a formal Meeting for Business to "consider the propriety of establishing a religious society, separate from the Society of Friends, upon their fundamental principles." Thus was established The Religious Society of Free Quakers, modeled on orthodox Friends' beliefs and practice. Though not yet disowned, perhaps William and Lydia Darragh could see the writing on the wall and aligned themselves in sympathy with the splinter group. That the Philadelphia Society of Friends began moving against the Darragh family that March was no accident. Women's Meeting members knew perfectly well why Lydia Darragh was not attending the meetings of the Southern District but were unwilling to say as much in their written records.[43]

With the rise of the Free Quakers, the meeting's elders, formerly complacent in their power and rectitude, suddenly found the very foundation of their moral and social superiority eroding. The upstarts posed a threat to the Quaker establishment in several ways. If disowned members had another way to worship collectively, the penalty of disownment lost its force. Further, an alternative religious society with a more open approach to its members' nonconformity might draw adherents away from the existing meetings. Coming at a time of Friends' increased emphasis on the evils of slavery, the very name this group chose created an insulting contrast implying that regular Quakers followed their religion's dicta in a slavish manner. But perhaps worst of all was the dissidents' extraordinary argument that they possessed residual rights to the physical property and meetinghouses, the construction and maintenance of which, for generations, they and their families had funded.

On July 9, the new Society of Free Quakers published a broadside challenging the disownment process and the Philadelphia Meeting's legal right to exclude members from sharing in its most tangible assets:

> The property of that society of which we and you were once joint members, is far from being inconsiderable, and we have done nothing which can afford even a pretension of our having forfeited our right therein. . . . As a place for holding our meetings for worship, and meetings for business relative to the society is become necessary for us, since you have separated yourselves from us, by testifying against us, and thereby rendering it highly improper for us to appear among you, as one people, at your meetings, we think it proper for us to use, apart from you, one of the houses built by friends in this city for those purposes.

While they requested an amicable discussion about which meetinghouse they could appropriate, they were peremptory in their statement about the burying ground: "We also mean to use the burial ground, whenever the occasion shall require it: For, however the living may contend, surely the dead may lie peaceably together."[44]

At the same time in late July that Friends began their proceedings against Lydia Darragh, delegations of Free Quakers visited various Friends' meetings. They sat through the Meetings for Worship, their objectionable presence quietly noted, hoping to deliver their demands, but were asked to "walk out" of the meetinghouses before the Meeting for Business began. The Philadelphia Meeting declined to read the representation, refusing even to record a minute acknowledging its receipt. After repeated evasions by the meetings' clerks, Free Quaker Timothy Matlack, the man who had beaten Thomas Fisher with his stick, called on James Pemberton, clerk of the Yearly Meeting, which oversaw the other meetings. Dispensing with decorum, Pemberton told Matlack, "The answer I am directed to make is short and I shall endeavour to deliver it in the very words in which I received it," adding, "it was not fit to be read, and this is all the answer I have to give."[45]

Stonewalled by the Friends Meeting and receiving no response, the Free Quakers set up a committee to draft a petition to the Pennsylvania Assembly to force the meetings to share their property, appointing William Darragh as one of its members. In the end, the assembly did not see it as within its purview to legislate on religious disputes. The Free Quakers finally decided to buy a piece of property and build their own meetinghouse, which was constructed in 1783 at the southwest corner of Fifth and Arch Streets. It took them a number of years to acquire a suitable piece of ground for their own cemetery, however, and they were permitted to continue burying their dead with the other Friends in the Arch Street Meeting House burial ground.[46]

Lydia Darragh's disownment played out against the backdrop of the Free Quaker movement. By "recommending" her transfer, Friends Meeting effectively challenged her to declare her allegiance. It took some time and some back and forth, but eventually Philadelphia Monthly Meeting recorded the outcome of this polite confrontation:

> Our Women Friends returned the Certificate given for Lydia Darragh in the 7th Mo. 1781, and reported that Lydia could not be prevailed with to attend the Mo Meeting of the So District to which it is directed, and also, that she has discovered a disunion

> with Friends by neglecting to attend our religious Meetings for Divine Worship and joining with a Number of Persons, associated under pretence of religious Duty, so far as to attend their Meetings; on considering her Circumstance Friends are of the Judgement it would be well to visit her from this Meeting, to which Isaac Lane and James Cresson are nominated.[47]

Lydia Darragh was a popular midwife and nurse. Her intimate involvement in the life of the female community was highly valued. That value was attested when the Women's Meeting chose to stand aside, at least partly, from the disownment decision. They wanted to leave the door open for her return, or at least for continued good relationships. Tempering the sterner judgment of the Men's Meeting, the Women's Meeting expressed a hope that Darragh might come back to the fold: "Our women Friends being desirous of some addition to the Conclusion respecting Lydia Darragh the following expressions were now agreed to be added thereunto—'nevertheless it is our desire she may become duly sensible thereof and qualified for restoration into religious Membership with us.'"[48]

This wish for reformation and reinstatement was a common part of most disownments. The fact that the Men's Meeting had curtly left it out in Lydia Darragh's case says much about how seriously they regarded the threat presented by the Free Quakers.

Lydia Darragh became an active member of the Free Quakers, as did her daughters and her youngest son, William. The Society attempted to extend its reach and form common cause by contacting other dissident organizations of outcast Friends. When they sent an epistle to a similar group in New England, the members signed their names to the letter. Echoing her Aunt Frances Barrington's assertive forthrightness, Lydia Darragh placed her signature at the very top of the women's column.[49]

Philadelphia Meeting was not quite done with the Darraghs, however. In 1787, it sent two members to treat with John Darragh for engaging in military exercises. Exactly when and in what capacity he served in the military is unclear. Because he was born in 1763, it is possible he performed military service during the Revolutionary War. He would have turned eighteen in December 1781, and though the fighting had largely died down after Yorktown in October, the war still had nearly two years to run. The meeting's visit may have been triggered by a letter signed by one John Darragh on August 1, 1786, in which the members of Eleazer Oswald's Philadelphia militia company volunteered to march to the frontier to dispossesses the British of the posts and garrisons they still held at the time. John Darragh rebuked the Friends sent to visit him, denying their authority to question him by saying he had never been a member of their Society in the first place. And so ended the Darragh family's involvement with the Religious Society of Friends in Philadelphia.[50]

It must have been with some sorrow in summer 1782 that Lydia Darragh received the news of Charles Craig's violent end. Everyone was talking about it. He had honored her request that he guard her secret transmission of the British plan to march against Whitemarsh. There was little for her to fear by this time. Though New York, eighty miles away, was still occupied, the war was waning, and another attempt against Philadelphia no longer seemed likely. She had left Philadelphia Meeting for the society of the like-minded Free Quakers, who would applaud her actions rather than censure them. But Craig's story was a sad one.

While the main army wintered at Valley Forge, the corps of dragoons was headquartered around Trenton, where it could monitor British activity at Philadelphia and New York. Count Casimir Pulaski, in overall command of the dragoons, turned his attention toward forming his own combined-arms unit, Pulaski's Legion, a mixed force of cavalry, infantry, and artillery. Looking for a capable officer to lead his lancers, Pulaski, with Washington's approbation, settled on Charles Craig.[51]

But this difficult winter was a time of discontent among the officer ranks. Resignations abounded, some for reasons of personal hardship, many over petty jealousies or magnified disputes about seniority and promotion. In this disgruntled atmosphere, Craig submitted his own resignation to Washington. Writing from Reading on March 5, he said his personal affairs were his principal reason for leaving the service but went on to enumerate concerns that he had been passed over for promotion and that his honor was in question, due to rumors about his activities on the Frankford lines. "In Justice to my reputation I must Likewise observe that many insinuations were thrown out at Head Quarters respecting my conduct at the Lines; which were extremely unjust & Malicious, And it gave me great Pain to find that they appeared to have some Weight with your Excellency."[52]

His friend, Charles Biddle, wrote that Craig "left the army at the request of Mark Bird." Craig's personal affairs may have involved some kind of employment with Bird, a Pennsylvania militia colonel and a Reading-area ironmaster involved in supplying the army. Craig remained in Reading, marrying Bird's young daughter, Charlotte, in 1781, apparently against her father's will. Without business experience, Craig found himself dependent on Bird for his livelihood. But the two men had a falling out. Another friend reported: "They were privately married, without Colonel Bird's Consent,—I believe without soliciting it. Craig himself was, however, very sanguine . . . that in a short Time the Parent would be reconciled to <u>both</u> his Children. In this, very unhappily, all were mistaken. Colonel Bird has always remained inflexible."[53]

By summer 1782, Craig was struggling financially. On June 26, he assisted John Jacob Faesch to inventory William Allen's Union Ironworks, operations of which had been taken over by Congress and the state of New Jersey. His relationship with his father-in-law continued to deteriorate. Biddle observed: "After the marriage, he [Bird] wanted Craig to retract something he had said about him. This Craig did not think, as a man of honor, he could do. On his refusing, Bird did everything in his power to injure him. Craig declared several times to me, before I left Reading, that Bird had used him so ill he had a great mind to shoot him."[54]

About this time, Charles Biddle was asked to captain a poorly constructed ship, the *Friendship*, then in the Chesapeake. He persuaded Craig to serve as captain of the *Friendship*'s marine contingent and awaited Craig's arrival in Baltimore. When Craig did not come, he finally appointed another former officer, Captain Whitehead, in his place. But just before sailing, he received shocking news: Instead of shooting his father-in-law, Charles Craig had shot himself. "Having spent all his money, and being bred to no business, he thought if he was gone Bird would take home his wife and infant child. He therefore determined to put an end to his own existence."[55]

His friends described Craig's melancholy state of mind. The hoped-for reconciliation with his father-in-law had not come about. His financial prospects were dim. Daniel Brodhead Jr., living in Reading at the time, noted that Craig was less cheerful than usual and that he avoided his friends. In early July, "he was seized with a violent fever" to which he seemed more susceptible due to his depression. His condition was so dangerous that physicians were brought from Philadelphia to save his life. Through their efforts, he appeared to be recovering, but was still distraught.

While acknowledging that he was recovering physically, Craig alarmed his family by revealing the underlying cause of his affliction: "My Disorder is of the Mind; it is here, (placing his Hand upon his Breast) my Heart is broke . . . it is suspended by a Thread. . . . I shall most Surely die. . . . [N]ever shall I go alive down Stairs . . . I shall disappoint the Doctors—I know I shall."[56]

Resolved to end his life, Craig planned his final moments carefully:

> He told his servant boy, who had been with him in the army, and had no idea of disputing any orders he gave him, to stay in the entry, and if any person came for him to tell them he was lying down. As there was a person asleep in the room where his pistols were he pulled off his shoes for fear of waking him; he put the pistols between two pillows, for fear he should be met in the entry.[57]

Daniel Brodhead Jr. arrived shortly afterward, immediate witness to a horrific scene:

> After taking such Precautions as were requisite to prevent Detection, he laid himself on the Bed, raising his Head, with several Pillows, to a convenient Height; he placed the Muzzle of the Pistol under one Ear, and discharged it's Contents, which went quite thro' his Head. The Report of the Pistol brought up his Brother Colonel Thos. Craig, who immediately burst open the Door (he having the Precaution to bolt it on the inner Side) but the unfortunate Charles was already quite dead.—I ought here to take Notice, that, least the Pistol should by any Means have proved ineffectual, he had provided his Sword, which lay across his Breast when his Brother entered the Room; so determined was he on the Perpetration of this shocking Deed.[58]

In heartrending terms, Brodhead related the anguish as Charlotte pleaded with Thomas Craig: "You will not leave me my Brother, my Friend,—my now, perhaps, only Friend; for have I not lost the best of Friends in the tenderest of Husbands? You must not leave me my dear Brother!"

Sensible of his need to care for his sister-in-law, Thomas struggled to contain his emotions. "[I]magine a most affectionate Brother,—his Heart just bursting with a manly Grief almost too violent to bear, & which was yet doubled by his Endeavors to suppress it from Motives of Compassion and Tenderness to his Widow-Sister."[59]

Strictures against suicide were still practiced. In some parts of America, suicides were liable to confiscation of their property, leaving their families destitute, and shameful interment, outside of consecrated ground, even, in some places, humiliation by burial at a crossroads with a stake through the corpse's heart. But attitudes had been easing throughout the eighteenth century, to the point that at least in the mid-Atlantic area, one of two possible legal interpretations could apply: *felo de se* (inexcusable self-homicide) or *non compos mentis* (essentially, a person out of his or her mind and unable to act rationally). Brodhead promulgated an account that would lead a coroner, who was required by law to judge the matter, to a merciful, *non compos mentis* decision, allowing the dead person to be buried in a churchyard and exempting the family from property confiscation.[60]

American officers conceived of a third, justifiable type of suicide, as practiced by the Romans and epitomized in Joseph Addison's influential drama, *Cato*, whose hero ends his own life by falling on his sword. The play, especially relevant at the time for its portrayal of honorable resistance to tyranny, was well known to Washington and his officer corps. It was performed at Valley Forge in May 1778.[61]

War grinds inexorably, damaging and destroying people regardless of merit. Innuendo can bring down the just as well as the unjust. Charles Craig was touchy on questions of personal honor and unable to let go of the ingratitude and wrongs he felt he had suffered; he was preyed on by a nagging sense of injustice. At the last, by placing his silver-mounted sword across his breast, he made a final, unanswerable statement about who he really was: a patriotic officer of the Revolution and, above all, a man of honor. Can we doubt him?[62]

Since the time when Christopher Marshall first ran ads for William Darragh's Scotch snuff back in 1764, the druggist appears to have acted as a sort of mentor or patron to the Darragh family. Marshall was ten years William Darragh's senior. He was also considerably wealthier, well connected, and possessed of a public reputation that lent weight to his powers of persuasion when he chose to argue on behalf of others, as we saw in the case of Rachel Hammer.

Benjamin Loxley's house proved to be an effective location for the Darragh family's store; they rented the property for nine more years. But the Darraghs were growing older. When paying taxes in 1782, William Darragh was listed as a shopkeeper, but by the following year, his health was failing. Instead of listing an occupation, he was shown as "Aged" in 1783. In thinking about their future, William and Lydia were alive to the need to provide for their children after their passing. Here, Christopher Marshall stepped in to help and advise.

Marshall and his sons owned several properties in the vicinity of their own well-established store in the 200 block of Chestnut Street, including seven of the twenty-three properties on Carters Alley, in the short block between Second Street and Goforth Alley. The Darraghs knew the area well, having rented Thomas Barclay's store at the corner of Carters and Goforth Alleys and having also rented their first store on Second Street directly across from the entrance to Carters Alley. A third of that block was taken up on the south side by their kinsman Blair McClenachan's home.

When, in 1782, William and Ann Watkins decided to sell their house on Carters Alley, the Darraghs got wind of it, either through Marshall, who owned the property next door, or through personal acquaintance with their former neighbors, the Watkinses. They chose to purchase the place as an investment. Though they didn't have enough capital to buy it outright, they were able to come up with £200 of the £550 asking price. They arranged with Christopher Marshall to take over the mortgage, in trust for three of their children, Susannah, who was thirteen at the time, William Jr., sixteen, and Ann, at age twenty-five a widow. Marshall would keep up the payments, presumably by renting out the house, and at a certain point, he and his heirs would own the property themselves.[63]

When William Darragh became seriously ill in April 1783, the family sent for Christopher Marshall. Whether they sought spiritual comfort or practical advice about his estate, Marshall's diary did not explain. He visited the sick man several times over the next two months, at one point encountering Samuel Wetherill at the Darraghs' house. Wetherill, in the role he had assumed as a minister with the Free Quakers, was almost certainly there tending to William's religious needs. Marshall also consulted with William's sister, Mary Eddy, at this time. Though he rallied a couple of times and for a while seemed to be improving, William Darragh passed away on June 8. Despite not being a member of Philadelphia Meeting, he was nonetheless recognized as a Friend and allowed to be buried in their ground at Fourth and Arch Streets. Friends charitably put aside their animosity toward the Free Quakers in the matter of burials. Samuel Wetherill, clerk of the Free Quaker Meeting, spoke at the funeral, which Marshall described as "very large and decent."[64]

William Darragh was memorialized in patriot printer John Dunlap's newspaper:

> On Sunday morning last departed this life, after a painful illness of ten weeks, Mr. William Darragh, in the 64th year of his age. This truly worthy man has left a wife and five children; Providence was pleased to spare him thus long to behold them with pleasure educated in a genteel and modest manner. On Monday evening his remains were decently interred in the Friends burial ground in this city, attended by a number of respectable inhabitants. His character was that of a humane and benevolent man, a tender father, an affectionate husband, a sincere friend, and a lover of his country.[65]

Lydia Darragh's children continued to live with her at the Loxley House, until the family moved a few blocks north on Second Street in 1786. Ann Darragh advertised her millinery business, operating out of the family shop. The death of her husband closed one chapter of Lydia Darragh's life and opened another, as she assumed a different position and status in the legal world. She was no longer a *feme covert*: Her being and public actions were no longer "covered" by her husband. She was suddenly free to make contracts, sell, purchase or own real estate, and appear in court. A determined woman used to taking actions and making things happen even when her husband could not, though obviously grieving for the loss of her loving partner of many years, she experienced a newfound freedom—a means of acting on her own. Following William's passing, Lydia Darragh continued to manage her finances carefully.

After renting property for so long, she was finally free to buy a house and store on her own say so. Though it took her three more years, presumably in order to accumulate enough money, she finally bought a house and storefront on Second Street on April 22, 1786. The deed notes that she paid for the property outright in cash, in a way that suggests careful savings from the proceeds realized in her shop. The lot and house were purchased "for and in consideration of the sum of £1,591 current money of Pennsylvania such there in hand well and duly paid in gold and silver coin by the said Lydia Darragh." Though her new place had a narrow frontage—only thirteen feet, four and a half inches—it was commodious, extending 141 feet west into Strawberry Alley. There was a well and a pump partway back along its north side, and a small alley extending west along the north side, as well as a workshop at the rear.[66]

Though ostensibly about rejoicing, illumination sometimes functioned as a public test of conformity and loyalty in times of domestic peace. By exposing nonconformity, dissidence and even mere difference could be punished by intolerant mobs. Illumination became a more sinister tool for social control during times of political polarization. Neutrality often troubles zealots. Public displays of allegiance, such as illuminations, unmasked dissenters and drove conformance, or at least acquiescence, to the dominant party through the threat of mob violence.

During the Revolution in America, both sides took advantage of illuminations to ferret out the disloyal and used their chastisement to force the rest to adhere to the dominant power's side or risk similar reprisal. A few examples suffice to make the point. Elizabeth Drinker noted that on the first anniversary of American independence in 1777, a great number of Quakers' windows were broken because they refrained from illuminating. The following year, their windows were spared because, in the wake of the British evacuation two weeks earlier, the city still faced a scarcity of all kinds of goods, and people in the streets recognized that "candles were too scarce and dear for Illuminations."[67]

The informal illumination test could be used by people of either faction to express animosity. In British-occupied Charleston, Elizabeth Mathews Heyward was ordered to illuminate her house to signify her rejoicing for the British victory at Camden, South Carolina. Meanwhile, her husband, Thomas Heyward, a signer of the Declaration of Independence, lay in a British prison in St. Augustine. When she refused, an officer is said to have threatened her, "I will return with a party, and before midnight level [your house] to the ground." He did not make good his threat, but several months later she was threatened again, and this time her house was damaged. Historian Alexander Garden related what transpired:

> On the anniversary of the surrender of Charleston, May 12th,1781, an illumination was again demanded, in testimony of joy for an event so propitious to the cause of Britain. Mrs. G. A. Hall (her sister-in-law), who laboured under a wasting disease, lay at the point of death. Again Mrs. Heyward refused to obey. Violent anger was excited, and the house was assailed by a mob with brickbats, and every species of nauseating trash that could offend or annoy. Her resolution remained unshaken, and while the tumult continued, and shouts and clamour increased indignity, Mrs. Hall expired.[68]

In America, as in Ireland, Quakers continued to resist what Dublin Friends had deemed "the precarious Test of Illuminations." In Philadelphia, on the first anniversary of the Declaration of Independence, the local celebration included illuminations. Some Tories and Quakers kept their houses dark. Congressman Henry Laurens got an earful about it and wrote that "an old friend of mine now a rigid Tory, complained to me, of the friends of Liberty who had on the 4 July broke the Glass Windows of Such quiet people as had refused to illuminate their Houses upon that anniversary."[69]

Christopher Marshall described the festive, and potentially destructive, atmosphere prevailing in the city on the 4th: "This being the anniversary of our freedom from English bondage, sundry vessels saluted the town. The company of Artillery and Invalids' Regiment marched to the State House, where the Congress, President of the State and Council with a number of officers attended; bell ringing, guns firing till the evening and until numbers were so drunk as to reel home."[70]

By 1781, when Philadelphians celebrated the victory at Yorktown with bonfires and illuminations, the Darragh family had repeatedly demonstrated their commitment to the American cause. Lydia Darragh had been disowned that summer for joining the Free Quakers, so there was no political bar to illuminating her prominent property. But other Friends, guided as ever by their Testimony against War, refrained, with predictable consequences.

Official Fourth of July festivities in Philadelphia became increasingly elaborate. Anticipating final confirmation of the war's end in summer 1783, John Dickinson, president of Pennsylvania's Supreme Executive Council, staged a grand celebration. The morning was ushered in by bells pealing throughout the town, followed by a commencement ceremony at the College of Philadelphia, at which George Washington was given a degree of LLD. Flags of all nations whose ships were in port, with the notable exception of Great Britain, were displayed in the harbor. Thirteen guns roared in the Pennsylvania State House yard at noon, followed by other salutes throughout the day. Dickinson entertained dignitaries from state and municipal government, as well as field officers in the army and state militia, while joyous citizens thronged the streets. That evening, the city was regaled with a special parade, highlighted by "Mr. Mason's Triumphal Car," a wagon bearing portraits of Washington, Gates, and French General Jean-Baptiste Donatien de Vimeur, comte de Rochambeau, who had led the French forces in America, pulled by eight white horses. Boys and girls dressed in white with blue ribbons accompanied the float, bearing lit candles. The procession passed along Second Street, between the city's two markets, directly before Lydia Darragh's house, where she, Christopher Marshall, and many others gazed on approvingly from her famous balcony. Having once watched alone as British soldiers marched past on their way to attack Whitemarsh, now, surrounded by friends, but missing her husband, Lydia's heart must have been full.[71]

EPILOGUE

Lydia Darragh survived her husband by six years. She died on December 28, 1789, after an illness of about a week. She had been well enough to walk with her daughter Nancy a few short blocks from her store on Second Street to visit eighty-year-old Christopher Marshall at his town house on Carters Alley on November 29. But when Marshall dropped by her home on December 22, she was "very poorly." He returned to see her each day through the 27th, reporting on her condition, but skipped his visit on the 28th, perhaps due to the rain. She passed away that evening. The next day, when her friend learned she was gone, he braved the heavy rain to console the family. "Went to the house of the late Lydia Darragh as its said she expired ½ after 10 oc last night without a sigh or a groan aged 61 years."[1]

On December 31st, three days after her passing, Lydia Darragh was buried. The Free Quakers had not yet managed to purchase a burying ground. Despite having disowned her in 1783, the Philadelphia Meeting, in keeping with their charitable practices, permitted Lydia Darragh to be buried in their cemetery at Fourth and Arch Streets, as they had her husband before her.

That morning, Marshall trudged through more heavy rain to console Ann Darragh, visiting "some time with her [and] the rest of the children."

Later in the day, he attended the funeral. The rain had let up, though conditions "kept cloudy, damp, very wet underfoot." Attesting to the regard in which Lydia Darragh was held, Marshall reported a large gathering of people, despite the weather. He walked back to his place in company with Caspar Haines, husband of his granddaughter Hannah, who had also been ill at the time.

Lydia Darragh's passing was reported in the city's newspapers, an honor accorded to relatively few women at the time.

> On Tuesday evening last, died Mrs. Lydia Darragh, and on Thursday her remains were interred in the Friends' burial ground attended by a numerous concourse of sorrowful citizens. She had experienced some share of those ills attendant on humanity, and applied herself, for the support of her family, to a profession, in which the female part of society experienced her skill, tenderness, and assiduity, —to all she extended her sympathy; the poor and unfortunate will long, and the wealthy do now, lament the loss of it. She found the rewards of decent competency, of universal respect, and "the blessings of many ready to perish." Let her example enliven the hope of the industrious, and give strength to the virtuous; trusting as she always did in her severest afflictions, that a good Providence will in due time, bless the labours of the compassionate and tenderhearted.[2]

Lydia Darragh was a woman who took care of business. Acting in her typically responsible manner, she was careful to leave a will. William Darragh had died intestate. He had been ill at least ten weeks before his death, so there was certainly opportunity for him to have tidied up his financial affairs. But the situation was straightforward—everything would be left to his wife—so the family may have felt no need to go to the trouble and expense. Lydia's case, however, was more complicated; she had five children to take care of. Written just three days before she died, the will carefully apportioned her wealth, property, and possessions among them. Proceeding under the guidance of a former neighbor, attorney Ashton Humphreys, she named daughters Ann and Susannah, and son, William, as her executors. Present that day as a witness was her nephew, George Eddy, who affirmed the document.[3]

An inventory of Lydia Darragh's possessions by John Townsend and Joseph Bacon, showed a total value of £1611 7s. 9d., of which £1200, or 74 percent, was the value of her house and lot in Second Street. A comparison of the property value with the average values listed on Philadelphia's 1789 tax assessment place this dwelling among the top 5 percent of house values in the city. Lydia had rented for many years, and her industry and frugality finally yielded a good standard of living.[4]

Perhaps judging her two older sons capable of looking after their own interests, Lydia Darragh left the largest portion of her wealth—the property on South Second Street—to her two daughters. At the time, Ann was a self-sustaining widow operating her millinery business out of the family shop. Susannah, who had just turned twenty-one, was still unmarried. Lydia gave John an indirect interest in the property by arranging that he be paid an annuity, the "Yearly rent or sum of Fifteen Pounds current money of Pennsylvania," by his sisters. She also provided, in case of John's passing, that this annuity be paid to her granddaughter and namesake, Lydia Barrington Darragh. John's other child, four-month-old Alexander Porter Darragh, was not mentioned in the will. Though she must have known of him, it is likely Lydia had never met her grandson, as John and his family were living in or near Baltimore at the time.[5]

To her youngest son, William, she left the rental property on Carter's Alley that had been managed in trust by Christopher Marshall. As an afterthought, perhaps suggested by her daughter Ann, she also carved off a piece of the Second Street lot for William, leaving him the use of the workshop she arranged to have erected at the rear of the property.[6]

Given his financial difficulties and previous insolvency, it was perhaps wisest not to give Charles an interest in the property, which would be liable to seizure in lieu of debts. Instead, she arranged for the daughters to pay him £50 after the space of a year. This was very close to the amount of cash she had on hand at the time of her death—£57 5s. 5d.

The contents of her home and "residue of my Estate not herein particularly mentioned," Lydia divided among her other four children, who were explicitly named. Some of these items were already in their hands, especially in the case of John and his young family. In this division of her personal possessions, Charles was notably absent. Again, the concern may have been to shield the assets from seizure. The danger was real: The Philadelphia sheriff had recently sold off the household effects of Charles's former business partners, the Shobers, including "*a large quantity of merchandise, jewellery, household furniture, wearing apparel, etc.*"[7]

William and Lydia Darragh did not keep enslaved persons, but they did use the labor of indentured servants and were accustomed to the presence of such persons in their household. Indentured servitude came in two varieties at the time. One type involved a person contracted as an apprentice for a period of time to learn a trade, after which they were free to pursue that trade. Such apprentices were often known to enter into the masters' business in partnership, and even to marry into the master's family. A typical example was Benjamin Loxley, who wanted to become a carpenter and joiner, and was bound apprentice by his uncle to W. Joseph Watkins. Free after five years, with his own set of tools, he worked briefly for his master, then went into partnership with another carpenter and married his former master's sister. The other type of servitude was a simple contract for unskilled labor in return for a consideration, such as a payment to the servant's parent or guardian, or payment of the person's passage to America. During the period of indenture, the servant was provided the necessities of life; domestic servants generally living in the homes of their masters. After serving out the duration of the contract, these servants were generally entitled to a cash payment of "freedom dues" and a suit of new clothes.[8]

Prior to Lydia Darragh's birth, her father had kept at least one young girl as an "apprentice," in this case really a servant laborer rather than someone learning a trade. Given his economic standing, he likely had others in his household throughout Lydia's childhood. Shortly after their arrival in Philadelphia, William's indentured servant, Michael Dunn, ran away—an irritating financial loss for the family. When Lydia made her famous walk to Frankford, William Darragh "insisted that she should take with her the servant maid," though she declined to do so. At the time of her death, she still had an indentured woman, whom she referred to in her will as "my Bought servant." The will provided that the woman's remaining time of servitude would belong to both daughters.[9]

Though Lydia Darragh's children would own the property on South Second Street for eleven more years, they did not continue living there. Both daughters appear to have moved out of the house shortly after her passing. The 1790 Census and Philadelphia City Directories show another shopkeeper, John Guest Jr., occupying the property.[10]

Susannah, who remained a member in good standing with Philadelphia Meeting, requested a Certificate of Removal to Duck Creek

Monthly Meeting, near current-day Smyrna, Delaware, which was granted on July 30, 1790, just seven months after her mother's death. It may be that she moved in with her brother, John, who seems to have lived near Duck Creek at that time. In November 1791, her certificate was returned to Philadelphia Meeting with a note that Susannah had been disciplined for marrying out of meeting to a man named Alricks. She did not live long after that, dying the next year on September 18 at age twenty-three. With her passing, her share of her mother's property on Second Street became legally vested in her brother John.[11]

About the same time, Ann Darragh married Clement Hall, a man from a Quaker family, near Salem, New Jersey, on January 13, 1792. Unfortunately for Ann, whose initial marriage to James Darrah had lasted only five months before she was widowed, this second marriage was even briefer; Hall died just four months after marrying her. In 1798, at age forty-one, Ann Darragh married a third husband, fifty-eight-year-old Edward Hall, of Mannington Township, Salem County, suggesting a familial relationship between the two Halls. This marriage lasted fifteen years before Edward, too, left Ann a widow.[12]

William Darragh Jr. may have continued to live in his mother's house until he died, sometime in 1796. He had retained, and perhaps labored in, the workshop she had left him at the rear of the property on Second Street. At some point, ownership of the workshop transferred to his brother Charles, whose financial problems continued to haunt him.[13]

By 1796, Charles Darragh's financial difficulties might have seemed a thing of the past, but they were not. The legal guidance Lydia Darragh had received while writing her will, which led her to keep tangible property out of Charles's hands, turned out to be solid advice. Nearly eleven years after the discharge of his debts in 1785, a piece of the Darragh family property—the workshop on Strawberry Alley—was seized by the Philadelphia sheriff. The workshop had been given initially to William Jr. in his mother's will, but it somehow came into Charles's possession. It may have been transferred from William to his brother to help him pay his debts, but details are scant. In February 1796, the workshop was seized from Charles to be sold at sheriff sale. After months of advertising the workshop property unsuccessfully, Sheriff John Baker finally sold it for $210 to Abraham Dubois, a goldsmith to whom Darragh and the Shobers owed money. Dubois seems to have bought the property himself only as a last resort when no one else would bid on it. However, five years later, he was able to sell it back to the Darragh family at a modest profit of $90, suggesting that the family had come to some kind of off-record arrangement with him, perhaps to keep Charles out of debtors prison.[14]

Charles's whereabouts at this time are uncertain. He was not living in his mother's property on South Second Street. The family continued to rent the property to other shopkeepers. There were two tenants in 1795: "Jeremiah Boone, Jeweller and Hair-worker" and "John Smith & Co., merchant." Given the tiny frontage on Second Street—only thirteen feet, four and a half inches—one of these renters may have been using the Strawberry Alley workshop. But Charles Darragh was still doing business in the city as late as 1796. He maintained relations with the Marshall family. The financial accounts for Benjamin Marshall's administration, show a payment to Darragh and some others, who may have been Charles's business partners, for writing and accounting services, which were paid for that year. However, Charles seems to have kept a low profile. He does not appear in the Philadelphia City Directories between 1785 and 1801, the year of his death. He may have spent some time at sea, an experience he was familiar with from crossing over to Pennsylvania as a young boy. A family tradition, collected by Henry Darrach, said that at some point "he made a voyage to China in connection with the tea trade."[15]

It is possible Charles Darragh moved in with his brother John in Delaware by 1799. He was present in New Castle that year, when he witnessed documents for John, but no record of where Charles was actually living in his last years has been found. His sister Ann, applying for Charles's bounty land on behalf of John's daughters, noted that he had died "without leaving a widow or children."[16]

Charles Darragh's death in June 1801 appears to have been the precipitating factor causing the family to sell the Philadelphia property. Neither of the two remaining siblings were living in the city by that time. They collaborated to sell the place. John reacquired the workshop at the rear from Abraham Dubois for $300, reuniting the property and helping ensure a clear title. He arranged an agreement of sale with a Philadelphia merchant, David Lapsley. In order to clear the property title, Ann Hall and her husband, Edward, sold their share of the property to John for $3,425, which was almost half the planned sale price of $6,950. Although calculations of value are somewhat imprecise, this amount appears to be very close to the price Lydia Darragh originally paid for the property. While it didn't appreciate much, it had provided a residence, a place of business, and probably rental income for the family for fifteen years.[17]

At final sale to Lapsley in November, John received $4,000 in hand and took Lapsley's five-year mortgage for the balance of $2,950, which netted John only $575 initially but paid him "lawful interest annually" in addition to the principal. Ann walked away fully reimbursed for her share, while John made money on the interest, which, at 6 percent per annum, would have yielded him close to an additional $530 over the next five years—a comfortable investment, backed up by Lapsley's bond. With the sale of this property, the Darragh family's direct connection with Philadelphia came to an end.[18]

On November 4, 1783, not yet twenty, John Darragh began advertising his services as an engraver. An ad for his services at the Loxley House ran at least seven times that month. Perhaps he had learned the value of advertising from his parents; throughout his life, he continued to use the newspapers to advertise his various businesses. Still in the city two years later, he advertised in the Philadelphia papers to return a man's silver watch he had found on the road to Lancaster. Sometime between 1786, when he showed up on Philadelphia's tax rolls as a single man, living with his mother, and 1787, John Darragh left the city and moved south. He married seventeen-year-old Margaret Stewart Porter on February 2, 1787. Their first child, named Lydia Barrington Darragh in honor of her grandmother, was born the following December. In August 1789, they had a second child, a boy, Alexander Porter Darragh, probably named for Margaret's father, who may have been living nearby. The 1790 US Census shows John Darragh and his young family living in Harford County, Maryland, not far from the great road and the ferry over the Susquehanna River. Within a few years, he shifted his base of operations east across the Susquehanna to Delaware.[19]

An enterprising person, John Darragh tried his hand at many different trades. By 1793, he was keeping a stable about twelve miles north of Duck Creek, where he offered his stallions to breed racehorses through newspaper advertisements. "The elegant full blooded horse Adonis will be let to mares this season at Cantwell's-Bridge, New-Castle county, and State of Delaware, at the sum of two guineas the season, and half a dollar to the groom." At the same time, he ran another ad for the less expensive services of "the noted horse Morwick . . . at six dollars the season, and one quarter of a dollar to the groom." The highly literate language Darragh used to praise his horses in these ads gives ample evidence of the quality of his education by his father.[20]

Two years later, John Darragh auctioned off some of his horses and other livestock, as well as "two excellent wagons and gears; with a variety of other articles too tedious to mention" in order to finance a new enterprise, an inn at the Sign of the Ship and Pilot Boat in New Castle. His inn was on the banks of the Delaware, where passengers could board the packet boats for Philadelphia. John described the new inn's amenities, touting its attractive location, which "commands an elegant prospect of the Bay and River." He also used the place as a venue for auctions of horses and land, and appears to have become involved in real estate sales in the late 1790s. That the inn was profitable can be seen in John Darragh's tax assessment for 1798, which showed him as one of the wealthiest people in New Castle, with an assessed value of $2,129.[21]

Though he operated a very active business in New Castle, John Darragh appears to have lived elsewhere in Delaware. The 1800 federal Census shows his growing family living in Mill Creek Hundred, a rural area in northwestern Delaware, where he likely engaged in farming. By 1810, the family was in the village of Newark, in White Clay Creek Hundred, where, according to his son, Alexander, John kept a farm. At some point, he gave up the inn and moved to this farm, where he died on July 23, 1822. He left the farm, which was heavily mortgaged, to Alexander. John Darragh was the only child of William and Lydia Darragh who had offspring; all surviving Darragh family members descended through John and three of his children: Lydia Barrington Darragh, Alexander Porter Darragh, and Eliza Constance Darragh.[22]

John's widow, Margaret, and several daughters left White Clay Creek and settled in New Castle, where members of the family remained for many years. His oldest daughter, Lydia Barrington Darragh, married James Short, and lived near Glasgow, Delaware, a bit south of Newark. They had one son, Alexander Darragh Short. John Darragh's daughter, Eliza, married John Janvier, of New Castle, and had a son, Julian, and a daughter, Margaret. John's other daughters, Margaret S., Ann H., and Susan, never married and left no descendants.[23]

Alexander Porter Darragh, a purser in the US Navy, married Eliza Tucker Armistead in Norfolk, Virginia, where he was stationed. He died at sea in 1831 and was buried in Gibraltar, leaving behind a single child, daughter Margaret Porter Darragh, who married Dr. Thomas Newton, of Norfolk. She can be identified as one of the informants, a third link in the chain, who learned Lydia's Tale from her great aunt, Ann Darragh, and possibly from her father. Margaret passed the family's version of the story to Henry Darrach, who then published it in 1916.[24]

Many affluent Quakers, including William Penn, were slaveholders from the time of their first settlement in Pennsylvania. Though as early as 1688 pious Friends from Germantown Meeting protested against their fellow coreligionists keeping slaves, only gradually did well-to-do Quakers begin to admit that the practice was cruel and inconsistent with their professed beliefs. Initially, when forced to confront their worldly embrace of personal economic benefit over righteous action by a few zealous, self-appointed preachers who refused to remain silent, wealthy Friends resisted the admonitions of the early abolitionists.[25]

Benjamin Lay was one of those who disturbed the Quaker status quo. Outraged at finding slavery so deeply entrenched in Philadelphia, he resorted to the older Quaker practice of demonstrative protest, shocking complacent Friends as they met for worship. At a major gathering of Philadelphia-area Friends, the Yearly Meeting at Burlington in 1738, he stunned the peaceful assembly when he rose to speak what was in his heart, as was the common way in Friends' religious meetings. In a booming voice, he launched into a ringing denunciation of the intolerable injustice of the slavery that many of the people in the room themselves were practicing at that very moment. To drive home his point, he suddenly threw off his plain coat, uncovering a military uniform beneath, whipped out a sword and plunged it into a book, representing the Bible, which spurted bright red "blood," spattering those seated near him with pokeberry juice. As often happened to those who insisted on disrupting Quaker meetings, Lay was carried bodily out of the meetinghouse through physical force—the violent reaction of professed pacifists, which showed he had gotten their attention and had certainly gotten under their skins.[26]

Though at the time self-interested Friends adamantly rejected criticism of their slaveholding, over the next two decades, the issue of slavery was one of the primary factors—along with a rejection of the military imperatives of governance generated by continued settlement of Native American lands—that led Quakers to begin religious reform. This movement saw Quakers reembrace their spiritual roots and withdraw from mainstream society rather than compromise their values. As revolution approached in the early 1770s, Friends expended increasing amounts of energy in testimony against slavery and in active efforts to discourage slaveholding among members. Influenced by Friends' arguments, Pennsylvania's radical government, while still in the throes of revolution, began the gradual abolishment of slavery by forbidding the importation of slaves and establishing a law that any child of a slave born in the state was automatically a free person.[27]

When delegates from Philadelphia Meeting came to treat with him for serving in the military, John Darragh had denied his membership in the Religious Society of Friends, but he remained a Quaker culturally, at least in some ways. For instance, when appearing before the judge to take up his brother William's administration, he did not swear an oath to perform the service faithfully; rather, he affirmed his intent. Sometime after moving south, though, and out of sync with the Quakers of his day, John Darragh took up the practice of keeping slaves.[28]

The 1790 Census shows John Darragh's small family of four living in Maryland without slaves. But by the following decade, when they had moved to Mill Creek Hundred, the family had grown to nine members, plus seven slaves. How John acquired title to these enslaved persons, whether through purchase or perhaps inheritance through his wife's family, is not known. In 1810, when they were living in the village of Newark, the household consisted of six family members and five slaves.

In 1799, John Darragh took legal action to free two of his slaves, at least partially. Because these manumissions were considered to be indentures that transferred the rights to property, they were recorded in the deed record books for New Castle County. Several of his neighbors also executed manumission documents at this time. Darragh and Whitehead Jones witnessed each other's manumissions of two young men before a justice of the peace on September 3. These documents, however, did not grant immediate freedom. Jones's slave, only twelve at the time, would be required to work sixteen more years. John Darragh's slave would be required to work for him nineteen more years before achieving his liberty:

> Be it remembered that I, John Darragh of the Town of New Castle, in the County of New Castle, and State of Delaware, for divers good causes and considerations me thereunto moving, have and by these presents do manumit and set free from the service of my-

> self, my heirs, executors, or administrators, my negro boy named Jesse from and after the term when he the said negro boy Jesse (now my slave) shall fully attain to and arrive at the age of thirty five years (he being at this time aged sixteen years) or when the said term of thirty five years from his birth shall be fully compleated and ended.[29]

Two days later, John Darragh returned to court, this time to free, once again conditionally, nineteen-year-old Musk, who would be released after laboring another sixteen years in bondage. Charles Darragh was present that day to witness his brother's act of limited magnanimity. He also served as witness for Thomas Farmer, who, more charitably, liberated a twenty-six-year-old man on the spot.[30]

John Darragh was sharp, a careful businessman who looked out for his own interests, not one to simply dispose of valuable resources without some recompense. In 1787, the state of Delaware had passed a law that the master of any manumitted slave, except for those freed during their prime working years, between ages eighteen and thirty-five, was required to post a manumission bond of $160. This bond guaranteed that if a slave was later unable to fend for himself or herself, he or she would not become a charge on the state, that is, liable to be supported by local community. Darragh's arrangement meant his slaves would work for him through their best years, then be freed just before he would be required to post the bond, thereby freeing up capital that could be used for other purposes, including the purchase of replacements for those persons he freed. The monetary value placed on enslaved people could vary considerably, but a boy might be purchased for less than the cost of a bond. As an example, John Darragh's son, Alexander, left behind at his death a young boy named Randel who was valued in the estate inventory at $150.[31]

Others of John Darragh's slaves, however, were not so fortunate as Jesse and Musk. They seem to have been passed down as property to his children. In addition to Randel, a "Colored Boy remaining with [the] family," at least one of John's daughters inherited a slave. Eliza C. Darragh manumitted a woman in 1826, "on condition that she the said Betsey Owens, shall well and faithfully serve me . . . during and to the full end and term of five years and five months," an act of relative generosity mirroring her father's legal actions.[32]

Ann Darragh followed in her parents' footsteps as a businesswoman, initially using their shop as her base of operations. At age twenty, while the British still occupied the city, she was already advertising herself as a wholesaler of European goods. Later, she was described as a milliner, selling accoutrements for ladies' fashions at the same location, while operating side by side with her brother John, who used the premises for his engraving business.[33]

Though disowned by Philadelphia Meeting for marrying contrary to discipline, Ann Darragh remained a Quaker, at least culturally, for the rest of her life. As a member of the Free Quakers, she was able to continue worshiping "in the manner of Friends," at least as long as she remained in Philadelphia. In relating the version of Lydia's Tale that came down through the family, Ann's grandniece described to Henry Darrach Ann's adherence to Friends' ways: "The dear old narrator of these events, herself a strict Quakeress, would always add: 'Ah! if my dear mother could only see the pictures of herself in the children's histories, flounced and furbelowed, how shocked she would be.'"[34]

As noted earlier, in 1792, Ann Darragh married, for the second time, into a family of Quaker descent living in Mannington Township, a little east of Salem, New Jersey, about twelve miles across the Delaware River from New Castle as the crow flies. Though Ann's second husband, Clement Hall died a few short months afterward, she remained in the area, eventually marrying Edward Hall six years later.

The close relationship that developed between the Darraghs' surviving children had a marked impact on the survival of Lydia's Tale. One indication that Ann stayed in close touch with her brother's family is her attempt to acquire bounty land due to Charles Darragh for his military service. During the Revolutionary War, as inducement for men to enlist in the army and navy, the United States offered bounty lands in unspecified locations. The amount of land depended on rank; as a lieutenant, Charles Darragh was eligible to receive two hundred acres. Much of the land later granted was in Ohio, federal territory that had been expropriated from the Native inhabitants through a series of military actions, most notably those ending in the treaty following the Battle of Fallen Timbers in 1795. Even if applicants had no intention of moving to Ohio, the warrants could be converted to cash by selling them to speculators, albeit at a discount from the land's potential value.[35]

As Charles's primary heir, Ann submitted an application on her own behalf in Philadelphia in 1829. When that did not pan out, she tried again four years later in New Castle, this time enlisting the aid of John Darragh's five daughters, each of whom appeared in court and signed the application. In this record, evidence can be seen that Ann retained her Quaker culture—rather than swear an oath that her application was truthful, she affirmed it. On the other hand, John's daughters, most of them by now Presbyterians, displayed no qualms about swearing. Like many other efforts to gain bounty land, there is no record suggesting that either of these applications bore fruit.[36]

Ann remained close to her brother John's descendants, especially the orphaned daughter of John's son, Alexander Porter Darragh, to whom she related her mother's story. That woman, Margaret Porter Darragh, became an important link in the story's survival, passing along the family's version of events to Henry Darrach late in the nineteenth century.

APPENDICES

Principal Lydia Darragh Narratives

Appendix A: Hannah Marshall Haines's Account, c. 1822

Wyck Association Collection, Series 3, Box 87, Folder 20: "Hannah Marshall Haines Prose," n.d., American Philosophical Society.

When the British had possession of Philadelphia, General Howe's Headquarters was in Second Street, the fourth door below Spruce Street (a house built by General Cadwalader). Directly opposite, resided William and Lydia Darach, members of the Society of Friends. One of the head officers of the army went to their house, & wished to look at their chambers, as they wanted one for their private use. He fixed on a back one, said it would not be wanted but once a week, unless something very particularly occurred, and they should wish to have a fire made & candles lit.

Two officers had frequently met there, one I think the Adjutant General. One day the latter came & told Lydia Darach they would be there, at seven o'clock, should stay late, & wished the family all to retire early to their chambers; said when they were going they would call her to let them out & take care of their fire & candles. She sent her family to bed, at 8 a clock also her husband. And as he had been so particular, her curiosity was excited. She took off her shoes & put her ear to the keyhole of the door. She then heard an order read for all the troops to march out, at 12 o'clock at night & attack General Washingtons Army, then Encamped at White Marsh. They were to go the night but one after.

When they had finished reading, & were getting ready to go, she went to her chamber & laid down. They soon came & knocked at the door. She did not answer till the third time feigning to be asleep. Her mind was so agitated that she could neither eat, drink or sleep, believing it was in her power to save the lives, perhaps thousands, but knew not in what way to give the information to General Washington, not daring to confide, even to her husband, the important secret she possessed. She was sensible that if discovered, her own life & perhaps that of her family would be taken. It was an awful situation & she fervently prayed to the Almighty to direct her what to do. The time was short & after much reflection concluded to go herself. She told her family that as they were in want of flour, she would go to Frankford & try to buy a quarter of a hundred. Her husband insisted on her taking their maid to carry it, to which she objected & went to General Howe & asked for a pass, to go through their troops, which he immediately granted, & she set off alone, left her bag att the mill & went on.

While between the two armies, an American officer stopped her, to inquire where she came from. She looked at him, but did not like his countenance, and was fearful he might betray her; though very desirous of returning home, that no suspicion might arise from her absence. She soon met Colonel Craig of the Light Horse who with some of his men was going on the lines to get what information he could procure. It was his daily practice. He immediately knew her, & inquired where she was going. She requested him to alight from his horse, & walk with her. He ordered his troops to keep in sight. She took his arm & then told him she was going to put her life into his hands. She then related to him the important information. He took her to a house near & requested the women to give her some thing to eat, & immediately set off to Headquarters.

A redoubt was dug, the cannon planted & every preparation made to receive them. That night, the men laid on their arms. She returned with her flour home. And the next night, she told her husband she had something that would occupy her till late & wished him to go to bed. She went into a front chamber, lowered the Shutters & set down to watch their movements. At 12, they marched from Headquarters without a word being spoken; she could only hear their footsteps.

When they returned she dare not ask a question, though very desirious to learn the event. That evening the adjutant came in, & asked Lydia Daragh to walk up to his room, as he had some questions to ask her. She followed him. He locked the door, placed a chair and requested her to be seated. Providently, the candle was behind her or, she said, he need not have said one word; her countenance would have betrayed her. Her hair felt, as though it arose under her cap when, he asked her if any of her family was up, the night they last met. She told him they had all retired at eight o'clock. He said, "I know you were asleep for I knocked three times before you heard me. I am at a loss to imagine who gave General Washington information of our intended attack, unless the walls of the house could speak. When we arrived at Whitemarsh, we found all their cannon mounted & the troops prepared to receive us, & we marched back like a parcel of fools, without firing a single gun."

Appendix B: Robert Walsh Jr.'s Account, 1827

Robert Walsh Jr., "American Biography," *American Quarterly Review* 1 (1827): 32-34.

When the British army held possession of Philadelphia, General Howe's head quarters were in Second street, the fourth door below Spruce, in a house which was before occupied by General Cadwalader. Directly opposite, resided William and Lydia Darrah, members of the Society of Friends. A superior officer of the British army, believed to be the Adjutant General, fixed upon one of their chambers, a back room, for private conference; and two of them frequently met there, with fire and candles, in close consultation.

About the 2d of December, the Adjutant General told Lydia that they would be in the room at seven o'clock, and remain late; and that they wished the family to retire early to bed; adding, that when they were going away, they would call her to let them out, and extinguish their fire and candles.

She accordingly sent all the family to bed; but, as the officer had been so particular, her curiosity was excited. She took off her shoes, and put her ear to the key-hole of the conclave. She overheard an order read for all the British troops to march out, late in the evening of the fourth, and attack General Washington's army, then encamped at White Marsh.

On hearing this, she returned to her chamber and laid herself down. Her mind was so much agitated, that, from this moment, she could neither eat or sleep; supposing it to be in her power to save the lives of thousands of her countrymen; but not knowing how she was to convey the necessary information to General Washington, nor daring to confide it even to her husband.

The time left, was, however, short; she quickly determined to make her way, as soon as possible, to the American outposts. She informed her family, that, as they were in want of flour, she would go to Frankford for some; her husband insisted that she should take with her the servant maid; but, to his surprise, she positively refused.

She got access to General Howe, and solicited what he readily granted,—a pass through the British troops on the lines.

Leaving her bag at the mill, she hastened towards the American lines, and encountered on her way an American Lieutenant Colonel (Craig) of the light horse, who, with some of his men, was on the look-out for information. He knew her, and inquired whither she was going. She answered, in quest of her son, an officer in the American army; and prayed the Colonel to alight and walk with her.

He did so, ordering his troops to keep in sight. To him she disclosed her momentous secret, after having obtained from him the most solemn promise never to betray her individually, since her life might be at stake, with the British. He conducted her to a house near at hand, directed a female in it to give her something to eat, and speeded for headquarters, where he brought

General Washington acquainted with what he had heard. Washington made, of course, all preparation for baffling the meditated surprise.

Lydia returned home with her flour; sat up alone to watch the movement of the British troops; heard their footsteps; but when they returned, in a few days after, did not dare to ask a question, though solicitous to learn the event.

The next evening, the Adjutant General came in, and requested her to walk up to his room, as he wished to put some questions. She followed him in terror; and when he locked the door, and begged her, with an air of mystery, to be seated, she was sure that she was either suspected, or had been betrayed.

He inquired earnestly whether any of her family were up the last night he and the other officer met:—she told him that they all retired at eight o'clock. He observed —"I know you were asleep, for I knocked at your chamber door three times before you heard me:—I am entirely at a loss to imagine who gave General Washington information of our intended attack, unless the walls of the house could speak. When we arrived near White Marsh, we found all their cannon mounted, and the troops prepared to receive us; and we have marched back like a parcel of fools."

Such is the substance of Lydia's narrative, heard from her mouth by several most respectable persons of our acquaintance, and implicitly believed by all of them, who knew her character and situation.

Marshall, in the third volume of the Life of Washington, says, in reference to Howe's scheme—On the fourth of December, Captain M'Lane, having discovered that an attempt to surprise the American camp at White Marsh was about to be made, immediately communicated the information to the Commander-in-chief. In the evening of the same day, Sir William Howe marched out of Philadelphia, with his whole force, &c. Mrs. Darrah's auditors, as we have stated, give Craig, as the name of the officer to whom she communicated the information. Whichsoever may have received it, the public benefit that she conferred, must be pronounced inestimable. The loss of many hundred American lives, and even more disastrous consequences, were, in all likelihood, averted by her courageous stratagem.

Appendix C. John Fanning Watson Version, 1829

The following narrative is transcribed from John Fanning Watson, Manuscript Annals, at the Historical Society of Pennsylvania, pages 23–24. Page 23 is part of a section titled "Miscellaneous Facts." Watson's version of Lydia's Tale is immediately preceded by summaries of two other stories he had received from Hannah Haines. The first was a description of a disinterment that Haines had heard from her mother, Sarah Marshall. The second was a note about David Rittenhouse's remarkable lack of education—remarkable because Rittenhouse turned out to be a much-admired savant. Following those two accounts, Watson recorded Lydia's Tale in much greater detail.

Lydia Darach

I have been well assured of a circumstance in 1777 which saved Genl Washington & his army, while at Whitemarsh. Mrs. Lydia Darach, a Friend & the wife of William Darach, a Teacher, while her house (Loxley's at the corner of 2nd & Little Dock St., see a drawing of it) was occupied as the business chamber of General Howe's adjutant General, had an opportunity one night to over-hear his reading of the order for the attack, & she made out to communicate it in time to Washington to put him on his guard. She related it herself afterwards to my particular friend, & may be relied on. The story is this: The Adjutant General called in the evening to say, he wished her & her whole Co. to go to bed by 9 O'Clock as he wished to have some company to examine some Papers free from noise etc. When he came with the sound of several Persons, she was in bed, and afterwards feeling an unusual & unexpected excitement to get up & listen, she did so, without awaking her husband who knew nothing of the arrangement. (The General kept his own Key to go in & out when he chose.) When she applied her Ear near the chamber door, she very distinctly heard the reading of the whole Plan of attack. The British were to march next night at midnight, in silent march. When she returned to her bed some time, the General rapped at the door to say he was withdrawing, & the front door might be locked. After this she lay meditating how she might prevent the effusion of blood. She executed her plan early next morning, by requesting a pass from General Howe to go to Frankford Mill for Flour (her husband knew no part of her design). It was granted. She went on foot. Near Frankford lines she met Allen McLane our celebrated Partizan officer on horse back, but not knowing him personally, & thinking his countenance was not encouraging, she did not communicate. Arrived at Frankford, she ordered 25 lbs Flour, & pushed on, hoping to meet some American officer to whom she might communicate. At some distance she met Colonel Craig (who shot himself) with about a dozen horse going to the lines for information. She knew him & begged him to send on his men, & speak with her alone. To him she revealed the whole, & he set off immediately to communicate to Washington. To make good her story on her return, she (although a woman of 40 & of weakly habit) actually carried her 25 lbs flour into Philadelphia. Next night, she arose, & at the appointed hour saw the silent march, through her window, & the arms beaming by moon light. She afterwards saw them return, wearied & chagrined. This was not all. The General came straightway & asked her into his Room, by candle light, & began solemnly to question her about there being a possibility of any person in her house to listen to & betray secrets. Happily her face was not to the light or it might have betrayed her. But before she could answer, he said "I know you were in bed, for I had to tap often to make you hear." She assured him her husband was asleep & her household had long before been to bed. He concluded by saying, "It is certain 'Walls have Ears' & we must have been exposed." All this event referred I presume to the battle of Edge Hill on the 5th December, & the return back to the city on the 8th following.

Such a heroine for her Country, should give fame to the name of Lydia Darach!

Mrs. Hannah Haines, who reads this, tells me she has heard the same from Lydia Darach in substance. She was a woman of excellent repute among Friends, as also her husband too.

[I find in confirmation of the above, from Capt. McLane, that he was apprised of this intention on the 4 December & his force in consequence was encreased to 80 additional men. He saw Howe's light troops on a Run, on the night of 5 December near to Washington's Camp & he succeeded to harrass & delay them till day light.]

[Marginal note:] x Mrs. D. Logan says she well remembers to have seen their march that night.

Appendix D. Henry Darrach Version, 1916

Henry Darrach, *Lydia Darragh One of the Heroines of the Revolution* (Philadelphia: City History Society of Philadelphia, 1916), 389-393.

Henry Darrach prefaced his transcription of Ann Darragh's version of Lydia's Tale with the following statement

1. Ann Darragh, at the time of the event, was 21 years old and resided with her mother Lydia, frequently related the event to her great niece, a great—grand daughter of Lydia, who recorded it for the family. [p. 388]

2. The great granddaughter was Margaret Porter Darragh Newton (1824–1891), who noted:

In my childhood the story was frequently related to me by daughter of Lydia Darragh. [p. 388, n. 6]

3. The age of Ann Darragh when she told the story is not stated, nor the time when the story is reduced to writing. [p. 388, n. 6]

4. Ann's account is the most satisfactory, while similar to that given by Walsh and Watson it omits Lydia's having gone to the mill, it also omits Craig's having taken Lydia to a house. These omissions will be noted in Ann's account to have a full statement of all Lydia is said to have narrated. [p. 389]

[In transcribing Newton's written version, Darrach inserted his own comments, within parentheses, to which I have added italics, below, to distinguish his comments from what he claimed to be Newton's text.]

Ann Darragh's Account

In the winter of 1777 and 1778 General Howe, commander of the British forces in Philadelphia, had his headquarters in the house of Mr. Cadwalader on Second Street, near Little Dock. The house occupied by William Darragh was nearly opposite. William Darragh was ordered to open his house for the accommodation of some of the troops and find other quarters for his family. It was a cold winter, the city was crowded and he knew not what to do, but finally Lydia determined to go herself to General Howe and ask for relief. While she was waiting for an audience one of the staff officers entered into conversation with her and finding she was as well as himself, a native of Ireland, became rather interested in her statement of her difficulties and asked General Howe to relieve her from the order. This he declined to do, saying they also were very much pressed for room, but at length decided to take only one room for a council chamber. This was large and at the back of the house. This quieted Lydia very much, for she had a son, her eldest, a lieutenant in General Washington's army, then at White Marsh, and all her sympathies were with these poorly clad and half-starved patriots, and to have her house used as a place in which to lay plans for their destruction was a bitter trial. She was, for want of room, obliged to send her younger children to the country home of a relative of her husband.

Councils were frequently held in the upper chamber, much to the distress of the mistress of the house. One day *(Tuesday, December 2d)* an officer came and told her to have all her family in bed at an early hour, as they wished to use the room that night free from interruption. She promised to do so, and when all was quiet lay down herself, but could not sleep. A presentiment of evil weighed down her spirits, and at last, hearing loud talking, went into a closet, separated from the council room by a thin board partition covered with paper, just in time to hear the reading of the minutes of the council, then concluding. The orders were: "The troops should march out on a certain night *(Robert Walsh, "late in the evening of the 4th")*, attack Washington's army, and with their superior force and the unprepared condition of the enemy victory was certain." A sharp pang shot through her heart. Patriotic she was, but perhaps motherly love had a large share in forming a resolution to do something to save the army of which her son was a member. She returned to bed, and when an officer knocked to waken her to fasten up the house after their departure she did not answer until the third summons.

The next day *(Wednesday, December 3d)* was spent in planning some mode of action. That night she told her husband she was going to use a pass she had obtained some time before to go to the country to see her children *(Robert Walsh states she was going to the Frankford mill for flour)*, and, starting early the next morning *(Thursday, December 4th)*, and going in the direction named in her pass *(Robert Walsh states she left her bag at the Frankford mill)*, but soon changing her course, after a long and weary walk, came near the American camp. She saw an officer approaching on horseback. It proved to be Colonel Craig, of the Light Infantry, whom she knew. He was greatly surprised to see her, and asked, "Why, Mrs. Darragh, what are you doing so far from home?" She asked him to walk beside her, which he did, leading his horse. In low tones she told him the important intelligence she had risked so much to bring, and he at once rode with it to headquarters. *(Robert Walsh states that before Craig left Lydia he took her to a house near at hand and directed a female in it to give her something to eat.)* Lydia then returned home, but did not tell her husband the real object of her errand to the country until she thought all danger over.

He little knew the part his wife had played in the drama of that eventful night. She feared the least suspicion of his having taken information out of the city might endanger his life and kept her secret. That night she sat at a front window, wrapped in a cloak, and watched the soldiery march by on their way to attack Washington. The next day was spent in an agony of fear, for even when the troops returned she was uncertain what the result was. There were many rumors, but she did not dare to ask a question.

When nearly dusk an officer came to the house, called her to the council room, and then locked the door. She was so faint she would have fallen if he had not handed her a chair and asked her to be seated. The room was nearly dark, and he could not see the pallor of her face. Then he inquired if any of her family were awake on the night of their last council. She replied: "No, they were all in bed and asleep." Then he said: "I need not ask you, for we had great difficulty in waking you to fasten the door after us. But one thing is certain; the enemy had notice of our coming, were prepared for us, and we marched back like a parcel of damned fools. The walls must have some ears." She retained her possession through all the interview. "I never told a lie about it," she would say, "I could answer all his questions without that." The dear old narrator of these events, herself a strict Quakeress, would always add: "Ah! if my dear mother could only see the pictures of herself in the children's histories, flounced and furbelowed, how shocked she would be."

NOTES

ABBREVIATIONS

APS	American Philosophical Society
Darrach CHS	Henry Darrach, *Lydia Darragh One of the Heroines of the Revolution,* Philadelphia: City History Society of Philadelphia, 1916
Darrach *PMHB*	Henry Darrach, "Lydia Darragh of the Revolution," *Pennsylvania Magazine of History and Biography* 23, no. 1, 1899, 86-91
FO	Founders Online, "Correspondence and Other Writings of Seven Major Shapers of the United States," National Archives, https://founders.archives.gov
HSP	Historical Society of Pennsylvania
ISOFCR	Ireland, Society of Friends (Quaker) Congregational Records, Findmypast.ie
NARA	National Archives and Records Administration
NDAR	*Naval Documents of the American Revolution,* https://www.history.navy.mil/research/publications/publications-by-subject/naval-documents-of-the-american-revolution.html
PMHB	*Pennsylvania Magazine of History and Biography*
USQMR	US Quaker Meeting Records, 1681–1935, Ancestry.com

INTRODUCTION

1. Laurel Thatcher Ulrich, *A Midwife's Tale: The Life of Martha Ballard, Based on Her Diary, 1785–1812* (New York: Vintage Books, 1990).
2. Alfred F. Young, *Masquerade: The Life and Times of Deborah Sampson, Continental Soldier* (New York: Vintage Books, 2004), 115.
3. For an example of exchange rates during the occupation of Philadelphia, see *Pennsylvania Evening Post,* November 6, 1777.

CHAPTER I: LYDIA'S TALE

1. Robert Walsh Jr., "American Biography," *American Quarterly Review* 1 (1827): 32-34.
2. Walsh, "American Biography," 34.
3. John Fanning Watson, "Annals of Philadelphia, being a collection of Memoirs, Anecdotes, & Incidents of the City & its Inhabitants from the days of the Pilgrim Founders," unpublished manuscript, 1829, Historical Society of Pennsylvania (hereafter HSP), box 5, 23-24.

4. Hannah Marshall Haines, untitled manuscript version of Lydia's Tale, n.d., Wyck Association Collection, ser. 3, box 87, folder 20, "Hannah Marshall Haines Prose," American Philosophical Society (hereafter APS).
5. Henry Darrach, *Lydia Darragh One of the Heroines of the Revolution* (Philadelphia: City History Society of Philadelphia, 1916) (hereafter Darrach CHS). Darrach was careful to note on the title page that he was "not related or connected with the family," though it is possible that the similarities of their names had driven him to research Lydia Darragh in the first place.

CHAPTER 2: THE BARRINGTON AND DARRAGH FAMILIES IN IRELAND

1. Jacob Hiltzheimer, *Extracts from the Diary of Jacob Hiltzheimer of Philadelphia, 1765–1798*, ed. Jacob Cox Parsons (Philadelphia: Wm. F. Fell, 1893), 32; An Abstract of the Records of Births, Deaths and Burial of Philadelphia Monthly Meeting 1688 to 1826, 323, US Quaker Meeting Records, Ancestry.com (hereafter USQMR). The record states Lydia Darragh's age at burial as sixty-one.
2. Richard Bauman, *For the Reputation of Truth: Politics, Religion and Conflict Among the Pennsylvania Quakers 1750-1800* (Baltimore: Johns Hopkins University Press, 1971), 231-234; William Penn, *A Brief Account of the Rise and Progress of the People Called Quakers* (London: James Phillips, 1794).
3. National Archives of Ireland, Betham Genealogical Abstracts, ser. 9-10 Miscellaneous collection, 24, Findmypast.ie; John O'Hanlon, Edward O'Leary, and Matthew Lalolr, *History of The Queen's County*, vol. 2 (Dublin: Sealy, Bryers & Walker, 1914), 491;J. Thomas Gilbert, ed., *History of the Irish Confederation and the war in Ireland, 1641 [–1649] containing a narrative of affairs of Ireland, by Richard Bellings*, vol. 1 (Dublin: M. H. Gill & Son, 1882), 91; John O'Hanlon and Edward O'Leary, *History of The Queen's County*, vol. 1 (Dublin: Sealy, Bryers & Walker, 1907), 187. For more information on the Queen's County Barringtons, see Jonah Barrington, *Personal Sketches of His Own Times* (Philadelphia: Carey, Lea and Carey, 1827), ch. 1.
4. National Archives of Ireland, Crossle Genealogical Abstracts, Military Records, Dec. 25, 1654, Findmypast.ie; National Archives of Ireland, Crossle Genealogical Abstracts, Parish Register Society of Dublin, Register of Derry Cathedral, 150 [1659], Findmypast.ie; National Archives of Ireland, Crossle Genealogical Abstracts, Calendar State Papers Relating to Ireland, 1660-2, Findmypast.ie; National Archives of Ireland, Betham's Genealogical Abstracts Prerogative Wills (Phillips Mss) B. 1581-1766. & Misc, 171, Findmypast.ie; Ian Gentles, *The New Model Army: Agent of Revolution* (New Haven, CT: Yale University Press, 2022), 175-204.
5. Oliver Cromwell to William Lenthall, September 17, 1649, in *Oliver Cromwell's Letters and Speeches* with Elucidations by Thomas Carlyle, vol. 2 (London: Chapman & Hall, 1871), 169-170. Cromwell and his soldiers displayed a knack for knocking people on the head. It was reported that after his victory at the Battle of Naseby in 1645, one hundred Irish women among the Royalist camp followers, were summarily murdered by being "knocked on the head." These women were likely Gaelic-speaking Welsh women rather than actually Irish. The distinction seemed to matter little to Cromwell and his followers, who viewed the Celtic people of the British Isles as subhuman. Ann Hughes, *Gender and the English Revolution* (Abingdon-on-Thames, UK: Routledge, 2011); Francis Charles Montague, *The History of England from the Accession of James I to the Restoration, 1603 to 1660* (London: Longmans, Green, 1907), 311; Veronica Wedgwood, *The King's War, 1641–1647* (London: Penguin, 1958).

6. Cromwell, *Letters and Speeches*, 170.
7. Letter of Hugh Peters, October 16, 1649, quoted in Philip Herbert Hore, *History of the Town and County of Wexford* (London: Elliot Stock, 1906), 298; Dennis Faul, "Cromwell in Ireland: The Massacres," *Seanchas Ardmhacha: Journal of the Armagh Diocesan Historical Society* 20, no. 1 (2004): 293–98. Traditional Irish accounts assert that scores of women who had assembled together to plead for mercy were also massacred by Cromwell's soldiery, who, as had been their wont in previous battles, had tacit license to murder the Catholic inhabitants. Anglophile apologists argue a lack of evidence for such atrocities, dismissing traditional sources.
8. Oliver Cromwell to the Governor of Ross, October 19, 1649, quoted in George Griffiths, comp., *Chronicles of the County Wexford, being a record of memorable incidents, disasters, social occurrences, and crimes, also, biographies of eminent persons, &c., &c., brought down to the year 1877* (Enniscorthy, Ireland: Printed at the "Watchman" Office, 1890), 129.
9. Hore, *Wexford*, 298-299.
10. National Archives of Ireland, Betham Genealogical Abstracts, ser. 9-10 Miscellaneous collection, 24-26, Findmypast.ie.
11. National Archives of Ireland, Betham Genealogical Abstracts, ser. 9-10 Miscellaneous collection, 24-26, Findmypast.ie.
12. Edward Smith, *The Life of William Dewsbury* (London: Darton and Harvey, 1836), 31; Hore, *Wexford*, 423; Irma Corcoran, *Thomas Holme, 1624–1695: Surveyor General of Pennsylvania* (Philadelphia: American Philosophical Society, 1992), 47-48; Griffiths, *Chronicles*, 133; "The Battle of Lambstown, 1650," Bree Heritage: The History of Bree, Co. Wexford, https://breeheritage.com/2017/02/02/the-battle-of-lambstown-1650/.
13. Thomas Barrington and Susan Nunn Marriage License, 1683: Henry C. Stanley-Torney, ed., "Ferns Marriage Licenses (1661–1806)," *Journal of the Kildare Archaeological Society*, vols. 9-10, 42; John Barrington Birth: Religious Society of Friends in Ireland Archives, Society of Friends (Quaker) Births, Register of Births, Dublin, 1859, ISOFCR. This document records John Barrington's birth in Wexford, at the home of parents Thomas and Susanna.
14. Religious Society of Friends in Ireland Archives, Half-yearly Meeting Minutes 1689–1707, September 8, 1705, 355, March 8–10, 1707, 406, ISOFCR; Michael Quane, "Quaker Schools in Dublin," *Journal of the Royal Society of Antiquaries of Ireland* 94, no. 1 (1964): 54-55.
15. Religious Society of Friends in Ireland Archives, Leinster Province 6-weeks Meeting Minutes 1706–1760, June 22, 1713, 109, ISOFCR.
16. John Roque, *An exact survey of the city and suburbs of Dublin: in which is express'd the ground plot of all publick buildings, dwelling houses, ware houses, stables, courts, yards &c, by John Rocque, chorographer to their Royal Highnesses the late & present Prince of Wales; A. Dury Sculp.* (Dublin: John Roque, 1756), Harvard Map Collection, Harvard College Library; Peter Wilson, *The Dublin Directory for the year 1751. Containing an Alphabetical List of the Names and Places of Abode of the Merchants and Traders of the City of Dublin* (Dublin: Peter Wilson, 1751); John Joseph Webb, *The Silk Industry in Dublin* (Dublin: Maunsel, 1913), 131.
17. Dublin Men's Meeting Minutes, September 23, 1714, ISOFCR. The document recording the couple's marriage intention says she has "noe parents" but that "her overseers signified their consent." A Book for Recording the Marriage Certificates of the

People called Quakers in the City of Dublin begun the 12th of the 6th Month 1701, MMIIM2, 397-398, ISOFCR. Note that the marriage date is recorded as January 11, 1714. In the Old Style or Julian calendar, the new year did not begin until March 25. Under that usage, January 1, 1714, was the day after December 31, 1714, which is confusing for modern readers. I have adjusted the date to 1715, under the New Style or Gregorian calendar, to reflect present usage. There is a garbled statement on the transcription of the marriage certificate that appears to indicate that her parents were deceased at the time of the wedding.

18. Ireland, Society of Friends (Quaker) Marriages, Registry of Marriages, Dublin Monthly Meeting to 1859, 5, ISOFCR; Ireland, Society of Friends (Quaker) Marriages, Registry of Deaths, Dublin Monthly Meeting, to 1859, 4, ISOFCR; Marriage of Andrew Jesop and Frances Barrington, July 27, 1714, Religious Society of Friends in Ireland Archives, Marriages, MM II M2, 382-383, ISOFCR.

19. See, for example, Family Search: Ireland Naming Customs: Traditional Naming Pattern, https://www.familysearch.org/en/wiki/Ireland_Naming_Customs. The Barrington family's first two daughters' names follow the traditional Irish pattern—the first daughter for the mother's mother, the second daughter for the father's mother.

Frances: born March 9, 1715. This name would have honored Mary Aldridge's mother, but it is worth noting first that Frances was the name of John Barrington's redoubtable sister, and second, that Francis was also a common male family name among the Barringtons of Queen's County, all of which, perhaps, made this highly suitable as a name for the firstborn daughter.

Susanna Barrington: born October 7, 1717, named for John's mother, Susanna Nunn.

Comfort Barrington, born April 16, 1719.

Thomas Barrington: born April 11, 1720. The first son was named after his paternal grandfather, in keeping with the traditional naming pattern.

John Barrington: born between December, 1721 and July, 1722, date not recorded. The second son was named after his father, instead of being named William, after his mother's father. Traditional naming patterns were not always followed explicitly, especially with regard to later children.

These birth records were taken from Ireland, Society of Friends (Quaker) Births: Register of Births, Dublin, 1859, ISOFCR. Because birth records for Lydia, and any other Barrington children, are not present in the same source, it is necessary to deduce her relationship to her birth family through circumstantial but compelling evidence, especially through detailed examination of her marriage record. An extract of the will of Lydia's sister, Susanna Barrington Webster, lists Lydia Darragh, Anna Barrington, and Mark Barrington as her siblings: Betham's Genealogical Abstracts. Prerogative Wills: (Phillips Mss.) W. 1779–1787 Series 1, wills: v. 76 "W" 1796–1799 "Y" 1703-1799, Findmypast.ie.

20. An obituary in the *Ariss Birmingham Gazette* for February 11, 1745, indicates that at least one other person bearing the uncommon name of Darragh, very possibly a relative of William's, was living on Pill Lane about the same time: "Dublin, Jan. 26. Last Saturday died at his House in Pill-Lane, Mr. Anthony Daraugh, an eminent Dealer in Hard-ware, and a Person of very fair Character."

21. Darrach, *Lydia Darragh*, 85-86; *Pennsylvania Packet or the General Advertiser*, Saturday, June 14, 1783, 3; Samuel L. Knapp, *The Life of Thomas Eddy; Comprising an Extensive Correspondence with Many of the Most Distinguished Philosophers and Phi-*

lanthropists of This and Other Countries (New York: Connor & Cook, 1843) 43; A Book for Entering the Names of [——]ting Friends Each Year . . . , D80 1748-1827, ISOFCR; Society of Friends, Dublin Meeting, Certificate of Removal for William and Lydia Darragh, July 12, 1763, ISOFCR.

22. Religious Society of Friends in Ireland Archives, Congregational Records, MM II F1, 508, ISOFCR.

23. The informant was Margaret Porter Darragh Newton, a great-granddaughter of Lydia Darragh, who received the description from her great aunt, Ann Darragh Hall. Darrach, CHS, 385.

24. Minutes of Dublin Mens Meeting, October 30, 1753, 236, ISOFCR.

25. *Dublin Gazette*, November 3, 1753; Society of Friends, Dublin Meeting, D59, Marriages 1738-1811, 99, ISOFCR. This is the meeting's record of the marriage, not the actual signed certificate, which, like most, was retained by the family. The certificate noted that Lydia was the daughter of John Barrington of Dublin, confirming their relationship despite the absence of a birth record. Lydia Barrington's mother, Mary Aldridge Barrington (I) of Dublin, wife of John (I), was buried on September 18, 1753, and so could not sign Lydia's marriage certificate on November 2, 1753. It was necessary to differentiate Lydia's mother from a second Mary Barrington (II) of Dublin, who passed away on October 14, 1757. Mary (II), whose maiden name was Mary Sutton, was also married to a John Barrington and is noted as his first wife. This John Barrington (II) was the son of Nicholas of Wexford, brother of John Barrington (I), who is later referred to in Dublin Meeting records as "the Elder" to distinguish him from his nephew. John (II) remarried in 1763 to Mary Ann Plummer.

26. John Barrington's older sister, Frances Barrington Jesop married the widower Robert Biker, weaver, a "near kinsman" of her deceased husband, Andrew Jesop. Though the Quaker population in Ireland at the time was not large, they practiced endogamy—members were permitted to marry only other Quakers. This created a limited pool of available mates and a tendency for families to be closely related in multiple ways. Concern about marrying too closely was reflected in an ongoing debate within the Society. For instance, many contended that marriages between first cousins should be prohibited. Others argued that as there was nothing specific in the scriptures that prohibited this, and it had long been their custom (through need), the practice could be countenanced. In addition, Biker had developed a reputation among Friends as a flirtatious libertine. After his first wife's death, Biker was having an affair with his servant, Rachel Dickinson, or, in the circumlocution of Friends, "committing uncleanness with her." Worse, amorous herself (and probably in search of financial security), Frances interrupted this adulterous affair, turning Robert's head. On learning that her daughter had secured the affections of this eligible man, Frances' mother, Susanna Nunn Barrington, advised her to close the deal quickly, skirting the Meeting's potential disapproval, following a time-honored proposition regarding worrisome marriages that "it is better to seek forgiveness than to ask permission." Frances and Robert decided to marry "after a disorderly manner," that is, outside the Meeting's jurisdiction and without its approval. Anticipating objections, the couple slipped away to be wed at a rural Meeting in neighboring Kilteel, about thirteen miles from Dublin, where they were not so well known. The entire sordid business brought dishonor to the Meeting, tarnishing the "Reputation of Truth" by which Friends were able to assert the superiority of their chosen way of life. Bauman, *Reputation of Truth*.

27. Religious Society of Friends in Ireland Archives: Registry of Marriages, Dublin Monthly Meeting to 1859, 43, ISOFCR. Susannah here is a variant spelling of Susanna. The name also appears sometimes as Susan.
28. Eddy Marriage: Friends Historical Library, Dublin: Ireland, Society of Friends (Quaker) Marriages, 1741, ISOFCR; Knapp, *Life of Thomas Eddy*, 42-43; Peter Wilson, *The Dublin Directory for the Year 1752* (Dublin: Browne and Nolan, 1752), 7; Religious Society of Friends in Ireland Archives: Dublin disownments, 1662–1756, MMII F1, 509, 9th of 1 mo. 1753, ISOFCR. Joseph Marshall was disowned for scandalous behavior: "[H]e became adicted to that hurtful Practice of keeping unprofitable company, thereby neglected his Business & in process of time failed in the payment of his just debts . . . & lastly hath absconded from his Creditors, leaving a Wife & several small Children in great Necesity & Want of subsistence." James Eddy's prominence in the meeting may be gauged by noting that his signature was first on the document. Eddy Certificate of Removal: dated May 1, 1753, ISOFCR; received September 28, 1753, recorded in Philadelphia Monthly Meeting Minutes, 1751–1756, 112, USQMR.
29. Henry Darrach, "Lydia Darragh, of the Revolution," *Pennsylvania Magazine of History and Biography* 23, no. 1 (1899): 90-91 (hereafter Darrach *PMHB*). John's birth after the Darraghs arrived in Philadelphia is borne out in a finding by the Philadelphia Monthly Meeting, which noted John as "having been born since the Arrival of his parents in this Country." Philadelphia Monthly Meeting, Arch Street, April 27, 1787, 314, USQMR. Some records show the year of John's death as 1822, but that seems to be incorrect.
30. Religious Society of Friends in Ireland Archives, Dublin Men's Meeting Minutes 1758-67, MM II A12, November 20, 1759, 133, 135, ISOFCR.
31. William Darragh also put his name to two Certificates of Removal in 1763. Religious Society of Friends in Ireland Archives: Dublin Men's Meeting Minutes 1750-54, MM II A10, March 8, 1754, 250, March 22, 1754, 252-253, ISOFCR; A Book for Entering the Names of [——]ting Friends Each Year . . . , D80 1748-1827, 1754. 9 mo. 17, ISOFCR; List of the Members of Dublin Mens Meeting & their Monthly Collections, 10, ISOFCR; Yearly Meeting Parliamentary Committee Minutes, 1731–1778, October 13, 1761, ISOFCR; Religious Society of Friends in Ireland Archives, Disownments, D50, 1756–89, 35-36, 43, 44, ISOFCR; Certificates 1715–1751, MM IV A2, Lydia Jaffray, January 1763, and Elizabeth Strettle, March 25, 1763, 196-197, ISOFCR.
32. Margaret Hope Bacon identified 141 minsters—47 of them women—who traveled from America to the British Isles from 1685 to 1835 to preach in this way. Margaret Hope Bacon, "Quaker Women in Overseas Ministry." *Quaker History* 77, no. 2 (1988): 94; Elizabeth Ashbridge, *Some account of the early part of the life of Elizabeth Ashbridge: who died, in the truth's service, at the house of Robert Lecky, in the County of Carlow, Ireland, the 16th of 5th month, 1755* (Philadelphia: Benjamin and Thomas Kite, 1807)
33. Philadelphia Yearly Meeting Minutes, 1755–1760, A Testimony from Goshen Monthly Meeting, July 18, 1757, 68, USQMR; Chester Monthly Meeting Women's Minutes, 1733–1779, March 26, 1753, 215, USQMR; Religious Society of Friends in Ireland Archives, MM VIII C1, Records of Ministers' Travels 1655–1775, 81, ISOFCR.

34. Philadelphia Monthly Meeting Minutes, 1646–1757, Memoirs Concerning Many Persons Eminent for Piety and Virtue among the People Called Quakers, Abraham Farrington, 71-76, USQMR.
35. Religious Society of Friends in Ireland Archives, QM II C1, Cork Ministers' Visits 1708-1877, September 25, 1756, 82-83, ISOFCR.
36. Religious Society of Friends in Ireland Archives, MM II K2, November 1-2, 1756, 14, ISOFCR; Religious Society of Friends in Ireland Archives, MM II A11, Dublin Men's Meeting Minutes 1754–1757, September 28, 1756, 162-163, ISOFCR.
37. Alfred W. Braithwaite, "Early Tithe Prosecutions: Friends as Outlaws," *Journal of the Friends' Historical Society* 49, no. 3 (1960): 148-156; Eric J. Evans found that "between 1690, and the passing of the Tithe Commutation Act in 1836, the Epistle of the Yearly meeting [in London] found it necessary to mention tithes, generally with further exhortations to refrain from payment on 47 occasions." Eric J. Evans, "A History of the Tithe System in England, 1690–1850, with Special Reference to Staffordshire" (PhD diss., University of Warwick, 1970): 179-180; Stephen Taylor, "Sir Robert Walpole, the Church of England, and the Quakers Tithe Bill of 1736," *Historical Journal* 28, no. 1 (1985): 51–77.
38. Religious Society of Friends in Ireland Archives, QM I G2, B9 Tithes 1706-1714, Leinster Quarterly Meeting Sufferings 1706–1714, County of Wexford, 213, ISOFCR; Gregory Clark, "Yields Per Acre in English Agriculture, 1250–1860: Evidence from Labour Inputs," *Economic History Review* 44, no. 3 (1991): 453. Generally speaking, a sheaf was an armful of cut stalks. A thrave was a bundle of 24 sheaves. In 1712, Barrington lost 8.6 thraves of wheat, which was equivalent to about 40 percent of what a man might cut in a day. He also lost 4.8 thraves of oats, about 15 percent of a day's work, plus perhaps another 30 percent of a day's work lost on barley and rye.
39. Religious Society of Friends in Ireland Archives, MM II G1, *The Sufferings of Friends belonging to Dublin Meeting, because for Conscience Sake they cannot pay Tithes, Priests Maintenance &c.*, 279, ISOFCR. Friends' intransigence was often made emphatically visible in their refusal to accept even commonly used names for things they objected to, prefacing such terms as *churchwarden* with "called" or "so-called."
40. *London Gazette*, June 9, 1759.
41. Dublin Monthly Meeting Minutes, August 28, 1759, September 11, 1759, October 23, 1759, November 6, 1759, ISOFCR; Dublin Monthly Meeting Minutes, October 23, 1759, ISOFCR.
42. Constantia Maxwell, *Dublin Under the Georges, 1714–1830*, 2nd ed. (London: Faber & Faber, 1945), 253.
43. *Dublin Courier*, June 15, 1763, 1.
44. *Dublin Courier*, July 18, 1763, 1.
45. Dublin Men's Meeting Minutes 1758-67, June 28, 1763, MM II A12, 352, ISOFCR; Dublin Monthly Meeting Certificates of Removals 1774–1776, MM II K2, 78, ISOFCR.
46. Dublin Women's Meeting Minutes 1757–1777, July 25, 1763, MM II B 1, ISOFCR. It should be noted that in Dublin, Lydia and William, along with Susanna Barrington, signed a document dated 11m. 1763—a Certificate of Removal for Lydia Jaffray, who was moving from Dublin to Moate. Moate MM minutes of Men's Meeting 1732–1755, MM IV A2; Sufferings 1660–1687, Certificates 1715-1751, 196, ISOFCR. But that seemingly anomalous date can be squared with other evidence sup-

porting the Darraghs' departure in August. Their absence from Dublin during fall 1763 is backed up both by Dublin Meeting records, which state that the Darraghs left in August (see below), and by the family record that their son, John, was born December 5, 1763, in America. It seems most likely that the Jaffray document was dated using the Old Style calendar—the Julian rather than the Gregorian calendar. Under the Old Style, 11th month 1763 was not November, but January, while First Month was actually March. While, officially, the New Style had gone into effect in Ireland on January 1, 1752, some people, especially those of a conservative bent, continued to use the Old Style in their dating for many years after the official transition. The next certificate recorded in the Moate book, following Jaffray's removal, was dated 25th 1 mo: 1763, also signed by William and Lydia Darragh.

47. Dublin Men's Meeting Minutes 1758-67, August 9, 1763, MM II A12, 360, ISOFCR.

48. Dublin Men's Meeting Minutes 1758-67, October 4, 1763, MM II A12, 369, ISOFCR.

49. Dublin Men's Meeting Minutes 1758-67, May 15, 1764, MM II A12, 399, May 29, 1764, 400, ISOFCR.

50. Dublin Men's Meeting Minutes 1758-67, July 9, 1765, MM II A12, 466, August 6, 1765, 469, ISOFCR.

51. Dublin Men's Meeting Minutes 1758-67, September 17, 1765, MM II A12, 476, ISOFCR; William Hodgson, ed., *The Life and Travels of John Pemberton, a Minister of the Gospel of Christ* (London: Charles Gilpin, 1844), 10-12; Philadelphia Monthly Meeting, Arch Street, Certificates of Removal, 1764–1767, 1733, USQMR. This appears to be the original signed document, not a copy.

52. Philadelphia Women's Meeting Minutes, 1757–1767, September 26, 1766, 210, USQMR.

CHAPTER 3: THE DARRAGHS MOVE TO PHILADELPHIA

1. See for instance Gottleb Mittelberger, *Gottleb Mittelberger's Journey to Pennsylvania in the Year 1750 and Return to Germany in the year 1754* (Philadelphia: German Society of Pennsylvania, 1898); Farley Grubb, "The Market Structure of Shipping German Immigrants to America," *PMHB* 111, no. 1 (1987): 27–48.

2. *Pennsylvania Journal and Weekly Advertiser*, September 1, 1763, 1; *Pennsylvania Gazette*, October 6, 1763, 2.

3. *Pennsylvania Gazette*, October 6, 1763, 3.

4. *Pennsylvania Gazette*, October 6, 1763, 3, October 13, 2.

5. *Report of the Commission to Locate the Site of the Frontier Forts of Pennsylvania, Vol. 1*, ed. Thomas Lynch Montgomery (Harrisburg: Wm. Stanley Ray, 1916), 164-174; Joseph J. Mickley, *Brief Account of the Murders by the Indians, and the Cause Thereof, in Northampton County, Penn'a., October 8, 1763* (Philadelphia: Thomas William Stuckey, 1875); Kevin Kenny, *Peaceable Kingdom Lost: The Paxton Boys and the Destruction of William Penn's Holy Experiment* (New York: Oxford University Press, 2009).

6. "Correspondence of the Children of Christopher Marshall," *PMHB* 17, no. 3 (1893): 336-347, https://www.jstor.org/stable/20083550.

7. Friends Historical Library, Dublin, Ireland, Society of Friends (Quaker) Marriages, ISOFCR; Knapp, *Life of Thomas Eddy*, 42.

8. Knapp, *Life of Thomas Eddy*, 42-43.
9. James and Mary Eddy, Certificate of Removal, Philadelphia Monthly Meeting, Minutes, September 20, 1753, USQMR; *Pennsylvania Gazette*, June 27, 1754.
10. Knapp, *Life of Thomas Eddy*, 42-43; *Pennsylvania Gazette*, June 27, 1754, December 5, 1754, November 6, 1755, for example.
11. City of Philadelphia, Department of Records, Philadelphia Deed: H 21.212, Christopher Marshall et ux to James Eddy, March 26, 1759; Certificate of Removal for Christopher Marshall, Philadelphia Monthly Meeting Minutes, April 3, 1736, USQMR; Marriage Certificate for Christopher Marshall Jr. and Ann Eddy, October 9, 1760, Philadelphia Monthly Meeting Minutes, 1759–1814, Book E27, 19, USQMR; *Pennsylvania Gazette*, August 20, 1761, 3, October 18, 1764, May 9, 1765.
12. Marriage Certificate for Christopher Marshall Jr. and Ann Eddy, October 9, 1760, Philadelphia Monthly Meeting Minutes, 1759–1814, Book E27, 19, USQMR; John W. Jordan, *Colonial Families of Philadelphia*, vol. 2 (New York: Lewis Publishing, 1911), 1027.
13. While I normalize the spelling of McClenachan's surname in the text, it was spelled in a variety of ways in the eighteenth century. Marriage of Blair Macclenachan and Ann Darragh, August 17, 1762, St. Paul's Church, Philadelphia, Pa., Parish Register, 1759–1835, 9; Henry Darrach, *Genealogical notes of Blair McClenahan and his children* (HSP, 1899), 2; Horace Wemyss Smith, *Life and Correspondence of the Rev. William Smith, D. D*, Vol. 2 (Philadelphia: Fergus Bros., 1880), 460-461; John T. Faris, *Old Churches and Meeting Houses in and around Philadelphia* (Philadelphia: J. B. Lippincott, 1926), 233-234.
14. Jordan, *Colonial Families,* 1027.
15. Barclay advertisement, *Pennsylvania Journal*, April 21, 1773, 2; *Pennsylvania Packet*, April 26, 1773, 1.

CHAPTER 4: THE DARRAGHS' LIVELIHOODS

1. Thomas M. Doerflinger, *A Vigorous Spirit of Enterprise: Merchants and Economic Development in Revolutionary Philadelphia* (Chapel Hill: University of North Carolina Press: 1986), 173-178; *Pennsylvania Gazette*, September 13, 1764.
2. US National Institutes of Health, National Library of Medicine, National Center for Biotechnology Information, "Description of Smokeless Tobacco Practices," 1.1.2 "Snuff taking," https://www.ncbi.nlm.nih.gov/books/NBK326503/; John Fitzgerald, "Lundy Foot & Company, Tobacco & Snuff Manufacturers," *Dublin Historical Record* 71, no. 2 (2018): 141–53; Peter Wilson, *The Dublin Directory for the Year 1760* (Dublin: Printed for Peter Wilson, 1760), 17. For Strasburgh Violet Rapee, see F. W. Fairholt, *Tobacco: Its History and Associations* (London: Chatto and Windus, 1876), 268.
3. Anonymous, *Ten Minutes' Advice in Choosing Cigars, with a Word or Two about Tobacco, and Something about Snuff. . .* (London: J. Meaden, 1833) 26-27.
4. *Pennsylvania Journal*, December 17, 1761; Catherine Snell Crary, "The Tory and the Spy: The Double Life of James Rivington," *William and Mary Quarterly* 16, no. 1 (1959): 61–72.
5. Lydia Darragh's "mortuary" advertisement noted that she lived on the corner opposite the Golden Fleece, which would place the Darraghs on the northeast corner, in the large property owned by John Taylor. *Pennsylvania Gazette*, December 4, 1766.

The Pennsylvania Journal and Weekly Advertiser, December 17, 1761, June 24, 1762; Juliette Gerhardt, *Life on the Philadelphia Waterfront 1687–1826: A Report on the 1977 Archaeological Investigation of the Area F Site, Philadelphia, Pennsylvania* (West Chester, PA: John Milnor Associates, 2006), appendix 1.1, 2; Samuel Rowland Fisher, "Journal of Samuel Rowland Fisher, of Philadelphia, 1779–1781 (continued)," *PMHB* 41, no. 4 (1917): 438. A Philadelphia Constable Return shows that William Darragh employed one female servant in 1775. City of Philadelphia Constables returns to Assessors for 1775, 68-69, https://therevolutionarycity.org/islandora/city-philadelphia-constables-returns-assessors-1775.

6. Peter Thompson, *Rum Punch and Revolution: Taverngoing and Public Life in Eighteenth-Century Philadelphia* (Philadelphia: University of Pennsylvania Press, 1999), 27; Philadelphia Mayor's Court Docket, July, 1768; July 1771, HSP. "Mayor's or Alderman's Court: The Mayor's Court convened quarterly at City Hall. The Mayor and two to ten Aldermen presided over cases such as larceny, assault and battery, running Tippling and Gaming houses, forgery, nuisances, riots, etc." Anne A. Verplanck, *Furnishings Plan for the Mayor's Court Chamber in Old City Hall, Philadelphia, PA* (National Park Service, 1988), 13, https://www.nps.gov/parkhistory/online_books/inde/mayor%27s_court_fp.pdf. Actual tavern license applications for William Darragh have not been located. Provincial summary lists exist that account for revenues received in Pennsylvania from license fees. In these records, fees from tavern license applicants are listed by month. The annual Mayor's Court records are sorted alphabetically by the initial letter of applicants' surnames. Though clerks for the city and province were operating out of the same building, working within feet of one another, they do not seem to have consulted closely with one another, as these two sets of records do not always agree. William Darragh's application for a tavern license in 1767: *Licenses for marriages, taverns and pedlars, 1761–1776 in the Province of Pennsylvania* [microform], MFilmXR 684, HSP. This was the only evidence of an application by Darragh on the annual provincial lists. 1768 exception list: Mayor's Court Doquet, July Sessions, 1768. Despite not being listed as an applicant on the provincial list for 1771, William Darragh is shown as having paid his fee on that year's Mayor's Docket "List of Publick Housekeepers recommended" for continuation.

7. City of Philadelphia, Department of Records, Deed D 10.86, July 8, 1766.

8. *Pennsylvania Ledger*, May 20, 1778; *Pennsylvania Packet*, November 20, 1783.

9. *Pennsylvania Gazette*, Thursday, November 28, 1765. The ad ran twice more, on December 5 and 12.

10. Darrach *PMHB*, 90-91. The birth records were extracted by Darrach from copies of Bible records furnished by two of Lydia Darragh's descendants, Julian D. Janvier, of New Castle, Delaware, and Lydia Barrington Darragh Short, of Baltimore.

11. *Pennsylvania Gazette*, December 4, 1766. The ad ran a second time, on December 11. This has led some writers to describe Lydia Darragh as a "mortician." Though the term *mortician* did not come into common usage to describe a "layer out of the dead" until the late nineteenth century, it serves as handy shorthand for the complex of services provided by Lydia Darragh and her colleagues. For instance, in 2005, when broadcaster Cokie Roberts called Lydia a "local mortician," she did so as a matter of convenience—a popularizer, Roberts wanted to summarize Darragh's occupation in a single phrase that her audience could relate to. Such descriptions have a tendency to stick with later writers. That capsulization, however, hardly captures the complexity

of how Darragh earned her living. Cokie Roberts, *Founding Mothers: The Women Who Raised Our Nation* (New York: Harper, 2005) 80.

12. Will of Mary Symonds, 1773, no. 297, Philadelphia Department of Wills, cited in Karin Wulf, *Not All Wives: Women of Colonial Philadelphia* (Philadelphia: University of Pennsylvania Press, 2000), 141n61. Symonds died June 9, 1773, and was buried in Christ Church Burial Ground. Samuel Johnson, *A Dictionary of the English Language* (1755, 1773), ed. Beth Rapp et al., https://johnsonsdictionaryonline.com; Mary Symonds advertisements: *Pennsylvania Gazette*, May 5, 1768, June 23, 1773;*The Philadelphia Directory by Francis White* (Philadelphia: Young, Stewart and McCulloch, 1785), 18.

13. John Fanning Watson, *Annals of Philadelphia, Being a Collection of Memoirs, Anecdotes, & Incidents of the City and Its Inhabitants from the Days of the Pilgrim Founders* (Philadelphia: E. L. Carey & A. Hart, 1830), 613. Catherine M. Scholten, "'On the Importance of the Obstetrick Art': Changing Customs of Childbirth in America, 1760 to 1825," *William and Mary Quarterly* 34, no. 3 (1977): 434.

14. *Pennsylvania Packet*, January 1, 1790.

15. *Pennsylvania Packet*, January 2, 1790.

16. Karol Weaver, *Medical Revolutionaries: The Enslaved Healers of Eighteenth-Century Saint Domingue* (Champaign: University of Illinois Press, 2006); Ulrich, *Midwife's Tale*, 64.

17. Mary Beth Norton, "'The Ablest Midwife That Wee Knowe in the Land': Mistress Alice Tilly and the Women of Boston and Dorchester, 1649-1650," *William and Mary Quarterly* 55, no. 1 (January 1998): 105-106.

18. *Pennsylvania Packet*, January 1, 1790.

19. Ulrich, *Midwife's Tale*, 197; Erin Allen, "Paying the Doctor in 18th-Century Philadelphia," Library of Congress blog, April 28, 2016, https://blogs.loc.gov/loc/2016/04/paying-the-doctor-in-18th-century-philadelphia/; Sara Collini, "The Labors of Enslaved Midwives in Revolutionary Virginia," *Women in the American Revolution: Gender, Politics and the Domestic World*, ed. Barbara B. Oberg (Charlottesville: University of Virginia Press, 2019), 22-24, 28.

20. Charles Lyon Chandler, *Early Shipbuilding in Pennsylvania, 1683–1812* (Philadelphia: Guild of Brackett Lectures, 1932), 23; Gary B. Nash, *The Urban Crucible: Social Change, Political Consciousness, and the Origins of the American Revolution* (Cambridge, MA: Harvard University Press, 1979), table 2, 394; Edward E. Curtis, *The Organization of the British Army in the American Revolution* (New York: AMS Press, 1969, originally published in 1926), 158; Joseph Galloway, *A True and Impartial State of the Province of Pennsylvania* (Philadelphia, 1759), 53.

21. Martha Ballard is a good example of how busy a midwife could be. During 34 years of practice, she recorded 996 deliveries—an average of at least one per week. Richard W. Wertz and Dorothy C. Wertz, *Lying-In: A History of Childbirth in America* (New York: Free Press, 1977) 9; Scholten, "Obstetrick Art," 426–445.

22. Johnson, *Dictionary*. Mary Beth Norton sketches what a lying-in might typically look like in *Founding Mothers and Fathers: Gendered Power and the Forming of American Society* (New York: Alfred A. Knopf, 1996), 362-363. Norton also provides a number of seventeenth-century examples of women's knowledge surfacing to the astonishment of men, especially during legal proceedings. *Founding Mothers and Fathers*, 222-39.

23. Hiltzheimer, *Extracts*, 32. A clyster was an enema. Johnson, *Dictionary*.

24. Karol K. Weaver, "'Painful Leisure' and 'Awful Business': Female Death Workers in Pennsylvania," *PMHB* 140, no. 1 (2016): 31–55.
25. *Pennsylvania Gazette*, January 5, 1769, 5.
26. *Pennsylvania Chronicle*, June 26, 1769.
27. John Westby-Gibson, *The Bibliography of Shorthand* (London: Isaac Pitman & Sons, 1887), viii; J. L. J. Hughes, "Dublin Shorthand Writers," *Dublin Historical Record* 13, nos. 3/4 (1953): 118–127.
28. *American Weekly Mercury*, June 17 and July 1, 1731.
29. Henry Darrach noted that William "was a skilled shorthand writer and specimens of the cipher used by him are in possession of a member of the family." Darrach's informant, who owned the shorthand samples, was Margaret Porter Darragh Newton of Norfolk, Virginia, a tradition bearer who learned Lydia's Tale directly from her great aunt, Ann Darragh. Darrach CHS, 385, 387-388.
30. E. Hodgson, *The Trial of Cosmo Gordon, Esq.; Commonly Called The Honourable Cosmo Gordon, for the Willful Murder of Frederick Thomas, Esq.; in a Duel in Hyde Park, on the Fourth of September, 1783* (London: J. Walmslay, 1784); Robert N. Fanelli, "A Fatal Dispute Among the Guards," *Journal of the American Revolution*, May 6, 2021, https://allthingsliberty.com/2021/05/a-fatal-dispute-among-the-guards/; William Darragh, *A Discourse Publickly Delivered by a female friend from Old England in the Friends Meeting-House in Pine Street, Philadelphia, on the third day of the 5th month, 1769: also a prayer, by another Friend: the whole taken down in characters (at the time they were spoken) by William Darragh: to which is added, a short preface, by the editor* (Philadelphia: 1769).
31. *Pennsylvania Chronicle*, June 19 and 26, 1769. The marriage he referred to, celebrated at the time of the sermon, was that of Benjamin Berry and Sarah Lightfoot, who were married at Pine Street Meeting on May 3, 1769. Though Darragh did not mention the preaching Friend's name, evidence shows that she was Rachel Wilson, who signed the marriage certificate. Others who signed included Samuel Wetherill, who lived across the street from the meetinghouse, and William Darragh's brother-in-law, James Eddy. Philadelphia Monthly Meeting Minutes, Marriage Certificate of Benjamin Berry and Sarah Lightfoot May 3, 1769. "Rachel Wilson of Kendal, 1722–1776: Notes and Incidents of Her Visit to America, 1768–1769," *Bulletin of Friends' Historical Society of Philadelphia* 8, no. 1 (1917): 25-35.
32. Abraham Mitchel, Philadelphia Tax List, 1769, HSP.
33. Will of Lydia Darragh, Philadelphia City Archives, U.413; *Pennsylvania Gazette*, September 27, 1764.
34. Irish Catholic Parish Registers, St. Catherine's, Dublin City, 1740-1749, 83, Findmypast.ie.
35. *Watson's Gentleman and Citizen's Almanack for 1755*, 72. The marriage bounty was part of the effort to extirpate Roman Catholicism.
36. Thomas Barclay, an Irish linen importer at the time, and later a prominent revolutionary, purchased the house at Sheriff Sale in August 1772 for £265. The property had belonged to one of his business partners, William Mitchell, an Irishman from Ulster. City of Philadelphia, Department of Records, Philadelphia Deed: D 33.192; Barclay advertisement in *Pennsylvania Journal*, April 21, 1773, 2; *Pennsylvania Packet*, April 26, 1773, 1. This ad ran several times in April 1773. The post alley is known over its course today as Ionic Street and Bank Street. William Darragh continued to rent

the property from Thomas Barclay through the end of 1776. Philadelphia County PA Archives Tax Lists, City of Philadelphia Provincial Tax List, Dock Ward 1774, http://files.usgwarchives.net/pa/philadelphia/taxlist/dockward1774.txt. In February 1777, Lydia Darragh advertised that she had moved to the Loxley House; *Pennsylvania Packet*, February 18, 1777.

37. Philadelphia Constable Returns for 1775 lists William Darrach as School Mast. living in a property owned by Thomas Bartley [Barclay], City of Philadelphia Constables returns to Assessors for 1775, 68-69, https://therevolutionarycity.org/islandora/city-philadelphia-constables-returns-assessors-1775. The large room in Barclay's house was later used as a school room by a dancing master, William McDougall. *Pennsylvania Gazette*, September 16, 1789, 3; Rebecca Yamin, *Archaeology of the City—The Museum of the American Revolution Site, Archaeological Data Recovery, Third and Chestnut Streets, Philadelphia, Pennsylvania*, vol. 1 (West Chester, PA: Commonwealth Heritage Group, 2016), 15-16.

38. "Battles Were Fought to Open American Revolution Museum," *Philadelphia Inquirer*, April 18, 2017, https://www.inquirer.com/philly/opinion/editorials/battles-were-fought-to-open-american-revolution-museum.html; National Park Service, *Statement for Management* (Philadelphia: Independence National Historical Park, 1993); Boundary Map 1A7, in Yamin, *Archaeology of the City*; Rebecca Yamin, *Archaeology at the Site of the Museum of the American Revolution: A Tale of Two Taverns and the Growth of Philadelphia* (Philadelphia: Temple University Press, 2019), 67, 78.

CHAPTER 5: LYDIA DARRAGH'S QUAKER FAITH

1. Rufus M. Jones, ed., *George Fox: An Autobiography* (Philadelphia: Ferris & Leach, 1909), 125n42. Though this was Fox's preferred explanation for the origin of the term *Quaker*, Jones points out that the word was already in use at the time to describe members of various religious sects who trembled and quaked in religious frenzy, noting that "Friends themselves were sometimes given to trembling, and that the name came into general use because it fitted." William Penn, *A Brief Account of the Rise and Progress of the People Called Quakers* (London: James Phillips, 1794); John Gough, *History of the People Called Quakers, From their first Rise to the present Time*, volumes 1-4 (Dublin: Robert Jackson, 1790). Gough, a well-respected Quaker educator, served as a recording secretary for Dublin Friends Meeting. He was well known to William and Lydia Darragh in Dublin and was the man charged with drawing up and transcribing their marriage certificate.

2. Richard Bauman, *Let Your Words Be Few: Symbolism of Speaking and Silence Among Seventeenth-Century Quakers* (Tucson, AZ: Cambridge University Press, 1983), 24-28.

3. Bauman, *Let Your Words be Few*, 85-88.

4. When Friends adopted their nontraditional names for the months of the year, the Julian calendar was still in use, so First Month would have been March until the adoption of the Gregorian calendar.

5. "Charles II, 1662: An Act for preventing the Mischeifs and Dangers that may arise by certaine Persons called Quakers and others refusing to take lawfull Oaths," *Statutes of the Realm,* vol. 5, 1628–80, ed. John Raithby (1819), British History Online, 350-351, accessed July 25, 2025, http://www.british-history.ac.uk/statutes-realm/vol5; Bauman, *Let Your Words Be Few*, 138.

6. "William and Mary, 1688: An Act for Exempting their Majestyes Protestant Subjects dissenting from the Church of England from the Penalties of certaine Lawes. [Chapter XVIII. Rot. Parl. Pt. 5. Nu. 15.]," *Statutes of the Realm,* vol. 6, 1685–94, ed. John Raithby (s.l., 1819), 74-76, British History Online, accessed July 25, 2025, http://www.british-history.ac.uk/statutes-realm/vol6/. Though persecution played a role in the migration to Pennsylvania, a more powerful motive was the establishment of a civil society governed by Quaker mores. For a summary of historians' discussions about the motives for Quaker migration, see David Hackett Fischer, *Albion's Seed: Four British Folkways in America* (New York: Oxford University Press, 1989), 425. *The "Great Law"—December 7, 1782,* Pennsylvania Historical and Museum Commission, http://www.phmc.state.pa.us/portal/communities/documents/1681-1776/great-law.html.
7. The closest thing to a Quaker manual of faith for the period might be the *Extracts from the Minutes and Advices of the Yearly Meeting of Friends Held in London*, published by the London Meeting for Sufferings in 1783, and shared with other meetings as a guide to organization and behavior. This became the basis for what later Friends called their *Book of Discipline*, the forerunner to today's *Faith and Practice*. It contained fifty-one chapters on such topics as affirmation, conduct and conversation, meetings of ministers and elders, plainness, and war.
8. Bauman, *Let Your Words be Few*, 26.
9. Matthew 5:34-37 (King James Bible). Richard Bauman detailed how Friends' refusal to swear oaths led to their persecution in seventeenth-century England, in *Let Your Words be Few*, 95-119.
10. As authority for the peace testimony, Quakers frequently cited a passage from the Bible: "And he shall judge among the nations, and shall rebuke many people: and they shall beat their swords into plowshares, and their spears into pruninghooks: nation shall not lift up sword against nation, neither shall they learn war any more." Isaiah 2:4 (King James Bible).
11. *Extracts from the Minutes and Advices of the Yearly Meeting of Friends Held in London, from Its First Institution* (London: James Phillips, 1783), 268-269; *Faith and Practice* (Philadelphia: Philadelphia Yearly Meeting, 2018).
12. Quaker Information Center, *What Do Quakers Believe?,* https://quakerinfo.org/quakerism/beliefs; George Fox, *The Works of George Fox*, vol. 4 (Philadelphia: Marcus T. C. Gould, 1831), 174.
13. Darragh, *Discourse*, iii.
14. Darragh, *Discourse*, 4-5.

CHAPTER 6: THE COMING OF THE REVOLUTION

1. Bob Ruppert, "A Fast Ship from Salem: Carrying News of War," *Journal of the American Revolution*, April 17, 2015, https://allthingsliberty.com/2015/04/a-fast-ship-from-salem-carrying-news-of-war/; William H. Hallahan, *The Day the American Revolution Began* (New York: William Morrow, 2000), 172, 247-251; *London Evening Post*, May 30, 1775, 2. As an illustration of the kinds of problems presented by this communication lag, it is worth noting that the British government printed an immediate rebuttal in which it griped: "A report having been spread, and an Account having been printed and published, of a Skirmish between some of the People in the Province of Massachusetts Bay and a Detachment of his Majesty's Troops; it is proper to inform the

Publick, that no Advices have as yet been received in the American Department of any such Event. There is reason to believe that there are Dispatches from General Gage on board The Sukey, Captain Brown, which, though she sailed Four Days before the Vessel that brought the printed Account is not yet arrived." *London Gazette*, May 30, 1775.
2. Bernard Bailyn, *The Ideological Origins of the American Revolution* (Cambridge, MA: Harvard University Press, 1992).
3. *The Autobiography of Benjamin Franklin*, 2nd ed. (New Haven: Yale University Press, 1964), 209-211.
4. Steven Craig Harper, *Promised Land: Penn's Holy Experiment, The Walking Purchase and the Dispossession of Delawares, 1600-1763* (Bethlehem: Lehigh University Press, 2006); James H. Merrell, *Into the American Woods: Negotiations on the Pennsylvania Frontier* (New York: W.W. Norton, 2000).
5. Benjamin Franklin, "Autobiography of Benjamin Franklin (Autograph manuscript signed) 1771–1789," Huntington Library, 142-143, https://hdl.huntington.org/digital/collection/p15150coll7/id/0.
6. Franklin, "Autobiography," 142-143.
7. "Lists of Pennsylvania Settlers Murdered, Scalped and Taken Prisoners by Indians, 1755–1756," *PMHB* 32, no. 3, (1908): 309-319; James H. Hutson, *Pennsylvania Politics 1746–1770: The Movement for Royal Government and Its Consequences* (Princeton: Princeton University Press, 1972), 24-26; Bauman, *Reputation of Truth.*
8. *Pennsylvania Gazette*, June 2, 1763.
9. *Pennsylvania Gazette*, June 9, 1763.
10. *Pennsylvania Gazette*, October 27, 1763, 3; C. M. Bomberger, *The Battle of Bushy Run* (Jeannette, PA: Jeannette Publishing, 1928); *Report of the Commission to Locate the Site of the Frontier Forts of Pennsylvania*, 164-174.
11. Kenny, *Peaceable Kingdom Lost*; Brooke Hindle, "The March of the Paxton Boys," *William and Mary Quarterly* 3, no. 4 (1946): 462–86; *Pennsylvania Gazette*, February 9, 1764.
12. Patrick Spero, *Frontier Rebels: The Fight for Independence in the American West, 1765–1776* (New York: W. W. Norton, 2018).
13. Samuel Morris to Samuel Powell, May 18, 1765, *PMHB* 19 (1895): 531-32; Marshall to John Scott, December 14, 1765, "Extracts from the Letter-Book of Benjamin Marshall, 1763–1766," *PMHB* 20 (1896): 211.
14. C. A. Weslager, *The Stamp Act Congress* (Newark: University of Delaware Press, 1976); Richard Alan Ryerson, *The Revolution Is Now Begun: The Radical Committees of Philadelphia, 1765–1776* (Philadelphia: University of Pennsylvania Press, 1978), 27.
15. Knapp, *Life of Thomas Eddy*, 44.
16. City of Philadelphia, Department of Records, Philadelphia County Deed Book: D 33.192; Priscilla H. Roberts, *Thomas Barclay (1728–1793) Consul in France, Diplomat in Barbary* (Bethlehem, PA: Lehigh University Press, 2008); *Pennsylvania Journal*, February 16, 1764.
17. J. Thomas Scharf and Thompson Westcott, *History of Philadelphia, 1609–1884*, vol. 1 (Philadelphia: L. H. Everts, 1884), 272-73; Roberts, *Barclay*, 36; Ryerson, *Revolution*, 80-81, 84, 275; Minutes of the Pennsylvania Supreme Executive Council, March 13, 1777; *Naval Documents of the American Revolution* (hereafter *NDAR*), vol. 8, 102; John H. Campbell, *History of the Friendly Sons of St. Patrick and of the Hibernian Society for the Relief of Emigrants from Ireland. March 17, 1771–March 17, 1892* (Philadelphia: Hibernian Society, 1892).

18. City of Philadelphia, Department of Records, Philadelphia County Deed Book: D 10.86, July 8, 1766. Markoe, a Danish citizen, was compelled to resign his commission when the king of Denmark issued a neutrality edict. *History of the First Troop of Philadelphia City Cavalry, 1774–November 17, 1874* (Philadelphia: Hallowell, 1875), 5.
19. Robert J. Chaffin, "The Townshend Acts Crisis, 1767–1770," *Blackwell Encyclopedia of the American Revolution*, ed. Jack P. Greene and J. R. Pole (Malden, MA: Blackwell, 1991), 126-145; *Pennsylvania Journal*, March 23, 1769.
20. James Boswell, *An Account of Corsica, The Journal of a Tour to That Island, and Memoirs of Pascal Paoli* (London: Edward and Charles Dilly, 1768); *Pennsylvania Gazette*, April 13, 1769.
21. Campbell, *History of the Friendly Sons*, 3-4; "The Friendly Sons of St. Patrick, of Philadelphia, More Manufactured History," *American Catholic Historical Researches* 19, no. 3 (1902): 98.
22. *Pennsylvania Gazette*, October 20, 1773, 3; Thomas B. Taylor, "The Philadelphia Counterpart of the Boston Tea Party," *Bulletin of Friends' Historical Society of Philadelphia* 2, no. 3 (1908): 86-110, http://www.jstor.org/stable/41944817; R. W. Kelsey, "Philadelphia Tea-Party Letter–773," *Bulletin of Friends' Historical Society of Philadelphia* 10, no. 2 (1921): 67-70, http://www.jstor.org/stable/45242191.
23. *Public Advertiser*, April 2, 1774, Founders Online (hereafter FO), https://founders.archives.gov/documents/Franklin/01-21-02-0073.
24. Alexander Graydon, *Memoirs of a Life Chiefly Passed in Pennsylvania, within the Last Sixty Years* (Harrisburg: John Wyeth, 1811), 111-112; Thompson, *Rum Punch*, 165; Ryerson, *Revolution*, 131-132; Timothy Compeau, *Dishonored Americans: The Political Death of Loyalists in Revolutionary America* (Charlottesville: University of Virginia Press, 2023).
25. Campbell, *History of the Friendly Sons,* 31-32.
26. *History of the First Troop*, 1, 11, 14. In testimony to his service, a bronze sculpture depicting McClenachan today guards the entrance to the Trenton Battle Monument.
27. Donald Grady Shomette, *Privateers of the Revolution: War on the New Jersey Coast, 1775–1783* (Atglen, PA: Schiffer Publishing, 2016), 132-133; John Adams to Charles Adams, December 20, 1794, FO; Charles Rappleye, *Robert Morris, Financier of the American Revolution* (New York: Simon and Schuster, 2010), 216; Thomas Paine, *The Complete Writings of Thomas Paine*, ed. Philip S. Foner (New York: Citadel Press, 1945), xx; Bonds of the Letters of Marque, *Naval Records of the American Revolution, 1775–1778* (Washington, DC: Government Printing Office, 1906), 339.
28. Christopher Marshall Certificate of Removal from Middletown Friends Meeting, April 3, 1736, USQMR; *Philadelphia Women's Monthly Meeting Minutes, 1728–1753,* October 26, 1735, January 26, 1736, USQMR.
29. Philadelphia Monthly Meeting Minutes, March 31, 1751, USQMR.
30. Philadelphia Monthly Meeting Minutes, December 22, 1750, January 29, 1751, February 26, 1751, USQMR.
31. Philadelphia Monthly Meeting Minutes, March 31, 1751, USQMR.
32. Kenneth Scott, "Counterfeiting in Pennsylvania," *Numismatic Notes and Monographs*, 1955, http://numismatics.org/digitallibrary/ark:/53695/nnan49620.
33. Philadelphia Quarterly Meeting Minutes, September 4, 1751; Philadelphia Yearly Meeting Minutes, September 29, 1752, USQMR; *Pennsylvania Archives*, ser. 3, vol. 10, September 22, 1752, 229, Fold3.com.

34. Philadelphia Monthly Meeting Minutes, August 29, 1760, USQMR; Diary of Christopher Marshall, Christopher Marshall Papers, Collection 395, box 1, June 24, 1783, HSP.
35. Marshall Brothers Account Book, 1776, https://therevolutionarycity.org/islandora/marshall-brothers-account-book-1776?search_api_fulltext=Marshall.
36. Ryerson, *Revolution*, 43, 80.
37. Ryerson, *Revolution*, 99.
38. Philadelphia Monthly Meeting Minutes, September 22, 1775, USQMR.
39. Philadelphia Monthly Meeting Minutes, February 23, 1776, USQMR.
40. John U. Rees, "'To Hold Thirty Six Cartridges of Powder and Ball': Continental Army Tin and Sheet-Iron Canisters, 1775–1780," https://www.academia.edu/87762425/_To_hold_thirty_six_cartridges_of_powder_and_ball_Continental_Army_Tin_and_Sheet_Iron_Canisters_1775_1780. Rees noted a report by the Continental Congress: "29 April 1776, The Committee of Claims reported, that there is due, To Benjamin Marshall, for tin cartouch boxes, the sum of £174 18 0." Benjamin Marshall did appeal his disownment, but the British occupation of Philadelphia interrupted the proceedings. In exile in Providence, he was unable to attend meetings in the city, and he died before the matter could be resolved. Philadelphia Monthly Meeting Minutes, May 31, 1776, July 27, 1776, November 4, 1776, August 4, 1777; Philadelphia Quarterly Meeting Minutes, November 3, 1777, February 2, 1778, USQMR.
41. Ryerson, *Revolution,* 113, 129, 131; Christopher Marshall, *Extracts from the Diary of Christopher Marshall, Kept in Philadelphia and Lancaster, during the American Revolution, 1774–1781*, ed. William Duane (Albany: Joel Munsell, 1877).
42. Benjamin Loxley, *Benjamin Loxley's Account of his Ancestors of his Parents and of himself and Family, Dated June 20, 1789*, HSP; Joseph Seymour, "Light the Match Load Away: The Ordnance and Organizational Structure of the Philadelphia Artillery, 1747–1777," *American Society of Arms Collectors Bulletin* 93, 32-47, https://americansocietyofarmscollectors.org/wp-content/uploads/2019/06/2006-B93-Light-the-Match-Load-Away-The-Ordnance-a.pdf; Graydon, *Memoirs*, 40.
43. Benjamin Loxley, *A Journal of the Campaign to Amboy, and Other Parts of the Jersies*, Am. 612, HSP.

CHAPTER 7: LYDIA DARRAGH'S NEIGHBORHOOD

1. While in more recent times Philadelphians have referred to a smaller area of South Philadelphia, below Oregon Avenue, as The Neck, in the eighteenth century the term was often applied to all of the land between the two rivers, south of the city. See, for instance, William Howe's orders of October 28, 1777, "The Troops are on no account to take any Article of property from the Inhabitants on the Neck without proper authority." "The Kemble Papers, Vol. I, 1773–1789," (General Sir William Howe's Orders 1777), *Collections of the New-York Historical Society for the Year 1883* (New York: Printed for the Society, 1884), 527.
2. *Pennsylvania Packet*, February 18, 1777.
3. David Price, "The Significance of John Cadwalader." *Journal of the American Revolution*, September 22, 2022, https://allthingsliberty.com/2022/09/the-significance-of-john-cadwalader/; Nicholas B. Wainwright, *Colonial Grandeur in Philadelphia: The House and Furniture of General John Cadwalader* (Philadelphia: HSP, 1964).
4. Watson, *Annals*, 1830, 124, 290-291, 357-358.

5. Lucius R. Paige, *History of Cambridge, Massachusetts, 1630–1877* (Boston: H. O. Houghton, 1877), 345-352.
6. Bowers Bath, *An Alarm Sounded to Prepare the Inhabitants of the World to Meet the Lord in the Way of His Judgments* (Printed by William Bradford, 1709), 9-10.
7. Jehu Curtis Clay, *The Life of Mrs. Robert Clay Afterwards Mrs. Robert Bolton (Née Ann Curtis) 1690–1738, in letters written by herself to her physician and now transcribed from the original manuscript by her great grandson, the Rev. Jehu Curtis Clay* (Philadelphia: n.d.), 41-42. Bolton's account of Bathsheba is corroborated by existing evidence, slim as that is. Bolton could be viewed as unfairly biased, but she was a careful and scrupulous writer who took account of her aunt's virtues as well as her flaws.
8. Clay, *Life*, 42-43.
9. Clay, *Life*, 41-50.
10. *The Statutes at Large of Pennsylvania from 1682 to 1801*, vol. 3, 1712 to 1724 (Pennsylvania: Clarence M. Busch, 1896), 345-357; Gary B. Nash, "The Free Society of Traders and the Early Politics of Pennsylvania," *PMHB* 89, no. 2 (1965): 147–73; Watson, *Annals*, 1830, 357.
11. Bolton, "Life," 44-45. Bolton was incorrect; the distance between the narrowly confined city center and Spruce Street was a little over half a mile. William John Potts thought that Bathsheba had lived in the Loxley House, as have other writers, but they seem to have misunderstood John Fanning Watson's account of the area. She lived across the way, on the west side of Little Dock Creek, near the property that eventually became the site of the Cadwalader house. William John Potts, "Bathsheba Bowers," *PMHB* 3 (1879): 110-113; Watson, *Annals*, 1830, 357.
12. Suzanne M. Zweizing, "Bathsheba Bowers (c. 1672–1718)," *Legacy* 11, no. 1 (1994): 65–73.
13. William L. Ramsey, *The Yamasee War: A Study of Culture, Economy, and Conflict in the Colonial South* (Lincoln: University of Nebraska Press, 2008); Clay, *Life*, 50.
14. Graydon, *Memoirs*, 107-108.
15. *Finding Aid to the Cadwalader Family Papers*, 1-3, HSP, https://hsp.org/sites/default/files/legacy_files/migrated/findingaid1454cadwaladerpart1.pdf; Charles Willson Peale, *Portrait of John and Elizabeth Lloyd Cadwalader and Their Daughter Anne*, 1772, Philadelphia Museum of Art, Accession Number 1983-90-3.
16. Walsh, "American Biography," 32; Darrach, *PMHB*, 386, 389. For the exact locations of the two properties, see J. M. Duffin, Mapping West Philadelphia: Landowners in October 1777, 2024, https://maps.archives.upenn.edu/WestPhila1777/map. php.
17. Watson, *Annals*, 1830, 357. Elizabeth Loxley, daughter of Benjamin, who was born about 1770, married Loyd Jones at the First Baptist Church of Philadelphia on October 1, 1792. Ann Loxley, another daughter of Benjamin, was born about 1775 and married Morgan John Rees in Philadelphia, February 22, 1796.
18. "I stood upon a Balcony on Society Hill, from whence I preached my Farewel-Sermon last Fall . . . " George Whitefield, *A continuation of the Reverend Mr. Whitefield's journal from a few days after his arrival at Georgia, to his second return thither from Pennsylvania* (Philadelphia: B. Franklin, 1740), 29.
19. *Pennsylvania Gazette*, April 10, 1740, 1-2.
20. Archibald Cummings, *Faith absolutely necessary, but not sufficient to salvation without good works. In two sermons, preached at Christ-Church in Philadelphia, April 20, 1740* (Philadelphia: Andrew and William Bradford, 1740), iii-iv.

21. Whitefield, *Journal*, 29-30; Mark 10:46-52 (King James Bible); John 9:34 (King James Bible).
22. Whitefield, *Journal*, 30.
23. Franklin, "Autobiography," 117.
24. John Pollock, *George Whitefield and the Great Awakening* (Garden City: Doubleday, 1972), 145-146; Joseph Belcher, *George Whitefield: A Biography, with special reference to his labors in America* (New York: American Tract Society, 1857), 356-357.

CHAPTER 8: THE SEAT OF WAR

1. Barnet Schecter, *The Battle for New York: The City at the Heart of the American Revolution* (New York: Walker, 2002), 258-271; Arthur S. Lefkowitz, *The Long Retreat: The Calamitous American Defense of New Jersey, 1776* (New Brunswick: Rutgers University Press, 1998), 98-126; David Hackett Fischer, *Washington's Crossing* (New York: Oxford University Press, 2004), 206-345; William L. Kidder, *Ten Crucial Days: Washington's Vision for Victory Unfolds* (Lawrence Township, NJ: Knox Press, 2018), 105-320; David Price, *The Road to Assunpink Creek: Liberty's Desperate Hour and the Ten Crucial Days of the American Revolution* (Lawrenceville, NJ: Knox Press, 2019), 3-196.
2. Much has been written blaming William Howe for the failure of Burgoyne's campaign. For a clear-eyed assessment of British strategy for 1777, and the responsibility for Burgoyne's defeat at Saratoga, see Kevin J. Weddle, *The Compleat Victory: Saratoga and the American Revolution* (New York: Oxford University Press, 2021), 49-72.
3. Sarah Logan Fisher, "A Diary of Trifling Occurrences, Philadelphia, 1776–1778," ed. Nicholas B. Wainwright, *PMHB*, 82 (1958): 437.
4. Fisher, "Diary," 439-440.
5. Marshall, *Extracts*, 121.
6. Henry Laurens to John Lewis Gervais, August 5, 1777, in Henry Laurens, *The Papers of Henry Laurens, Volume 11: Jan. 5, 1776-Nove. 1, 1777*, ed. David R. Chesnutt et al. (Columbia: University of South Carolina Press, 1988), 418.
7. Robert N. Fanelli, "HMS Roebuck on the Delaware," *Journal of the American Revolution*, May 25, 2023, https://allthingsliberty.com/2023/05/hms-roebuck-on-the-delaware/.
8. Fisher, "Diary," 443.
9. Thomas Gilpin, *Exiles in Virginia: with Observations on the Conduct of the Society of Friends during the Revolutionary War, Comprising the Official Papers of the Government Relating to that Period. 1777–1778* (Philadelphia: G. Sherman, 1848); Paige L. Whidbee, "The Quaker Exiles: 'The Cause of Every Inhabitant,'" *Pennsylvania History: A Journal of Mid-Atlantic Studies* 83, no. 1 (2016): 28–57; Norman E. Donoghue II, *Prisoners of Congress: Philadelphia's Quakers in Exile, 1777–1778* (University Park: Pennsylvania State University Press, 2023).
10. Knapp, *Life of Thomas Eddy*, 44.
11. Minutes of the Pennsylvania Council of Safety, September 26, 1776, *NDAR*, vol. 6, 1009-1010. "For the sake of regularity, we think it necessary for you to employ a person to act in the capacity of Steward and Clerk (the wages allowed is 14 dollars P month) who shall give receipts for all the provisions he receives, shall superintend the delivery of them and keep lists of the men employed, which lists are to be returned to this Board." *NDAR*, vol. 8, 181. The board may have urged filling this position again, having felt the lapse of such accounting after Darragh's departure.

12. National Archives and Records Administration (hereafter NARA), "Compiled Service Records of Soldiers Who Served in the American Army during the Revolutionary War, 1775–1783," M881, Fold3.com. Darragh's commission, which made him the most junior officer in his company, was backdated to January 1, a common practice.
13. John B. B. Trussell Jr., *The Pennsylvania Line: Regimental Organization and Operations, 1776–1783* (Harrisburg: Pennsylvania Historical and Museum Commission, 1977), 42, 49-50; *Pennsylvania Archives,* ser. 5, vol. 2, 773; NARA, M246, US Revolutionary War Rolls, 2nd Pennsylvania Regiment, folder 15, roll 0081, 5, Stayner's Company Payroll, June 1777.
14. Thomas J. Maguire, *Battle of Paoli* (Mechanicsburg: Stackpole Books, 2000); Case Files of Pension and Bounty-Land Warrant Applications, W.7876, NARA, M804, Fold3.com.
15. Trussell, *Pennsylvania Line,* 44. After Stayner's capture, command of Darragh's company went to Captain Peter Gosner. It was also listed as the "Colonel's company."
16. Trussell, *Pennsylvania Line,* 50; muster rolls, payrolls, strength returns, and other miscellaneous personnel, pay, and supply records of American army units, 1775–83, Pay Roll for Captain Roger Stayner's Company for the months of November and December (1777), NARA, M246, Fold3.com.
17. On December 29, 1777, Congress authorized an extra month's Extraordinary Pay that was disbursed during February. At that time, Charles Darragh was again on command. Pay Extraordinary for Captain Roger Stayner's Company, NARA, M246, 27, Fold3.com.
18. Marshall, *Diary*, 96.
19. Neil Hanson, *The Great Fire of London in that Apocalyptic Year, 1666* (Hoboken, NJ: John Wiley & Sons, 2002).
20. Preservation Society of Charleston, 1778 (January 15) Fire, http://www.halseymap.com/flash/window.asp?HMID=30.
21. Deposition of William Barry, June 11, 1776, *NDAR*, vol. 5, 483, https://www.history.navy.mil/content/dam/nhhc/research/publications/naval-documents-of-the-american-revolution/NDARVolume5.pdf.
22. Benjamin L. Carp, *The Great New York Fire of 1776: A Lost Story of the American Revolution* (New Haven, CT: Yale University Press, 2023), 123.
23. Thomas J. Maguire, *The Philadelphia Campaign,* vol. 1, *Brandywine and the Fall of Philadelphia* (Mechanicsburg: Stackpole Books, 2006); Michael C. Harris, *Brandywine: A Military History of the Battle for Philadelphia, October 4, 1777* (El Dorado Hills, CA: Savas Beatie, 2014); Gary Ecelbarger, *George Washington's Momentous Year: Twelve Months that Transformed the Revolution*, vol. 1, *The Philadelphia Campaign, July to December 1777* (Yardley: Westholme, 2024), 130-141.
24. Robert Morton, "The Diary of Robert Morton," *PMHB* 1, no. 1 (1877): 7.
25. Elizabeth Drinker, *The Diary of Elizabeth Drinker, Volume I: 1758—1795,* ed. Elaine Forman Crane (Boston: Northeastern University Press, 1991), September 23, 1777, 234.
26. Marshall, *Diary*, 130.
27. Drinker, *Diary,* September 25, 1777, 235; Morton, *Diary*, 7.
28. Drinker, *Diary*, September 25, 1777, 235; Fisher, "Diary," 450; Morton, *Diary*, 7.
29. Drinker, *Diary*, September 25, 1777, 235. A fire did actually break out in the city

a few weeks later, on October 12. The occupying troops appear to have doused it, preventing its spread. Robert Morton reported: "About 1 o'clock this morning, the inhabitants were alarmed by the cry of fire, which happened at a stable above the Barracks, supposed to have been occasioned by a number of Hessians lodging in the Stable, but was happily extinguished notwithstanding the inactivity of the inhabitants, and a 3 story adjoining house which caught 3 Times, in less than 2 hours." Morton, *Diary*, 18.

30. *Pennsylvania Evening Post*, October 11, 1777; John Miller's Journal, in Watson, *Annals*, 1844, vol. 2, 68.

31. Morton, *Diary*, October 20, 1777, 22.

32. Morton, *Diary*, 9. The planation became the site of the Naval Asylum on the Schuylkill.

33. Morton, *Diary*, 10.

34. Morton, *Diary*, 10-11; John Fanning Watson, *Annals of Philadelphia and Pennsylvania in the Olden Time*, vol. 2 (Philadelphia: John Penington and Uriah Hunt, 1844), 285.

35. Drinker, *Diary*, November 5, 1777.

36. Morton, *Diary*, 20.

37. Morton, *Diary*, 22.

38. "An account of the Number of Houses, and Inhabitants, &c in the city of Philadelphia, the Northern Liberties, and District of Southwark," in B. F. Stevens, comp., *Facsimiles of Manuscripts in European Archives Relating to America, 1773–1783*, vol. 24 (London: Mallby & Sons, 1895), 2085. Galloway's tallies for males 18 to 60 were calculated incorrectly. Two separate math errors in the subtotals for the city and the suburban districts gave a net result of plus 10, which was then carried over to give a total population of 21,767. To correct for the errors, I have adjusted the number here to 21,757.

39. Darrach CHS, 389.

40. Darrach PMHB, 86. It appears that on hearing the family story about a cousin aiding Lydia Darragh, someone dug around to see if there was a British officer named Barrington serving in 1777. Because Barrington was Lydia's maiden name, it was logically the first name that might be checked, the surnames of most other cousins still being undocumented in the latter part of the 1800s. This inquiry was most likely launched by Henry Darrach himself, but his statements created a conundrum. No work by the title cited in his footnote has been found. It could have been a misattribution for a regimental history published in 1847: Richard Cannon, *Historical Record of the Seventh Regiment, or The Royal Fusiliers, Containing an Account of the Formation of the Regiment in 1685, and of its subsequent services to 1846* (London: Parker, Furnival & Parker, 1847). This was a volume in the series Historical Records of the British Army, Comprising the History of Every Regiment in Her Majesty's Service. But Cannon's work did not detail Barrington's service record. A later book, *British Officers Serving in America 1774–1783*, published by Worthington Chauncey Ford in 1897, does give partial details of Barrington's service (p. 24), but not the retirement date cited by Darrach. There is yet a later history that matches more closely the title listed by Darragh: Percy Groves, *Historical Records of the 7th or Royal Regiment of Fusiliers Now Known as the Royal Fusiliers (The City of London Regiment) 1685–1903* (Guernsey: Frederick B. Guerin, 1903). While it does include Barrington's retirement

date (p. 290), it did not see print until 1903. The most likely explanation is that Darrach corresponded with Groves, who had already published several other regimental histories, and that Groves shared with him additional information that would be found later in his forthcoming work. Though his conclusion about Barrington turned out to be incorrect, the episode points to the thoroughness of Darrach's inquiries, especially considering the limitations of his day.

41. Tony Hayter, ed., *An Eighteenth-Century Secretary at War: The Papers of William, Viscount Barrington* (London: Bodley Head, 1988), 16.

42. *London Gazette*, March 4, 1775; Peter Force, *American Archives*, "List of the Prisoners taken at Chambly and St. John's," Vol. 3/1426, 1427; Muster Rolls of the 7th Regiment of Foot, 1772, Dec 1775–Dec 1776, and Dec 1776–June 1777, WO12/2474, https://7thregimentoffoot.weebly.com/fort-chambly-pows.html; Names of the Officers, non-commissioned officers and private men, brought prisoners from Chambly, quoted in Kenneth Baumgardt, *The Royal Army in America During the Revolutionary War: The American Prisoner Records* (Report for the US Army Corps of Engineers, 2008); John Adams, *The Adams Papers, Diary and Autobiography of John Adams*, vol. 2, 1771–1781, ed. L. H. Butterfield (Cambridge, MA: Harvard University Press, 1961), 223–226.

43. Ken Miller, "'A Dangerous Set of People': British Captives and the Making of Revolutionary Identity in the Mid-Atlantic Interior," *Journal of the Early Republic* 32, no. 4 (2012), 593. Some sources, such as the *Pennsylvania Journal*, June 19, 1776, say five officers escaped, but the highly detailed examinations of two Americans who served as guides for the fugitives describe only four. "The Examination of William Poor, in respect to the British Officers (prisoners of war) who broke their Parole, and escaped from Lebanon, Pennsylvania, in June, 1776," and "The Examination of John White," Force, *American Archives*, 5th ser., vol. 1, 596-599. One of the four officers who escaped can be identified with certainty: Lieutenant George Cuppaidge, an Irishman of the 26th Regiment. Another was most likely Captain Walter Home or Hume, like Barrington from the 7th Regiment, who seems to have been the leader of the group, according to testimony of Americans who were forced—at gunpoint—to guide them. Lieutenant William Richardson of the 26th was probably another. The fourth officer has not been identified. Each of these men seems to have been accompanied by a soldier who acted as a personal servant. Steven M. Baule with Stephen Gilbert, *British Army Officers Who Served in the American Revolution, 1775–1783* (Westminster, MD: Heritage Books, 2004), 4.

44. Force, *American Archives*, 5th ser., 1, 411-412, 761; Miller, "Dangerous," 571; NARA, Lancaster Committee to President of Congress, Dec. 21, 1775, *Papers of the Continental Congress*, reel 83.

45. Force, *American Archives*, 5th ser., 1:411-412; Letter from Lebanon Committee to Lancaster Committee, July 16, 1776, 401, cited in David Library of the American Revolution: Finding Aid on Prisoners of War, https://www.amphilsoc.org/sites/default/files/2020-01/attachments/Prisoners%20of%20War.pdf.

46. George Washington to Benjamin Franklin, August 18, 1776, FO, https://founders.archives.gov/documents/Franklin/01-22-02-0336; Force, *American Archives*, 5th ser., 1:1325; Christian McBurney, *Kidnapping the Enemy: The Special Operations to Capture Generals Charles Lee & Richard Prescott* (Yardley, PA: Westholme, 2014), 122.

No record of the actual exchange has been found. McBurney suggested that Barrington was freed in late August 1776, but the document referred to seems to be Barrington's parole after being jailed at Lancaster. McBurney, *Kidnapping*, 117. Don Hagist, *General Orders, Rhode Island: December 1776–January 1778* (Berwyn Heights, MD: Heritage Books, 2019), 42.

47. McBurney, *Kidnapping*, 136, 149-150; Jonathan Trumbull Sr. to George Washington, July 25, 1777, FO, https://founders.archives.gov/documents/Washington/03-10-02-0411. In June 1777, William Barrington had received a promotion to captain in the 70th Foot, though it is not clear that the news from England reached him before his capture. Nonetheless, he continued to serve as an aide-de-camp to Prescott through 1778. *London Gazette*, June 28, 1777; McBurney, *Kidnapping*, 185.

48. McBurney, *Kidnapping*, 162; Joseph Webb Jr. to George Washington, January 30, 1778, FO https://founders.archives.gov/documents/Washington/03-13-02-0342; *New York Gazette and Weekly Mercury*, April 6, 1778. Curiously, *The Complete Peerage* does not mention this marriage, though it does list a later marriage. Teresa Clarke was the daughter of the late Thomas Clarke, Esq. *Independent Chronicle* (Boston), January 7, 1779.

49. What became of Barrington's first wife is unknown. Thomas Banks's succeeding Barrington as captain in the 70th Foot is from *Scots Magazine*, February 1, 1780; Baule, *British Army Officers*, "Thomas Banks, Captain, 70th Foot, September 2, 1779," 9; *The Complete Peerage*, V. I, 433-434. Barrington of Beckett House, Viscounts Barrington, https://landedfamilies.blogspot.com/2020/03/409-barrington-of-beckett-house.html. On William's death, his younger brother, Richard James Barrington, succeeded to the viscountcy. He appears to have been somewhat unstable, as revealed in an unusual letter he wrote to Benjamin Franklin while he was in France (or, possibly, to William Temple Franklin, Benjamin's grandson, the recipient is unclear). In this remarkable communication, Richard introduced himself, lamented his own "unfortunate turn for extravagance and dissipation," and, having resigned his commission in the British Horse Guards, incredibly asked to be given a commission in the American army. Later that year, he sailed to Philadelphia and married Susan Budden, a daughter of William Budden. Richard Barrington to William Temple Franklin[?] (unpublished), January 16, 1783, The Revolutionary City, https://therevolutionarycity.org/islandora/barrington-richard-unknown-recipient-1783-january-16.

50. William Howe had a number of aides de camp in 1777, including Nisbet Balfour, Cornelius Cuyler, Valentine Gardiner, William Gardiner, Henry Knight, Friedrich von Muenchhausen, John Montresor, and James Patterson, but none of these known aides was Irish.

51. Alexander Garden, *Anecdotes of the American revolution, illustrative of the talents and virtues of the heroes and patriots, who acted the most conspicuous parts therein; second series* (Charleston, SC: A. E. Miller, 1828), 44.

52. "Staff Officers in North America . . . Lt.-Col. James Paterson, of 63d, foot, to be Adjutant General," *Scots Magazine* 38 (July 1776): 399; Evan W. H. Fyers, "General Sir William Howe's Operations in Pennsylvania, 1777 (Continued)," *Journal of the Society for Army Historical Research* 9, no. 35 (January 1930): 32. James Paterson returned to Philadelphia at an unknown time. A pass signed J. Paterson, Adjutant General, dated January 15, 1778, suggests that either he was present in Philadelphia at

that time or that he had not formally relinquished the title and that someone in an acting capacity signed his name in absentia. Friedrich von Muenchhausen, *At General Howe's Side, 1776–1778, The Diary of General William Howe's aide de camp, Captain Friedrich von Muenchhausen*, trans. Ernst Kipping, annotated by Samuel Smith (Monmouth Beach, NJ: Philip Freneau Press, 1974), 47; Mark Urban, *Fusiliers: The Saga of a British Redcoat Regiment in the American Revolution* (New York: Walker, 2007), 134-135; John Graves Simcoe, *Simcoe's Military Journal: A History of the Operations of a Partisan Corps, Called the Queen's Rangers* (New York: Bartlett & Wellford, 1844), 56. In June, 1778, Henry Clinton, by then commanding the British army in North America, who did not get along with Balfour, appointed Francis Rawdon-Hastings to the position of adjutant general. Mark M. Boatner, *Encyclopedia of the American Revolution* (New York: D. McKay, 1966), 919.

53. The earliest attempt to connect André with Lydia Darragh was made by Theodore W. Bean in his *History of Montgomery County Pennsylvania, Illustrated* (Philadelphia: Everts & Peck, 1884), 167; D. A. B. Ronald, *The Life of John André, the Redcoat Who Turned Benedict Arnold* (Philadelphia: Casemate, 2019). For a thorough discussion of the Meschianza and André's role, see John W. Jackson, *With the British Army in Philadelphia* (San Rafael, CA: Presidio Press, 1979), 235-249.

54. Baule, *British Army Officers*, 4; Deborah Logan, "Books taken from Dr. Franklin's Library by Major André—M. du Simitiere's statement," *PMHB* 8, no. 4 (December 1884): 430.

55. George Washington to Thomas Mifflin, April 10-12, 1777, FO.

56. Trussell, *Pennsylvania Line,* 149, 211-220. The village of Frankford grew up around a mill established by Swedish settlers in the 1660s, before the arrival of English settlers led by William Penn. The mill and village were on the north bank of a tidal creek that ran into the Delaware River two miles to the east. The creek itself continues to be known by various names along its length, from east to west: Frankford, Tacony, and Tookany Creek.

57. Excellent summaries of the events leading up to the British movement against Whitemarsh can be found in Thomas J. Maguire, *The Philadelphia Campaign,* vol. 2, *Germantown and the Roads to Valley Forge* (Mechanicsburg: Stackpole Books, 2007), 221-233; Michael C. Harris, *The Philadelphia Campaign, 1777* (Havertown, PA: Casemate, 2023); Ecelbarger, *George Washington's Momentous Year*; Michael C. Harris, *Fighting for Philadelphia: Forts Mercer and Mifflin, the Battle of Whitemarsh, and the Road to Valley Forge, October 5–December 19, 1777* (El Dorado Hills, CA: Savas Beatie, 2025).

58. Thomas Sullivan, *From Redcoat to Rebel: The Thomas Sullivan Journal,* ed. Joseph Lee Boyle (Warminster, MD: Heritage Books, 1997), December 4, 1777.

CHAPTER 9: LYDIA DARRAGH EAVESDROPS ON THE BRITISH

1. Walsh, "American Biography," 32.

2. "William Howe Orderly Book, March 9, 1776–May 1, 1778," William L. Clements Library, University of Michigan Library digital collections, https://quod.lib.umich.edu/h/howew/howew.0001.001.

3. Carl Baurmeister, "Letters of Major Baurmeister during the Philadelphia Campaign, 1777–1778," pt. 2, ed. Bernhard A. Uhlendorf and Edna Vosper, *PMHB* 60, no. 1 (1936): 41.

4. Archibald Robertson, *Archibald Robertson: His Diaries and Sketches in America, 1762–1780* (New York: New York Public Library, 1971), 158; Morton, *Diary*, 31-32; Drinker, *Diary*, December 1, 1777, 290.
5. Allen McLane to George Washington, November 28, 1777, FO, https://founders.archives.gov/documents/Washington/03-12-02-0428; John Clark to George Washington, December 1, 1777, FO, https://founders.archives.gov/documents/Washington/03-12-02-046; Robert Smith to George Washington, December 2, 1777, FO, https://founders.archives.gov/documents/Washington/03-12-02-047; John Clark to George Washington, December 3, 1777, FO, https://founders. archives.gov/documents/Washington/03-12-02-0481;
6. William Dewees Jr. to George Washington December 4, 1777, FO, https://founders.archives.gov/documents/Washington/03-12-02-0496. John Nagy, writing about espionage in 2011, mistakenly attributed authorship of the Dewees letter to William Darragh, as part of his argument that the Darragh family were active participants in an organized spy network. John Nagy, *Spies in the Continental Capital* (Yardley: Westholme, 2011), xii.
7. "William Howe Orderly Book," December 3, 1777, December 4, 1777; Robertson, *Diaries*, 158.
8. Ira D. Gruber, ed., *John Peebles' American War, The Diary of a Scottish Grenadier, 1776–1782* (Mechanicsburg, PA: Stackpole Books, 1998), December 4, 1777, 152.
9. Johann Ewald, *Diary of the American War: A Hessian Journal*, ed. Joseph P. Tustin (New Haven, CT: Yale University Press, 1979), 108.
10. See appendices for each of these narratives. Johnson, *Dictionary*, defines *closet* as "a small room of privacy and retirement."
11. *Valley Forge Orderly Book of General George Weedon* (New York: Dodd, Mead, 1902); Diagram of Troop Dispositions at Whitemarsh, November 28 1777, John Cadwalader Papers, folder 24, HSP.
12. *Pennsylvania Ledger: or the Philadelphia Market-Day Advertiser*, December 3, 1777. Though this report, given from the British perspective, doubled the number of American casualties, it was, at the time, the most accurate printed account available to citizens of Philadelphia, depicting one of the war's more ferocious and sanguine encounters.
13. Drinker, *Diary*, October 4, 1777, 239-240.
14. Walsh, "American Biography," 32-33.
15. Watson, *MS Annals*, 1829, 24; John Fanning Watson, *Historic Tales of Olden Time, Concerning the Early Settlement and progress of Philadelphia and Pennsylvania* (Philadelphia: E. Littell and Thomas Holden, 1833), 294-295; Watson, *Annals*, 1844, 327.
16. Darrach CHS, 390.
17. Walsh, "American Biography," 33.
18. Haines, untitled manuscript version of Lydia's Tale.
19. See Watson's account in appendix C below.
20. Darrach CHS, 390.

CHAPTER 10: LYDIA DARRAGH'S WALK TO THE AMERICAN LINES

1. Darrach CHS, 391.
2. Henry Leffmann, *Notes on the Secret Service of the Revolutionary Army Operating Around Philadelphia* (Philadelphia: City History Society of Philadelphia, 1910).

3. Henry Leffmann, *Outline Autobiography of Henry Leffmann, A. M., M. D., PH. D., D. D. S., of Philadelphia, with a Reference Index of Contributions to Science and Literature* (Philadelphia: n.p., 1905).
4. Leffmann, *Notes*, 169.
5. Central Intelligence Agency, *Intelligence During the War of Independence,* accessed August 20, 2025, https://www.cia.gov/resources/csi/static/Intelligence-in-the-War-of-Independence-web.pdf.
6. Scharf and Westcott, *History of Philadelphia,* 368.
7. "Correspondence of the Children of Christopher Marshall," 343; Marshall, *Extracts*, May 10, 1778, 179-180.
8. George Washington to Henry Laurens, December 15, 1777, FO, https://founders.archives.gov/documents/Washington/03-12-02-0553.
9. Drinker, *Diary*, September 16, 1777, 231.
10. Victor S. Clark, *History of Manufactures in the United States: 1607–1860* (Washington, DC: Carnegie Institution of Washington, 1916), 598-599.
11. Drinker, *Diary*, November 12, 1777, 253; Hiltzheimer, *Extracts*, December 13, 1777, 37; Samuel Emlen, *Extract of a letter from several Friends in Philadelphia, to John Fothergill, David Barclay, Daniel Mildred, Jacob Hagen, Thomas Corbyn, Mark Beaufoy, John Eliot, and Richard Chester*, December 16, 1777, Haverford College Quaker and Special Collections; Fisher, "Diary," December 6, 1777, 458.
12. John K. Alexander, "The Philadelphia Numbers Game: An Analysis of Philadelphia's Eighteenth-Century Population," *PMHB* 98, no. 3 (1974): 314–24; Michael C. Harris and Gary Ecelbarger, "The Numerical Strength of George Washington's Army During the 1777 Philadelphia Campaign," *Journal of the American Revolution*, October 5, 2021, https://allthingsliberty.com/2021/10/the-numerical-strength-of-george-washingtons-army-during-the-1777-philadelphia-campaign/.
13. Hoping to overcome British merchants' insistence on being paid in specie, several Philadelphia businessmen who had remained in the city during the British occupation signed a subscription stating that they would honor Pennsylvania's paper currency. In the process, they announced exchange rates for various kinds of specie. This ended up carrying little to no weight. *Pennsylvania Evening Post*, Philadelphia, PA, Saturday, November 6, 1777.
14. Journal of HMS Liverpool, November 1, 1777, *NDAR* 10:370-371; Richard Howe to Hamond, December 2, 1777, *NDAR* 10:653-654; Journal of Captain James Parker, December 1, 1777, *NDAR* 10:645. Sturdy and dangerous, *chevaux de frise* continue to turn up occasionally. One thirty-foot *cheval de frise* washed up in the Delaware River at Bristol as recently as 2012 in the aftermath of Hurricane Sandy. See *The Brandywine Dispatch*, Summer 2017, https://www.brandywinebattlefield.org/wp-content/uploads/2012/05/BBPA-Summer-2017-Newsletter.pdf.
15. Timothy Pickering to Allen McLane, November 15, 1777, Allen McLane Collection, MS 2958.6269, New-York Historical Society; Elias Boudinot, *Journal or Historical Recollections of American Events during The Revolutionary War* (Philadelphia: Frederick Bourquin, 1894), 50.
16. Albert Cook Myers, *Sally Wister's Journal* (Philadelphia: Ferris & Leach, 1902), 166-172.
17. Simcoe, *Simcoe's Military Journal*, 27-28.
18. This area between the lines was a particularly hazardous location in 1777, the site of frequent attacks by troops from both sides, especially cavalrymen, who could approach

swiftly, strike, then ride off quickly if outnumbered by the enemy. The surviving account of a British attempt to surprise American vedettes near the Jolly Post in Frankford provides a glimpse of this dangerous small-scale warfare. See: *Simcoe's Military Journal*, 25-27.

19. "Kemble Papers," 1:533.

20. Howe's Orders, November 20, 1777, "William Howe Orderly Book," 391.

21. "Captain Jacob Coats' Account, Written from Frankford, January 5th, 1826," in Watson, "Annals of Philadelphia," 409-411. An 1808 map locates the Dover property directly south across Frankford Creek from the Swedish Mill, adjacent to Abel James's Chalkley Hall. John Hills, William Kneass, and Joseph B Varnum, *A Plan of the City of Philadelphia and Environs* (Philadelphia: Published by the author, 1808).

22. Fisher, "Diary," December 6, 1777, 458.

23. Drinker, *Diary*, December 6, 1777, 261.

24. Robert Smith to George Washington, December 2, 1777, FO, https://founders.archives.gov/documents/Washington/03-12-02-0475.

25. Drinker, *Diary*, November 24, 1777, 257.

26. Howe's official proclamation appointing Galloway came in early December. However, several of his subordinates were already conducting their duties by that time. Carlile had taken up his duties at least by November. *Dunlap and Claypoole's American Daily Advertiser*, December 31, 1777.

27. Philadelphia Monthly Meeting Minutes, August 24, 1753, 272, December 25, 1761, January 16 and 19, 1762, 381-382, USQMR; undated memorandum, *Philadelphia Yearly Meeting for Sufferings, Miscellaneous Papers, 1779–1780*, Haverford box B5.3, item 73, quoted in David W. Maxey, *Treason on Trial in Revolutionary Pennsylvania: The Case of John Roberts, Miller* (Philadelphia: American Philosophical Society, 2011), 197n41.

28. Testimony of Jacob Weaver, *PA Archives*, ser. 1, vol. 7, 48 (1778); Records of Pennsylvania's Revolutionary Governments 1775–1790 (Record Group 27), Pennsylvania State Archives, roll 42, p. 734. On June 14, 1779, Thomas Hale, one of the agents for estates forfeited to the Commonwealth of Pennsylvania by conviction for treason, seized from Carlile's estate "one frame building 2 Stories high 16 feet by 12 ½ feet, found on the ground of Jacob Weaver of the Northern liberties Farmer." Redoubt no. 2, occupied by the 1st Battalion of Guards, was only a couple of hundred yards from Weaver's house. For the unfortunate fate of Captain Frederick Thomas, see Fanelli, "Fatal Dispute."

29. Philadelphia Yearly Meeting Minutes 1777–1780, Respublica vs Abm. Carlile, Testimony of Peter Stonemetz, USQMR. This document is an alternate transcription of the trail testimony written by a Quaker who attended the proceedings, most likely Henry Drinker. Its details differ from the testimony taken down for the official court record.

30. Philadelphia Yearly Meeting Minutes 1777–1780, Respublica vs Abm. Carlile, Testimony of Margaret Sueeble, 72, USQMR.

31. Testimony of Jacob Weaver, Philadelphia Monthly Meeting Minutes, Meeting for Sufferings, 1778, Respublica vs Abrm. Carlile, 73, USQMR.

32. Testimony of John Paul, Philadelphia Monthly Meeting Minutes, Meeting for Sufferings, 1778, Respublica vs Abrm. Carlile, 74, USQMR.

33. Testimony of George Bruner, Daniel Hoffman, and Peter Stonemitz, PA Archives, ser. 1, vol. 7, 45-47; Philadelphia Yearly Meeting Minutes, 1777–1780, 126-127, USQMR.

34. Edward J. Gibbon, "Transfer of Land from the Swedes," in *A History of Frankford* (Philadelphia: Frankford Lions Club, c. 1990), 5-6.
35. Drinker, *Diary*, September 30, 1777, 237.
36. Drinker, *Diary*, October 4, 1777, 239-240. The Paul family owned a large property adjacent to the Frankford mill, across the creek from Abel James's Chalkley Hall, and next door to Edward Stiles's mansion, Port Royal.
37. Heading to New York, a traveler had the option of crossing over the Delaware at Bristol to the town of Burlington, once the capital of West Jersey, or at Trenton, the town that grew up at the Falls of the Delaware. The name New York Road was used to distinguish it from Old York Road, which made its way to New York by a route that crossed the Delaware River at Coryell's Ferry. Both of these roads were laid out along preexisting Indian paths, in use long before European settlement. Paul A. W. Wallace, *Indian Paths of Pennsylvania* (Harrisburg: Pennsylvania Historical and Museum Commission, 1965), 45, 90.
38. Simcoe, *Journal*, 23.
39. For a description of the devastation, see Maguire, *Philadelphia Campaign,* 2:234-236.
40. Darrach CHS, 389, 391.
41. Pennsylvania, US, Land Warrants and Applications, 1733–1952, Warrant of Charles Darragh, Cumberland County, Pennsylvania, September 29, 1766, Ancestry.com; Marriage of Blair Macclenachan and Ann Darragh, June 17, 1762, Episcopal Diocese of Pennsylvania Archives, Record of Marriages 1759–1824, St. Paul's Church, Philadelphia, 8; Deed of Blair McClenahan, 1766, City of Philadelphia, Department of Records, Philadelphia Deed Book D 10.86;Darrach, *Genealogical notes*; Franklin L. Burns, "The Story of the Glassley Commons," *Tredyffrin Easttown History Club Quarterly* 5, no. 3 (1943): 51, https://www.tehistory.org/hqda/html/ v05/v05n3p050.html.
42. For the relationship between William Darragh and Mary Darragh Eddy, see ch. 4 above. "Correspondence of the Children of Christopher Marshall," 343. For more details on the Darraghs visits with the Marshalls in 1778, see ch. 13 below.
43. For the Haines manuscript, see appendix A.
44. Walsh, "American Biography," 33.
45. Watson, *MS Annals*, 24.
46. Darrach CHS, 391.
47. Haines, *MS.*, see appendix A below.
48. Haines, *MS.*, see appendix A below; Watson, *MS Annals*, 1829, 24; Walsh, "American Biography," 33. Walsh cited his fact checking in an article published in his *National Gazette and Literary Register*, March 10, 1828. For more biographical information on Charles and Thomas Craig, see Robert N. Fanelli, "Charles Craig's Final Statement," *Journal of the American Revolution*, July 10, 2018, https://allthingsliberty.com/2018/07/charles-craigs-final-statement/.
49. *Pennsylvania Archives,* ser. 2, vol. 14, 595; Charles Craig to William Thompson, September 25, 1775, Library of Congress, George Washington Papers, cdn.loc.gov/master/mss/mgw/mgw4/034/0100/0197.jpg; Thomas Craig to William Thompson, September 25, 1775, Library of Congress, George Washington Papers, cdn.loc.gov/master/mss/mgw/mgw4/034/0100/0199.jpg; William Thompson to John Allen, No-

vember 14, 1775, *Pennsylvania Archives,* ser. 1, vol. 4, 680. By this time, the Northampton Rifle Company, which was among the very first US Army units authorized by Congress on June 14, 1775, had been incorporated into Thompson's Pennsylvania Rifle Battalion.
50. Craig was appointed a captain of dragoons January 10, 1777. The unit is generally referred to today as the 4th Regiment of Continental Light Dragoons. Revolutionary War Rolls, 1775–1783, National Archives, M246, roll 0115, Fold3.com. Colonel Stephen Moylan to George Washington, July 12, 1777, FO, https://founders.archives.gov/documents/Washington/03-10-02-0254.
51. George Washington to Elias Boudinot, April 1, 1777, FO, https://founders. archives. gov/documents/Washington/03-09-02-0035.
52. Anonymous letter, "Accusation of Captn. Craig," December 11, 1777, FO, https://founders.archives.gov/documents/Washington/03-12-02-0483.
53. Charles Craig to George Washington, December 2, 1777, FO, https:// founders. archives.gov/documents/Washington/03-12-02-0469; Charles Craig to George Washington, December 3, 1777, FO, https://founders.archives.gov/documents/Washington/03-12-02-0483. A Pennsylvania ironmaster wrote from Frankford on December 4, exposing the British intent to trick Washington into shifting his ground. William Dewees to George Washington, December 4, 1777, FO, https://founders.archives.gov/documents/Washington/03-12-02-0496.
54. For more on Charles Craig, see Fanelli, "Charles Craig's Final Statement."
55. Walsh, *American Biography*, 33.
56. Haines, *MS*; Watson, *MS Annals*, 1829. Note that Watson confused the weight. See page 171 above.
57. Howe's Orders, November 20, 1777, "William Howe Orderly Book," 391.
58. Watson, *Historic Tales*, 295.
59. "William Howe Orderly Book," November 20, 1777.
60. Haines, *MS.*
61. Darrach CHS, 391.
62. William Faden, *A plan of the city and environs of Philadelphia: with the works and encampments of His Majesty's forces under the command of Lieutenant General Sir William Howe, K.B.*, London, 1779, https://www.loc.gov/resource/g3824p.ar132700/?r=0.298,0.5,0.59,0.507,0.
63. Library of Congress, *Philadelphia and Neighborhood*, manuscript map, 1778, https://www.loc.gov/item/gm71000682/.
64. Howe's orders for December 2, 1777, note, "49th Regt., Ens. Joshua Roche to be Lieutenant, Vice Robinson, Appointed to the Invalid's 26 Nov. 1777." Sullivan, *Redcoat to Rebel*, "Return of the killed, wounded and missing, in the different skirmishes, from the 4th, to the 8th, December, 1777," 160-161.
65. Watson, *MS Annals*, 24.

CHAPTER 11: WHITEMARSH AND THE BATTLE OF EDGE HILL

1. Charles Craig to George Washington, December 3, 1777, FO, https://founders. archives.gov/documents/Washington/03-12-02-0483.
2. John Clark to George Washington, December 3, 1777, FO, https://founders. archives.gov/documents/Washington/03-12-02-0481.

3. George Washington to Elias Boudinot, April 1, 1777, FO, https://founders.archives.gov/documents/Washington/03-09-02-0035.
4. "A Magazine for Miscellaneous Pieces and Publications collected & preserved by Elias Boudinot," quoted in George Adams Boyd, *Elias Boudinot, Patriot and Statesman, 1740–1821* (Princeton, NJ: Princeton University Press, 1952), 46-47.
5. Robert Smith to George Washington, December 2, 1777, FO, https://founders.archives.gov/documents/Washington/03-12-02-0475. The author, from North Carolina, was a captain in George Baylor's 3rd Continental Light Dragoons. Francis B. Heitman, *Historical Register of Officers of the Continental Army During the War of the Revolution, April, 1775, to December, 1783*, new, revised, and enlarged edition (Washington, DC: Rare Book Shop Publishing, 1914), 506.
6. Henry Darrach communicated with Lydia Darragh's great niece Margaret Porter Darragh Newton before her death in 1894. "The description of Lydia Darragh was received from Ann Darragh by Margaret Porter Darragh (Mrs. Dr. Thomas Newton), deceased, Norfolk, Va.," Darrach CHS, 385n3.
7. Hiltzheimer, *Extracts*, 32; Watson, *MS Annals*, 24; Watson, *Historic Tales*, 295.
8. Boudinot, *Journal*, vii, 50; Elias Boudinot, *A Magazine for Miscellanious Pieces & Publications collected & preserved by Elias Boudinot from 1775*, John Carter Brown Library, Codex Eng 82, 44.
9. Boudinot, *Journal*, iii.
10. Diagram of Troop Dispositions at Whitemarsh, November 28, 1777, Cadwalader Papers, folder 24, "Miscellaneous 1777," HSP; *Valley Forge Orderly Book of General George Weedon*, 146; Watson, *MS Annals*, 24, "I find . . . from Capt. McLane, that he was apprised of [Howe's] intention on the 4 December & his force in consequence was encreased to 80 additional men." Allen McLane, note on letter, Richard Kidder Meade to McLane, December 4, 1777, Allen McLane Collection, MS 2958.6269, New-York Historical Society.
11. Garry Wheeler Stone and Paul W. Schopp, *The Battle of Gloucester, 1777* (Yardley: Westholme, 2022), 46; Howe Orders, December 3, 1777, December 4, 1777, William Howe Orderly Book.
12. Carl Baurmeister to Von Jungkenn, December 19, 1777, "Letters of Major Baurmeister," pt. 2, 43.
13. Sullivan, *Redcoat to Rebel*, 157; Allen McLane, December 4, 1777, Allen McLane Collection, MS 2958.6269, New-York Historical Society; Elias Boudinot to Thomas Wharton, December 9, 1777, New-York Historical Society, Reed Papers no. 4, reel no. 2, 133.
14. Joseph Plumb Martin, *A Narrative of a Revolutionary Soldier: Some of the Adventures, Dangers, and Sufferings of Joseph Plumb Martin* (New York: Signet Classic, 2001), 85.
15. Sullivan, *Redcoat to Rebel*, 157-158; *Pennsylvania Packet*, December 17, 1777, 2-3.
16. Beggarstown, known originally as Bebberstown after early landowner Mattias Van Bebber, stretched along Germantown Road through a neighborhood now called Mount Airy, itself named for William Allen's fine country estate.
17. Robert N. Fanelli, "The 2nd Connecticut Regiment at Edge Hill," *Journal of the American Revolution*, June 15, 2021, https://allthingsliberty.com/2021/06/the-2nd-connecticut-regiment-at-edge-hill/.
18. Enoch Edwards to George Washington, December 7, 1777, FO, https://founders.archives.gov/documents/Washington/03-12-02-0521.

19. Anne de Benneville Mears, *The Old York Road and Its Early Associations of History and Biography, 1670–1870* (Philadelphia: Harper & Brother, 1890), 205.
20. Samuel Fitch Hotchkin, *The York Road, Old and New* (Philadelphia: Binder & Kelly, 1892), 205; Anonymous letter, "Accusation of Captn. Craig," December 11, 1777, FO, https://founders.archives.gov/documents/Washington/03-12-02-0483.
21. Martin, *Narrative*, 85.
22. Deana D. Hurd, "Sergeant Lewis Hurd's Account of the American Revolution," in *A History and Genealogy of the Family of Hurd in the United States* (New York: privately printed, 1910), 73; William F. Buck, "The Battle of Edge Hill," in *Historical Sketches: A Collection of Papers Prepared for the Historical Society of Montgomery County, Pennsylvania* (Norristown: Published by the Society, 1900), 223.
23. Watson, *MS Annals*, 24.
24. Darrach CHS, 391.
25. Walsh, "American Biography," 33-34.
26. Haines, *MS*.
27. Watson, *MS Annals*, 24.
28. Darrach CHS, 391.
29. It was no accident that Friends named several of their early settlements for the sacred notion of Providence. For Quakers, this idea carried more than just a sense of benevolent intervention; Providence could also be seen as God's just retribution against those who antagonized Friends. Naomi Pullin, "Providence, Punishment and Identity Formation in the Late-Stuart Quaker Community, c.1650–1700," *Seventeenth Century* 31, no. 4 (2016): 471-494.
30. *Parcel* definition is from Johnson, *Dictionary*.
31. Simcoe, *Journal*, 56. One of Balfour's successors, John André, ended up being executed for pursuing the role of spymaster too zealously.

CHAPTER 12: THE AFTERMATH OF LYDIA DARRAGH'S ADVENTURE

1. "Correspondence of the Children of Christopher Marshall," 343.
2. "Correspondence of the Children of Christopher Marshall," 343.
3. "Correspondence of the Children of Christopher Marshall," 344.
4. Administration of Benjamin Marshall, Philadelphia Administration Files, no. 54, 1778; Philadelphia Monthly Meeting, Births, Deaths and Burials, 1688–1826, April 20, 1779, USQMR.
5. Philadelphia Quarterly Meeting Minutes, February 2, 1778, USQMR.
6. "Before the American Revolution, Philadelphia was still a 'pedestrian city,' 'not only a walking city, but a talking city' where important social knowledge was formed at intimate distances." Peter Thompson, quoted in Karin Wulf, "Assessing Gender: Taxation and the Evaluation of Economic Viability in Late Colonial Philadelphia," *PMHB* 121 (1997), 201-235; Nash, *Urban Crucible*, 4-5; Marshall, *Extracts*, 179.
7. *Pennsylvania Ledger*, May 20, 1778, 3. Knyphausen was occupying John Cadwalader's house at the time.
8. Marshall, *Extracts*, 198-200. Polly could seldom be counted on to contribute any effort to the household, but in this case she may have been stimulated to make a good show by the arrival of the young men. Her wayward career and the angst it caused the Marshalls shows through plainly in Christopher Marshall's diary between January 1775, and July 1780.

9. Marshall, *Extracts*, 177.
10. Fred Anderson Berg. *Encyclopedia of Continental Army Units* (Harrisburg: Stackpole Books, 1972), 99. Walter Stewart, who took over the 2nd Pennsylvania, would later become Blair McClenachan's son-in-law.
11. George Washington, *The Papers of George Washington*, Revolutionary War Series, vol. 15, *May–June 1778*, ed. Edward G. Lengel (Charlottesville: University of Virginia Press, 2006), 429–431.
12. Robert N. Fanelli, "One Famous, One Forgotten: John Eager Howard and Patrick Duffey," *Journal of the American Revolution*, June 8, 2017, https://allthingsliberty.com/2017/06/john-eager-howard-forgotten-patrick-duffey/.
13. Samuel Rowland Fisher, "Journal of Samuel Rowland Fisher, of Philadelphia, 1779-1781," *PMHB* 41 (1917): 411, 415. This journal was published in three parts in 1917. "Extracts from Letterbooks of Lieutenant Enos Reeves of the Pennsylvania Line," *PMHB*, 9 (1897): 82; Diary of George Nelson, February 5, 1781, HSP; Daniel Newton Journal, February 4, 1781, February 20, 1781, New-York Historical Society; Richard Peters to Gen. Irvine, February 6, 1781, Lane Collection, Yale University, cited in John D. R. Platt, *Historic Resource Study: The City Tavern* (Philadelphia: Independence National Historical Park, 1973), 179-182.
14. *Pennsylvania Archives*, ser. 6, vol. 1, 94.
15. Bonds of the Letters of Marque, *NDAR, 1775-1778*, 339; William Bell Clark, "That Mischievous Holker: The Story of a Privateer," *PMHB*, 79, no. 1 (1955): 29-30. McClenachan named the ship to honor a man who could aid his enterprises, John Holker, the French consul to Pennsylvania, who at the time lived in the Masters House on High Street, formerly occupied by William Howe after the Battle of Edge Hill. Privateering was especially profitable for him. "Blair McClenaghan is a principal owner of the Holker privateer," wrote Timothy Pickering. "He has made an incredible estate during the war." Timothy Pickering to John Pickering, September 24, 1779, Pickering Papers, vol. 5, 125, Massachusetts Historical Society, quoted in Clark, "Mischievous Holker," 34.
16. Holker, Letter of Marque, April 14, 1779; Library of Congress, *Naval Records of the American Revolution, 1775–1788* (Washington, DC: Government Printing Office, 1906), 339.
17. Darrach CHS, 387. Henry Darrach was in a position to know such things. A Mason himself, he was the librarian responsible for the archives of the Masonic Grand Lodge of Pennsylvania. In 1783, Charles Darragh signed a receipt for the sale of painting supplies sold by the Marshalls to the US military. National Archives, Receipt Books of Samuel Hodgdon, Commissary General of Military Stores and Assistant Quartermaster, 10/1778—11/1789, Catalog ID: 606909A.
18. Christopher Marshall's Diary, 1783, Collection 395, box 1, March 12-19, 1783, HSP.
19. *Freeman's Journal: or, The North-American Intelligencer*, September 17, 1783, 2; *Independent Gazetteer*, Saturday, November 15, 1783, 3; *Freeman's Journal*, May 25, 1785, 3, *Pennsylvania Evening Herald and the American Monitor*, August 27, 1785, 38; *Pennsylvania Evening Herald*, June 29, 1785, 2; *Philadelphia Gazette & Universal Daily Advertiser*, February 10, 1796, 3.
20. Carlton F. W. Larson, "The Revolutionary American Jury: A Case Study of the 1778–1779 Philadelphia Treason Trials," *SMU Law Review* 61, no. 4 (2016): 1441-1524; Carlton F. W. Larson, *The Trials of Allegiance: Treason, Juries and the American*

Revolution (New York: Oxford University Press, 2019), 150-176; Maxey, *Treason*, 87-90; Rene J. Silva, "Pennsylvania's Loyalists and Disaffected in the Age of Revolution: Defining the Terrain of Reintegration, 1765–1800" (PhD diss., Florida International University, 2018), 334n5, https://digitalcommons.fiu.edu/etd/3670.

21. Fisher, "Journal," *PMHB* 41 (1917): 438, July 7, 1781.

22. USQMR, Philadelphia Monthly Meeting, Southern District Minutes, January 27, 1779, 276. "The Overseers acquainted the Meeting that William Matlack has been frequently treated with for his deviation from our religious testimony against war, by assuming a military appearance and associating as one of the Militia; but that he does not discover a proper sense of his deviation. Thomas Fisher & John James are appointed to treat further with him and report to next meeting." Fisher, "Journal," *PMHB* 41 (1917): 145-146.

23. Fisher, "Journal," *PMHB* 41 (1917): 306, 318.

24. Fisher, "Journal," *PMHB* 41 (1917): 305-306, 438; James Lenox Banks, *David Sproat and Naval Prisoners in the War of the Revolution* (New York: Knickerbocker Press, 1909), 4.

25. Fisher, "Journal," *PMHB* 41 (1917): 443.

26. Larson, *Trials*, 221.

27. Transcript of Christopher Marshall's Diary, February 8, 1783, Collection 395, box 1, HSP.

28. Transcript of Christopher Marshall's Diary, May 15, 1783, Collection 395, box 1, HSP.

29. *Pennsylvania Packet*, June 17, 1780, 3.

30. The Ladies Association is described in excellent detail in Mary Beth Norton, *Liberty's Daughters: The Revolutionary Experience of American Women, 1750–1800* (Boston: Little, Brown, 1980), 178-188.

31. "Account of donations 'for the Soldiers of the American Army,' undated [1780]," Joseph Reed Papers, 1757–1874, New-York Historical Society.

32. Norton, *Daughters*, 183-186.

33. Philadelphia Monthly Meeting, Arch Street Minutes, 1777–1781, USQMR.

34. Philadelphia Yearly Meeting Minutes, 1779, 426, USQMR.

35. Philadelphia Monthly Meeting Minutes, March 31, 1775, 299, March 29, 1776, 366, January 29, 1779, 101-102, USQMR; Andro Linklater, *An Artist in Treason: The Extraordinary Double Life of General James Wilkinson* (New York: Walker, 2009), 31.

36. Philadelphia Monthly Meeting, March 30, 1781, 303-304, April 27, 1781, 309, June 29, 1781, 317, USQMR.

37. Philadelphia Monthly Meeting, Women's Minutes, April 27, 1781, 433, USQMR.

38. Philadelphia Monthly Meeting Minutes, April 27, 1781, 306, USQMR.

39. Philadelphia Monthly Meeting, Women's Minutes, May 25, 1781, 437, June 29, 1781, 2, July 27, 1781, 6, USQMR.

40. Philadelphia Monthly Meeting, Women's Minutes, February 25, 1780, 395, May 5, 1780, 400-401, USQMR.

41. Philadelphia Monthly Meeting, Women's Minutes, June 29, 1781, 1, USQMR. Different Friends' clerks recorded this procedure in various ways, describing the action as a "recommendation" and the document as a "Minute of recommendation," a "minute of Removal," or, sometimes, a "Certificate."

42. Philadelphia Monthly Meeting, Women's Minutes, July 27, 1781, 6, USQMR.
43. *Religious Society of Free Quakers Records, 1781–1975*, box 1, APS. A list of those who joined the Free Quakers during the first year includes William and Lydia Darragh, and their daughters Ann and Susanna. The Junior League of Philadelphia, *Religious Society of Free Quakers, list updated 4 November 2021*, unpublished manuscript courtesy of Maria Thompson.
44. "From the Monthly Meeting of Friends, Called by Some the Free Quakers, Held by Adjournment at Philadelphia, on the 9th Day of the 7th Month, 1781: To those of our Brethren who have disowned us," *Religious Society of Free Quakers Records, 1781–1975*, APS.
45. *Religious Society of Free Quakers Records, 1781–1975*, August 6, 1781, September 3, 1781, APS.
46. *Religious Society of Free Quakers Records, 1781-1975,* January 7, 1782, APS; Charles E. Peterson, *Notes on the Free Quaker Meeting House, Fifth and Arch Streets, Philadelphia, Built 1783–84* (Washington, DC: Ross & Perry, 2002).
47. Philadelphia Monthly Meeting Minutes, October 25, 1782, USQMR.
48. Philadelphia Monthly Meeting, Women's Minutes, June 29, 1781, July 27, 1781, USQMR; Philadelphia Monthly Meeting, Arch Street Minutes, October 25, 1782, August 29, 1783, September 26, 1783, USQMR. The value midwives brought to the community was exemplified in the case of Alice Tilly a century earlier. See Norton, *Founding Mothers and Fathers*, 204-206, 224-225.
49. *Religious Society of Free Quakers Records, 1781–1975*, February 2, 1785, APS.
50. Philadelphia Monthly Meeting Minutes, March 30, 1787, April 27, 1787, USQMR; Scharf and Westcott, *History of Philadelphia,* 442-443. There may have been two other Pennsylvania men named John Darragh of approximate military age around this time, and it is difficult to distinguish them. One, a private, served in the 8th, and later 9th, Pennsylvania Regiment during the war, and is probably the man who received two hundred acres of bounty land from the state in 1787. Another was a carpenter from Philadelphia. One John Darragh enlisted as a private on August 10, 1780, in Captain John Barker's militia company, in the Philadelphia City 3rd Regiment of Foot, but because Lydia Darragh's son John was only sixteen at that time, it seems unlikely that this was him. Lloyd DeWitt Bockstruck, *Revolutionary War Bounty Land Grants Awarded by State Governments* (Baltimore: Genealogical Publishing, 1996), 133; Pennsylvania Veterans Card Files, 1775–1916, ser. 13.5, Ancestry.com. After the war, in 1785, a John Darragh served as a matross (a gunner's mate who assisted in loading, firing, and sponging cannon) in the 3rd Company of the Philadelphia Militia's artillery battalion. Given the timing of Philadelphia Meeting's attempted disownment, it seems most likely that this man was Lydia Darragh's son John. Pennsylvania Archives, ser. 6, vol. 3, 1245.
51. Casimir Pulaski to George Washington, January 20, 1778, FO, https://founders.archives.gov/documents/Washington/03-13-02-0259; George Washington to Casimir Pulaski, January 26, 1778, FO, https://founders.archives.gov/documents/Washington/03-13-02-0312.
52. Charles Craig to George Washington, March 5, 1778, FO, https://founders.archives.gov/documents/Washington/03-14-02-0047. Although Craig formally left the service at this time, he continued to act in the American military's interest. During spring 1779, he was a scout or liaison in the dangerous wilderness near the juncture

of Pennsylvania, New Jersey, and New York. John Sullivan to George Washington, May 8, 1779, FO, https://founders.archives.gov/documents/Washington/03-20-02-0348.

53. Daniel Brodhead Jr. to Walter Jenifer Stone, July 12, 1782, Gratz Collection, case 4, box 11, HSP.

54. Keith W. Wright, *A History of the Andover Iron Works: Come Penny Go Pound* (Charleston, SC: History Press, 2013), 73; Charles Biddle, *Autobiography of Charles Biddle* (Philadelphia: E. Claxton, 1883), 172.

55. Biddle, *Autobiography*, 168-172.

56. Brodhead to Stone, July 12, 1782, Gratz Collection, case 4, box 11, HSP.

57. Biddle, *Autobiography*, 172.

58. Brodhead to Stone, July 12, 1782, Gratz Collection, case 4, box 11, HSP. It seems unlikely that Craig actually planned to "fall on his sword"; rather, his placing the sword across his breast was a symbolic act.

59. Brodhead to Stone, July 12, 1782, Gratz Collection, case 4, box 11, HSP.

60. Bradley Chapin, "Felony Law Reform in the Early Republic," *PMHB* 113 (1989): 163-183. Chapin notes: "The common law regarded suicides as felons punishable by forfeiture of chattels and ignominious burial. Inquest juries generally avoided at least the forfeiture by finding insanity. . . . The infamy [of "shameful interment"] consisted of being buried in or near the king's highway with a stake driven through the heart. Whether or not suicides should have a Christian burial was a vexed question in colonial jurisdictions." Two weeks afterward, alluding to Craig's death, Jacob Hiltzheimer noted the ignominious burial, in a potter's field, of another suicide, Major William Galvan. Jacob Hiltzheimer, *Extracts from the Diary of Jacob Hiltzheimer of Philadelphia, 1765–1798*, ed. Jacob Cox Parsons (Philadelphia: Wm. F. Fell, 1893), 162.

61. Joseph Addison, *Cato* (Edinburgh: Printed for John Wood, 1713), act 5, scene 1.

62. Administration of Charles Craig, Berks County Pennsylvania, Familysearch.org. The inventory lists "1 Silver Mounted Sword" valued at £4.

63. William Watkins to William and Lydia Darragh, August 27, 1782, City of Philadelphia, Department of Records, Philadelphia Deed Book D, no. 6, 37; William Darragh to Christopher Marshall in Trust, August 31, 1782, City of Philadelphia, Department of Records, Philadelphia Deed Book D, no. 6, 40.

64. Transcript of Charles Marshall's Diary, April 1783, Collection 395, box 1, HSP; Pennsylvania, U.S., Tax and Exoneration, Philadelphia, Dock Ward, 1782 and 1783, Ancestry.com.

65. *Pennsylvania Packet*, June 14, 1783, 3.

66. Unfortunately, an administration for William Darragh has not been located. Wulf, *Not All Wives*, 2-6; Peter Stretch to Lydia Darragh, April 22, 1786, City of Philadelphia, Department of Records, Philadelphia Deed Book EF, no. 7, 444-445.

67. Elizabeth Drinker, *The Diary of Elizabeth Drinker, Volume I: 1758—1795*, ed. Elaine Forman Crane (Boston: Northeastern University Press, 1991), 225, 314. Grace Growden Galloway noted on that July 4, "great rejoicing (but No Illuminations,) it being the annaversery of independence." Raymond C. Werner, "Diary of Grace Growden Galloway," *PMHB* 55, no. 1 (1931): 38.

68. Alexander Garden, *Anecdotes of the Revolutionary War in America, with Sketches of Character of Persons the Most Distinguished, in the Southern States, for Civil and Military Services* (Charleston, SC: A. E. Miller, 1822), 227-228.

69. Dublin MM II A12, August 28, 1759, 121, ISOFCR; Henry Laurens to John Lewis Gervais, August 5, 1777, in Laurens, *Papers,* 427.
70. Marshall, *Extracts,* 251.
71. Transcript of Charles Marshall's Diary, July 4, 1783, Collection 395, box 1, HSP; *Pennsylvania Journal, and the Weekly Advertiser,* July 5, 1783, 3; Hiltzheimer, *Extracts,* July 4, 1783; Scharf and Westcott, *History of Philadelphia,* 432.

EPILOGUE

1. Marshall Diary, November 29 and December 29, 1789.
2. *Pennsylvania Mercury and Universal Advertiser,* January 2, 1790; *Independent Gazetteer,* January 2, 1790. That two newspapers ran her obituary suggests her popularity.
3. Philadelphia Department of Wills, Will of Lydia Darragh, December 26, 1789, Philadelphia Will Book U, no. 168, 413.
4. Since Lydia Darragh had purchased the property only three and a half years prior for £1,591, it appears that the property had declined in value by £391. That apparent drop may have been attributable to the carving off of the Strawberry Street end of the lot for William Darragh Jr.'s workshop. Doerflinger, *Vigorous Spirit,* 37-39.
5. Christopher Marshall's diary for January 12, 1790, noted, "Nancy Darragh sett off for her brother John Yesterday morning on Stage for Baltimore." He also mentioned her return with John the morning of January 24.
6. Ann may have had a hand in the addition of the codicil, which began, "I the within named ~~Ann~~ Lydia Darragh considering my aforegoing will do in addition to what I have therein given & devised to my Son William give devise & bequeath unto my said son William his Heirs & Assigns forever a Frame Tenement or shop lately built by me on the Lot of Ground given to my Daughters Ann & Susannah fronting on Strawberry Alley with the Ground whereon the same stands." Philadelphia Department of Wills, Will of Lydia Darragh, December 26, 1789, Philadelphia Will Book U, no. 168, Codicil.
7. *Freeman's Journal; or the North American Intelligencer,* May 25, 1785, 3.
8. Sharon V. Salinger, *"To Serve Well and Faithfully": Labor and Indentured Servants in Pennsylvania, 1682–1800* (New York: Cambridge University Press, 1987); Loxley, *Account* 2-3.
9. *Pennsylvania Gazette,* September 27, 1764.
10. 1790 US Census for South Second Street, Philadelphia, 91; Clement Biddle, *Philadelphia Directory* (Philadelphia: James & Johnson, 1791), 51.
11. William Wade Hinshaw, *Encyclopedia of American Quaker Genealogy,* vol. 2 (Ann Arbor, MI: Edwards Brothers, 1938), 500; Darrach PMHB, 91.
12. The dates for Ann Darragh's three marriages derive from genealogical information that Henry Darrach transcribed from copies of Bible records furnished him by descendants of John Darragh. Darrach PMHB, 90-91. Clement Hall was a generational name in a Quaker family near Salem, New Jersey. Will of Edward Hall of Mannington Township, Salem County, New Jersey, September 21, 1813.
13. Henry Darrach listed William's death date as December 11, 1790. This seems to be an error, because William's administration was filed in 1796, probably not long after his death. Philadelphia Register of Wills, Administration Files, book H, file 113, Letters of Administration, July 1, 1796.
14. *Philadelphia Gazette & Universal Daily Advertiser,* February 10, 1796, 3; John

Baker to Abraham Dubois, June 5, 1796, City of Philadelphia, Department of Records, Philadelphia Deed Book EF, no. 10, 496.

15. Edmund Hogan, *The Prospect of Philadelphia, and Check on the Next Directory*, vol. 1 (Philadelphia: Robert Bailey, 1795), 121. David Lapsley, who would buy the Darragh property in 1801, maintained a shop six doors north of there at the time. On June 1, 1796, the Marshalls paid $100 to "Darragh, Ferriss, Craig & Brown for posting up Books, drawing out accots & other writing from time to time, writing paper &c." City of Philadelphia, Administration Files, Administration of Benjamin Marshall; Darrach CHS, 387.

16. Manumission of Musk, New Castle, Delaware Land Records, September 5, 1799, 182-183; Bounty Land Application for Charles Darragh, December 4, 1833, Revolutionary War Pension and Bounty-Land Warrant Application Files, M804, roll 0742, Fold3.com.

17. Lydia Darragh originally paid £1,591 for the property on South 2nd Street in 1786. Using the estimated exchange rate of $4.38 per pound for 1801, the value of £1,591 would have been about $6,968, very close to the actual sale price of $6,950. See the dollar-pound exchange rate calculator at https://measuringworth.com/datasets/exchangepound/result.php.

18. Abraham Dubois to John Darragh, October 16, 1801, City of Philadelphia, Department of Records, Philadelphia Deed Book EF, no. 7, 448-449; Edward Hall et ux to John Darragh, October 15, 1801, Philadelphia Deed Book EF, no. 10, 498; John Darragh and Wife to David Lapsley, November 14, 1801, Philadelphia Deed Book EF, no. 7, 446-448. See also EF, no. 10, 358.

19. *Pennsylvania Packet*, November 4, 1783; *Philadelphia Directory by Francis White*, 18; *Freeman's Journal*, April 20, 1785; Darrach PMHB, 90; John Darragh and Alex Porter, 1790 US Census, Harford County, Maryland.

20. *Delaware Gazette*, March 23, 1793. Cantwell's Bridge is modern-day Odessa. Duck Creek Crossroads is called Smyrna today.

21. *Delaware and Eastern-Shore Advertiser*, March 4, 1795; *Delaware and Eastern-Shore Advertiser*, April 25, 1795. The name of this port town morphed over time from the Dutch, New Amstel, to an English near-homophone, New Castle. Liam Riordan, Annotated tax records for New Castle, 1798, http://nc-chap.org/census/riordan/tax1798.php.

22. John Darragh, 1800 Census, Mill Creek Hundred, New Castle County, Delaware; John Darragh, 1810 Census, White Clay Creek Hundred, New Castle County, Delaware. Note that a "hundred" is a subdivision of a county, more or less the equivalent to a township in Pennsylvania and some other states. Will of Alexander Porter Darragh, New Castle, Delaware, book S 414, November 12, 1829; Darrach PMHB, 90.

23. Darrach PMHB, 90. Henry Darrach compiled his genealogy of Lydia Darragh's descendants from Bible records shared with him by Julian Darragh Janvier, a great-grandson, and Lydia Barrington Darragh Short, a third great-grand daughter. Other than a few minor discrepancies with exact dates, Darrach's information is substantiated by public records.

24. *National Gazette and Literary Register*, March 9, 1831, 2; Darrach CHS, 388.

25. 1688 Germantown Quaker Petition Against Slavery, Haverford College Quaker and Special Collections.

26. Marcus Rediker described this scene vividly in *The Fearless Benjamin Lay: The Quaker Dwarf Who Became the First Revolutionary Abolitionist* (Boston: Beacon Press, 2017), 1-2; Roberts Vaux, *Memoirs of the Lives of Benjamin Lay and Ralph Sandiford* (Philadelphia: Solomon W. Conrad, 1815), 25-28.
27. Jack D. Marietta, *The Reformation of American Quakerism, 1748–1783* (Philadelphia: University of Pennsylvania Press, 1984); Bauman, *Reputation of Truth;* Jean R. Soderland, *Quakers and Slavery: A Divided Spirit* (Princeton, NJ: Princeton University Press, 1980); Donna McDaniel and Vanessa Julye, *Fit for Freedom, Not for Friendship: Quakers, African Americans, and the Myth of Racial Justice* (Philadelphia: Quaker Press of Friends General Conference, 2009); Pennsylvania Supreme Executive Council, *An Act for the Gradual Abolition of Slavery*, March 1, 1780.
28. William H. Williams, *Slavery and Freedom in Delaware 1639-1865* (Wilmington, DE: Scholarly Resources, 1996).
29. Manumission of Jesse, Delaware Public Archives, Dover, Delaware, Recorder of Deeds, New Castle County, RG 2555, subgroup 000, ser. 011, 173-174.
30. Manumission of Musk, Delaware Public Archives, Dover, Delaware, Recorder of Deeds, New Castle County, RG 2555, subgroup 000, ser. 011, 182-183.
31. Benjamin Joseph Klebaner, "American Manumission Laws and the Responsibility for Supporting Slaves," *Virginia Magazine of History and Biography* 63, no. 4 (1955): 443–53; Will of Alexander Porter Darragh, New Castle, Delaware, book S 414, Estate Settlement, 1839.
32. Manumission of Betsey Owens, Delaware Public Archives, Dover, Delaware, Recorder of Deeds, New Castle County, November 15, 1826, 69.
33. *Pennsylvania Ledger*, May 20, 1778, 3; *Philadelphia Directory by Francis White*, 18.
34. Darrach CHS, 392.
35. Library of Congress, *Journals of the Continental Congress, 1774-1789*, vol. 5, 1776, June 5–October 8 (Washington, DC: Government Printing Office, 1906), September 16, 1776; US House of Representatives, Land Ordinance of 1785, https://history.house.gov/HouseRecord/Detail/25769822302.
36. Bounty Land Warrant #1997-200, November 2, 1829, November 27, 1833, Revolutionary War Pension and Bounty-Land Warrant Application Files, M804, Fold3.com.

BIBLIOGRAPHY

Primary Sources

MANUSCRIPTS

American Philosophical Society. *Religious Society of Free Quakers Records, 1781–1975*, box 1.

Boudinot, Elias. "A Magazine for Miscellanious Pieces & Publications collected & preserved by Elias Boudinot from 1775." John Carter Brown Library, Codex Eng 82.

Cadwalader, John. *John Cadwalader Papers,* folder 24, Historical Society of Pennsylvania.

City of Philadelphia Constables returns to Assessors for 1775, 68-69.

https://therevolutionarycity.org/islandora/city-philadelphia-constables-returns-assessors-1775.

Craig, Charles. Charles Craig to George Washington, December 2, 1777. Founders Online, National Archives.

Craig, Charles. Charles Craig to George Washington, December 3, 1777. Founders Online, National Archives.

Darrach, Henry. "Genealogical notes of Blair McClenahan and his children." Historical Society of Pennsylvania, 1899.

Darragh, Charles. Pension File. https://www.fold3.com/image/16866723.

Darragh, William. Runaway Notice. https://www.ancestry.com/imageviewer/collections/61028/images/gpc_runawayservants-0062?pId=500001606&lang=en-US.

Dewees, William, Jr. William Dewees Jr. to George Washington, December 4, 1777. Founders Online, National Archives.

Emlen, Samuel. *Extract of a letter from several Friends in Philadelphia, to John Fothergill, David Barclay, Daniel Mildred, Jacob Hagen, Thomas Corbyn, Mark Beaufoy, John Eliot, and Richard Chester.* December 16, 1777. Haverford College Quaker and Special Collections.

Extracts from the Minutes and Advices of the Yearly Meeting of Friends Held in London, from Its First Institution. London: James Phillips, 1783. https://books.googleusercontent.com/books/content?req=AKW5QaeveUdnrbLOtWm7tk6Bnq-ycxxvsg8cbxLWLHK0fMJc3qcoqpwqRva9bo6yRA8uTSnDoOu8fXtSBckt50Pzrcm9O4XbOUlNM2FFXULlS_SVMdO16_gcF9WF6TiN-WExHWD6m2-Uyf_nkiwCYAxhXv7pVFQa-ye3lkcsyQUNoYSFxdzl1n47w0WQ1VHqKv470uEWphlFtLyWv2aOLE6RWwvp5_dvD5uP0Zd7j2teYmNQlzowGG0V0gg8M09vvE9LZ684YvB3o0gp0qwrnwyVUoJi5ivJAp1DXHiZSmHcvMVtiC52IJw.

Faden, William. *A plan of the city and environs of Philadelphia: with the works and encampments of His Majesty's forces under the command of Lieutenant General Sir William Howe, K.B.*, London, 1779. https://www.loc.gov/resource/g3824p.ar132700/?r=0.298,0.5,0.59,0.507,0.

Franklin, Benjamin. "Autobiography of Benjamin Franklin (Autograph manuscript signed), 1771–1789." Huntington Library.

https://hdl.huntington.org/digital/collection/p15150coll7/id/0.

Haines, Hannah Marshall. Untitled manuscript version of Lydia's Tale, n.d. American Philosophical Society, Wyck Association Collection, ser. 3, box 87, folder 20, "Hannah Marshall Haines Prose."

Hills, John, William Kneass, and Joseph B Varnum, *A Plan of the City of Philadelphia and Environs* (Philadelphia: Published by the author, 1808). https://www.phmc.state.pa.us/bah/dam/mg/di/m011/Map0106Interface.html.

Howe, William. "William Howe Orderly Book, March 9, 1776–May 1, 1778." In the digital collection William Howe Orderly Book, 1776–1778. William L. Clements Library, University of Michigan Library Digital Collections. Accessed September 18, 2024. https://quod.lib.umich.edu/h/howew/howew.0001.001.

ISOFCR: Ireland, Society Of Friends (Quaker) Congregational Records. Findmypast.ie.

Library of Congress. *Philadelphia and Neighborhood*, manuscript map, 1778. https://www.loc.gov/item/gm71000682/.

Loxley, Benjamin. "A Journal of the Campaign to Amboy, and Other Parts of the Jersies." Historical Society of Pennsylvania, Am.612.

Loxley, Benjamin. "Benjamin Loxley's Account of his Ancestors of his Parents and of himself and Family, Dated June 20, 1789." Historical Society of Pennsylvania.

Marshall Brothers Account Book, 1776. https://therevolutionarycity.org/islandora/marshall-brothers-account-book-1776?search_api_fulltext=Marshall.

Marshall, Christopher. Diary of Christopher Marshall, Christopher Marshall Papers, Collection 395. Historical Society of Pennsylvania.

Marshall, Hannah. "Hannah Marshall her Book 1781." Wyck Association Collection, American Philosophical Society. https://therevolutionarycity.org/islandora/object/apsrevcity%3A7781#page/6/mode/2up.

McLane, Allen. Allen McLane Collection, MS 2958.6269. New-York Historical Society.

Moylan, Stephen. Colonel Stephen Moylan to George Washington, July 12, 1777. Founders Online, National Archives.

Murray, James. James Murray to Charles Steuart, December 21, 1777. *Charles Steuart Papers*, National Library of Scotland.

Nicole, Pierre, and John Montrésor. *A survey of the city of Philadelphia and its environs shewing the several works constructed by His Majesty's troops, under the command of Sir William Howe, since their possession of that city 26th. September, comprehending likewise the attacks against Fort Mifflin on Mud Island, and until it's reduction, 16th November, 1777.* Map. https://www.loc.gov/item/gm71000933/.

Papers of the Continental Congress, 1774–1789. Library of Congress.

Philadelphia City Archives. Will of Lydia Darragh, No. U.413.

Reed, Joseph. *Joseph Reed Papers 1757-1874.* New-York Historical Society.

USQMR: US Quaker Meeting Records, 1681–1935. Ancestry.com.

Washington, George. George Washington Papers. Series 4, General Correspondence: British Prisoners, December 31, 1779, List of Officers. Library of Congress. https://www.loc.gov/item/mgw456439/.

Watson, John Fanning. "Annals of Philadelphia, being a collection of Memoirs, Anecdotes, & Incidents of the City & its Inhabitants from the days of the Pilgrim Founders." Unpublished manuscript, 1829. Historical Society of Pennsylvania, box 5.

PUBLISHED PRIMARY SOURCES

Adams, John. The Adams Papers, Diary and Autobiography of John Adams. Vol. 2, 1771–1781. Edited by L. H. Butterfield. Cambridge, MA: Harvard University Press, 1961.

Addison, Joseph. *Cato.* Edinburgh: Printed for John Wood, 1713.

Allen, James. "Diary of James Allen, Esq., of Philadelphia, Counsellor-at-Law, 1770–1778." *Pennsylvania Magazine of History and Biography* 9 (1885): 191-193.

Angel, Israel. "The Israel Angell Diary, 1 October 1777–28 February 1778." Edited by Joseph Lee Boyle. *Rhode Island History* 58 (2000): 107–38.

Ashbridge, Elizabeth. *Some account of the early part of the life of Elizabeth Ashbridge: who died, in the truth's service, at the house of Robert Lecky, in the County of Carlow, Ireland, the 16th of 5th month, 1755.* Philadelphia: Benjamin and Thomas Kite, 1807.

Barrington, Jonah. *Personal Sketches of His Own Times.* Philadelphia: Carey, Lea and Carey, 1827.

Baurmeister, Carl. "Letters of Major Baurmeister during the Philadelphia Campaign, 1777–1778." Pt. 1. Edited by Bernhard A. Uhlendorf and Edna Vosper. *Pennsylvania Magazine of History and Biography* 59, no. 4 (1935): 392–419.

Baurmeister, Carl. "Letters of Major Baurmeister during the Philadelphia Campaign, 1777–1778." Pt. 2. Edited by Bernhard A. Uhlendorf and Edna Vosper. *Pennsylvania Magazine of History and Biography* 60, no. 1 (1936): 34–52.

Baurmeister, Carl. "Letters of Major Baurmeister during the Philadelphia Campaign, 1777–1778." Pt. 3. Edited by Bernhard A. Uhlendorf and Edna Vosper. *Pennsylvania Magazine of History and Biography* 60, no. 2 (1936): 161–183.

Biddle, Clement. *Philadelphia Directory.* Philadelphia: James & Johnson, 1791.

Boudinot, Elias. *Journal or Historical Recollections of American Events during The Revolutionary War.* Philadelphia: Frederick Bourquin, 1894.

Boudinot, Jane J., ed. *The Life, Public Services, Addresses and Letters of Elias Boudinot, President of the Continental Congress.* Vol. 1. Boston: Houghton, Mifflin, 1896.

Bowers, Bath. *An Alarm Sounded to Prepare the Inhabitants of the World to Meet the Lord in the Way of His Judgments.* Printed by William Bradford, 1709.

Clay, Jehu Curtis. *The Life of Mrs. Robert Clay Afterwards Mrs. Robert Bolton (Née Ann Curtis) 1690–1738, in letters written by herself to her physician and now transcribed from the original manuscript by her great grandson, the Rev. Jehu Curtis Clay.* Philadelphia: n.d.

"Correspondence between William Penn and James Logan, secretary of the province of Pennsylvania, and others, 1700–1750: from the original letters in possession of the Logan family." *Memoirs of the Historical Society of Pennsylvania.* Vols. 9-10. Philadelphia: Historical Society of Pennsylvania, 1870–1872.

"Correspondence of the Children of Christopher Marshall." *Pennsylvania Magazine of History and Biography* 17, no. 3 (1893): 336-347. https://www.jstor.org/stable/20083550.

Cromwell, Oliver. Letter to William Lenthall, September 17, 1649. In *Oliver Cromwell's Letters and Speeches with Elucidations by Thomas Carlyle.* vol. 2. London: Chapman & Hall, 1871, 166-173.

Cummings, Archibald. *Faith absolutely necessary, but not sufficient to salvation without good works. In two sermons, preached at Christ-Church in Philadelphia, April 20, 1740.* Philadelphia: Andrew and William Bradford, 1740.

Darrach, Henry. "Lydia Darragh of the Revolution." *Pennsylvania Magazine of History and Biography* 23, no. 1 (1899): 86-91.

Darrach, Henry. *Lydia Darragh One of the Heroines of the Revolution.* Philadelphia: City History Society of Philadelphia, 1916.

Darragh, William. *A Discourse Publickly Delivered by a female friend from Old England in the Friends Meeting-House in Pine Street, Philadelphia, on the third day of the 5th month, 1769: also a prayer, by another Friend: the whole taken down in characters (at the time they were spoken) by William Darragh: to which is added, a short preface, by the editor.* Philadelphia: 1769. Located at the Library Company of Philadelphia.

Derounian Kathryn Zabelle, ed. *The Journal and Occasional Writings of Sarah Wister.* London: Associated University Presses, 1987.

DeSilver's Philadelphia Directory and Stranger's Guide for 1828. Philadelphia: Robert Deliver, 1828.

Drinker, Elizabeth. *The Diary of Elizabeth Drinker, Volume I: 1758-1795.* Edited by Elaine Forman Crane. Boston: Northeastern University Press, 1991.

Essay on the Art of War: in which the General Principles of the Operations of War in the Field Are Fully Explained. London: A. Millar, 1761.

Ewald, Johann. *Diary of the American War: A Hessian Journal.* Edited by Joseph P. Tustin. New Haven, CT: Yale University Press, 1979.

Fisher, Samuel Rowland. "Journal of Samuel Rowland Fisher, of Philadelphia, 1779–1781." *Pennsylvania Magazine of History and Biography* 41, no. 2 (1917): 145-197; 41, no. 3 (1917): 274–333; 41, no. 4 (1917): 399-457. This was published in three parts.

Fisher, Sarah Logan. "A Diary of Trifling Occurrences, Philadelphia, 1776–1778." Edited by Nicholas B. Wainwright. *Pennsylvania Magazine of History and Biography* 82 (1958): 454.

Force, Peter. *American Archives.* 5th ser., vol. 1. Washington, DC: M. St. Clair Clarke and Peter Force, 1848.

Franklin, Benjamin. *The Autobiography of Benjamin Franklin.* 2nd ed. New Haven: Yale University Press, 1964.

Garden, Alexander. *Anecdotes of the Revolutionary War in America, with Sketches of Character of Persons the Most Distinguished, in the Southern States, for Civil and Military Services.* Charleston, SC: A. E. Miller, 1822.

Garden, Alexander. *Anecdotes of the American revolution, illustrative of the talents and virtues of the heroes and patriots, who acted the most conspicuous parts therein.* 2nd ser. Charleston, SC: A. E. Miller, 1828.

Gough, John. *History of the People Called Quakers, From their first Rise to the present Time.* Vols. 1-4. Dublin: Robert Jackson, 1790.

Graydon, Alexander. *Memoirs of a Life Chiefly Passed in Pennsylvania, within the Last Sixty Years.* Harrisburg: John Wyeth, 1811.

Gruber, Ira D., ed. *John Peebles' American War: The Diary of a Scottish Grenadier, 1776–1782.* Mechanicsburg, PA: Stackpole Books, 1998.

Hagist, Don. *General Orders, Rhode Island: December 1776–January 1778.* Berwyn Heights, MD: Heritage Books, 2019.

Hayter, Tony, ed. *An Eighteenth-Century Secretary at War: The Papers of William, Viscount Barrington.* London: Bodley Head, 1988.

Hiltzheimer, Jacob. *Extracts from the Diary of Jacob Hiltzheimer of Philadelphia, 1765–1798.* Edited by Jacob Cox Parsons. Philadelphia: Wm. F. Fell, 1893.

Hogan, Edmund. *The Prospect of Philadelphia.* Vol. 1. Philadelphia: Robert Bailey, 1795.

Jones, Rufus M., ed. *George Fox: An Autobiography*. Philadelphia: Ferris & Leach, 1909.

"The Kemble Papers, Vol. I, 1773–1789" (General Sir William Howe's Orders 1777). *Collections of the New York Historical Society for the Year 1883.* New York: Printed for the Society, 1884.

Laurens, Henry. *The Papers of Henry Laurens, Volume 11: Jan. 5, 1776–Nov. 1, 1777.* Edited by David R. Chesnutt and James C. Taylor. Columbia: University of South Carolina Press, 1988.

Library of Congress. *Journals of the Continental Congress, 1774–1789.* Vol. 5, 1776, June 5–October 8. Washington, DC: Government Printing Office, 1906.

Library of Congress. *Naval Records of the American Revolution, 1775–1788.* Washington, DC: Government Printing Office, 1906.

Logan, Deborah Norris. "Books taken from Dr. Franklin's Library by Major Andre—M. du Simitiere's statement." *Pennsylvania Magazine of History and Biography* 8 (1884): 430.

Marshall, Benjamin. "Extracts from the Letter-Book of Benjamin Marshall, 1763–1766." *Pennsylvania Magazine of History and Biography* 20 (1896): 204-212.

Marshall, Christopher. *Extracts from the Diary of Christopher Marshall, Kept in Philadelphia and Lancaster, during the American Revolution, 1774–1781.* Edited by William Duane. Albany: Joel Munsell, 1877.

Martin, Joseph Plumb. *A Narrative of a Revolutionary Soldier: Some of the Adventures, Dangers, and Sufferings of Joseph Plumb Martin.* New York: Signet Classic, 2001.

Mittelberger, Gottleb. *Gottleb Mittelberger's Journey to Pennsylvania in the Year 1750 and Return to Germany in the Year 1754* (Philadelphia: German Society of Pennsylvania, 1898).

Morton, Robert. "The Diary of Robert Morton." *Pennsylvania Magazine of History and Biography* 1, no. 1 (1877): 1-39.

Muenchhausen, Friedrich von. *At General Howe's Side, 1776–1778, The Diary of General William Howe's aide de camp, Captain Friedrich von Muenchhausen.* Translated by Ernst Kipping, annotated by Samuel Smith. Monmouth Beach, NJ: Philip Freneau Press, 1974.

Myers, Albert Cook. *Sally Wister's Journal.* Philadelphia: Ferris & Leach, 1902.

Naval Documents of the American Revolution. https://www.history.navy.mil/research/publications/publications-by-subject/naval-documents-of-the-american-revolution.html.

Paine, Thomas. *The Complete Writings of Thomas Paine.* Edited by Philip S. Foner. New York: Citadel Press, 1945.

Penn, William. *A Brief Account of the Rise and Progress of the People Called Quakers.* London: James Phillips, 1794.

Pennsylvania State Archives.

Pennsylvania Supreme Executive Council. *An Act for the Gradual Abolition of Slavery.* March 1, 1780.

Purver, Anthony. *A New and Literal Translation of All the Books of the Old and New Testament; with Notes Critical and Explanatory.* London: W. Richardson and S. Clark, 1764.

Rees, John U. "Eyewitness to Battle: Alexander Dow's Account of a 1777 Skirmish and the 1778 Battle of Monmouth." *Brigade Dispatch* 29, no. 1 (Spring 1999): 15-16.

Roach, Hannah Benner. "Philadelphia's Colonial Poor Laws; Taxables in Chester, Walnut and Lower Delaware Wards, Philadelphia, 1767." In *Colonial Philadelphians.* Philadelphia: The Genealogical Society of Pennsylvania, 1999.

Robertson, Archibald. *Archibald Robertson: His Diaries and Sketches in America, 1762–1780.* New York: New York Public Library, 1971.

Rocque, John. *An exact survey of the city and suburbs of Dublin: in which is express'd the ground plot of all publick buildings, dwelling houses, ware houses, stables, courts, yards &c, by John Rocque, chorographer to their Royal Highnesses the late & present Prince of Wales; A. Dury Sculp.* Dublin: John Roque, 1756. Harvard Map Collection, Harvard College Library.

Ross, Charles, ed. *Correspondence of Charles, First Marquis Cornwallis.* Vol. 1. London: John Murray, 1859.

Simcoe, John Graves. *Simcoe's Military Journal: A History of the Operations of a Partisan Corps Called the Queen's Rangers, Commanded by Lieut. Col. J. G. Simcoe during the War of the American Revolution.* New York: Bartlett and Welford, 1844.

Stanley-Torney, Henry C., ed. "Ferns Marriage Licenses (1661–1806)." *Journal of the Kildare Archaeological Society.* Vols. 9-10.

The Statutes at Large of Pennsylvania from 1682 to 1801. Vol. 3, 1712 to 1724. Pennsylvania: Clarence M. Busch, 1896.

Stevens, B. F., comp. *Facsimiles of Manuscripts in European Archives Relating to America, 1773–1783.* Vol. 24. London: Mallby & Sons, 1895.

Sullivan, Thomas. *From Redcoat to Rebel: The Thomas Sullivan Journal.* Edited by Joseph Lee Boyle. Warminster, MD: Heritage Books, 1997.

The Trial of the Right Honourable Lord George Sackville at a Court-Martial Held at the Horse-Guards, February 29, 1760, for an Enquiry into His Conduct, Being Charged with Disobedience of Orders, while He Commanded the British Horse in Germany. Together with His Lordship's Defense. London: W. Owen, 1760.

US House of Representatives. Land Ordinance of 1785. https://history.house.gov/HouseRecord/Detail/25769822302.

Valley Forge Orderly Book of General George Weedon. New York: Dodd, Mead, 1902.

Varle, Charles. *To the citizens of Philadelphia, this new plan of the city and its environs is respectfully dedicated by the editor.* Philadelphia: Charles Varle, 1802. Map. https://www.loc.gov/item/2018590113/.

Walsh, Robert, Jr. "American Biography." *American Quarterly Review* 1 (1827): 32-34.

Walsh, Robert, Jr. Robert Walsh to Edward Everett, November 12, 1858, *Proceedings of the Massachusetts Historical Society* 4 (1858): 231–34.

Washington, George. *The Papers of George Washington.* Revolutionary War Series, vol. 3, *1 January 1776–31 March 1776.* Edited by Philander D. Chase. Charlottesville: University of Virginia Press, 1988.

Washington, George. *The Papers of George Washington.* Revolutionary War Series, vol. 15, *May–June 1778.* Edited by Edward G. Lengel. Charlottesville: University of Virginia Press, 2006.

Werner, Raymond C. "Diary of Grace Growden Galloway." *Pennsylvania Magazine of History and Biography* 55, no. 1 (1931): 32-94.

White, Francis. *The Philadelphia Directory by Francis White.* Philadelphia: Young, Stewart and McCulloch, 1785.

Whitefield, George. *A continuation of the Reverend Mr. Whitefield's journal from a few days after his arrival at Georgia, to his second return thither from Pennsylvania.* Philadelphia: B. Franklin, 1740.

Wilson, Peter. *The Dublin Directory, for the Year 1751. Containing an Alphabetical List of the Names and Places of Abode of the Merchants and Traders of the City of Dublin.* Dublin: Peter Wilson, 1751.

Wilson, Peter. *The Dublin Directory, for the Year 1752. Containing an Alphabetical List of the Names and Places of Abode of the Merchants and Traders of the City of Dublin.* Dublin: Browne and Nolan, 1752.

Wilson, Peter. *The Dublin Directory, for the Year 1760. Containing an Alphabetical List of the Names and Places of Abode of the Merchants and Traders of the City of Dublin.* Dublin: printed for Peter Wilson, 1760.

Secondary Sources

Acosta, Ana M. "Pregnant Silence and Mystical Birth: Quaker Worship in the Seventeenth Century and the Subversive Practices of Silence." *Restoration: Studies in English Literary Culture, 1660–1700* 43, no. 1 (2019): 51–72.

Alexander, John K. "The Philadelphia Numbers Game: An Analysis of Philadelphia's Eighteenth-Century Population." *Pennsylvania Magazine of History and Biography* 98, no. 3 (1974): 314–24.

Allen, Erin. "Paying the Doctor in 18th-Century Philadelphia." Library of Congress blog, April 28, 2016. https://blogs.loc.gov/loc/2016/04/paying-the-doctor-in-18th-century-philadelphia/.

Anonymous. "Lists of Pennsylvania Settlers Murdered, Scalped and Taken Prisoners by Indians, 1755–1756." *Pennsylvania Magazine of History and Biography* 32, no. 3, (1908): 309-319.

Anonymous. "Rachel Wilson of Kendal, 1722–1776: Notes and Incidents of Her Visit to America, 1768-1769." *Bulletin of Friends' Historical Society of Philadelphia.* Vol. 8, no. 1 (1917): 25-35.

Anonymous. *Ten Minutes' Advice in Choosing Cigars, with a Word or Two about Tobacco, and Something about Snuff. . .* London: J. Meaden, 1833.

Bacon, Margaret Hope. "Quaker Women in Overseas Ministry." *Quaker History* 77, no. 2 (1988): 93–109.

Bailyn, Bernard. *The Ideological Origins of the American Revolution.* Cambridge, MA: Harvard University Press, 1992.

Banks, James Lenox. *David Sproat and Naval Prisoners in the War of the Revolution.* New York: Knickerbocker Press, 1909.

Barnes, Howard Lee. "Frankford Is More Than Three Centuries Old." In *A History of Frankford.* Philadelphia: Frankford Lions Club, c. 1990.

Baule, Steven M. with Stephen Gilbert. *British Army Officers Who Served in the American Revolution, 1775–1783.* Westminster, MD: Heritage Books, 2004.

Bauman, Richard. *For the Reputation of Truth: Politics, Religion and Conflict Among the Pennsylvania Quakers 1750–1800.* Baltimore: Johns Hopkins University Press, 1971.

Bauman, Richard. *Let Your Words Be Few: Symbolism of Speaking and Silence Among Seventeenth-Century Quakers.* Cambridge: Cambridge University Press, 1983.

Bauman, Richard. "Quaker Folk-Linguistics and Folklore." In *Folklore Performance and Communication.* Edited by Dan Ben-Amos and Kenneth S. Goldstein. The Hague: Mouton, 1975.

Baumgardt, Kenneth. *The Royal Army in America During the Revolutionary War: The American Prisoner Records.* Report for the US Army Corps of Engineers, 2008.

Beatty, Jacqueline. *In Dependence: Women and the Patriarchal State in Revolutionary America.* New York: New York University Press, 2023.

Belcher, Joseph. *George Whitefield: A Biography, with special reference to his labors in America.* New York: American Tract Society, 1857.

Berg, Fred Anderson. *Encyclopedia of Continental Army Units.* Harrisburg: Stackpole Books, 1972.

Berkely, Edmund, and Dorothy Smith Berkely. *Dr. Alexander Garden of Charles Town.* Chapel Hill: University of North Carolina Press, 1969.

Berkin, Carol. *Revolutionary Mothers: Women in the Struggle for America's Independence.* New York: Alfred A. Knopf, 2005.

Bezanson, Anne. *Prices and Inflation During the American Revolution: Pennsylvania, 1770–1790.* Philadelphia: University of Pennsylvania Press, 1951.

Biddle, Charles. *Autobiography of Charles Biddle.* Philadelphia: E. Claxton, 1883.

Bockstruck, Lloyd DeWitt. *Revolutionary War Bounty Land Grants Awarded by State Governments.* Baltimore: Genealogical Publishing, 1996.

Bomberger, C. M. *The Battle of Bushy Run.* Jeannette, PA: Jeannette Publishing, 1928.

Boyd, George Adams. *Elias Boudinot, Patriot and Statesman, 1740–1821.* Princeton, NJ: Princeton University Press, 1952.

Braithwaite, Alfred W. "Early Tithe Prosecutions: Friends as Outlaws." *Journal of the Friends' Historical Society* 49, no. 3 (1960): 148-156.

Braithwaite, William C. *The Beginnings of Quakerism.* London: Macmillan, 1912.

Brandt, Susan H. *Women Healers: Gender, Authority, and Medicine in Early Philadelphia.* Philadelphia: University of Pennsylvania Press, 2022.

Brown, Gerald S. "The Court Martial of Lord George Sackville, Whipping Boy of the Revolutionary War." *William and Mary Quarterly* 9, no. 3 (1952): 317–337.

Buck, William F. "The Battle of Edge Hill." In *Historical Sketches: A Collection of Papers Prepared for the Historical Society of Montgomery County, Pennsylvania.* Norristown: Published by the Society, 1900.

Burns, Franklin L. "The Story of the Glassley Commons." *Tredyffrin Easttown History Club Quarterly* 5, no. 3 (1943): 50-59. https://www.tehistory.org/hqda/html/v05/v05n3p050.html.

Campbell, John H. *History of the Friendly Sons of St. Patrick and of the Hibernian Society for the Relief of Emigrants from Ireland. March 17, 1771–March 17, 1892.* Philadelphia: Hibernian Society, 1892.

Cannon, Richard. *Historical Record of the Seventh Regiment, or The Royal Fusiliers, Containing an Account of the Formation of the Regiment in 1685, and of its subsequent services to 1846.* London: Parker, Furnival & Parker, 1847.

Central Intelligence Agency. *Intelligence During the War of Independence.* Central Intelligence Agency. March 15, 2007. Accessed October 16, 2022. https://www.cia.gov/static/Intelligence-in-the-War-of-Independence.pdf.

Chaffin, Robert J. "The Townshend Acts Crisis, 1767–1770." *Blackwell Encyclopedia of the American Revolution.* Edited by Jack P. Greene and J. R. Pole. Malden, MA: Blackwell, 1991.

Chandler, Charles Lyon. *Early Shipbuilding in Pennsylvania, 1683–1812.* Philadelphia: Guild of Brackett Lectures, 1932.

Chapin, Bradley. "Felony Law Reform in the Early Republic." *Pennyslvania Magazine of History and Biography* 113 (1989): 163-183.

Clark, Gregory. "Yields Per Acre in English Agriculture, 1250–1860: Evidence from Labour Inputs." *Economic History Review* 44, no. 3 (1991): 445-460.

Clark, Victor S. *History of Manufactures in the United States: 1607–1860.* Washington, DC: Carnegie Institution of Washington, 1916.

Clark, William Bell. "That Mischievous Holker: The Story of a Privateer." *Pennsylvania Magazine of History and Biography* 79, no. 1 (1955): 27-62.

Claussen, W. Edmunds. *Wyck: The Story of an Historic House, 1690–1970.* Philadelphia: Mary T. Haines, 1970.

Cokayne, George Edward. *The Complete Peerage of England, Scotland, Ireland, Great Britain and the United Kingdom, Extant, Extinct, or Dormant.* Edited by Vicary Gibbs. Vol. 1. London: St. Catherine Press, 1910.

Collini, Sara. "The Labors of Enslaved Midwives in Revolutionary Virginia." In *Women in the American Revolution: Gender, Politics and the Do-*

mestic World. Edited by Barbara B. Oberg. Charlottesville: University of Virginia Press, 2019.

Compeau, Timothy. *Dishonored Americans: The Political Death of Loyalists in Revolutionary America.* Charlottesville: University of Virginia Press, 2023.

Connerley, Jennifer. "Fighting Quakers: A Jet Black Whiteness." *Pennsylvania History: A Journal of Mid-Atlantic Studies* 73, no. 4 (2006): 373–411.

Corcoran, Irma. *Thomas Holme, 1624–1695: Surveyor General of Pennsylvania.* Philadelphia: American Philosophical Society, 1992.

Cowell, Patti. *Women Poets in Pre-Revolutionary America, 1650–1775: An Anthology.* Troy, NY: Whitson Publishing, 1981.

Crary, Catherine Snell. "The Tory and the Spy: The Double Life of James Rivington." *William and Mary Quarterly* 16, no. 1 (1959): 61–72.

Curtis, Edward E. *The Organization of the British Army in the American Revolution.* New York: AMS Press, 1969. Originally published in 1926.

David Library of the American Revolution: Finding Aid on Prisoners of War. https://www.amphilsoc.org/sites/default/files/2020-01/attachments/Prisoners%20of%20War.pdf.

Derounian-Stodola, Kathryn Zabelle. "Sarah Wister (1761–1804)." *Legacy* 10, no. 2 (1993): 128–34.

Doerflinger, Thomas M. *A Vigorous Spirit of Enterprise: Merchants and Economic Development in Revolutionary Philadelphia.* Chapel Hill: University of North Carolina Press, 1986.

Donoghue, Norman E., II. *Prisoners of Congress: Philadelphia's Quakers in Exile, 1777–1778.* University Park: Pennsylvania State University Press, 2023.

Dorr, Benjamin. *A Memoir of John Fanning Watson, the Annalist of Philadelphia and New York.* Philadelphia: Collins, Printer, 1861.

Dripps, Matthew, publisher, Augustus Kollner, lithographer. *Map of the Township of Oxford, Boroughs of Frankford & Bridesburg: with parts of Bristol, N. Liberties and Cheltenham Townships.* Philadelphia: Matthew Dripps, 1849. Map Collection, Free Library of Philadelphia. https://libwww.freelibrary.org/digital/item/11763.

Duffin, James. Mapping West Philadelphia. https://maps.archives.upenn.edu/WestPhila1777/view-parcel.php?pid= 792&popup=1.

Durbin, Chris. "The Sad Fate of Admiral Byng." *Naval History* 33, no. 4 (2019). https://www.usni.org/magazines/naval-history-magazine/2019/august/sad-fate-admiral-byng.

Ecelbarger, Gary. *George Washington's Momentous Year: Twelve Months that Transformed the Revolution.* Vol. 1, *The Philadelphia Campaign, July to December 1777.* Yardley: Westholme, 2024.

Evans, Eric J. "A History of the Tithe System in England, 1690–1850, with Special Reference to Staffordshire." PhD diss., University of Warwick, 1970.

Fagan, Patrick. "The Population of Dublin in the Eighteenth Century with Particular Reference to the Proportions of Protestants and Catholics." *Eighteenth-Century Ireland/Iris an Dá Chultúr* 6 (1991): 121–156.

Fairholt, F. W. *Tobacco: Its History and Associations.* London: Chatto and Windus, 1876.

Fanelli, Doris Devine, and Karie Diethorn. *History of the Portrait Collection, Independence National Historical Park.* Philadelphia: American Philosophical Society, 2001.

Fanelli, Robert N. "Charles Craig's Final Statement." *Journal of the American Revolution*, July 10, 2018. https://allthingsliberty.com/2018/07/charles-craigs-final-statement/.

Fanelli, Robert N. "A Fatal Dispute Among the Guards." *Journal of the American Revolution*, May 6, 2021. https://allthingsliberty.com/2021/05/a-fatal-dispute-among-the-guards/.

Fanelli, Robert N. "HMS *Roebuck* on the Delaware." *Journal of the American Revolution*, May 25, 2023. https://allthingsliberty.com/2023/05/hms-roebuck-on-the-delaware/.

Fanelli, Robert N. "One Famous, One Forgotten: John Eager Howard and Patrick Duffey." *Journal of the American Revolution*, June 8, 2017. https://allthingsliberty.com/2017/06/john-eager-howard-forgotten-patrick-duffey/.

Fanelli, Robert N. "The 2nd Connecticut Regiment at Edge Hill." *Journal of the American Revolution*, June 15, 2021. https://allthingsliberty.com/2021/06/the-2nd-connecticut-regiment-at-edge-hill/.

Fanelli, Robert N. "William Allen and His Family: Tories or Patriots?" *Journal of the American Revolution*, December 2, 2020. https://allthingsliberty.com/2020/12/william-allen-and-his-family-tories-or-patriots/.

Faris, John T. *Old Churches and Meeting Houses in and Around Philadelphia.* Philadelphia: J. B. Lippincott, 1926.

Faul, Dennis. "Cromwell in Ireland: The Massacres." *Seanchas Ardmhacha: Journal of the Armagh Diocesan Historical Society* 20, no. 1 (2004): 293–298.

Fischer, David Hackett. *Albion's Seed: Four British Folkways in America.* New York: Oxford University Press, 1989.

Fischer, David Hackett. *Washington's Crossing.* New York: Oxford University Press, 2004.

Fitzgerald, John. "Lundy Foot & Company, Tobacco & Snuff Manufacturers." *Dublin Historical Record* 71, no. 2 (2018): 141–153.

Ford, Worthington Chauncey. *British Officers Serving in America 1774–1783.* Brooklyn: Historical Printing Club, 1897.

Fox, George. *The Works of George Fox.* Vol. 4. Philadelphia: Marcus T. C. Gould, 1831.

Fyers, Evan W. H. "General Sir William Howe's Operations in Pennsylvania, 1777 (Continued)." *Journal of the Society for Army Historical Research* 9, no. 35 (January 1930): 27-42.

Gentles, Ian. *The New Model Army: Agent of Revolution.* New Haven, CT: Yale University Press, 2022.

Gerhardt, Juliette. *Life on the Philadelphia Waterfront 1687–1826: A Report on the 1977 Archaeological Investigation of the Area F Site, Philadelphia, Pennsylvania.* West Chester, PA: John Milnor Associates, 2006.

Gibbon, Edward J. "Transfer of Land from the Swedes." In *A History of Frankford.* Philadelphia: Frankford Lions Club, c. 1990.

Gilpin, Thomas. *Exiles in Virginia: with Observations on the Conduct of the Society of Friends during the Revolutionary War, Comprising the Official Papers of the Government Relating to that Period. 1777–177*8. Philadelphia: G. Sherman, Printer, 1848.

Griffiths, George, comp. *Chronicles of the County Wexford, being a record of memorable incidents, disasters, social occurrences, and crimes, also, biographies of eminent persons, &c., &c., brought down to the year 1877.* Enniscorthy, Ireland: Printed at the "Watchman" Office, 1890.

Groves, Percy. *Historical Records of the 7th or Royal Regiment of Fusiliers Now Known as the Royal Fusiliers (The City of London Regiment) 1685–1903.* Guernsey, UK: Frederick B. Guerin, 1903.

Grubb, Farley. "The Market Structure of Shipping German Immigrants to America." *The Pennsylvania Magazine of History and Biography* 111, no. 1 (1987): 27–48.

Hallahan, William H. *The Day the American Revolution Began.* New York: William Morrow, 2000.

Hanson, Neil. *The Great Fire of London in That Apocalyptic Year, 1666.* Hoboken, NJ: John Wiley & Sons, 2002.

Harper, Steven Craig. *Promised Land: Penn's Holy Experiment, The Walking Purchase and the Dispossession of Delawares, 1600–1763.* Bethlehem, PA: Lehigh University Press, 2006.

Harris, Michael C. *Brandywine: A Military History of the Battle for Philadelphia, October 4, 1777.* El Dorado Hills, CA: Savas Beatie, 2014.

Harris, Michael C. *Fighting for Philadelphia: Forts Mercer and Mifflin, the Battle of Whitemarsh, and the Road to Valley Forge, October 5–December 19, 1777.* El Dorado Hills, CA: Savas Beatie, 2025.

Harris, Michael C. *Germantown: A Military History of the Battle That Lost Philadelphia but Saved America, September 11, 1777.* El Dorado Hills, CA: Savas Beatie, 2020.

Harris, Michael C., and Gary Ecelbarger. "The Numerical Strength of George Washington's Army During the 1777 Philadelphia Campaign." *Journal of the American Revolution*, October 5, 2021. https://allthingsliberty.com/2021/10/the-numerical-strength-of-george-washingtons-army-during-the-1777-philadelphia-campaign/.

Harvey, Oscar Jewell. *A History of Wilkes-Barré, Luzerne County*. Wilkes-Barré, PA: Raeder Press, 1909.

Heitman, Francis B. *Historical Register of Officers of the Continental Army During the War of the Revolution, April, 1775, to December, 1783.* New, revised, and enlarged edition. Washington, DC: Rare Book Shop Publishing, 1914.

Hinshaw, William Wade. *Encyclopedia of American Quaker Genealogy.* Vol. 2. Ann Arbor, MI: Edwards Brothers, 1938.

Hirst, Margaret E. *The Quakers in Peace and War: An Account of Their Peace Principles and Practice.* London: Swarthmore Press, 1923.

Historical Society of Pennsylvania. *Finding Aid to the Cadwalader Family Papers.* https://hsp.org/sites/default/files/legacy_files/migrated/findingaid1454cadwaladerpart1.pdf.

History of the First Troop of Philadelphia City Cavalry, 1774–November 17, 1874. Philadelphia: Hallowell, 1875.

Hodgson, E. *The Trial of Cosmo Gordon, Esq.; Commonly Called The Honourable Cosmo Gordon, for the Willful Murder of Frederick Thomas, Esq.; in a Duel in Hyde Park, on the Fourth of September, 1783.* London: J. Walmslay, 1784.

Hodgson, William, Jr. *Life and Travels of John Pemberton, A Minister of the Gospel of Christ.* London: Charles Gilpin, 1844.

Hore, Philip Herbert. *History of the Town and County of Wexford.* London: Elliot Stock, 1906.

Hotchkin, Samuel Fitch. *The York Road, Old and New.* Philadelphia: Binder & Kelly, 1892.

Hughes, Ann. *Gender and the English Revolution.* Abingdon, UK: Routledge, 2011.

Hughes, J. L. J. "Dublin Shorthand Writers." *Dublin Historical Record* 13, nos. 3/4 (1953): 118–127.

Hurd, Deana D. "Sergeant Lewis Hurd's Account of the American Revolution." In *A History and Genealogy of the Family of Hurd in the United States.* New York: Privately printed, 1910.

Hutson, James H. *Pennsylvania Politics 1746–1770: The Movement for Royal Government and Its Consequences.* Princeton, NJ: Princeton University Press, 1972.

Intel.gov. *Lydia Darragh: Neighbor & Spy.* https://www.intelligence.gov/evolution-of-espionage/revolutionary-war/new-nations-first-spies.

Jackson, John W. *With the British Army in Philadelphia, 1777–1778.* San Rafael, CA: Presidio Press, 1979.

Jones, Rufus M. *The Later Periods of Quakerism.* Vol. 2. London: Macmillan, 1921.

Jordan, John W. *Colonial Families of Philadelphia.* Vols. 1 and 2. New York: Lewis Publishing, 1911.

Junior League of Philadelphia. "Religious Society of Free Quakers." Unpublished manuscript courtesy of Maria Thompson, 2021.

Katcher, Philip R. N. *Encyclopedia of British, Provincial, and German Army Units 1775–1783.* Harrisburg: Stackpole Books, 1973.

Kelsey, R. W. "Philadelphia Tea-Party Letter–1773." *Bulletin of Friends' Historical Society of Philadelphia* 10, no. 2 (1921): 67–70.

Kenny, Kevin. *Peaceable Kingdom Lost: The Paxton Boys and the Destruction of William Penn's Holy Experiment.* New York: Oxford University Press, 2009.

Kerber, Linda K. *Women of the Republic: Intellect and Ideology in Revolutionary America.* Chapel Hill: University of North Carolina Press, 1980.

Kidder, William L. *Ten Crucial Days: Washington's Vision for Victory Unfolds.* Lawrence Township, NJ: Knox Press, 2018.

Klebaner, Benjamin Joseph. "American Manumission Laws and the Responsibility for Supporting Slaves." *Virginia Magazine of History and Biography* 63, no. 4 (1955): 443–53.

Knapp, Samuel L. *The Life of Thomas Eddy; Comprising an Extensive Correspondence with Many of the Most Distinguished Philosophers and Philanthropists of This and Other Countries.* New York: Connor & Cook, 1843.

Larson, Carlton F. W. "The Revolutionary American Jury: A Case Study of the 1778–1779 Philadelphia Treason Trials." *SMU Law Review* 61, no. 4 (2016): 1441-1524.

Larson, Carlton F. W. *The Trials of Allegiance: Treason, Juries and the American Revolution.* New York: Oxford University Press, 2019.

Leffmann, Henry. *Notes on the Secret Service of the Revolutionary Army Operating Around Philadelphia*. Philadelphia: Printed for the City History Society of Philadelphia, 1910.

Leffmann, Henry. *Outline Autobiography of Henry Leffmann, A. M., M. D., PH. D., D. D. S., of Philadelphia, with a Reference Index of Contributions to Science and Literature*. Philadelphia: 1905.

Lefkowitz, Arthur S. *The Long Retreat: The Calamitous American Defense of New Jersey, 1776.* New Brunswick, NJ: Rutgers University Press, 1998.

Linklater, Andro. *An Artist in Treason: The Extraordinary Double Life of General James Wilkinson*. New York: Walker, 2009.

Lippincott, Horace Mather. *A Portraiture of the People Called Quakers.* Philadelphia: Walter H. Jenkins, 1915.

Lochemes, M. Frederick, Sister. *Robert Walsh: His Story.* New York: American Irish Historical Society, 1941.

Mackesy, Piers. *The Coward of Minden: The Affair of Lord George Sackville.* New York: St. Martin's Press, 1979.

Maguire, Thomas J. *Battle of Paoli.* Mechanicsburg, PA: Stackpole Books, 2000.

Maguire, Thomas J. *The Philadelphia Campaign.* Vol. 1, *Brandywine and the Fall of Philadelphia.* Mechanicsburg, PA: Stackpole Books, 2006.

Maguire, Thomas J. *The Philadelphia Campaign.* Vol. 2, *Germantown and the Roads to Valley Forge.* Mechanicsburg, PA: Stackpole Books, 2007.

Marietta, Jack D. *The Reformation of American Quakerism, 1748–1783.* Philadelphia: University of Pennsylvania Press, 1984.

Marshall, John. *The Life of George Washington, Commander in Chief of the American Forces, during the War which Established the Independence of His Country, and First Presidency of the United States.* Vol. 3. Philadelphia: C. P. Wayne, 1805.

Maxey, David W. *Treason on Trial in Revolutionary Pennsylvania: The Case of John Roberts, Miller.* Philadelphia: American Philosophical Society, 2011.

Maxwell, Constantia. *Dublin under the Georges, 1714–1830.* 2nd ed. London: Faber & Faber, 1946.

Mayer, Holly A. *Belonging to the Army: Camp Followers and Community During the American Revolution.* Columbia: University of South Carolina Press, 1996.

McBurney, Christian. *Kidnapping the Enemy: The Special Operations to Capture Generals Charles Lee & Richard Prescott.* Yardley, PA: Westholme, 2014.

McDaniel, Donna, and Vanessa Julye. *Fit for Freedom, Not for Friendship: Quakers, African Americans, and the Myth of Racial Justice.* Philadelphia: Quaker Press of Friends General Conference, 2009.

McGhee, Shawn David. *No Longer Subjects of the British King: The Political Transformation of Royal Subjects to Republican Citizens, 1774–1776.* Yardley: Westholme, 2024.

Mears, Anne de Benneville. *The Old York Road and Its Early Associations of History and Biography, 1670–1870.* Philadelphia: Harper & Brother, 1890.

Merrell, James H. *Into the American Woods: Negotiations on the Pennsylvania Frontier.* New York: W.W. Norton, 2000.

Mickley, Joseph J. *Brief Account of the Murders by the Indians, and the Cause Thereof, in Northampton County, Penn'a., October 8, 1763.* Philadelphia: Thomas William Stuckey, 1875.

Miller, Ken. "'A Dangerous Set of People': British Captives and the Making of Revolutionary Identity in the Mid-Atlantic Interior." *Journal of the Early Republic* 32, no. 4 (2012): 565-601.

Mishoff, Willard O. "Business in Philadelphia During the British Occupation, 1777–1778." *Pennsylvania Magazine of History and Biography* 61, no. 2 (April, 1937): 165-181.

Montague, Francis Charles. *The History of England from the Accession of James I to the Restoration, 1603 to 1660.* London: Longmans, Green, 1907.

Myers, Albert Cook. *Immigration of the Irish Quakers into Pennsylvania, 1682–1750, With Their Early History in Ireland.* Swarthmore, PA: Published by the author, 1902.

Nagy, John. *George Washington's Secret Spy War: The Making of America's First Spymaster.* New York: St. Martin's Press, 2016.

Nagy, John. *Spies in the Continental Capital.* Yardley, PA: Westholme, 2011.

Nash, Gary B. "The Free Society of Traders and the Early Politics of Pennsylvania." *Pennsylvania Magazine of History and Biography* 89, no. 2 (1965): 147–173.

Nash, Gary B. *Quakers and Politics: Pennsylvania, 1681–1726.* 2nd ed. Boston: Northeastern University Press, 1968.

Nash, Gary B. *The Urban Crucible: Social Change, Political Consciousness, and the Origins of the American Revolution.* Cambridge, MA: Harvard University Press, 1979.

Nash, Gary B., and Billy G. Smith. "The Population of Eighteenth-Century Philadelphia." *Pennsylvania History* (July 1975): 362-368.

National Park Service. *Statement for Management.* Philadelphia: Independence National Historical Park, 1993.

Norton, Mary Beth. "The Ablest Midwife That Wee Knowe in the Land": Mistress Alice Tilly and the Women of Boston and Dorchester, 1649–1650." *William and Mary Quarterly* 55, no. 1 (January 1998): 105-134.

Norton, Mary Beth. *Founding Mothers and Fathers: Gendered Power and the Forming of American Society.* New York: Alfred A. Knopf, 1996.

Norton, Mary Beth. *Liberty's Daughters: The Revolutionary Experience of American Women, 1750–1800.* Boston: Little, Brown, 1980.

O'Hanlon, John, and Edward O'Leary. *History of The Queen's County.* Vol. 1. Dublin: Sealy, Bryers & Walker, 1907.

O'Hanlon, John, Edward O'Leary, and Mathew Lalor. *History of the Queen's County.* Vol. 2. Dublin: Sealy, Bryers & Walker, 1914.

Paige, Lucius R. *History of Cambridge, Massachusetts, 1630–1877.* Boston: H. O. Houghton, 1877.

Peterson, Charles E. *Notes on the Free Quaker Meeting House, Fifth and Arch Streets, Philadelphia, Built 1783–84.* Washington, DC: Ross & Perry, 2002.

Platt, John D. R. *Historic Resource Study: The City Tavern.* Philadelphia: Independence National Historical Park, 1973.

Pollock, John. *George Whitefield and the Great Awakening.* Garden City, NY: Doubleday, 1972.

Portraits in Delaware, 1700–1850. Wilmington, DE: National Society of Colonial Dames of America in the State of Delaware, 1951.

Potts, William John. "Bathsheba Bowers." *Pennsylvania Magazine of History and Biography* 3 (1879): 110-113.

Price, David. *The Road to Assunpink Creek: Liberty's Desperate Hour and the Ten Crucial Days of the American Revolution.* Lawrenceville, NJ: Knox Press, 2019.

Price, David. "The Significance of John Cadwalader." *Journal of the American Revolution,* September 22, 2022. https://allthingsliberty.com/2022/09/the-significance-of-john-cadwalader/.

Pullin, Naomi. "Providence, Punishment and Identity Formation in the Late-Stuart Quaker Community, c.1650–1700." *Seventeenth Century* 31, no. 4 (2016): 471-494.

Quane, Michael. "Quaker Schools in Dublin." *Journal of the Royal Society of Antiquaries of Ireland* 94, no. 1 (1964): 47–68.

Ramsey, William L. *The Yamasee War: A Study of Culture, Economy, and Conflict in the Colonial South.* Lincoln: University of Nebraska Press, 2008.

Rappleye, Charles. *Robert Morris, Financier of the American Revolution.* New York: Simon and Schuster, 2010.

Rediker, Marcus. *The Fearless Benjamin Lay: The Quaker Dwarf Who Became the First Revolutionary Abolitionist.* Boston: Beacon Press, 2017.

Rees, John U. "'To Hold Thirty Six Cartridges of Powder and Ball': Continental Army Tin and Sheet-Iron Canisters, 1775–1780." https://www.academia.edu/87762425/_To_hold_thirty_six_cartridges_of_powder_and_ball_Continental_Army_Tin_and_Sheet_Iron_Canisters_1775_1780.

Report of the Commission to Locate the Site of the Frontier Forts of Pennsylvania, Volume 1. Edited by Thomas Lynch Montgomery. Harrisburg: Wm. Stanley Ray, 1916.

Roberts, Cokie. *Founding Mothers: The Women Who Raised Our Nation.* New York: Harper, 2005.

Roberts, Priscilla H. *Thomas Barclay (1728–1793) Consul in France, Diplomat in Barbary.* Bethlehem, PA: Lehigh University Press, 2008.

Rose, P. K. *The Founding Fathers of American Intelligence: George Washington, John Jay, and Benjamin Franklin.* Washington, DC: Central Intelligence Agency, 1998. https://www.cia.gov/static/4c28451b90165b446ac948e3dd47c972/The-Founding-Fathers-of-American-Intelligence-.pdf.

Ruppert, Bob. "A Fast Ship from Salem: Carrying News of War." *Journal of the American Revolution*, April 17, 2015. https://allthingsliberty.com/2015/04/a-fast-ship-from-salem-carrying-news-of-war/.

Ryerson, Richard Alan. *The Revolution Is Now Begun: The Radical Committees of Philadelphia, 1765–1776.* Philadelphia: University of Pennsylvania Press, 1978.

Salinger, Sharon V. "*To Serve Well and Faithfully*": *Labor and Indentured Servants in Pennsylvania, 1682–1800.* New York: Cambridge University Press, 1987.

Scharf, J. Thomas, and Thompson Westcott. *History of Philadelphia, 1609–1884.* Vol. 1. Philadelphia: L. H. Everts, 1884.

Schecter, Barnet. *The Battle for New York: The City at the Heart of the American Revolution.* New York: Walker, 2002.

Scholten, Catherine M. "'On the Importance of the Obstetrick Art': Changing Customs of Childbirth in America, 1760 to 1825." *William and Mary Quarterly* 34, no. 3 (1977): 426–445.

Scott, Kenneth. "Counterfeiting in Pennsylvania." *Numismatic Notes and Monographs*, 1955. http://numismatics.org/digitallibrary/ark:/53695/nnan49620.

Seymour, Joseph. "Light the Match Load Away: The Ordnance and Organizational Structure of the Philadelphia Artillery, 1747–1777." *American*

Society of Arms Collectors Bulletin 93, 32-47. https://americansocietyofarmscollectors.org/wp-content/uploads/2019/06/2006-B93-Light-the-Match-Load-Away-The-Ordnance-a.pdf.

Shammas, Carole. "The Female Social Structure of Philadelphia in 1775." *Pennsylvania Magazine of History and Biography* 107 (1983): 69-83.

Shomette, Donald Grady. *Privateers of the Revolution: War on the New Jersey Coast, 1775–1783.* Atglen, PA: Schiffer Publishing, 2016.

Silva, Rene J. "Pennsylvania's Loyalists and Disaffected in the Age of Revolution: Defining the Terrain of Reintegration, 1765–1800." PhD diss., Florida International University, 2018. https://digitalcommons.fiu.edu/etd/3670.

Smith, Billy G. *The "Lower Sort": Philadelphia's Laboring People, 1750–1800.* Ithaca, NY: Cornell University Press, 1990.

Smith, Edward. *The Life of William Dewsbury.* London: Darton and Harvey, 1836.

Smith, Horace Wemyss. *Life and Correspondence of the Rev. William Smith, D. D.* Vol. 2. Philadelphia: Fergus Bros., 1880.

Snift, Dean, of Brazen-Nose [Benson Earle Hill]. *A Pinch—of Snuff: Composed of Curious Particulars and Original Ancedotes of Snuff Taking; as Well as a Review of Snuff, Snuff-Boxes, Snuff-Shops, Snuff-Takers, and Snuff-Papers; with the Moral and Physical Effects of Snuff.* London: Robert Tyas, 1840.

Soderland, Jean R. *Quakers and Slavery: A Divided Spirit.* Princeton: Princeton University Press, 1985.

Spero, Patrick. *Frontier Rebels: The Fight for Independence in the American West, 1765–1776.* New York: W. W. Norton, 2018.

Stone, Garry Wheeler, and Paul W. Schopp, *The Battle of Gloucester, 1777.* Yardley: Westholme, 2022.

Sullivan, Aaron. *The Disaffected: Britain's Occupation of Philadelphia During the American Revolution.* Philadelphia: University of Pennsylvania Press, 2019.

Taylor, Thomas B. "The Philadelphia Counterpart of the Boston Tea Party." *Bulletin of Friends' Historical Society of Philadelphia* 2, no. 3 (1908): 86–110. http://www.jstor.org/stable/41944817.

Thomas, Gilbert J., ed. *History of the Irish Confederation and the war in Ireland, 1641 [–1649] containing a narrative of affairs of Ireland, by Richard Bellings.* Vol. 1. Dublin: M. H. Gill & Son, 1882.

Thompson, Peter. *Rum Punch and Revolution: Taverngoing and Public Life in Eighteenth-Century Philadelphia.* Philadelphia: University of Pennsylvania Press, 1999.

Trussell, John B. B, Jr. *The Pennsylvania Line: Regimental Organization and Operations, 1776–1783.* Harrisburg: Pennsylvania Historical and Museum Commission, 1977.

Tuckey, Francis H. *The County and City of Cork Remembrancer; or Annals of the County and City of Cork.* Cork, Ireland: Osborne Savage & Son, 1837.

Ulrich, Laurel Thatcher. *A Midwife's Tale: The Life of Martha Ballard, Based on Her Diary, 1785–1812.* New York: Vintage Books, 1990.
Urban, Mark. *Fusiliers: The Saga of a British Redcoat Regiment in the American Revolution.* New York: Walker, 2007.
US National Institutes of Health, National Library of Medicine, National Center for Biotechnology Information. "Description of Smokeless Tobacco Practices," 1.1.2 "Snuff taking." https://www.ncbi.nlm.nih.gov/books/NBK326503/.
Vaux, Roberts. *Memoirs of the lives of Benjamin Lay and Ralph Sandiford: two of the earliest public advocates for the emancipation of the enslaved Africans.* Philadelphia: Solomon W. Conrad, 1815.
Wainwright, Nicholas B. *Colonial Grandeur in Philadelphia: The House and Furniture of General John Cadwalader.* Philadelphia: Historical Society of Pennsylvania, 1964.
Wallace, Paul A. W. *Indian Paths of Pennsylvania.* Harrisburg: Pennsylvania Historical and Museum Commission, 1965.
Watson, John Fanning. *Annals of Philadelphia and Pennsylvania in the Olden Time*, Vol. 2. Philadelphia: John Penington and Uriah Hunt, 1844.
Watson, John Fanning. *Annals of Philadelphia, Being a Collection of Memoirs, Anecdotes, & Incidents of the City and Its Inhabitants from the Days of the Pilgrim Founders.* Philadelphia: E. L. Carey & A. Hart, 1830.
Watson, John Fanning. *Historic Tales of Olden Time, Concerning the Early Settlement and progress of Philadelphia and Pennsylvania.* Philadelphia: E. Littell and Thomas Holden, 1833.
Weaver, Karol K. *Medical Revolutionaries: The Enslaved Healers of Eighteenth-Century Saint Domingue.* Champaign: University of Illinois Press, 2006.
Weaver, Karol K. "'Painful Leisure' and 'Awful Business': Female Death Workers in Pennsylvania." *Pennsylvania Magazine of History and Biography* 140, no. 1 (2016): 31–55.
Webb, John Joseph. *The Silk Industry in Dublin.* Dublin: Maunsel, 1913.
Weddle, Kevin J. *The Compleat Victory: Saratoga and the American Revolution.* New York: Oxford University Press, 2021.
Wedgwood, Veronica. *The King's War, 1641–1647.* London: Penguin, 1958.
Werner, Raymond C. "Diary of Grace Growden Galloway." *Pennsylvania Magazine of History and Biography* 55, no. 1 (1931): 32–94.
Wertz, Richard W., and Dorothy C. Wertz. *Lying-In: A History of Childbirth in America.* New York: Free Press, 1977.
Weslager, C. A. *The Stamp Act Congress.* Newark: University of Delaware Press, 1976.
Westby-Gibson, John. *The Bibliography of Shorthand.* London: Isaac Pitman & Sons, 1887.
Westcott, Thompson. *The Historic Mansions and Buildings of Philadelphia, with Some Notice of Their Owners and Occupants.* Philadelphia: Porter & Coates, 1877.

Whidbee, Paige L. "The Quaker Exiles: 'The Cause of Every Inhabitant.'" *Pennsylvania History: A Journal of Mid-Atlantic Studies* 83, no. 1 (2016): 28–57.

Wight, Thomas. *A History of the Rise and Progress of the People Called Quakers, in Ireland, from the Year 1653 to 1700.* 2nd ed. London: George Yard, 1800.

Williams, William H. *Slavery and Freedom in Delaware 1639–1865.* Wilmington, DE: Scholarly Resources, 1996.

Wright, Keith W. *A History of the Andover Iron Works: Come Penny Go Pound.* Charleston, SC: History Press, 2013.

Wright, Robert K., Jr. *The Continental Army.* Washington, DC: Center of Military History, US Army, 1986.

Wulf, Karin. "Assessing Gender: Taxation and the Evaluation of Economic Viability in Late Colonial Philadelphia." *Pennsylvania Magazine of History and Biography* 121, no. 3 (July 1997): 201-235.

Wulf, Karin. *Not All Wives: Women of Colonial Philadelphia.* Philadelphia: University of Pennsylvania Press, 2000.

Yamin, Rebecca. *Archaeology at the Site of the Museum of the American Revolution: A Tale of Two Taverns and the Growth of Philadelphia.* Philadelphia: Temple University Press, 2019.

Yamin, Rebecca. *Archaeology of the City—The Museum of the American Revolution Site, Archaeological Data Recovery, Third and Chestnut Streets, Philadelphia, Pennsylvania.* Vol. 1. West Chester, PA: Commonwealth Heritage Group, 2016.

Young, Alfred F. *Masquerade: The Life and Times of Deborah Sampson, Continental Soldier.* New York: Vintage Books, 2004.

Zweizing, Suzanne M. "Bathsheba Bowers (c. 1672–1718)." *Legacy* 11, no. 1 (1994): 65–73.

ACKNOWLEDGMENTS

For aid in researching this book, I am indebted to many people and institutions, among them:

Russell D. Brindley, Valley Forge National Historic Park, and my good friend Ed Wimble, for information on Charles Darragh's court-martial. Lisa B. Davis, regent, Great Bridge Chapter, National Society Daughters of the American Revolution. Karie Diethorn, supervisory museum curator, Independence National Historical Park, National Park Service, US Department of the Interior, for information and photographs of the Lydia Darragh Cradle. James Duffin, archivist, University of Pennsylvania Archives, for his incredibly useful work on Mapping West Philadelphia, https://maps.archives.upenn.edu/WestPhila1777/map.php and for sharing information from the Philadelphia Constables Returns. Grace Ford-Dirks, manager of interpretation and public outreach, Wyck Historic House, Garden, and Farm, for the Hannah Marshall Haines Portrait. Laura C. Keim, curator of Stenton, Deborah Norris Logan's home. Kelly Kinzle, for letting Doris and I examine the Lydia Darragh mahogany chair and for sharing the provenance and photos of the chair. Mary Jo Larkin, SSJ, Logue Library, dean for library and information resources, Chestnut Hill College. Carlton F. W. Larson, for information on Abraham Carlile and his copy of the DeShong Trial notes. Bruce Laverty, former curator of architecture, Athenaeum of Philadelphia, and Kristina Wilson, current curator, for images of the Loxley House.

My friends at the American Philosophical Society, including Michelle McDonald, librarian and director, Adrianna Link, curator of history of science, Brenna Holland, assistant director of library and museum programs, and Caroline O'Connell, exhibitions curator, for their help in locating Hannah Marshall Haines's manuscript, accessing the Free

Quaker papers, and more. Matt Nelson, Beinecke Library Public Services, Yale University Library. Lexy Nilles, access services librarian, Historical Society of Pennsylvania. Matthew Skic, director of collections and exhibitions, Museum of the American Revolution. Billy G. Smith, for his spreadsheet of Philadelphia tax lists. Rick Taraborrelli of the Philadelphia Register of Wills. Maria Thompson of the Free Quaker Society. Don Waldo for many insights into Charles Craig's service in the Light Dragoons. Darragh Walker, sixth great-granddaughter of Lydia Darragh, for sharing information about the Darragh family. Sarah J. Weatherwax, senior curator of graphic arts, The Library Company of Philadelphia, for help confirming the Lydia Darragh engravings. Emily Winters, The Carpenters' Company. Karin Wulf, director and librarian, Mark Armstrong, rare material research and reference librarian, and Kimberly Nusco, associate librarian for research and reference, John Carter Brown Library of the Early Americas, for locating and sharing the manuscript of Elias Boudinot's "Reminiscences." LuLen Walker, art curator, and Christen E. Runge, assistant curator, Art Collection, Booth Family Center for Special Collections, Georgetown University, for the Robert Walsh Jr. portrait.

I am also grateful to Don Hagist, editor of the *Journal of the American Revolution*, for guidance in publishing my articles, to Bruce H. Franklin, publisher of Westholme, for his thoughtful suggestions on this book, and to Westholme's copy editor extraordinaire, Ron Silverman. Thanks, too, to Gary Ecelbarger for pointing me toward Westholme in the first place.

A number of people have stimulated and sustained my interest in the American Revolution. I am grateful to the members of the Washington Crossing American Revolution Round Table, especially our late founder, Joseph F. Seliga, and longtime members John Fabiano, Joseph E. Wroblewski, and Robert Wong. Many thanks are due to my fellow trustees of the Swan Historical Foundation, most especially my friend of half a century, Colonel Richard J. Kane, chairman, James C. Beachell, treasurer, and especially Deborah Hvizdos, vice chairman, who, in her former role as New Jersey state historian for the National Society Daughters of the American Revolution and current role as national chair of the NSDAR's Volunteer Information Specialists, has a long record of service to others. Also, my thanks to the members of our informal American Revolution touring group, led with enthusiasm by Gary Ecelbarger and including Doug Bonforte, Jim Christ, Sue Cory,

Mike Harris, Tom McAndrew, Greg Pusak, John Resto, Bill Welsch, and Roger Williams.

I owe a special debt of gratitude to my childhood buddies Jim McCormick, who has encouraged my writing since high school, and Dave Comeaux, who always sparks my intellect and curiosity.

Thanks to my lovely daughters, Catherine and Anna, for listening to my endless yammering about local history. Finally, and most importantly, I want to thank my wonderful wife and best friend, Doris Devine Fanelli, former chief of cultural resources management, Independence National Historical Park, who generously shared her knowledge of eighteenth-century Philadelphia, who informed my scholarship at every turn, and who lived patiently for several years with this other remarkable woman, Lydia Darragh.

INDEX

Note: LD stands for Lydia Darragh; WD for William Darragh